NEVER NEVER GIVE UP

Ross Z. Pierpont, MD, F.A.C.S.

© Ross Z. Pierpont, M.D. 2,000

All rights reserved.

However, the author intends to grant permission to interested persons to reproduce parts of this book, especially those parts dealing with health care and the Pierpont health Care System. Please direct any questions or submit written reproduction requests to Ross Z. Pierpont, M.D. F.A.C.S. , 215 Belmont Forest Court, Suite 408, Timonium, Maryland 21093.

Dedication and Foreword

This book, Never, Never, Ever Give Up! has been long in the making — roughly my life — and I wish to dedicate it to all of my family.

My stalwart mother, Ethel Zimmerman Pierpont, headed a single-parent household and educated four sons: an entomologist, Roger, B.S.; two physicians, Edwin and myself; and one entrepreneur, Philip.

Her support defies my skill to describe it.

Each of us grew up individualists, but there was never a time we four, along with Mother, our wives and our children, did not pull together as one when help was needed.

My wife, Grace, deserves every accolade this husband can muster for her tolerance and unswerving support, as does my daughter, Christine, and her husband Lippold von Klencke.

Together, Christine and Lippold have raised four grandchildren: Ludolf, 21, now studying law; Anna, 20, beginning University at Passau; Celeste, 16, finishing high school in Hameln and an expert horsewoman; followed by Henry age 14 and a budding musician-singer.

I never forget God, our maker, who has been good in ordaining to me a precious gift of recall, without which this book would never have been written.

So many others have touched this lifetime of mine. My thoughts and thanks to each and everyone of you. I have never forgotten you.

Distinguished author and editor, Blaine Taylor, rendered sage advice and direction at critical times, for which many thanks.

The support of two friends, Claude and Shirley Gerard, with whom I have been privileged to work on this and many other projects in business and political life has been constant and superior.

Their patience and encouragement knew no bounds in the use of time, energy and advice to clear high hurdles.

Finally, for everyone I have failed to identify at this time and place, for your friendship and support — my everlasting thanks to each of you.

May God bless every one as we continue to move through this life to improve America for all Americans. Not least of my dreams is a health care system worthy of this great nation.
Never, never, ever, give up!

Ross Z. Pierpont, M.D.

The Beginning

During my life as a surgeon practicing medicine in a Baltimore that was then a collection of ethnic and amiable neighborhoods, I had no hint that one day I would be at home in a German castle named Schloss (Castle, in English) Haemelschenburg — much less begin to write this book here.

Unexpected it is, yet here I sit in an apartment in this enormous, centuries-old castle high above a single, narrow, curving street. Across the street is a building used generations ago to collect and store the grain harvested each year. Adjacent to that building is another that houses the castle's electrical system. Beside it, a one-story-high water wheel turns as I watch. Beside and below the buildings, stretching to a river, are the estate's farmlands. Behind the castle are stables and a riding hall built to train the estate's horses. Beyond the stable and climbing for nearly a mile are the estate's dense forests harvested only by permit, still filled with game, and the source of the castle's pure water.

It is easy to understand why some architects have called this castle the finest example of Weser Renaissance architecture privately owned in western Europe. Privately owned it is. My host and hostess are my only daughter, Christine, and her husband Lippold von Klencke. Today, he is at work as a staff member of the German Government office in nearby Hannover. Christine is busy managing the castle's numerous affairs. My wife, Grace, is occupied elsewhere with the smallest of our four grandchildren and more than content to leave me to my thoughts, and my writing.

My thoughts lead me on. What inspired me to begin this while visiting in Germany? Why didn't it occur to me in our home in Baltimore? The answer comes without thought. Here I sense a continuity — an endlessness — I had never sensed in my own United States. The vista is timeless, somehow linking me to both past and future, connecting me with Lippold's ancestors who built and lived in this castle and now moving into the future through my grandchildren.

I respect continuity. I admire stability. Here, in a culture much older than I knew at home in the United States, I feel those qualities as I had never felt them in the mobility of our Maryland life. This old castle speaks to me of stability of place, continuity of circumstance.

What has been in the past moves forward in the history of where I sit and portends what will be, tomorrow, and untold years of the tomorrows after that. The lives of countless others who once walked the halls of this castle now link with my half-century of living with birth, sickness and death. Or is it death, birth, and sickness? The continuum need not be described. It is enough to know it exists.

Life teaches me that all things are possible to one who stays able and stable.

But life becomes a series of impossibilities to the unstable person who responds to adversity by flutter and waffle.

Events beginning in my earliest childhood taught me, unforgettably, that a combination of ability and stability were the foundation of my survival. As I matured, those qualities became the keystone of my medical career and living — an altogether different proposition.

Happenings beyond anything I wanted to face, or could do anything about, built the proposition of ability and stability into my character and enabled me to persevere when events declared me to be down and out.

Here I now sit articulating the guiding principle of my life: never, never, ever give up.

Chapter One
Life as a child in Baltimore County, Maryland

You never miss what you never had, and I never had a father.

I was three years old when he died; I remember nothing of any lasting significance about him. When I look at his likeness in a photograph, it is only a two-dimensional shadow of a man who remains a stranger to me. For a reason I cannot explain, my one remembrance of him that remains alive is when I pushed a little red wheelbarrow behind him one day when he was inspecting our stone house in Woodlawn, Baltimore County. That is all.

When I became a physician, I looked up the sickness that took him. It was staph/viridans bacterial endocarditis engrafted on his mitral valve. This followed a post-rheumatic fever mitral stenosis. Why do I mention it so many years later? Because it's worth remembering, today, that in 1920 death was nearly inevitable from a continuously-fed septicemia. My father was virtually condemned to death the day he became ill. Today, antibiotics would have cured his illness in days.

My mother, Ethel Zimmerman Pierpont, spoke almost nothing to us about my father. She did not live in the past. Also, the necessities of caring for four young boys filled her waking hours. At the time my father died, we were Roger age 9, Philip age 6, Ross (that's me), age 3, and Edwin age 18 months. Not once did any of us feel she resented our demands or shorted our care. Even as a child I sensed that she fully accepted what had happened to her life, and she measured up to her responsibilities without question. Fortunately for us, she was a physically strong, stable, self-reliant and educated woman. She had completed her formal education at what was then the "Model School for Teachers" and which is now Towson University. The admired "Model School" has been updated into the "Lida Lee Tall" teaching division of the University.

As debates about today's education rage on with more heat than illumination, I find it amusing to look back at my own education in the 1920s. My mother had been a teacher when she married my father, Edwin L. Pierpont, an auditor, but marriage and four children in seven years took her from the classroom. After my father died, she was fortunate in being able to return to teaching as a means of supporting us in a one-parent family.

My mother taught in a one-room school at Hernwood in a rural part of Baltimore County known as Randallstown. About 2,500 people lived in this area at the time, and most were farmers or related to farming. To reach Randallstown, my mother drove a horse and buggy seven miles on raw dirt or one-lane, gravel "roads" to and from the school. Every school morning, after she had fed and entrusted the youngest of us to relatives, and every school afternoon for the nine months of the school year, mother, horse and buggy defied every kind of weather that came upon us. She went through scorching heat, below-zero cold, rain, sleet, ice, snow — and those beautiful, bracing spring and fall mornings that helped make it all worthwhile.

How she managed to teach all seven grades, male and female alike, all in that one room school, I'll never hope to know. Most of her students were from nearby farms, and some of the young men were larger and even older than my mother. In spite of relative size, gender, age differences, and what today's teachers would call unacceptable crowding, there was never any lack of respect for my mother and her teaching. She was there to educate, and her pupils knew it. She got the job done.

Since two of us were too young for school in those early years, Mother turned to relatives to care for us while she taught school. As soon as we looked old enough to go to school with her, she fudged on the county's age requirements to accommodate our presence in her classroom. At age five, I started in the first grade of Mother's school with no previous preparation. Pre-school and kindergarten were unknowns to our school system and the Pierponts in those (primitive?) times. A few years after I began school, Woodlawn opened a small school with some splitting of classes, and Mother gained a teaching appointment at the new school. That change seems not worth mentioning now that it's history, but that change in Mother's life cut her horse and buggy travel by six and a half miles each way. The time and energy she saved made a difference in the lives of the four young Pierponts almost beyond calculation. Oblivious of the importance of such things at the time, I now recognize that one change in the demands on my mother's time affected me for the rest of my life.

At the time of Mother's changed position, she had become known in the school system as "Miss Ethel." It was natural for her to become "Miss Ethel," my school teacher, for part of the day, and then after school become my Mother who loved me as her third son. For me to start school at age five with no preparation for it was a daring proposition, to say the least. Today, I doubt anyone could get away with it. But Mother had become close to the principal, who in those times was totally in charge of what went on in her school. Mother was positive beyond a doubt that I was better off with her in school than footloose, and it is obvious, now, that starting school as young as I did was to control the development of the rest of my life. I am sure I produced more than an occasional difficult moment in those first school years. With the benefit of hindsight, it is clear that five-year old Ross tended to be aggressive, or as some kindly souls might put it, "strong-willed." Less generous people would call me bull-headed.

Maybe I just had the strength of my early convictions.

Once school began for me, it never stopped. In my boyhood days, no one had invented magnet or accelerated schools; advanced students simply skipped a grade. One of my later teachers wanted me to skip a grade, but Mother stopped that in its tracks. I was the youngest child in the class, and skipping a grade would have aggravated the age difference. As it was, I completed the seven grades at Woodlawn by age 11.

The Zimmerman Influence

My mother, as a Zimmerman, belonged to a family considered one of the pillars of Woodlawn's 2,500-or so people. Considering the rural nature of Woodlawn, the prestige of that position is not especially impressive, except that one of the impressions I absorbed as a child was I belonged to a pillar of my world. I had no awareness of the relative size of the Woodlawn community. My early impression of my place in the world is as much a part of my character as being a man, and a surgeon.

My maternal grandfather, William S. Zimmerman was nothing if not prolific. He and my maternal grandmother produced 10 children, including my mother who was sixth in the line and the third of the four girls. The Zimmerman family in my grandfather's time roamed on a huge tract of land that had been bought in pre-Civil War years. One boundary of the original tract ran along Windsor Mill Road northerly to Gwynn Oak Avenue, a total distance of almost two and one-half miles. This farm included what is now Leakin Park and Lorraine Cemetery in Baltimore County. The Zimmermans farmed this huge tract with the help of a number of slaves. I mention this as a fact of the times and my family history, not as something for me to be proud of, or for that matter ashamed of. My ancestors did what was accepted all around them at the time and is a simple fact of my life and upbringing, just like the Zimmermans being "pillars of Woodlawn."

As a child, my world consisted of the farms and houses of Woodlawn, and the Woodlawn of my childhood years continues as a large part of the world I now occupy as an adult. Originally, Woodlawn existed as an Indian settlement on the east bank of the swift-running stream called Gwynns Falls. The Indians were the Pow Ha Tans, a basically friendly tribe white settlers easily dealt out of their land. For all practical purpose, Pow Ha Tans do not exist as a tribe today. As a boy, I had yet to learn to think in such adult terms as fairness and cheating, so the treatment of the Pow Ha Tans was another of those things that somehow happened to other people. At the same time, what other people can do to hurt you made an impression that affected my contact with others throughout the rest of my life.

When a road from Baltimore was built on the west side of Gwynns Falls Creek to accommodate horse-drawn trolleys, people on the east side decided to relocate close to the new road. It was a mark of the times that relocating the homes became a community effort. When winter froze Gwynn Falls into a solid bridge of ice, everyone joined together to pick up the houses and carry them to the west bank. It was community work everyone did at his own risk, for liability and injury insurance were unknown. If hurt, the community would help but staying whole was each individual's personal responsibility.

After marrying my mother, my father bought 12 acres of the Zimmerman tract and built a house of native stone on it. An uncle, Fred Loos, married Mother's sister, Ruth, and built their home on land next to ours. Other Zimmermans bought parcels of Grandfather's tract and built more homes nearby. Mother's sister, Harriet, never married and lived with my Grandfather on the last parts of the land eventually shrunken to about 20 acres.

Although I grew up without a father, the closeness of our families, both personally and physically, did much to fill the vacuum of his absence. Somehow, my Mother always managed to preserve a feeling we were one, together, and we would make it. That feeling permeated Mother's life not only with us children, but with other men. My memory of her in her thirties is how she always stood perfectly erect, feminine, and completely poised. Her skin was smooth with no need for cosmetics; her dark brown, almost black hair worn nearly shoulder length without a part was a striking contrast with her wide, blue-hazel eyes. In spite of the stress she had to feel from the tremendous responsibilities of managing a home alone with four boisterous sons, she smiled easily, and hearing her laugh was a delight that still sounds in the halls of my memory.

From time to time, she naturally attracted eligible men who asked her to marry them. She rejected all offers. Once when I was still very young, I heard her explain her thoughts to a friend: "I am not sure another man would take care of my boys as Ed and I want it done. No, I'm not going to make another man their father."

My mother's family history became part of me. Grandfather Billy Zimmerman, at age 15, led a horse from the barn and rode off to join two of his brothers in the Confederate Army. He fought only one battle — at Gettysburg — where he was captured by the Union Army and imprisoned at Point Lookout, Maryland.

Word reached Billy's mother, Great Grandmother Zimmerman, that her son was dying in a Yankee prison. Loading a wagon with food, clothing, straw and other essentials, my Great Grandmother hitched up a horse and drove 40 miles to Washington to see President Abraham Lincoln. For several days, she sat vigil in the muddy road as close to the White House as she could get. She refused to give up, and eventually, someone told Lincoln about her. Lincoln issued his personal pardon for Billy's release. Having what she came for, this unyielding woman immediately set out for Point Lookout prison, a trip of another hundred miles or more.

No one ever recorded what happened when she reached the Federal prison, for my Great Grandmother never made much of her story. We know only that she secured Billy's release with Lincoln's pardon and bedded her sick son in the wagon for the four-day journey back to Woodlawn. Billy not only survived the rough trip, he lived to 92. Alas, Lincoln's pardon of Billy — what would have been a precious family treasure — has never been found. I have often wondered if a family member, perhaps Grandfather Billy himself, bitter over the family's losses during the war, despised the capture, sickness, and imprisonment represented by the pardon, had deliberately destroyed it. No one will ever know.

In the post-World War 1920s, the Zimmerman family fortunes prospered. Old enough by then to help, I and others trucked farm-fresh produce grown on the farm to Lexington Market in Baltimore City where we sold it to consumers and wholesale buyers. The business helped to teach me early hours, for most wholesale deliveries took place starting at 4:00 A.M.

Great Grandfather Zimmerman's partner in the produce business drove it into bankruptcy through gambling losses then stealing to make them good. Characteristically, Great Grandfather Zimmerman immediately did what honor demanded. He sold off his entire estate, paid off the debts, and impoverished his family. Once he completed that little job, he set about rebuilding the family fortunes . It was a lesson in converting stunning instability into the stability, even prestige, as he eventually acquired land running nearly two miles along Windson Mill Road to St. Lukes Lane. This was the property inherited by Grandfather Billy Zimmerman, and the source of the acres bought by my father for our own house. All of this was a lesson I never forgot when I, too, became victim of events I could not control.

With my mother as a working teacher, education became central to my earliest years. I had no way of realizing it then, but education dominated, shaped my life. In those days, where we lived in rural Baltimore County, large numbers of children growing up on farms were home taught, and even self-taught. For luckier others, education was a room, pencils, books, and the teacher who ruled the school world. Educational materials were scarce or did not exist. But if you wanted to learn, you could. You did. If you did not care to learn, your mind could not keep up and you failed — a drop out. Many boys I knew in Woodlawn never completed high school; some never finished grammar school. It was a time when no one really thought much about such things; they just happened and everybody's life went on for those who were lucky.

Time brought improvements. As transportation by car, bus and trolley became available, Baltimore County began to consolidate the one-room and two-room schools. High schools were added to various communities. My school destination when I finished grade school at age 11 was Catonsville High School six miles from home. Bus time to school was about an hour and a half each way. Bus fare, for children affording a bus, was each one's personal problem. Many of the boys and girls my age walked to school or rode bicycles. Others unable to afford bus fare quit school and settled for a job where schooling wasn't required.

That was the story of my Zimmerman uncles. Not one had a formal education of any kind. Yet all six became financially successful. Three uncles, Albert, Philip, and Seth Zimmerman, climbed from farm boys and local growers of fresh fruits and vegetables to the brokerage of fresh produce. As Zimmerman Brothers, they capitalized on the increasing availability of refrigerated truck and railroad delivery to ship fresh fruits and vegetables coast to coast. The brothers absorbed other purveyors and grew to sell carloads and trainloads of citrus from Florida, California, and Mexico to fast-growing chain stores like A&P, American, and Safeway. At one point in their careers, their business grew so large that these three young, uneducated men in Baltimore County controlled the entire lettuce crop of the Imperial Valley in California! All three men lived and died wealthy merchants.

Frank, Walter and William Zimmerman went their own ways. The west had a powerful lure for them; they saw opportunity and adventure beyond the Mississippi. It became clear that their zeal for going west had become a family matter. As was the practice in the Zimmerman family, their mother called a family council to discuss the brothers' ideas. When it became clear the boys were dead set on leaving home, Grandmother Zimmerman formalized the decision. Always in character, she issued a family directive often quoted in the Zimmerman family lore. "If you are going west, go all the way. Do not stop in Chicago. That city is a den of sin, crime, and lawbreakers. Have none of it. If you leave this house, go till you reach the west coast!"

All three obeyed their marching orders and did not stop until they reached Portland, Oregon. There, they went into the logging business, and Zimmerman Bros. became a growing, very prosperous enterprise. In time, Zimmerman, Wells, Brown & Co. became a leader in providing logging equipment throughout the Pacific Northwest. As they prospered, they built imposing residences on fashionable Multnomah Hill in Portland, and summer homes on the Pacific. Their wives and childen traveled the world.

As happens so often, the children of the three brothers became social butterflies. By the time I was old enough to know about them they had gone full cycle — the modest fortunes of the parents were spent. As the money vanished, all male descendants of both the Atlantic and Pacific branches of the Zimmermans disappeared with it. Those now left to carry on are named Pierponts, Loos, McCauslands, Sack, and others.

This was the past that was, and is, the threads of my legacy as we descendants of Zimmermans and Pierponts wove the fabrics of our lives.

Learning that crying won't help.

Events in 1916-1917 leading up to the American entry into World War I had a sobering effect on the families of Woodlawn, especially families of German descent. I missed that experience because I wasn't born until 1917, and my father was exempt from service due to his rheumatic heart disease and family responsibilities.

Before and during the war years, Father built a large blue-stone bungalow and a barn on our 12-acre farm. Other Zimmermans and their wives or husbands had also built homes on the Zimmerman family tract. Mother's sister and her husband built next to us on a half-acre, and early in my life I came close to learning real life saints were possible. Ruth and Fred Loos were just that to me. They loved me, I know not why even now, and I adored them.

Next door to the Loos was "the old home place," a farm of 28 acres where Grandfather Billy and his daughter Aunt Hattie lived.

The early '20s brought a surge in the national economy. But it was downhill for the Pierpont family following my father's death two years after the Armistice in 1918. At my age of three, I as well as my three brothers were still burdens, not a help. There was no welfare to meet basic needs. No food stamps. No social workers to turn to. No Aid for Dependent Children. Four boys and one mother, we were on our own!

Somehow the others made me understand what we had to do to survive. We had our own strength and next of kin. It was pitch in. Everybody does his share. Work. Don't ask others to take care of you; take care of yourself. Root hog or die!

It was a time of survival on its cruelest terms.

One of my earliest lessons of wanting and denial came at Christmas 1923 when I was six. Christmas had never brought us gifts of games, or toys, or bikes. Our gifts were hand-me-downs from older boy to younger boy, or from someone else. We got a pair of pants. Some socks. Underwear. Necessities were king.

In my sixth Christmas, prosperity seemed all around us. The florist across the road was especially jolly after a big year. On Christmas morning, the florist's four boys pushed four new bikes out their door showed them off throughout the neighborhood. We four Pierpont boys were almost the same age as his four boys. My mother gave me a pair of pants and a scooter. It was a struggle for her to manage the scooter.

Trying to understand what others could have, but I couldn't have, I hid my disappointment as best I could. But it didn't work and of course Mother saw it. Though neither of us said anything, I know now she felt far worse than I did. The hurting of that one Christmas became so much a part of me the emotion tries to return even now: Why is Ross Pierpont so inferior to our neighbors' boys? Why can't we Pierponts have what others have? I had no answers, could not answer. That Christmas day taught me, never to be forgotten, that my life must be lived as it is. Not as I wish it to be. Self-pity and tears change nothing. My envy of the florist's sons made clear that the harshest terms of life are competition and comparison. The determination that I would never let disappointment matter when I can make things different became as much a part of me, that day, as breathing. Denial and comparison instilled in me a competitive approach and a never-say-never attitude which became the building blocks of my character. That part of me has not changed even at advanced years.

Looking at our social structure today from the vantage point of what Christmas at age six taught me, I see we have become compassionate, though many argue we do not do enough. But what has our compassion wrought? As a physician, I look at the psychological assertion of childhood scarring the adult personality as a basis for antisocial behavior and ask where does such an understanding lead us? I understand the need to heal. I also see that our social system is breeding out of many people the toughness that helps to conquer adversity. Are we losing the toughness needed to cope with life's inevitable setbacks?

Toughness! Caring for four boys demanded every ounce of it my mother possessed. Her responsibility for our well-being continued around the clock, seven days a week, 52 weeks a year. To provide food, clothes, security, and care for us through the inevitable childhood sicknesses could have made her buckle and collapse. Had it happened, I think my brothers and I would have understood. But not once did she waver. Not once, not ever, did I hear her complain.

One winter three years after Father died, my brother Philip went out to sled on snow-covered Lewis Hill. This is a very steep hill, great for sledding. All along the hill that winter, gas and water pipes lay strewn awaiting the introduction of water and gas. Philip saw Winnie Ditman belly flop on his sled, and as Winnie flew by Philip jumped on Winnie's back. The jolt knocked Winnie's hat over his eyes, and the boy lost control of his sled. Both boys rammed into the steel pipes head on.

Winnie's skull split open. Philip flew about 10 feet through the air and landed on the pipes. Winnie lay for days between life and death, but finally recovered. My brother suffered severe bruises of his right leg and left arm. While recovering from his injuries, he developed a strep throat. Then he suddenly developed an acute blood infection and a hematogenous osteomyelitis in his right shin bone. He underwent emergency surgery to unroof the shin bone from knee to ankle and scrape the infected marrow. That was standard treatment in the days before antibiotics.

He seemed to improve, then suddenly his left elbow became infected. Surgery like that on his leg had to be done on his left ulna. The progress of successive infections was so alarming, and the need for complete rest of the infected parts considered so important, little or no attention was devoted to his joints and their motion. He finally recovered from his primary infections, but infections also occurred in other bones as late as his senior years.

A boy's unthinking exuberance on an icy hill disabled him for the rest of his life.

This was my first real contact with the medical profession. Our family doctor was A.C. Smink, and a prince through it all. He understood what we were up against and called in a specialist only when there was no other choice. Even though I was only six, I was there when one day he said to my Mother: "Ethel, I'll send you a bill. Pay what you can and don't worry." His word was good. No bill ever came.

Through it all, my Mother's love of her sons was her strength. Though every one of us, and others in the Zimmerman families, felt her stress, she never passed any of it on to us. The costs of Philip's care was a daily concern mentally as well as financially. Health insurance? What was that? Hospital payments were not high, but they had to be paid. Somehow Mother managed. To this day, I don't know how.

Dr. Smink's treatment of Philip affected the rest of my life. In addition to his competence and humanity, I saw that Dr. Smink drove a fine car, dressed well, and never seemed to have a worry about money. The way my life seemed to be going, it would make sense to do as Dr. Smink did. Help people. Be independent. Have money. Be looked up to. Be your own boss. Somehow, even at age six, the beginnings of my later career had begun to take shape.

By 1925 in our Woodlawn neighborhood, farmland was being replaced by houses. But my Mother's oldest sister, Lulu, and her husband, Truman Sauter, still ran the largest farm in our vicinity. Truman and his two sons, Brent and Webster Sauter, raised all kinds of vegetables. Their orchards brought in bountiful crops of peaches, apples, pears, and plums that won prizes at Baltimore County fairs. My own fortunes rested in my own cow. I had grown from close to a six-year old midget into a straw-haired maturing boy at age eight. I probably weighed about 40 pounds.

By five-thirty every morning of my life, seven days a week, I was up to milk my cow and take her to pasture. I delivered the morning's raw milk to my customers, then walked the half-mile to the elementary school in Woodlawn. After school, I brought in my cow, milked her and readied the milk for delivery the next morning.

By this time, Brent and Webster Sauter had built up huckster routes for selling their farm-fresh fruits and vegetables — known as "arabing" in Baltimore and the counties. But I saw they were missing sales in the close-in areas next to us. It was an opportunity I could not miss. I put together a series of pull wagons with sides high enough to hold fresh fruits and vegetables, and as soon as they were ready Ross Pierpont, the entrepeneur, was in the huckstering business, too.

Friday evenings as soon as I could after milking my cow, I pulled my empty wagons to Granite in Baltimore County. On the five or six mile trip to Granite, I bought the best seasonal fruits and vegetables I could find on farms along the way. On the way back, I loaded my purchases into the wagons. When I got back home with the loaded wagons, my brother, Ed, would help me clean my purchases for sale the next morning. Ed was a help, too — he was big for his age of six.

Every trip from the first one on, I learned what it meant to buy the best at the lowest prices. If I could buy sweet corn for two cents less per dozen ears by walking two more miles to get it, I walked two miles. Two cents? I could mail a letter for two cents. I could buy two sticks of gum for two cents. No one I knew had ever heard of something called inflation; "sound as a dollar" meant exactly that, and I loved the sound of those words.

Saturdays went fast. After milking and pasturing my cow, Ed and I traveled my route of customers in Woodlawn and nearby Broadacres starting as soon as my customers were up and about. By noon, the wagons were empty. On a good day we earned about five dollars. Sometimes it was more; rarely was it less.

Five dollars was real money when I was eight. I could buy a shirt for a dollar. A pair of pants, or a pair of low shoes, sold for less than five dollars. Everyday people seldom bought soft drinks by the case in those days, but a dollar would buy a case of Coca Cola if anyone wanted that much. You could buy a new car with the income of a hundred days' work. The main thing was, by clothing myself and buying necessities, I was no longer a drain on my Mother's modest income from teaching. I was not only a solvent eight-year old, I even extended small loans and gifts to Mother and my brothers. With minor exceptions, I have never lost the financial independence I acquired when I was a child pulling my produce wagons and milking my cow.

Looking back, I guess I should have noticed and told Mother about Ed's unusual need for water and his tendency to put on excess weight. Every place we stopped, he asked for and drank some water. It was a early sign of a pre-disposition for polydypsia and the severe diabetes he eventually developed, but I was too young for Ed's behavior to mean anything. He was much younger — only six — and even so there was little I could have done about Ed's symptoms at the time.

Activities gravitate to active people, and before I reached my teens and high school, I continued to add to my ventures. The Union News, a newspaper in Towson, Baltimore County's capital, offered a new bicycle or a thoroughbred Holstein heifer to anyone who sold 20 subscriptions to the paper. I sold all 20 subscriptions to customers on my "arab" route. Thinking that bicycles wear out and make no money, while a heifer produces milk and eventually meant profit, I took a heifer registered under the unforgettable name of "Glenham Konigen Cornelia."

Meanwhile, one of my produce customers had a cow that delivered twin calves, one male and one female. She offered me the heifer, and I took her, giving me what seemed almost a herd of cattle, in my young life. The barn had plenty of space for all three animals, and feeding three was little more work than feeding one or two. Things were looking up!

It seemed that way, but hopes and realities often turn out different, which taught me another lesson. I had just turned 12, and high school was in Catonsville, 6 miles away. A bus to the school came by our house, and most of the time I could afford the fare. Before climbing on the bus at 8 A.M., my routine was to milk the cow, add the morning's raw milk to the production of the evening before, and deliver it to my loyal customers. Most of the time this routine was so habitual I never thought much about it. When the weather turned rainy, however, my cow became extra smelly, and I became a walking smell of cow and barn. I used to hate the looks on the faces of others on the bus as they saw me climb aboard. My reception in the crowded, humid classroom at school wasn't any better.

My two heifers had grown into cows that ate, but delivered no milk. Neither of the heifers had ever been bred and delivered a calf, so they had yet to "come fresh." Something had to give, so I decided to sell the heifers and stick to my one milk cow. Fortunately, both animals looked prime and I had no trouble selling them.

A retired policeman lived on a small farm just up the road from our house. He happily bought the registered Holstein for $37.50. The owner of the bus I rode to school bought the twin heifer for a little less, $35.00. I had done well!

Before two months had gone by, both purchasers came to me and asked for their money back. According to the purchaser of the registered Holstein, the heifer had eaten barbed wire which naturally enough proved indigestible. The wire also perforated the animal's stomach bringing her to an untimely end. The question was, when and where had the Holstein gotten her fatal meal. Twelve-year old boy or no, I led the unhappy ex-policeman around our barn and pasture to show we had never used barbed wire. Then we went to his small farm where I picked up lose pieces of barbed wire from a barbed wire fence he had put up. My case closed, I wished my neighbor well, but not well enough to return his money. Grumbling and reluctantly accepting his fate, my neighbor watched me leave his farm and end that complaint.

After settling the case of the barbed wire eating cow, the buyer of the twin calf began complaining to me while I rode his bus to Catonsville High School. He said he had his heifer serviced by four bulls, but the heifer never came pregnant. I replied he had not asked for a guarantee of fertility, and I had never given him one. The problem with his heifer was his, not mine. Later, I learned that when a twin birth occurs with one male and one female, the female is often sterile. Trivial players may like to know this is called a "Free Martin" in the cattle trade. The bus owner eventually stopped complaining. I kept that money, too.

Reminders of my venture into dairy farming kept coming to me until just a few years ago. Every year I got an annual letter from the Holstein/Freisian Association of dairy cattle, addressed to one "Master Ross Pierpont." I guess I should have told them I never wanted to be a cattleman anyway.

Another of my early ventures took place as a willing associate of my cousin, Brent Sauter. Brent was a strapping young man with a ready grin and an even readier imagination. He loved idle conversation with the customers on his huckster route, and came up with stories about Baltimore County as far-fetched as they were amusing. This venture, never to be forgotten as a practicing physician, taught me the power of mind over the physical body. People who need help are often ready to believe anyone who promises to deliver it.

Marsha Myers was a very nice lady of middle age troubled by severe arthritis. One day I went with Brent Sauter to cover his huckster route, and we called on "Lady" Myers. Mrs. Myers wanted to know if Brent could supply her with fresh spring water. Brent thought a moment. "Yes, ma'am, we can do that. But it's hard right now to reach the spring." Mrs. Myers wanted spring water very badly. "I'll pay you for your trouble, young man. I want eight one-gallon jugs a week. One for each day and a spare."

"That's a lot of jugs, Mrs. Myers."

"What would you charge me?"

Brent looked at me. I looked at Brent. Brent turned to Mrs. Myers. "I'll do it for $2 a week."

"That will be just fine! Bring the first jug as soon as you can."

When we were out of her hearing, Brent looked at me and burst into laughter.

"What's so funny?"

Still chuckling, Brent said, "Ross, all water comes from springs somewhere. Let's get eight jugs, fill them with water for her and see what happens."

The week following the spring water conversation, we got eight empty jugs and started off toward Mrs. Myer's house. On, the way, there was a house with a high porch, and under the porch we saw an outdoor water spigot. We filled the jugs with nice, clear water from the spigot and delivered them to a waiting Mrs. Myers. She smiled to see the jugs and paid Brent his two dollars. Both of us felt some pangs of conscience about taking this nice old lady's money, because Brent said, "You know, Mrs. Myers, you shouldn't expect anything from your water for — oh, six weeks or so." Where he got the idea of waiting six weeks, I'll never know. Call it just one of those ideas that happen.

We faithfully delivered Mrs. Myers her water, exchanging full jugs for empty ones, for exactly six weeks and 48 jugs' worth. On the sixth delivery, Mrs. Myers gave each of us a cake and kissed us on the cheeks. "You boys have made me feel so much better!" she said. "I'm so glad you helped me."

Brent and I were frauds, and we both knew it. However, Mrs. Myers also felt better. For whatever reason, her faithful ingestion of a gallon of water a day, taken from a spigot under a neighbor's porch, had resulted in some relief from her painful arthritis. I asked myself, should we tell Mrs. Myers the truth, give back her money, and let her go back to her pre-spring water days? No, somehow even as mischievous boys we knew that telling her the truth would be devastating. So as long as Mrs. Myers wanted the water, we took it to her. Nor did it hurt that every $2 she paid us was pure profit!

Every physician encounters "the Myers' phenomenon" — the power of suggestion, or mind over matter — thousands of times. The effect has yet to be fully understood. Sometimes in my own practice, I had to make a conscious effort to avoid disillusioning patients hoping desperately that something of no medical value was an answer to their pain. In cases where patients had to know the truth to avoid hurting themselves, I have had no choice but to tell them that "Mrs. Myers' spring water" was not a substitute for medical care.

Suggestion has another side to it. One of our family's favorite stories came from an episode at the Zimmerman stall in Lexington Market. One day, they brought in two bushels of radishes which they emptied on the stall's counter. Grandfather soon noticed a nicely dressed young woman standing with her back against the counter holding the radishes. Strange! Unobserved by the woman, he watched as she reached behind her back and took a radish from the counter display. She placed the radish in a handkerchief which she carried to the proper place for a handkerchief, her nose. But the radish in the handkerchief popped into her waiting mouth.

The action fascinated Grandfather Zimmerman, and he continued to watch as the woman repeated exercise twice, three times, then four. The loss of four radishes meant nothing, but he could not let her get away with her sneaky thievery. He thought a moment, then called loudly to his son: "Albert! Albert, come here with that water hose. Get these radishes off the counter and wash them again! That darn stall cat of yours just climbed on the counter and peed all over them!"

When he got to this part of his story, Grandfather always laughed as he told how the woman began to choke, sending bits of radishes flying out of her mouth as she dropped her handkerchief and fled gagging and spitting out of the market and into Lexington Street.

Lexington Market provided another episode of family lore. This time it was cucumbers. A fastidiously dressed matron was picking over the Zimmerman cucumber display and trying to make her selections by squeezing the cucumbers. When she found one firm enough to satisfy her, she probed it with a thumbnail. When it got too much for Grandfather, he caught the woman's eye and said, "Madam, I must tell you that the more you squeeze some things the harder they get." The matron gaped as Grandfather continued in his best confidential tone. "Unfortunately, Madam, cucumbers are just not one of them."

Approaching age 12, I entered two new phases of my young life in Woodlawn. One new phase was to start my high school studies at Catonsville High School which drew students from an area of perhaps 100 square miles. Going to school was never a problem for me. Somehow, by then, I had become convinced my future contained a position in medicine, but I hadn't the faintest idea how that would come about. I just felt it would happen. I loaded my schedule with all the academically-oriented subjects I could find. To me these studies were like mental meals to be ingested, digested and filed away in my mind.

While studies had never given me problems I couldn't handle, I suddenly found my whole outlook on life changed. Girls!

Until I changed my outlook, girls were, well, girls. They were there, as all the other things in life were there, but we paid no more attention to them than was necessary. What I discovered at age 14 was that girls my age were nothing like girls I saw when I was 10 or 12. They didn't even look the same! I suddenly became attracted — no, fascinated! — with soft round curves that looked so touchable, and the way girls' bodies moved this way, that way, when they walked. I think girls were on my mind even as I slept. In fact, there was no doubt girls were on my mind as I slept.

My imaginative pleasures almost totally absorbed me in my deepest, secret self until the temptations of early sexual attraction ran smack up against the demands of school work. My grades suffered terribly.

My third year in high school became the absolute bottom of my entire educational life. Fortunately, the requirements of entering college and earning a medical degree had enough power to pull me back from potential disaster. With an increased appreciation of feminine attraction, especially in the girls of my senior high school year tempered by determination to keep such distractions in their place, I was able to re-concentrate on my studies. Fortunately, if not without some regrets over missed opportunities, my efforts succeeded. I finally graduated well up in my class. (I find myself smiling as I write this, for the memories of those heady times are fun to recall, even at these late years of my life. Surely, this is a tribute to the power of imagination. Alas! what's left now is mostly just that — imagination.)

A part of the discipline learned in my childhood, and then as a boy in my teens, was to address people in their proper titles. Children did not call adults by their first names. Acquaintances did not call each other by first names. Only equals and intimate friends were spoken to in first names. The use of last names showed respect, and also distance.

People who did not know my mother well enough to call her by her first name, but did not want to be so formal as to call her Mrs. Pierpont, came to call her "Miss Ethel." Although I never called her that, as I have mentioned she was also "Miss Ethel" to me when I was one of her pupils in her one-room school.

The title was a combination of neighborly affection and respect. The name suited her well. Miss Ethel at that time of her life was a tall, erect woman of no-nonsense bearing. Her smile was quick to light up her strong features, and her frown and tightly closed jaw served her well as mental punishment. Physical cleanliness and neatness, self-control, empathy for the needs of others, and a total love of education were the building blocks of her character. Not until I was grown and left home did I fully realize how our neighbors in Woodlawn, and her students at our county elementary school, appreciated her as a friend and confidant. It was common for neighbors with little education to bring her documents to read and explain. They also often asked for her advice.

One reason Mother understood and respected the need of help for others is that she needed so much help herself. Without being asked, my three uncles in Oregon put her on their payroll at $100 a month. Her brothers in Maryland sent us fresh fruits and vegetables in season, and gave money, too, from time to time. With such care and help, we survived.

One day after studying our finances, Mother decided that our unfinished attic could be turned into a source of income to supplement her schoolteacher's pay. She borrowed money and turned the second floor into an apartment. It was rented instantly and was never vacant as long as I lived there. That led to another survival-based decision. We had three bedrooms, one for Mother, and two for four boys. Mother kept one bedroom for herself, put the four of us boys in one bedroom, and cleared the third bedroom to take in a boarder. One of our boarders was a smart, good-looking woman who taught with Mother at Woodlawn Elementary. She lived with us for only a few weeks before Webster Sauter, a cousin, discovered the attraction. He became a steady visitor, and we soon lost our boarder while gaining a new relative.

Renters in the apartment, a boarder in a bedroom, plus four energetic boys in the house could have become bedlam. When you have only one bathroom and that many people, you either enforce mutually accepted controls or life becomes chaos. The fact is, we not only managed, we kept our lives on a fairly even keel because Mother organized our activities with patience, respect for privacy, and aplomb. Indeed, her management of the Pierpont household earned her yet another name, "The Madam."

To understand growing up in our German-based culture in Woodlawn of the 1920s, it is necessary to understand the role and function of religious practice at the times. Probably the easiest way to explain our community's religion is the word "practice," for our religion in Woodlawn included a prescribed, thoroughly understood ritual. Everything went according to undeviating schedules. You knew what your religion expected of you, and you did it. If you were not faithful to what you learned in Sunday School, and from a thundering pulpit, you would pay a great price for your sins. Not the least of these were eternal suffering and torment from the fires of Hell. This was redemption religion. There were no in-betweens.

When it came to our religion, Mother was a dedicated church-going woman. She served on the Board of our church (almost unknown for a woman in those days), helped select our preachers, and spent precious hours working the oyster and chicken patty dinners to raise money.

It was never a question about what we would do on Sundays. We got up, dressed in our "Sunday clothes," and went to church. When Uncle Fred Loos did not pick us up in his car, we walked as a group to St. Luke's Methodist Episcopal Church on St. Luke's Lane, about a mile and a half away. Uncle Fred liked church and sang in the choir. He also played the banjo, mandolin, and guitar on request. For Sunday School, we divided our family into different sections of the one-room church according to age and subject matter.

For the Sunday sermon following Sunday School, nine of us sat together in one pew. Every year, the church rewarded us for our faithfulness; the first year, a pin; the second year a wreath, then a series of bars for the next years up to fifteen. The Loos, Zimmermans, and Pierponts were a thoroughly decorated, dedicated group that took going to church seriously.

The weekly rituals were only one part of our religion and times. An equally important part centered upon Dr. Cook, an evangelist. Dr. Cook traveled a well-known evangelistic circuit that included spending the last two weeks of August and the first two weeks of September with our Woodlawn congregation. For his special services, the church erected a big white tent on the Emmert property just outside Woodlawn. The tent held about 250 people sitting, and another hundred or so standing. Throughout the tent were vessels where people grateful for saving their souls acknowledged their redemption with suitable donations. Sometimes I watched how people gave way to their deepest emotions as they were being saved, then the gratitude measured by their contributions, and I could not help wondering how many would make it through purgatory and into the promised land.

I do not question Dr. Cook's religious sincerity when I say he was a professional, conducting a professional group experience. I can still see the people in that tent shoulder to shoulder, all united in their desire to believe; I can feel the throbbing power of the organ, and the congregation standing and singing, some as loudly as possible, then others humming and singing ever so softly... Electricity charged the very air one breathed as hundreds of voices joined in singing "When the Roll Is

Called up Yonder," "Amazing Grace," "Onward Christian Soldiers," "Bringing In The Sheaves," and "The Old Rugged Cross."

So many years later, the experience of hundreds of religiously-charged voices and the throbbing organ preparing the faithful for "the message" is something I will never forget..

What messages those were! The scene is a frock-coated Dr. Cook thundering from the pulpit about God's forgiveness of the worst sinners...and the need for all sinners to ask for His redeeming grace. The evangelist flings his arms outstretched to their limit as he begs attending sinners to come to the altar of redemption. "Come! Come, give yourself to God!" The evangelistic fervor of Dr. Cook arouses those moved by his appeal. Some rise, go forward, and kneel head down over the altar. Dr. Cook, face shining with perspiration, beams in approval. Alas, others waver. Some clearly want to go, but are not ready for the commitment. The organ comes alive. The choir softly sings "Nearer My God To Thee." More come forward. The choir sings and Dr. Cook implores every sinner to find redemption over the words to "What a Friend We Have In Jesus."

You could breathe pure religious emotion in Dr. Cook's tent.

Dr. Cook always visited us when he came to Woodlawn, and I was given a part in the nightly services. I can still see myself where Dr. Cook and Mother stationed me at the back of the tent to watch the people. By now I had grown into a thin, some would say gangly, boy of 14. For the evening services, I put on a freshly ironed white shirt, a blue serge suit with knickers, my pair of black patent leather shoes, and combed my unruly tow hair into a semblance of order. At my station, I looked for tears to fill eyes, or a person with body-language indicating a readiness to be saved. Then I gently and firmly took that person by the arm and led him or her to the altar. Not for nothing do the religious refer to their followers in terms of pasture and sheep. The more who went forward, the more others followed.

When the altar was full, Dr. Cook would go forward to lay his hands on each person and say a prayer. As each one rose and returned to his or her seat, each donated in thankfulness for their salvation. The glow on these persons' faces never failed to impress me. It was real. It was, in some ways, holy.

Dr. Cook's evangelism lasted just about three hours, but he was as tireless at the end as he was at the beginning. Not even the town drunk wore him down. Night after night, this lost soul came to be saved all over again. Alas, John Barleycorn was more powerful than Dr. Cook's redemption. Dr. Cook never failed to meet the man with limitless forgiveness and compassion. The drunk truly meant well, I suppose, for he always made a contribution upon being saved.

Being involved in the collection of nightly donations, I could not help but notice that the contributions became smaller and smaller as the week's services went on. I don't think redemption became cheaper. Why did people donate less? Perhaps it was the repetition of the experience. Perhaps something else. Who's to say?

I am sure no one in our families would have been so faithful to our church without the inspiration of my Mother. She believed in God's good will and her religion without doubt or question, and she wanted to share her faith with us. Somehow we understood, without thinking about it, that her belief in the goodness of God was a strength that kept her going through strains that surely would have broken a weaker person. We knew she was only doing her best to open a door for us to find the same kind of strength, to show us a right way to go. In general, Mother's vaccination took. None of us became intensely religious, nor did any of us turn away from the teachings and beliefs of our youth. Religion was there. We accepted it. It colored our lives and made them more meaningful. We had no need to say anything more.

Although religion dominated our Sunday mornings, we had the rest of our Sundays to fill. At such times, Mother turned into Miss Ethel, the educator. We had a second-hand upright piano in our living room, and Mother saw to it I took lessons from age 5 to age 11. None of my brothers could be persuaded to study music although Roger toyed with a trumpet until he tired of it. The best that can be said of Mother's musical effort was it planted in me a seed of music appreciation which has brought me uncounted hours of pleasure. Rarely do I miss an opportunity to attend Baltimore opera, or performances of the Baltimore Symphony orchestra.

When I was still in high school, Miss Ethel's passion for education led to enrolling my oldest brother, Roger, into the University of Maryland at College Park as a boarding student. I followed his progress enviously, and all of us were proud to see him graduate with a degree in Entomology.

After graduation and getting a job, Roger returned some of Mother's investment in his education by sending us money. Nothing was said, but we three boys still at home always knew it when Roger's funds arrived.

One of Roger's early jobs was to direct the spraying of New Jersey with DDT to get rid of mosquitoes. A more interesting though unsavory job came later when he became a Captain in the U.S. Army. The Army sent him to Naples, Italy to run a service which de-loused Naples prostitutes. Whores infested with lice were a threat to spread typhus among soldiers on shore leave, and the Army's solution to that threat was practical enough: dis-infest the whores. In the inscrutable ways of the military, it became inevitable that Roger would become known as "King of the Whores of Naples."

Our knowledge of DDT and other pesticides was limited, and Roger eventually paid a price for his part in using them. Contracting asthma and emphysema from inhaling DDT, he eventually died at age 77 of respiratory failure.

My next oldest brother, Philip, was a Pierpont aberration academically. Philip simply refused to study. He was a good athlete, and his basic goal in life was to have a good time. If that meant playing cards, playing golf, or playing baseball, so be it. Of course his sledding injury and subsequent illnesses permanently handicapped him, but he made the most of it. He trained himself to use his right arm so successfully he became an excellent baseball pitcher. In one game in a good amateur league, he struck out 21 of 22 batters facing him. Since he could not run well with his handicap, he took up golf with a different kind of handicap. He was so good at golf he had a scratch (0) handicap, to 2 or 3 for a long period of his adult life. He was even a good pool player, but a student he was not.

Philip's ability to make an independent livelihood was always somewhat of a question mark with us, and when he finally decided he wanted to build a gasoline service station, Mother could not have been happier. Between them, they found a good location, and Mother borrowed money to build it using our property as collateral. When the station was finished, she deeded it to Philip. My brother was a good mechanic, and we all pitched in to get the station into profitability. The station did well, and taught me how to grease a car, change the oil, change a wheel with a flat tire, and other acts of maintenance.

With Roger a graduate entomologist pursuing a military career and second-oldest Philip established in his own business, that left Ed and me to be accounted for. In 1940, the year before the Japanese attacked Pearl Harbor, I greeted Mother with my medical diploma. I was 22, and still looked like a gangling, tow-head kid. Well, shoot! I was a gangling, tow-head kid.

Youngest brother Ed brought Mother's maternal responsibilities to an end with his own M.D. three years later. Whatever Mother's secret thoughts through all the years of our struggles, whatever doubts she had felt and hidden, were now resolved. After Ed's graduation ceremonies, she looked at him with pride. "Three out of four!" she exclaimed, her respect for education never far below the surface. "That's not so bad. That's one job that's finished." A great smile warmed her face, and I longed for a way to tell her I understood her sacrifices, her love for us, and her pride. But I was still just 22, and there was much for me to learn before I could truly understand the woman I loved as Mother, and cared for in other ways I lacked the words to describe.

Chapter Two
"Nothing to Fear But Fear Itself"

Who knows better than a doctor how nature can be both cruel and kind? One of nature's kindest acts is the way memories can soften our worst experiences. It is impossible to re-live — who would want to! — the terrible and gloomy days of the early 1930s in the United States. Jobless men sat in cheerless homes day after day, or wandered the streets desperately looking for work that wasn't there. Anxiety drained the natural warmth from family relationships in homes by the millions. Fear spared no one. Uncertainty loomed like the pall of an untreatable illness replacing security and stability in families in neighborhoods still rich and newly poor.

Nor was it easy on the families of men who still had jobs. Each day a man went to work he knew it could be his last one. Day after day, men lost their jobs; there was no end to it, and downcast breadwinner after breadwinner walked the streets with other unfortunates to beg or stand in breadlines. Perhaps worst of all was the feeling that no one seemed to know what to do to make things right again. Helplessness destroyed hope.

Prudent families who had built up savings lived on them until the money ran out. Banks foreclosed mortgages on properties they could not re-sell, while people lost everything they owned. Families doubled up to avoid being on the street. Theaters ran specials where admission was a can of food or even a single potato. Fathers and grandfathers alike took work in the Government's "Work Progress Administration" wielding a pick and shovel. It was better than nothing. Unemployable young men went into camps called the Civilian Conservation Corps. High school graduates loafed on the streets because looking for a job of any kind was a waste of time. In one of President Franklin Roosevelt's famous "fireside chats," the outwardly confident Roosevelt delivered his famous, meant-to-be inspiring declaration, "We have nothing to fear but fear itself!"

In some ways, the Pierpont family was lucky in the days of the Great Depression. Poverty and struggle every day of our of lives had trained us for it. When you are looking at life from the bottom, the only way is up. As for young Ross Pierpont, I continued with my cow, my huckster route, and any odd jobs I could come across. One of my odd jobs was a family affair consisting of helping to run a pool room in back of the Woodlawn gasoline service station, a predecessor of the gasoline station my brother, Philip, would open years later. During the three years from 1929 to 1932, when the owners of the pool room weren't there, Philip, Ed and I took turns keeping it open.

There were three tables in the pool room. Most mornings at 8 A.M., we came in and woke up the homeless men we had let sleep on the tables the night before. We took off the covers, brushed the cloth, checked and chalked the cue sticks and were ready for business. Sometimes the homeless men had garnered a few bucks the day before, and would use it to shoot pool. Men without money were allowed to stay out of the cold and watch. We three brothers often played as house men. We always split the take with the room's owners, and sometimes we got $5 for the day. Often, of course it was less. On really good days, it was a little more. But man, $5 in cash when you could ride a bus for a nickel was big money. It was also big money compared to what I came to earn only a few years later!

Money was so scarce in one of my years at Catonsville Senior High that I couldn't come up with the bus fare so I rode the bicycle I had bought from earlier earnings. When it snowed it was take the bus or stay home. With no other choice, I tapped my savings for the bus fare; I would not let weather keep me from school.

As my graduation from high school neared, my goal of becoming a doctor like Dr. Smink became a question mark. Where could I go? Where would I get the money to pay tuition and live on? Mother and I studied what we could do with the savings I had put aside during my high school years very, very carefully. My options were limited to the University of Maryland School of Pharmacy and the School of Medicine. The School of Pharmacy charged about $250 per year for tuition. If I was good enough, and lucky enough, to be selected for a three-year pharmacy course, pre-med, I could apply for the School of Medicine. If my grades in Pharmacy School were high enough, I would be on a preferred basis for acceptance in the Medical School. Tuition at Medical School was a little higher than for Pharmacy School. The two schools were right across the street from each other at Lombard and Greene Streets in downtown Baltimore. Not only was the tuition within my possibilities, if I worked while going to college, I could get to either school on the Woodlawn trolley for a nickel one way! The School of Pharmacy was my only answer.

With the blind confidence only a 15-year old product of the Zimmerman-Pierpont families could muster, I never thought for a moment I might not be accepted by both schools. I was Ross Zimmerman Pierpont. I was able. I was stable. I wanted to become a doctor. I would be admitted and graduate. Blind arrogance? Refusal to admit a possible rejection? Probably both. It did not matter. I had fought my way upward for every one of my 15 years, and failure was something that happened to others, not to me. I didn't ask how I would succeed. It was not a question.

I was right. I entered Pharmacy School in the fall of 1933, and began earning my way through. My education in pharmacy became my life for the next three years. Earning my education is not a mistaken choice of words. While in my first college year and going on age 16, I applied for admittance to the National Youth Administration Program. This was one of President Roosevelt's attacks on "fear itself," and it was good news when I was accepted, for it brought me fifteen dollars, sometimes more, every month.

My first NYA job was to help the man who ran the school stockroom. Then I graduated to be a monitor of the physics class taught by Drs. Pillsbury and Ashbury. While I watched and helped the class, Pillsbury found time to work on his thesis for his doctorate. I always admired the title of his opus: "The effect of moonlight on the pineal gland to impart that 'lovey dovey' feeling." My last job at the Pharmacy School was to clean the workroom and office of the school's professor of organic chemistry. Did that make me, Pierpont the embryonic physician, a janitor? It sure did. But janitoring also earned me 35 cents an hour. Allowed a maximum of 10 hours a week, that came to $3.50. Cash! It was a lifesaver when the government later raised my rates to a loftier level: 50 cents an hour.

My weekly NYA income combined with my savings did not provide enough for me to continue Pharmacy School, but weekends and summers were still open. As soon as my first year of Pharmacy School was over, I found a job as a clerk in Stagmers Drug Store in Catonsville. I had passed the milestone of age 16, marking one of the big years of my life, for I had not only finished one full year of graduate education successfully, I was now old enough to get my driver's license! A sympathetic Philip listened to my needs and lent me his "renovated," second-hand Chevrolet to go to work at the drug store. Each Friday, I worked from 4 in the afternoon till 11 at night. I fell into bed when I got home Friday night, slept fast, and got up Saturday morning early enough to feed, milk and pasture my cow, and be at the store by 7, thanks to Philip's car.

My workday on Saturdays ended once again at 11, but Sundays were a breeze. They started at 8 in the morning and I was off by 10 that night. Over only three days, I accumulated 37 hours of paid work, for which I received $12. Cash! To that I added my 10 hours with the NYA at 50 cents an hour, and golly! I pocketed $17 a week. Every week! Was I slave labor working at Stagmer's Drug Store 37 hours for 32 cents an hour? I didn't think so then. I was happy to get the money I needed for my education. I guess Philip thought the same way too, or he wouldn't have lent me his precious car.

Even at my wages, and with Stagmer father and son working the store, it was touch and go to stay open. In those depression times, people used their money only for bare necessities, and sometimes not even the necessities. The competition of growing chain drug stores drove down prices, and my job was always a question mark.

Activities happen to active people, and one day a customer I knew named Charley Fisher called me to one side. "I've been watching you, and you've got a lot on the ball. I do a lot of business with Peoples Drug Stores in Washington, and they are hiring drug clerks. What do you think about working for Peoples?"

"I don't know — never thought about it. But I checked Reads and they pay $14 a week for 10 hours a day 6 days a week. I can't work hours like that and go to school, too."

Charley nodded. "You're right. But Peoples is better. They pay $18 and commissions, and their commissions are higher than Reads. What do you say I recommend you?"

It was too rich to turn down. Somehow I would manage the hours and my studies, no matter what it took. However, I got lucky at Peoples Drug. Instead of having to take a regular, full time job, I got a job to fill in for clerks on vacation, sick, or anything else, at a store on Georgia Avenue between Emerson and Farragut Streets in northwest Washington. I started during the vacation season, so I immediately found myself working every day.

I needed a place to stay, and I asked others in the store about a room to rent. A customer in the store at the time heard my question and said he had an apartment in the Colony Theater building at the end of the block and had a room he didn't need. He would rent it to me if I wanted it. Did I want it! His apartment looked beautiful to me — large and roomy and well kept, with three bedrooms and two baths. The rent of the spare room was in my league at $3.50 a week, so I rented it on the spot.

My ten-hour days varied because I was a relief man. One day I would work 10 hours from 1 P.M. to the 11 P.M. closing. Another day, I might work 8 A.M. to 6 P.M. Seventy hours a week brought $18 for my base salary. However, the Peoples chain had a commission on its own brand of products, products purchased at special prices, and close-out items. I often wondered what people did with all that awful Ben Hur perfume they bought because it was so cheap. My commission ran 10% to 20%, and I recorded every "P.M" or "Blue" sale on a special sheet kept by the cash register. I really worked at moving commission items, and it paid. off. On an average week, I added about $25 in commissions to my base salary. If we had some really hot close outs to sell, I could earn as much as $50 to $60 additional. No income tax to pay, either. That kind of income far exceeded anything I had ever imagined possible. It surely put to shame my $12 a week earned at the neighborhood drug store in Catonsvile.

With the possibility of losing my job and finding enough money to pay for my education always nagging my mind, I never missed a day of work at Peoples. I worked all free time at Christmas, at Easter, at other holidays, during other clerks' vacations, and absence due to illness. Everywhere Peoples needed a relief man, I was ready for the job. Before I finally had to quit, I had worked at just about every Peoples Drug Store in Washington.

My trust in people, combined with a total lack of sophistication, brought me close to disaster in Washington. Between work and college, I went to my room in the theater building only long enough to sleep, bathe and leave. If I worked the 8 to 6 shift, I ate dinner at Mrs. Telford's "Buffeteria" a distance away at Columbia Road and 14th Street Northwest. With my 17-year old appetite to guide me, my goal in food was as much as I could get for the least money. Mrs. Telford's gave me all I could eat for 75 cents. There were times I ate enough dinner there to last me for a second day. That didn't hurt my budget, either.

Intimately familiar with animal life all around me at Woodlawn, not to mention the need to bring my cow fresh, and with the normal interests of a 17-year old, sex was hardly a strange phenomenon to me. Peoples Drug Stores sold condoms every day. However, nothing prepared me for what happened when I went to my room one night. About midnight after we had cleaned up and closed the drug store following the 1 to 11 shift, I dragged myself, bone weary, up Georgia Avenue and into the apartment. The door to the kitchen stood wide open and I stopped dead in my tracks staring at a scene I couldn't believe. My landlord, George, nude from the waist down, and a woman about age 20 I recognized as the daughter of another occupant of our apartment, were making violent love on the kitchen floor. Neither heard me come in, or if they did, they were too occupied to care. George continued thrusting, and his partner continued heaving until I turned away, shaking my head over what I had just seen. It was the first time I had ever been a visual participant at human intercourse.

I quietly closed the door to my room behind me and tried to fall asleep, but noises I'd never noticed before came through the wall from the room next to mine. George's partner on the kitchen floor normally occupied this room with her mother. Sounds of unusual motion, punctuated by an occasional moan or sigh, told me I was not hearing the mother talking in her sleep or fighting a nightmare.

I left early the next morning to make an 8 A.M. starting time at the drug store. The day after that I worked the shift ending when the store closed, and I wondered what I would encounter when I got to my room. All was quiet. I slept until mid-morning, when I found I was all alone in the apartment. My fellow female residents, Mother Jane and daughter Monique, had gone to their jobs with the Federal Government. George, who had no job I knew about, also was nowhere to be seen. As I stood there wondering just what I was in the middle of, prudence told me I needed to check things out. Doors were not locked, and when I looked in Monique's empty room, very large photographs of this attractive young woman in different nude poses sat here and there. My 17 year old mind recorded one of the photographs indelibly on my memory. Monique, standing and totally nude, had bent down until her long brown hair touched the floor. The photographer took the picture showing her face framed by her spread legs. With a big smile, she seemed to be laughing at my juvenile gaping at female anatomy customarily hidden between female legs.

A further look around showed that daughter Monique had taken lessons from Mother Jane, who had similar photographs on display. Neither Playboy nor Penthouse was in existence when I saw my first nude female photographs, but both women could have made these magazine's pages had they been in existence at the time. Landlord George wasn't left out, either. His room had plenty of similar photographs, though he hadn't gone in for the enlargements. I had seen enough. Now I had to find out what I was into.

I wasted no time getting to the drug store. Fair Dry, the fountain manager, was making sandwiches for the day and with only one customer, he was not busy. When the customer left, the store was empty. Fair came over with toast and coffee for the two of us. "Fair," I burst out, "I need to know something. What the dickens is going on in that apartment I'm in?" I hesitated to tell him more, because I just wasn't sure how far I should go in telling him what I had run into.

Fair laughed hilariously. Instead of answering me, he called to George Wiard and Andy Johnson at the store's back counter: "Wiard, Johnson, stop what you're doing and come over here. Pierpont has something to ask you."

As Wiard and Johnson joined us, they were both smiling broadly, as though they were in on a secret joke. I looked at them, puzzled. Fair said, "Pierpont wants to know what's going on in that apartment where he lives."

They were laughing at me, having their own little joke. I failed to see the fun. Wiard said, "Pierpont, are you sure you're not part of the action?"

"What action?"

All three laughed. Johnson said to the other two, "You know, fellows, this kid isn't gettin' any!"

Fair Dry had sense enough to know the fun was over. "Pierpont, we've never said anything to you because we thought you were smart enough to see what's going on where you live. Fact is, we began wondering if the temptation was enough to get you into George's operation. George is the pimp for the women. How could we know if he hadn't gotten you to join him?"

"Yeah! Sort of assistant pimp!" said Johnson. They laughed as if that was funny. I was too young to be really insulted, and these men had been good to me, but I wanted no more of it. Fortunately for me, perhaps, a customer came in and Johnson and Wiard, still enjoying their little joke, went back to their work elsewhere in the store.

"Fair," I said to Dry, "I'm living in a damn' whorehouse, is that it?"

"That's it, Pierpont. Don't think it's a small time game, either. George hustles those two women hard, and takes his cut, even though both the Mother and daughter work for the Government. Maybe I should have said something before, but I didn't want to mess with your business."

"What business!" I exploded. "I've only been working here for a few months. I've never had anything like this happen to me before."

Fair looked at me a minute while I wondered what he was thinking. I knew only that I was in a bad situation, but I was too inexperienced to know how bad. "I believe you," Fair said. Then he told me he and his unmarried sisters — in those times, the words were "old maids" — lived about two blocks from the store. They had rented out a room, but the renter had moved out, so it was vacant. If I wanted it, he would rent it to me for $3 a week.

"You're lucky, Pierpont," Fair said. "If you hadn't come to me today, and stayed in that apartment with George and his women, you stood a good chance of being arrested."

"What!" Arrested? My stomach turned over.

"George is greedy and from what I see not very careful. If the police raided that apartment while you're living there, you wouldn't have a snowball's chance in hell proving you were an innocent bystander. I don't have to tell you what would happen to you if you were caught, convicted and sent to jail as a pimp." He paused and the tone of his voice became deadly. "Or do I have to tell you what happens to pimps in jail?"

My skin crawled. My world hadn't taught me anything about pimps, much less pimps in jail. But cold fear grabbed me by the throat as I now realized my predicament. Fair was dead right about what would happen to me if the police raided the apartment and found me in it. They would laugh at my denials as Fair and the others had just laughed at my ignorance... My ambition to become a doctor, gone! ... My mother... She would believe me, but what about everyone else in Woodlawn, ready to believe a juicy scandal about the Zimmermans and Pierponts? When such thoughts stopped tumbling through my head, I said, "You don't have to tell me anything else now. Except, I'll get my first week's rent and be at your place within an hour!"

I did just that, and Fair Dry and the two sisters were wonderful friends to me for almost two years. I came to feel I had almost become a member of their family.

If I once lived in a whorehouse without knowing it, no doubt it could have happened another time, in another place, but I doubt it. Many times, oh so very many times, I thought how lucky I was, and that, as the saying goes, "God looks out for fools, drunks, and children..." To which I add, "and 17 year olds too damn dumb to look out for themselves!"

Once I recovered from my shock, I realized George had given me an indirect warning, but I had been too inexperienced to realize its significance. Out of nowhere, he had once said to me, "Pierpont, in Washington be careful if you ever pick up a woman in your car. There are good looking women who are police decoys who would really like to pick up someone like you."

"What are you talking about? I don't pick up women."

George smiled. "You're dumb enough to offer a woman a ride if she looks like she needs one. If that woman's a decoy, she'll hop in all right. When you ask where she wants to go, she gives you a fake address. Then she puts on a little act to say she's available and if you take the bait, you're dead. When you get to where she says to stop, you'll be looking at the front of a police station. And when you look at your attractive companion, you will notice a small gun pointed at your belly. She will politely ask you to join her in the police station where you will be booked and fined for soliciting."

This whole speech had puzzled me, and I had tactfully ended the conversation.

What I didn't know at the time, of course, was George's role in sex-for-pay, and the possibility he was testing me as potential pimp. Later, I learned he was a two-time loser as a pimp, and one of his larger failings was he couldn't resist personal sex with the women he pimped for. Something that puzzled me at the time, and still does to some degree, is the motivation of the two women George kept in his Washington apartment. In my brief and limited contacts with them, they were personable, were unusually attractive physically, and had good government jobs. What drove them to do sex for pay? Why did they let George dominate their lives? Never once did they make an advance toward me; could it have been that the idea of sex with an inexperienced teen-age boy had no appeal for professional purveyors of sex? I'll never know because I never went back to ask.

My innocence in sex-for-pay matched my ignorance in union organizations. Both saved me from what could have become a total disaster.

As a relief man for Peoples Drug Stores, I constantly moved from store to store according to needs. My focus was keeping my job and saving as much money as I could, so as I moved to different stores I never got to know other employees very well. Nor did I notice that very often after I left a store an employee I had worked with was transferred and later fired. Any remarks about someone quitting, or being fired, were so common in those hard times they meant little to me.

I did my best to be pleasant on the job, and be helpful, so I didn't find it unusual when a really nice middle manager for the chain, Henry Dexter, often chatted with me and seemed interested in my background and family. Our conversations were always just manager-to-young man chit-chat, except that once in a while he would mention someone who had lost his job at Peoples, and ask if I had ever heard what happened to him. One day it occurred to me he might like to meet my family. I invited him to dinner in Woodlawn, and he agreed to go with me the first afternoon we were both free.

That happened the following week, and I suggested we go by a cousin's place in Severna Park, in Anne Arundel County, where we could go for a swim in the Severn River. Then we would have dinner with my family before heading back to Washington. He picked me up at my rooming house in his car, and we started for Severna Park. As Henry drove, he became more and more preoccupied. I then noticed he seemed nervous about something, and wondered if he was uncomfortable about having dinner with people he'd never met before. I said some friendly things I hoped to be reassuring, but his conversation turned to some of the men who had been fired by Peoples. I had never been told why the men had been fired, or what they did after losing their jobs, so I had little to add to his remarks. Out of the blue, Henry pulled the car into a gas station and said he needed to make a call. I thought nothing of it and after he came back we went on to Severna Park where we had a very pleasant swim. Henry was his old self by this time and whatever had been troubling him was gone.

Mother fixed a family dinner of old-fashioned, Maryland friedchicken with mashed potatoes and gravy, and Henry and I scooped up more than our share. It was a very pleasant, and I was not looking forward to returning to my empty room in Washington, but it had to be. We were no sooner on the road back when Henry stopped the car and said very abruptly: "Ross, I almost made the biggest mistake of my life today."

He hesitated. I said, "What was it?"

Again he hesitated before saying, "I'm going to give it to you straight. I am in charge of organizing the union at Peoples Drug. They are fighting us every way they know how." He let that sink in for a minute. "In your job the company sent you from store to store. In three stores, three good inside union men were transferred then fired right after you left them. We talked about those men getting fired, and you came up as the connection to the firing in every case."

"Why me? I had nothing to do with it!"

"No one could think of any other explanation than that you were the company's 'union buster.' There just wasn't any other connection."

I started to protest, but Henry said: "Hold your hat. Once we decided you were the union buster, we had to do something to stop you."

"But — "

"My orders were to bring you to Rock Creek Park tonight for the beating of your life. I don't know how that would have turned out — men fighting for their jobs and dealing with a kid like you they think is their enemy — " He broke off in mid-sentence and left me to think about what he was suggesting. Then he said, "The more I thought about what could happen to you, the more worried I got. That was what I was thinking about when we were on the road to Severna Park."

I remembered how anxious he had appeared. Now I knew why.

"Somehow as we talked today I knew I couldn't go through with it. The better I got to know you, the more open you were with me, the more I was convinced you had nothing to do with union busting. The company firing those men had no connection with you. It was coincidence."

Something told me not to say anything. I waited, and Henry pulled out a cigarette and took a few puffs. "Ross, it wasn't easy to call off your beating. Other men were depending on me to bring you there. But I couldn't go against my conscience. I decided today on the road to call it off, and that was the telephone call I made. After seeing you together with your family this evening, I know I was right. You are not the 'union buster'."

Thoughts tumbled through my mind. Today I was on the way to the "beating of my life. Maybe worse." What's worse? Maiming. Crippled. Beaten to a pulp and left lying at night in an empty park — would I have lived? My skin crawled. How had they picked me as their "union buster?" Of course they were wrong. But I had worked those stores. George Wiard, Alex Young, Izzy Goldstein...all three fired after I left the stores. All three were older than I was, and with my work, sleep and study schedule we had very little in common. All three, as I looked back, were conscientious workers, nice guys, too. But getting fired in the depression happened all the time. I had no reason to ask any questions about why they had been fired. Henry had smoked in silence; now I said, "Henry, I can't tell you how much I appreciate your confidence in me — what you have done for me — calling off the beating... but I want you to know I had nothing to do with anyone getting fired." My voice rose. "I am not a company sneak!"

"I know that, Ross. Now I want you to forget any of this ever happened. And whatever you do, don't talk to anyone — anyone! — about it."

At 17, your dreams always look better than the present. Terrible things only happen to others; that's them, not me. No one had ever talked to me about a Peoples Drug Store union. The only thing I was guilty of was working hard, and concentrating on what mattered to me. With the help of a clear conscience and youthful confidence, I recovered from the scare quickly. It was all over. Henry put the car in gear, and as we rode back to Washington and my room near the Georgia Avenue Peoples Drug store, I had plenty of time to think. Chance and circumstance, what a difference they make in life. No matter how we try, no matter what we do, life just goes on from one situation to another where your fate — your grades, your job, your success or failure — is in the hands of someone else.

Earlier, I mentioned how I earned extra money from the commissions Peoples Drug Stores paid for selling special products. Most of these products were Peoples' own brands of merchandise, called Promotion Merchandise. Since they cost Peoples less than national brand merchandise, the company paid an extra commission to employees who persuaded customers to buy them rather than the products they might otherwise buy. Some of the more profitable items, which paid bigger commissions, are what we at one time called "unmentionables."

Hardly anything is beyond mentioning in the most polite company today, and surely stores do not hide intimate merchandise. I wonder if anyone would really be shocked to see a video showing how to insert a tampon, manipulate a douche, or put on a condom. In the 1930s, we kept condoms inside a drawer under the counter, usually in small nondescript brown envelopes easy to "palm" to the customer. As a drug store clerk, I always got a bit of a "kick" to handle a condom sale. I learned very early how to spot the condom buyer as soon as he approached. His first move was to look around to make sure no female was within sight or hearing. The coast being clear, he would say almost in a whisper: "Give me three Trojans, Doc."

Now, I can't say I am proud of how I handled these sales. But my age 17 ethics were governed by survival, and survival in the '30's meant making enough money to live. Selling "Dash" condoms, the Peoples private label, earned me a full 10% sales commission, so I pushed "Dash" condoms every chance I got. There was no way to sell customers Dash condoms by talking about them, but I also knew that rarely if ever did a customer look at his purchase at the time of buying. When a man asked for three Trojans, I usually reached inside the condom drawer for a pack of "Dash" condoms and slipped them to him while palming the half-dollar in payment. Without another word, I would write up my "Dash" sale on the PM sheet to collect my five cents commission, and ring up the sale on the cash register.

By this time the customer was invariably on his way out, and almost always every one would sneak peek at his purchase to make sure of what I had given him. Not once did anyone ever bring back his purchase to claim Trojans instead of Dash. However, I do remember one man irate enough to look at me and mutter, "You dirty son-of-a-bitch! You gave me the wrong rubbers!" He didn't speak loud enough for me to hear, but I surely could read his lips. Fortunately, he turned and left the store and I never saw him again.

As may be easily understood, my work in Peoples Drug Store brought me into close contact with all types of people and human needs. In less than three years, I learned more about human bowel movements than I really cared to know. Today, people manage their evacuation with an almost unlimited range of medications. In the 1930s, many people relied on mineral oil. Some people, especially women, took an ounce or two of mineral oil every night.

I was working in the Takoma Park drug store when the company's "PM Advisor" announced a real special on Peoples Mineral Oil. The commission was 20% of the regular price, and we put up a large display featuring one gallon of mineral oil for $2.49. The first day of the sale, a very patrician and elderly lady, elegantly dressed including gloves, came to my counter and spoke in a voice of no nonsense: "Young man, I would like a quart of Nujol."

Nujol mineral oil sold for much more than the Peoples brand,

and did not pay a PM commission. I said, "Ma'am, do you use the oil regularly?"

"I most certainly do."

"Every night?"

"Every night. But why is this any business of yours?"

"Ma'am, I'd like to show you something. Most people don't know this, but Peoples Mineral Oil is manufactured by the same people that make Nujol. It's the same thing, and it costs a lot less."

"I never heard that. Are you sure?"

"Let me show you." I got out a bottle of Nujol, and a gallon jug of Peoples mineral oil. "Please take off your gloves. I will show you these two oils are the same."

I had piqued her curiosity enough for her to remove her gloves. I said, "Hold out both hand while I put a drop of these oils on them."

She did as requested and I carefully placed a drop of Nujol on one thumb, and Peoples mineral oil on her other thumb. I said, "Rub your thumbs and fingers together and you will see there's no difference."

She did as I asked and said, "Young man, you are right. They are the same."

"Except for the price," I said. "Look at the special price on Peoples' mineral oil. It's a real bargain today, only $2.49 for a full gallon."

She thought, as she wiped her hands with the tissue I gave her. "Is there any limit on how much I can buy on sale?"

"How much do you want?"

"Could you let me have seven gallons?"

I'm sure my jaw dropped. I could have whistled. 20% commission on seven gallons — "Just a moment until I see if we can do that." I made a few notes on a piece of paper, smiled and said, "Madam, the seven gallons will be fine. We have it."

To my amazement, she said "Just a moment, please," turned, and walked back to the front door. She beckoned to someone outside, and in came a man in full chauffeur's uniform. She spoke briefly to him; he nodded, and came to the counter and said, "I'll take it." Without another word, I wrote up the sale, and helped the chauffeur load the nine gallons of mineral oil into the biggest, blackest, shiniest Cadillac I had ever seen.

I stood there watching and thinking happily of my $2 PM commission as she got in and they drove away. It was the biggest commission of my drug store career, not to mention probably the biggest sale of mineral oil to one person ever rung up.

Other clerks in the store were somewhat dazzled by the whole episode. One said, "If that lady ends up taking all that mineral oil, you guys better watch where you walk on the slippery slopes of Takoma Park!" I had no problem joining in the laughter.

In 1937, I reached the biggest milestone of my young life — I was all of 18 — by transferring to the University of Maryland Medical School. This was the year the nation's economy had turned sour again, in a downturn labeled the "1937 recession," so I was more than pleased to get my National Youth Administration job back at the U. of M. Medical School. The pay had been increased to 75 cents an hour, still with a 10-hour limit, but $7.50 was good money in 1937. I needed every cent of it.

Since I was a veteran of the programs in the Pharmacy School, I qualified for a job in the Medical Library. Miss Briscoe was in charge of the library, and it was pretty much her life. She almost instantly recognized my deep interest in medicine, and she increasingly trusted and encouraged me.

During my hours in the Library, I checked books in and out, obtained reference lists, and catalogued some of the archives. Miss Briscoe gave me her signature stamp and pad, and allowed me to requisition library materials. Eventually I became "boss man" of the Library.

A special opportunity to make some money arose when the Medical School had to get out some mass mailings to alumni numbering well into the thousands. I asked for the job and got it. I then asked for 10 National Youth Administration students to assist in the mailing, and put them on piece work. I said, "This is a 10-hour job but I don't care how long you take. If you take 15 hours to get out your part of the mailing, I will put you down for 10 hours. I will also put you down for 10 hours if you get your mailing out in five hours."

Do incentives work? Those 10 students never took more than five hours, and the bulletins never missed a mailing deadline.

My need for money to pay tuition and live on without burdening my Mother gave me no choice but to continue at Peoples Drug in Washington until 1939. Then fortune smiled on me once again in the form of an award of a Junior Internship at Maryland General Hospital in Baltimore for that summer. I reviewed the status of my savings. Putting it mildly, accepting the internship would be very close financially. Always the optimist, I told myself that if I ran a tight budget I would make it work. I quit my job at Peoples Drug Store, and that became the last time I ever clerked in a pharmacy. Looking back through the prism of a half-century of surgical practice, I believe my experience as a drug store clerk taught me more than I realized at the time. My work for Peoples was probably a good bargain for the both of us.

Chapter Three
Pharmacy As My Key To Enter Medical School

As a teen-age boy in Pharmacy School, I didn't realize that I was getting an education in more than chemistry and medicines. Fellow students in Pharmacy exposed me to a world made up of people and ways of life I had never encountered before.

When I grew up in the Woodlawn section of Baltimore County, it was a land-oriented, very rural community made up of large landowners, farmers, hired farm workers, and tradesmen. The people I and my family associated with were almost totally Anglo-Saxon, Germanic, and Protestant. I knew people who belonged to different Protestant denominations, but as a boy I never saw a Catholic church, and had yet to meet a Jew or Asiatic, or to hear of a synagogue. I finally did get to know a Jewish boy, Abe Scop, when I was going to Catonsville High School. This high school was diverse for the times, with pupils enrolled from Catonsville itself and widely scattered communities to the west of Baltimore City: Woodlawn, Randallstown, Granite, Rockdale, Franklintown, Ingleside, Landsdowne, Relay, and Arbutus. Not one black boy or girl attended Catonsville High.

In Woodlawn of the 20s and 30s, black and white were totally segregated into separate communities identified by churches, schools, and types of work performed. The only black people I knew lived in small pockets of houses dating back to the days of plantations and slavery. So far as I knew, nearly all of the blacks in Woodlawn were direct descendants of former slaves. Mobility was not a characteristic of Woodlawn at the time, and most blacks depended on employment with the descendants of former plantation owners. At least they were free to work for whomever paid them best, and most of them were proud owners of the properties in which they lived.

In those days we never discussed black and white racial cultures. People just accepted the differences as "that's how things are." Black and white, we played together when children, commonly worked beside each other, and developed friendships which remained as we grew older. However, we also separated into different ways of life as our education and responsibilities moved us apart, and rarely indeed did the twain come together. When we saw one another, old friendships endured, but mainly as memories.

Everything I knew about people changed in a hurry beginning with my first day in Pharmacy School.

The student body of Pharmacy School of the University of Maryland was enormously diversified. I rubbed shoulders every day with Poles, Ukrainians, and Italians mostly from East Baltimore City, but also from south and west within the city limits. Greeks came from "Greektown" further east of the section dominated by the Poles, Ukrainians, and Italians. Some Jews came from "Corned Beef Row" where their parents had settled as immigrants mostly from Russia and Germany. Others came from an area called "the Golden Ghetto" of northwest Baltimore City. Today, as black Americans choose to identify themselves as African-Americans, it is a bit of irony to remark that I studied long ago with a different type of African-Americans. These were whites repatriated to the United States for their schooling.

Religious beliefs mirrored ethnic origins: Very quickly, those of us who were practicing Protestants became acquainted with faithful Catholics, orthodox Hasidic Jews, Quakers, and even some agnostics or atheists.

It is easy to remember the names, and how they illustrate the student diversity. Some professors' problems in pronouncing the names were often good for a chuckle: Wasilewiki, Kosakowski, Miedwieski, Rabinowitz, Scherr, Silverman, Nurkin, Schmidt, Zimmerman, Knecht, Cosmos, Paderakis, Kamkorski, plus a Pierpont, Traband, McNally, and Henry. We spoke the English language differently; our inheritances were different, and our features were different.

Noses became one of the more interesting identifiers of ethnic origins.

A sea of multi-cultures engulfed my self-confident Ango-Saxon identity — I had become a minority! This new and demanding world gave all of us much to think about, for we were universally in the same ocean regardless of our personal differences. Two common denominators helped to bind us together. We were determined to better ourselves and in doing so better the world we were living in. Second, most of us would have called church mice rich compared to our status. Pharmacy

School in 1933 was the very pit of the Great Depression.

No doubt our common ambitions helped us to accept our differences. No one tried to change anyone else. I can't recall anyone trying to impose his way of life, or beliefs, on another. (I can say "his" because we had only a very few women would-be pharmacists.) Our adjustments were abrupt, yet they came without notable friction. We studied and worked together. We made lasting friendships in a genuinely undemanding way.

As the saying goes, "You can take the kid out of the country, but you can't take the country out of the kid." That proved true with us as school friends. When we finished school and returned to our homes, we also settled back into "the country of our lives." In spite of everything we had learned to appreciate about each other's cultures, we were most comfortable when we were with our own kind. This phenomenon is familiar to everyone, yet poorly understood. I still think about it. Writing now from a castle a thousand miles from the United States, distance gives me a clear view of the cultural conflicts tearing holes in the fabric of our society. This vantage point reveals "political correctness" to be the irrational, near-fanaticism it actually is. The anger generated by "affirmative action," and especially female hostility toward men cloaked in garments labeled "equality of opportunity" and liberating feminism, seem to me terribly divisive and destructive. Is cultural cohesion a force for good or evil? Is it possible, or desirable, to sponge away ethnic, racial, and cultural differences? Clearly, these differences are pitting American against American, men versus women. The near future could see younger generations pitted against older generations. In the hands of white, black, or religious fanatics, cultural differences can — and have — become threats to life itself. I pretend no answers to such questions. However, my experience in Pharmacy School, and later as a physician, tells me that the more educated we become as a people, the greater becomes our ability to understand and tolerate human differences. The converse appears true: The more ignorant the social group, the more its members approach "gang mentality" and hostility to anything, and anyone, foreign to them. Perhaps the answer is not to try to sponge away racial and cultural differences, but to find ways to teach understanding and accepting them. Whatever the answers may be, one thing is certain: they won't come easy.

My social learning in Pharmacy School was not limited to the discovery of human differences. I also got lessons in economic survival from my Mother and Dr. Frank Slama, Professor of Botany and Pharmacology.

Mother in her role as "Miss Ethel" had become familiar with the fee structures of the University of Maryland in the process of overseeing the courses in entomology taken by Roger, my oldest brother. When the book of curriculum of the School of Pharmacy came in, she sat down with it at the kitchen table. Her dark brown hair was long and straight, and she pushed it back from her high forehead with both hands as if this would help her to focus on her reading. Scanning the pages for course offerings and fees, she suddenly said, "Well!" That was it, but Mother was a disciplined woman, and for her that was quite an exclamation. I looked to see what had moved her, and her eyes, clear and hazel, were gleaming as she looked up at me from her reading. "I don't understand this at all. Inorganic Chemistry at College Park is $30. Inorganic Chemistry in Baltimore is $45." She looked from the curriculum book to me. "What do you make of that, Ross?"

I had no idea. I shrugged in dismissal of the question. "I don't know."

She closed the book, smiling at my innocence, and patted me on the shoulder. On registration day, Mother and I went to see the Dean of the Pharmacy School, Dr. DuMay. After the customary greetings, Mother and I sat down. Erect and imposing, completely composed, she spoke in a voice that was characteristically genteel, but at the same time authoritative. "The University at College Park and the Pharmacy School here in Baltimore have courses in Inorganic Chemistry. Is one course better than the other? Or are both the same?"

The Baltimore and College Park campuses competed with each other for prestige. Dr. DuMay's pride in his school was evident in his answer. "I assure you, Mrs. Pierpont, absolutely, the two courses are the same." He modified his tone to indicate confidentiality. "Ours could be just a little better."

Mother handed Dr. DuMay both schools' curriculum books opened to the fees for Inorganic Chemistry. "There must be a mistake in the fees, then. As you can see, the course in Inorganic Chemistry at College Park is $30. Your fee in Baltimore is $45. Since both schools are part of the University of Maryland, I would think both fees should be the same? Don't you agree?"

I glanced from Dr. DuMay to Mother. I swear her hazel eyes were twinkling.

Understandably, Dr. DuMay was not ready for the question. He did a couple of "H'mmms" as he studied the two books. "This has never come up before." He appeared to be thinking about his options, and Mother watched and waited. I was not about to open my mouth about anything. Finally, the Dean looked at both of us and bit the bullet. The School of Pharmacy was going to lose $15 in tuition, and there was no way out of it.

"Mrs. Pierpont, you are right. Our fee should be the same as College Park's. I will see that the difference is refunded."

Mother smiled graciously. Hers was a smile you earned, and when it came it was worth it. "Thank you very much, Dr. DuMay. That's very kind of you." She wasn't through. "One of my friends, Doctor, has a son here, Charles Farley. I'm sure this would apply to him, too, wouldn't it?" Dean DuMay's normal composure disappeared momentarily as Mother added very sweetly. "The boy needs help so very much. He tries so hard."

Dr. DuMay had no way out and he was a gentleman about it. "Of course, Mrs. Pierpont." He scribbled on a piece of paper. "I will see that young Charles Farley gets a refund of $15, too." Whether he was thinking how much more this could go on, I'll never know. He asked to be excused to attend a meeting and, leaving us where we stood, he left his office and disappeared down the hall.

Dr. DuMay had just met "Miss Ethel" Pierpont.

How trivial this episode may appear today! What was all the big fuss about cutting $15 in tuition? For one thing, there was a principle involved. In those days, we paid what was right and due, and not a penny more. Our family scraped not for dollars, but nickels and dimes. Sheer survival when I was a very small boy, and even more so during the Great Depression, meant making things go farther, spending money only when it was absolutely necessary. It was not unusual for an older brother, sometimes a parent, to borrow 50 or 75 cents from a younger brother, or child, with a newspaper or "a-rab" route.

Then there was the money itself. When you could buy a car for $35, or even less, $15 was one heck of a lot of money. Saving that much was worth almost any amount of effort.

One more extra-curricular lesson in Pharmacy School has never dimmed in my mind. Dr. Frank Siama taught Botany and Pharmacology during my first and second years at the Baltimore City campus. Every student had the same assignment of collecting and preserving 25 fresh botanical specimens. Preservation included drying, pressing, and mounting the specimens with identifications in Latin, English, family, and species. This was not an easily accomplished assignment for students who had grown up and lived in row-house neighborhoods of Baltimore.

I knew the Woodlawn countryside as only someone who had tramped nearly every square foot of the fields and woods would know it. I knew every stream and their wet areas where Jack in the Pulpit, violets, Forget-me-nots, mushrooms and knotweed flourished. Daisies, bloodroot, Mayflowers, cornflowers, and many other plants of all varieties grew abundantly in sunny, well-drained soil. It was as easy to gather hundreds of plants as to gather one. It only took a little more time.

Stored in our attic were magazines left over from my days of selling subscriptions to raise money. I put old copies of Country Gentleman, The Ladies Home Journal, The Saturday Evening Post, and others, to good use pressing freshly collected plant specimens. I told some of my classmates about my botanical resources, and some joined me in gathering expeditions. Others with more money than ambition offered to buy dried specimens from me to complete their collections. More than a few obtained complete collections from me. For awhile it was great! I charged a nickel for a pressed Forget-me-not, but handsome tubers, May apples or Jack-in-the Pulpit were prized and worth 10 times as much — a full 50 cents each!

The end came when Dr. Siama caught his first sight of his students' collections. His next botanical lecture focused on the experience of collecting specimens as well as presenting the finished work in class. As he warmed to his subject, he commented on the fine quality of the mounted specimens, but it soon became clear he was unhappy about my enterprise."The similarity of these collections is too great to be an accident. The assignment is to learn botany, not run a business. If I find that anyone is making a business out of collecting and selling plant specimens," he paused, his eyes scouring the waiting students, "there will be hell to pay!"

I got the message and felt that, once again, I had skated too close to an icy body of water. Only good luck had kept me from falling in. Nothing to do but clean out my locker and drop the botanical venture. Even my own handsome collection had to go, lest I trigger an angry response from Dr. Siama. Fortunately for my ambitions, I managed to scrape up other ways to help pay my way to my Pharmacy degree.

In 1938, the mood of the nation had improved and my mood kept pace. In fact, I was upbeat. I had finally made it into the University of Maryland Medical School. Glad to be there, I also had no illusions about the hardships I would face throughout the next three years. The demands of the professors of the University of Maryland Medical School were too well known to permit complacency. What I had going for me was the confidence I had built up by weathering the lean years of high school and pharmacy school. We med students got some comfort and a laugh from a well-known quotation by a previous med student of unknown place and circumstance:

"To survive academically in medical school, it is necessary to have a head and a tail. The more you have of one, the less you need the other."

My first two years, in the late 30s, were pre-clinical, followed by the clinical training. It seems a bit strange, now, but one of all of the med students' biggest problems in those days was transportation. We had to go to lectures, clinical training, and other duties (read night duty) at University Hospital in the business district of Baltimore City, at Mercy Hospital a 15 minute walk from the Medical School, and at City Hospitals about seven miles away. Public transportation was out of the question to reach City Hospital; time was much too short.

An automobile was the only answer, but buying and running one on my existing income and savings was out of the question. However, other students had the same problem I had, which inspired me to start a "Pierpont-City Hospitals Shuttle." By getting a quarter per student per round trip, I hoped to offset the price of a car and buy gasoline for it. A dollar bought six or seven gallons of gas at the time; the price of the car became the question.

I shopped for a used car until I finally found a 10-year-old model-A Ford four-door sedan. They let me test drive the car, and while it had the natural aches and pains that come with age, it ran. I wasn't interested in cosmetic appeal; I needed a car that would take me and my riders to City Hospital and back on time. 1928 Fords were really quite reliable. Alas, the seller wanted a mind-boggling $50! No way. I finally convinced him my total bankroll was $35, and that he would be helping some very grateful medical students who were out to help humanity. He let me have the car.

Winter came, as of course it always does in Baltimore. My Ford had no heater, so I scraped together $4.95 — more than 10% of the purchase price of the entire car! — and bought a heater that was a work of some engineering genius. The idea was to cut a hole in the floor of the car and install a slotted piece of metal over the hole. Then I connected one end of a large metal pipe to the underside of the register. I connected the other end of the pipe to the exhaust pipe of the car. When the exhaust pipe of the car got hot, heated air from the connection on the exhaust flowed up the metal pipe to the hole in the floorboards of the car. Behold, it worked! We could ride to and from City Hospital in middle-class comfort. That does not mean we weren't aware of carbon monoxide poisoning. But we were sure we weren't meant to suffocate with CO, and we rode our steed with nary a thought of possible suffocation.

However, thoughtlessness came close to our undoing. Two of my regular riders were Bill Pico and Luis Rowerto Guzman from Puerto Rico. The three of us became good friends, and my trusty Ford became a constant source of jokes, comments on my driving skills, and the need for vehicle improvements. Such shoddy transportation for three future medical giants!

In those days, railroad tracks ran down the center of Fleet Street. Running on a split-second schedule as usual one afternoon, the three of us were rushing to City Hospital. A long freight train was slowly puffing along the tracks in the same direction we had to travel. It was about to block our way and make us late. The challenge was too much for Pico. "Don't let that bum make us late! Take the sidewalk and pass him."

The curb was low. I ran the car with two wheels on the sidewalk and speeded up to pass the train. The train by now had gained speed of its own and was steadily going faster. Side by side we raced, the car bouncing high as the wheels hit one curb and dropped down another. "Pierponne!" yelled Pico. "You're losing! Faster, faster!"

Up to then it had been a crazy adventure. Ahead of us, we saw a truck parked at an angle. The railroad tracks veered toward the truck. Another large truck was rumbling along toward us on our side of the street. We had only one chance. Get through the gap between the locomotive and the parked truck or wreck the car. At our speed, the wreck would be total, with who knows what injuries, possibly death.

"Hold on!" I shouted and turned the car off the sidewalk and on the cobblestone street. The car protested its treatment but held together and we made the passage with inches to spare on either side. Total silence in the car permitted us to hear the curses aimed at us by the truck driver as we passed.

Irrepressible Pico found his voice. "Pierponne, I don't want to see you ever do that again."

Trembling but regaining poise, I said, "You bet your sweet ass you'll never see that again!" And he never did.

My Ford had happier memories, too. On nights when I had completed my National Youth Administration chores (now paying me 75 cents an hour), I often drove Miss Briscoe, the Medical librarian, home. She was a gracious, lovely person and a friend. Without telling me how she did it, she had learned my schedule, and let me nap on the second floor of the library, using a large piece of shelf paper to protect my clothes. Between naps, I used the time to complete my homework.

Much happier times were generated with the help of my Ford when it made dates with Grace Schmidt possible. Grace was a student nurse at Maryland General Hospital about a mile from my medical school. I really impressed Grace by taking her, another student nurse named Dolly Foster, and others, to their psychiatry training at Sheppard Pratt, the well-known psychiatric hospital in Baltimore County.

Good memories or not, the Ford eventually had to go. I sold it for $5 more than I had paid for it — after all, it had a $4.95 heater by that time. Then I turned around and bought an even cheaper car. I was an intern making $10 a month plus room and board when I bought my second car. That was really upscale living, for I no longer had to pay tuition. The $10 a month was mine to spend! The car was a Willys roadster, purchase price $27.50. In spite of that price, its Continental motor ran beautifully, and did so for 40 years including use as a truck hauling fresh vegetables and fruit on a nearby farm. People meeting the Willys for the first time always got a laugh when they saw me start it by pulling up the horn. The biggest problem with the Willys was the top and curtains; they continuously sprang leaks. By the time I had the Willys a few years, its top was a mosaic of adhesive tape scrounged from the emergency room and covered with waterproof paint.

From the anatomy of Ford and Willys automobiles to the anatomy of human beings is a bridge to be walked when you're a medical student. Knowledge of the human body is indispensable for a physician, and anatomy was the bedrock of studies at the University of Maryland Medical School. In my days there, we even carried the subject into our third year.

I assure you that anatomy studies at University of Maryland Medical School were strictly no nonsense. The head of anatomy was Professor Uhlenhuth, imported from Germany to teach the subject. He was a man in his early fifties, several inches shorter than six feet tall, gray hair parted in the middle, fierce blue eyes beside a prominent nose, and lean and muscular in appearance. The man actually looked like an anatomy professor imported from Germany! As he stood under an overhanging bright light in the pit of the amphitheater and observed our expressions, there was no question who was in charge. Our schedule was nine to noon in the dissecting laboratory, plus an hour lecture. Professor Uhlenhuth's classes began on time, ran on schedule, and ended on time. I looked forward to his demonstrations, which were invariably highly organized, clear, and without wasted time or effort. For his demonstrations, he had a wealth of skeletons, boxes of individual bones of all types and conditions, and perfectly dissected specimens of human body parts. We learned to pay attention to him, too. When he finished a lesson and aimed his questions at often nervous students, he tolerated only answers direct and to the point.

I never got to know Professor Uhlenhuth very well. I suspect no one did, but I got to know anatomy. This was my favorite study even before I entered medical school. In my pre-med training, I had dissected two embalmed cats. Most of my cat-dissection I completed at home, which did not make me a favorite of the family. The odor of formaldehyde is so powerful nothing will contain it outside a glass bottle. Its odor permeates clothing, soaks into your hands and forearms, and clings to you for days no matter how much you scrub the flesh. I rode the Woodlawn trolley to and from school, and the only way to get my embalmed cats home was to carry them in a paper bag. I was not a popular passenger but must say I was never crowded on the trolley. The problems of formaldehyde odor continued throughout my medical training no matter how hard I tried to get rid of it. I don't like to be shunned any more than any other human being likes it, but I just had to get used to people sniffing and looking around then moving away from the source of the unpleasant odor — me.

From smelling like a cow to smelling of formaldehyde — I'd made progress!

My affinity for anatomical studies made this one of my strengths in medical school. I seemed to have a natural, photographic memory for tissue structure, the position and shape of normal and diseased organs, bone and ligament connections, and the other parts of the human body. On the rare occasions when I got less than a perfect score in my examinations, whether practical or written, I was really hurt. How could it have happened! Anyway, I was proud of completing all required premedical courses in anatomy and zoology weeks to months ahead of my classmates. Anatomy was my game!

Other courses in Medical School varied from painful drudgery to the discovery of challenging ideas and information. The course in Organic Chemistry was run — not taught — by a professor who was pedantic, dull and ineffective. On a basis of one to 10, he deserved no more than a four. Required courses in pathology and clinical medicine were worthwhile, and a couple were superior. In every subject, the professor in charge made the difference.

Professor Maurice Pincoff, head of internal medicine, and an associate, Dr. Arthur Shipley, were two top men at the University. Dr. Pincoff was known for identifying the tumor Pheochromocytoma, a tumor of the adrenal gland. This tumor periodically injects a hormone into the blood stream that causes extreme high blood pressure, accompanied by extremely painful headaches. Strokes can also occur. Before Dr. Pincoff's identification of the tumor, there was no known connection between the tumor and resulting headaches, strokes, and high blood pressure. Pincoff's research showed that the adrenal tumor was a cause of such symptoms and that removing it would eliminate them. Dr. Shipley, Professor of Surgery, developed the procedure for removing the tumor.

The University supplemented classroom and laboratory studies in medical school with actual practice, most particularly OB-Gyn. Women who could not afford a doctor or hospital care could call on University Hospital for medical assistance in giving birth at home. Third and fourth year students were assigned to these calls under the supervision of the senior obstetrics resident in charge of home-delivery services.

A real problem in providing home-delivery services was the gypsies of Baltimore. Tribes or families of gypsies would cluster in rundown sections of the city, usually living in empty stores or row houses, wherever they could find them. Any medical student answering a gypsy call was likely to be surrounded by any number of skeptical or even hostile people. They didn't trust us to help them, and we didn't trust them under conditions that demanded mutual trust. The tension created a surreal atmosphere at the scene of a gypsy birth. It was far from unusual for a student attending a gypsy birth to be held a virtual captive until the delivery was over. There was no way to call for help, because the gypsies had no telephones. If a student ran into a problem beyond his capability, getting help varied from difficult to impossible.

To avoid impossible problems with gypsy births, we refused in-home delivery and insisted that the woman come to the hospital; but they learned about this and found ways to hide their identity. I guess it was inevitable that one day they would ensnare third-year student Ross Pierpont.

Early one afternoon, a call came in for help in an in-home delivery, and I was on call. I went to the address given and found myself at a store front on West Lexington Street, a rundown section of Baltimore with abandoned houses and empty stores. As soon as I stopped my car and saw I had a problem, I was surrounded by gypsies, men and women of many ages, shapes, and visual expressions. They opened my car doors and some climbed inside, all chattering in English I had trouble understanding. I reached for my physician's bag and waved vigorously for them to get out of my car. They did so reluctantly. One helpful fellow made sure I would not think of driving off by snatching the key from the ignition. I was trapped. My only choice was to make the best of it.

Mustering all of the professional presence possible for a gangling 20-something facing the delivery of a baby in an abandoned store, I entered the building. The surroundings couldn't have been worse! The gypsies had created cubicles for their families with brightly colored sheets, or makeshift partitions of cardboard or plywood. A man led the way to a cubicle and pulled aside a hanging sheet, where I looked down upon my patient, the mother-to-be. She was a dark-haired and very pregnant woman lying on blankets and pillows on the floor. I judged her to be in her late twenties, with dark, gleaming eyes wide in fear. As we stared at each other, it was a question of which one was frightened the most.

A dirty, middle-aged woman sitting beside the mother-to-be looked me over with neither welcome nor dismissal. I asked, ""When did her labor pains start?" No answer. "How far apart are the labor pains now?" Both women were silent. I guessed that neither one knew what I was asking.

"Has her water broken?"

The older woman thought as she studied me. She finally said something I guessed to be, "Pee?"

"No. Not pee. Baby water."

"Oh." She shook a mop of unkempt hair that ran half way down her back. "No baby water."

I took my patient's blood pressure and temperature. Both were normal. As I checked her chest, she shrieked violently. The older woman jumped. Was I hurting her? No, labor pains had begun. Gypsies poked their heads into the cubicle as I palpated her abdomen. Damn! Damm, damm, damm! The length of the shriek and the palpation told me this was only a short contraction and early labor.

Knowing I might as well get on with it, I used my authority to clear the sightseers from the cubicle. With the older woman watching me, I did a rectal examination. More damn the luck. Her cervix was not completely effaced; dilation was about half-programmed. This situation called for me to return to the hospital and come back hours later when the delivery was no more than two hours away. It wasn't going to happen and I knew it. They had the key to my car. I had no way to reach a telephone. My only hope was that someone would wonder why I did not return and would guess what had happened. If so, the hospital might send police and get me out of this mess. I no more than thought that thought to know I was kidding myself. I was trapped until this gypsy woman had her baby.

Actor I'm not but this was a time to be nonchalant, and I sat down beside my patient. Two dark-eyed children came in, and I played a little children's game with them for a few minutes thinking it would ease everyone's concerns. I tried to explain to the young woman what was going on inside her body, and how she could help the birth, but she either did not understand or did not want to understand. Our efforts at communication finally gave me a feeling that she and her attendant now liked me and was sure I would stay until "Consuela" delivered — what else?

A man brought in a mattress and pillow and laid it beside my patient. I was now their physician-in-residence.

Close to midnight, the woman's labor pains became longer, more intense, and closer together: about eight minutes apart. I checked the fetal heartbeat and the presentation of the baby's head. The heart was beating normally and the head now properly engaged. I could do nothing now but wait. It was going to be a long night. I sat down on the mattress and leaned against the wall. My early fear for my safety had left me, but I also had to realize I was in a precarious situation. If the birth did not go normally and exceeded my capabilities, if the baby or mother died, or if both died, my life would be in serious danger. Stories about gypsies gave them a reputation for being extremely emotional and violent. But I was doing everything I could. Everything seemed normal, and, incredibly, it seems now, I drifted into an uneasy sleep.

Someone shaking my shoulder woke me up. It was the older woman attending the birth. "Water!" she said exclaimed. ""Lots of water."

I nodded to show I understood and glanced at my watch: 4:30 a.m. Putting on a rectal glove, I checked my patient's condition and found a completely effaced and fully dilated cervix, a mid-descent, and a pelvic engagement of the baby's head. The fetal heart was fine — thank Heaven, I thought. Contractions now came every two minutes, full, hard, prolonged.

Everyone who has ever seen movies knows births call for hot water, so it was no problem to get my gypsy assistant to boil water and bring clean towels and blankets. These came with surprising speed; things were now moving well. I had one woman sit at the patient's head and hold both of the young woman's hands. "Pull on her hands!" I told my patient. "Pull hard. Push your stomach as hard as you can. Bear down and push out your baby."

Another woman mopped my patient's forehead. As many gypsies as could cluster around the curtain were peering in. Well, nothing I could do about that right now. About 45 minutes went by as my patient's cries from labor pains came almost continuously. The black occiput appeared (the back of the baby's head; this is usually the first part of babies to become visible.) The fetal heart was normal. More of the baby's head appeared.

Within only a minute or two more, the head had entirely appeared. As the woman cried out in pain, I grasped the baby's head and pulling down on it saw the right shoulder appear; then the left, and all at once the baby was born. A loud cheer went up, and I couldn't help but look up. From appearances, the entire tribe had seen the birth take place.

I cleaned the amniotic fluid from the baby's mouth and holding him head down gently slapped his buttocks. A shuddering first breath quickly changed to a newborn wail. I clamped and cut the cord and handed the baby to my faithful, and now beaming, assistant. The next step was to massage the abdominal wall to extrude the placenta. It checked out fine with a minimum of bloody drip from the vagina. As I took off my gloves, another cheer went up and I found a bottle of red wine in my hand. Definitely, this was not my sort of celebration, but I saw other bottles of red wine and realized discretion called for dissimulation. I never tasted a bottle of wine as bad as that one in my life. But they whooped when I sipped it, so I took a deep breath and had some more. Ecccch. I still remember that sour taste.

Hugs (many of them smelly) and smiles later, I headed for my car at the break of dawn. At the door, the gypsy chief waited for me. I had just delivered the heir of the head man. Once safely in my car, I checked my bag and was not surprised to find everything except my instruments had been taken. Oh well, I still had my bag, it was a new day, and I was alive.

Experiences both rewarding and frightening are part of life as a physician, especially a surgeon. I think such human lessons helped me a great deal when I taught surgical anatomy from 1945 to 1967. During that period of my life, I developed into an authority when anatomical anomalies occur in the operating room. Hardly ever did we encounter a variation I had not seen first-hand in the dissecting laboratory. On a purely personal note, the years of owning a photographic memory of human anatomy in all its enormous ramifications helped me to help an old friend, Dr. Phil Heuman. After pulling a fairly long tour of duty in the Korean War (police action?), Phil returned to resume his civilian career. He knew he was rusty and needed to go back to medical school, but the mere idea of becoming a student at his age really bothered him. I helped him with his anatomical studies, and thought no more about it.

On Phil's 50th wedding anniversary, he took the occasion to describe how I had put him at ease. "Ross Pierpont gave me the lift of my life in medicine," he said. "With me at the dissecting table, in a few hours he took me from uncertainty to confidence by making human anatomy so easy to understand I had no problems from then on!"

It is obvious that knowledge of human anatomy is absolutely essential in the correct practice of medicine. What is happening, however, is that some medical schools have begun to short-change anatomy in favor of other, perhaps more glamorous subjects. I find it inexcusable that students in some medical schools today have a problem locating organs as gross as the kidneys, pancreas, and adrenals.

Perfect knowledge of human anatomy can mean the difference between success and failure in diagnosing a disease, or conducting a surgical procedure. The anomalous development of arteries, veins, and organs is not uncommon. These anomalies can be seen very clearly in dissecting the body. What happens in a situation when a physician poorly trained in anatomy encounters physical anomalies he or she has never seen? The answer is obvious, as well as unpleasant to contemplate.

Chapter Four
Winning, Losing, Winning

Thinking about my formative years, I can see that my dedication to achievement was a primary force in shaping the personality of the skinny kid and determined young man who eventually grew into Ross Z. Pierpont, M.D. Never in all those early years did I dare to take my eyes off what it takes to succeed in a world defined by one's resources — or lack of them. As I grew from boy to man, only two resources occupied my mind: ability and money. I had little time, and less energy, for the pursuit of happiness as I completed high school at age 15, worked about 60 hours a week to pay my way through Pharmacy School by 18, and earned my M.D. four years later. At age 22 I could call myself "Doctor!" You bet I was proud.

My size in those formative years had much to do with my life both in school and to this day. I was a tow-headed, very thin kid — maybe even a bit scrawny — as far back as I can remember. My size, since I was one or two years younger than my classmates, put me at a real disadvantage in anything athletic. Just one attempt as a team player in basketball, baseball, soccer, or football was all it took to write me off forever as a team competitor. The other boys were simply older, stronger, taller, and heavier. On the field or court, I was duck-pin in a game of ten-pins.

I compensated for my physical disadvantages by fighting as hard as I could in activities where size and strength did not rule me out. Concentrating my efforts in less physical sports — golf and tennis — became my best bets. I found that in these sports a competitive attitude and learned skills could go a long way in overcoming sheer size and strength.

Busy though I was throughout high school and college, I found time to play tennis in local tournaments with enough success to keep me in the game. However, my favorite game when I was in high school was golf. In my last two years at Catonsville High, I became friends with a fellow golfer named Conrad Swearer. Connie was two years older than I, a tall, thin, almost aesthetic-looking young man with skin so clear he had almost no need to shave. He was easy to get along with, lived about a mile from my house, and — wonder of wonders! — owned a Model T

Ford. Owning a car made Connie more than any BMIS ("Big Man in School"). He was virtually a merchant prince.

Connie was a natural golfer, and I was a notch better than acceptable, so we played golf together when we had the time. The high spot of our golf was when we got together for a summer day of golf at All View Country Club in what is now Columbia City in Howard County, Maryland. For most golfers, All View was "in the middle of nowhere," and not at all popular. When I drive past that site these days I smile to remember what was there as I look at an apartment-townhouse complex where I once spent happy hours.

Our "golf day" began at four a.m., when we crammed in some breakfast and strapped our golf clubs and repair parts on our bicycles. Repair parts on the golf course? A golfer needed spare parts because club heads of wood often came off their wood shafts, or the wrapping would loosen. When this happened, we simply glued the parts together and borrowed each others clubs until the glue hardened. I still remember the hours I spent making up my mind about my first set of golf clubs, bought with my own savings, when I was 10. Western Auto had a sale and I bought a brassie, a 2 iron, a 5 iron, a 9 iron and a putter, complete in their own bag. These cost me $4.95 — no sales tax, either.

Cycling to All View was enough to test our desire to play. We had one way to go, and that was an hour of pedaling and coasting up and down one hill after another. Our pre-dawn start was not without reason. We aimed to reach All View and wait for the sun to come up before normal golfers got there. As soon as dawn arrived, with no one else around to say anything, we teed off. The fifth hole at this course was a water hole and as often as not we hit a drive into the water. The water was only a few feet deep, with a muddy bottom. Stripping down to bare feet, we got into the water and "dived" for our missing ball. We never found just the ball we had hit into the hole, but we surely found lots of others. Once we collected a dozen or more balls, it was our signal to move on. We knew the golf pro, understandably, did not look kindly on kids cutting into his source of additional income. Through the grapevine, we had heard that he had caught some other boys collecting lost golf balls and had barred them from the course.

Armed with all the balls we might need, and ready to fix any clubs that came apart, we pressed on with our game. When we reached the clubhouse after 18 holes, a not-so-nice golf pro was waiting. He was a lean, sunburned, unsmiling man of about 30 who seemed never happy about anything including pocketing our green fees. I think the idea of boys our age playing his game of golf cheapened the sport in his eyes. If so, it didn't stop our fun. He grudgingly accepted the 75 cents we paid to cover us for the rest of the day, and by noon we had finished another 18 holes.

The sun overhead meant it was time to open the lunch we had brought with us. Fairly well dried out from 18 holes of golf, and not counting any immersion in the fifth hole, we downed our lunch with a quart of "soda pop" each. Rejuvenated, we played two more rounds of 18 holes each, making 72 holes for the day. Most days that was it, but eager beaver and bargain hunters as we were, it wasn't unusual to tag on another nine holes running our total to 81 holes. Well, you have to have a limit when you have to pedal 8 up-and-down miles back home!

A real challenge came in my last year of high school. Connie was joking about our golf, and out of nowhere he said, "Ross, let's do something different."

"Like what?"

Connie grinned and that look made me think: "Oh, oh!"

"How would you like to take a trip to Canada?"

"To what!"

"To Canada! Listen, Dad's had a good year and he's upgrading me to a Model A Ford. I really want to take it somewhere this summer. Do you think your mother will let you drive with me to Niagara Falls? Think about it, Ross! You and me watching Niagara Falls! Then we could go to Quebec."

I had only a general idea of Canada being somewhere above New York state on the map, and for me to go to Canada was roughly like going to, say, Florida or maybe South America.

"I don't have that kind of money, Connie."

"You won't need much money. We'll share. Look, ask your mother and if she says no, forget it. But ask her. OK?"

His enthusiasm was catching. I thought about my savings, and maybe it would work if we shared expenses. I said, "Let me think about it."

I looked up the trip. 500 miles just to reach Canada, then another hundred miles or more to Quebec, and back. A thousand miles at least! I was only 15. Connie was 17. I had never dreamed of anything like such a trip, and it was exciting. I studied my savings, and somehow it would be enough if Mother would say yes.

The proposed trip called for a Zimmermann-Pierpont-style family conference. Mother, Ed and I sat in our kitchen, the family conference room. Roger was away studying entomology at the University of Maryland, Philip was somewhere else, and so it came down to the three of us at the kitchen table. As I described Connie's idea for the trip, Mother was both Mother and "Miss Ethel." I can remember as though it were an hour ago how her hazel eyes peered into mine, reading my thoughts, balancing my youth against my competence.

"You know you will have to pay your share of the expenses, Ross. Are you sure you are able to do that?"

Money, always money! Was there nothing else? I said, "I've saved enough, Mother. Yes, I can pay my share."

At the time of the family conference, my share of the trip had been cut by a third traveler. Word of Connie's grand excursion had gotten around and another classmate wanted to join us. The idea was for Connie to provide the car, and Bud Farley and I would put up $25 each. There was no need to spend our hard-earned money on hotels and restaurants because we would sleep in a tent available from friends. Meals? What's wrong with taking our own food with us and cooking it over camping utensils, plus anything else we needed to buy along the way? Our big cost would be gasoline for the Ford, which cost a dollar for six or seven gallons.

My $25 share of the cost reassured Mother, but by now my brother Ed was beside himself with excitement. "Mother, I can find my share and I want to go, too! Please let me go!"

Ed was only 14 and letting both of us go gave Mother a lot to think about. She closed our conference promising Ed to think about it, and Ed kept me awake that night chattering about the trip and asking me to tell Mother to let him go, too. Since Bud Farley was just 14, and his family had let him go, so why couldn't he go? I didn't take sides, and the next day Mother gave in after Ed's reassuring promises well meant and mostly kept. I never found out where Ed got his $25, but if Mother helped out a bit I wouldn't have been surprised.

How can I describe a trip of boys our age let loose on a thousand-mile "safari?" It was school left out, nothing to do but watch the trees go by, the sun come up and set, no parents, no bedtime, no girls, total freedom! Leaving Woodlawn in the middle of a scorching hot July, we tooled along a blacktop road just wide enough for cars to pass in different directions. With our hair blowing wildly in the open car, we joked and laughed at nothing and everything and felt like explorers on a great adventure. To us, it was a great adventure for we had never been more than a few miles beyond our homes, and now we were on our way to Canada, a place never seen before.

Connie held a steady foot on the throttle of the rough-riding Ford, as we bounced along north and east along the Susquehanna Trail, up and down one tree-covered Allegheny mountain after another, through 200 miles of Pennsylvania, until we entered New York State. We were now in the state with Niagara Falls!

But we would not reach our goal this day. The sun had begun sinking behind some low-lying New York hills as we drove beside a picture-card pasture and lake. "Hey! Why don't we stop here?" asked Bud Farley.

"Why not?" replied Connie slowing down as we looked for a nearby farm house. Right out of the picture books came a farmer bringing his cows in from pasture. We waited beside the road, putting on our most demure behavior, and the farmer let his cows wander on while he paused to see why we were sitting there in the car. I called out, "Mister, they're sure fine looking Holsteins you got there. That chunky one there looks a little like my own cow."

Connie turned to look at me appreciatively, and the farmer said, "You got cows, young feller?"

I guess a skinny, tousle-haired boy as a milk-cow farmer seemed a little strange.

"Just one," I said, knowing the need to tell the truth. "Had her for nine years now. I belong to the Holstein/Fresian Association, too." The truth didn't extend to describing my brief ownership of a twin, sterile heifer, and another heifer that died on a lunch of barbed wire.

No one said anything for a minute, but I had broken the ice. Connie said, "Mister, we're on our way to Canada, and we need a place to pitch our tent for the night. Would it be all right if we stayed beside the lake? We won't make any mess or leave any trash or anything."

The farmer scratched the stubble on his sweaty chin, pushed back his hat and pondered. Then he measured his words. "For your ages, looks like you young fellers are havin' yourselves a trip. But I reckon no harm's done lettin' you stay by the lake." Another peering look at all of us. "Sure, go ahead." As he started after his cows, he called back, "Remember your promise — clean up after you!"

"We will," all four of us chorused back. And we meant it.

Nothing illustrates the frightening loss of ordinary civility in our nation better than our unprotected, overnight stay in a stranger's pasture, and all the other unprotected stops we made during our 10 days of the trip. Not once did we fear for our safety, not once were we threatened. In my boyhood, and through World War II, money for travel was scarce, and hitchhiking was commonplace. No one hesitated to pick up a stranger. People trusted each other and helped each other. Many families, ours included, left their doors unlocked in Woodlawn except at night. Muggings, rapes, robberies, theft — no one worried about them. I don't recall a single case of rape in Baltimore County during the years I grew up there. For a man to remain seated while a woman stood just wasn't done. In those hard times, men became hoboes, but they were decent hoboes, not bums, and when one came to our door asking for food we did not hesitate to give what we could. What would have surprised us when we asked to pitch our tent in the farmer's pasture would have been his turning us down. We never doubted he would let us stay and not ask for money.

We were sweaty and tired, and the cool lake was inviting. After an outdoor bath, we set up our tent, two single cots, and one double cot. Our first "dinner" called for a decision. Since Connie had done the driving, I offered my services as resident chef. Bud Farley and my brother were assigned to clean up after our meal. This consisted of soup, beans, and bread which never tasted better. Cleaning up went fast, and almost as soon as dinner was over we were sound asleep on our cots with the stars far above watching over us.

We went to sleep fast, but it was not long before the heat of the day gave way to nighttime chill, and we were soon shivering under our blankets. Lesson number one was that no number of blankets on top of you will keep you warm when the bottom of your cot is exposed to the cold. After that first night, we carried newspapers to line the cots and insulate them from the cold air.

We were on our way to Niagara Falls by 8 o'clock the next morning, and the road seemed to go on forever. We grew more and more anxious to reach it by the afternoon, then, suddenly, there it was! The sight of that white, roaring, foaming water is awesome even to teen-age boys. The picture is fixed in my memory. You look at the smoothly flowing river as it reaches the top of the Falls, then plunges violently over the rim, a torrent literally roaring as it hits bottom nearly two hundred feet below. The water moves on but the scene never changes, and I wondered how much water had poured endlessly over the Falls for century upon century. We didn't talk about it, but I remember thinking, "How can this go on, never ending, night and day, with no end to the water? Where does it all come from? Where does it go? What makes it happen?"

As I watched the ever-changing, never-changing water, the beginnings of what I now call stability...continuity...stirred within me. What we look on as the past was once the future, and what we are now will become the past, all of going on and on and ever-on in some great cycle, like the Falls, beyond human explanation.

Ready to see the Falls from the Canadian side, we walked across Peace Bridge. We neared the border between our two countries expecting various inquiries, some identification or where we came from, or what we were doing there all by ourselves. It must have happened to the custom official before because he laughed at our obvious concerns and waved us on. "Go ahead!" I felt a little disappointed that entering a foreign country could be so unexciting. I also felt let down when I saw that the vista on the Canadian side of the Falls is bigger and more impressive than the American view. How come the Canadians have a better Falls than do Americans?

How long can you look at Niagara Falls? We soon had enough of the scene and pointed the Ford toward Toronto. The city was disappointing, looking to us like nothing more than a collection of big buildings, so we soon turned our backs on Toronto and headed for Montreal. The "Royal Mountain City" of Canada was truly a different kind of city, cosmopolitan, even then considered by some as the "Paris of the Western Hemisphere." Our high school French helped with the signs and when trying to chat with the French-speaking Montrealers, but not by much. Although those Canadians were very friendly, we really felt, for the first time, to be in a foreign nation. Anyway, the city was no place for us to pitch our tents, so we headed for the countryside and found a place to stay for the night. We wanted a break in our diet by this time, and near our campsite was a farm with chickens. We bought a dozen eggs for 20 cents, and Connie cooked scrambled eggs on our Sterno stove. No gourmet meal ever tasted better than that open-air meal in the fields just outside Montreal!

I know of no other automobile trip that ranks with the drive from Montreal to Quebec City at that time. The wide open countryside seemed to be endless. Land beside the road was cultivated but the only signs of human habitation were an occasional small farmhouse with a nearby resident animal. Church spires alerted us to our approach to each town, usually one desperately in need of fixing up. When we drove into one of the infrequent towns, more accurately a village, we saw depressingly small houses in sorry disrepair. What struck us most was how the villages centered around their churches with steeples so large the churches seemed out of proportion.

We loved Quebec! This city looked as if a part of Europe illustrated in our schoolbooks had been picked up and set down on the cliffs overlooking the great St. Lawrence River, which I, at least, viewed with great respect. We visited the famous fort and the equally famous Plains of Abraham, where at one time the fate of North America hung in the balance. Chateau Frontenac was a delight, and so were the imposing churches. These were made almost entirely of native wood, and their Catholicism, and their "Frenchness," could not be missed or misunderstood. The people of Quebec were not about to lose even a fraction of their religion, or their European heritage.

Leaving Quebec, we found a campsite on the banks of the St. Lawrence, near the Thousand Islands. It was to be our last night in the adventure, and by now we were ready to go home. Up at dawn the next morning, we drove non-stop through the rest of Canada, through Maine and part of New Hampshire, down to Boston, and on to Springfield, Massachusetts. Someone noticed a YMCA in the center of Springfield and called out, "There's a YMCA! Let's stop!"

Sweaty and very tired of driving, Connie eased the Ford to a stop at the entrance. I looked in my wallet and found a YMCA card I had won years earlier in a potato bag race. "Hey! Look at this," I said showing the card to Connie.

Connie looked at the beaten-up card and laughed. "That thing won't get you anywhere."

"What do we have to lose? Let's try it."

Bud Farley and Ed were ready to try anything but walking. "C'mon, Connie, let's try it. I'm beat."

We trooped into the YMCA about as sweaty, bedraggled, and disheveled a group of four as one can imagine. A gray-haired, skinny man about 60 years old and sporting a bushy gray mustache looked up as we approached and took us in silently one at a time. He seemed in charge so I showed my card. Barely looking at the card, he grinned a little and winked. "Get your stuff and come in."

Hot showers! Cool swimming pool! A good night's sleep in on a real mattress! We hated to give it up but wanted to get on with our trip home even more. We were on our way so early the next morning — I missed not being able to say thank you to our gray-mustached friend — we reached New York City by 9:00 o'clock. Navigating through New York with Connie at the wheel was an experience in its own right, but we made it out of town and onto Route 1 into New Jersey. This was just a two lane blacktop road at the time.

The sun went down, shadows crept over the road, and we knew we would never make it to Woodlawn at night. The road now passed through an unpopulated area of New Jersey, and Connie said, "Look for a place where we can stop and pitch our tents." Just then, I saw a dirt road and pointed it out. Connie turned into it, went over a railroad crossing, and then turned the Ford into an empty field. We piled out thinking only of getting some sleep after more than 12 hours on the road from Springfield.

It was so dark by this time that we used flashlights to find a level spot to pitch our tents one more time. The soil was so loose and sandy the tent pegs would not hold. We looked for another way to anchor the tents, and Bud Farley pointed out a place where the railroad tracks were elevated. "Why don't we tie the tent ropes to the track? That'll hold 'em."

"Who the hell ever tied tent ropes to a railroad?" I growled, but everyone was much too tired to debate the point. Anyway, the tracks were rusty and it didn't look like the railroad had been used in a long time. So we tied the ropes on one side of our tents to the tracks and the ropes on the other side to some scrub roots. In minutes all four of us were sound asleep.

Part way through that night, a bright light flashed through our tents. A bell clang-clanged and a loud train whistle shrieked so loudly we jumped to our feet without thinking. "My God! What is it?" The answer was, naturally, a train doing what trains always do: travel on the railroad tracks. We must have been a sight, standing there in our underwear, mouths agape as a freight train rumbled past our tents. It missed my tent by no more than a foot or two, and no one said anything until the train had disappeared in the darkness.

Connie looked at the rest of us and said, "It's a damn good thing we tied tent ropes to roots or this tent would be wrapped around the wheels of that train!"

The excitement subsided and we bundled ourselves back into our cots still a little apprehensive about the safety of our site. But nothing else happened, and it was all forgotten by the time we packed up to hit the road for the rest of the way home.

Three relieved families greeted us when we drove into Woodlawn, where we gave the adults what was probably the most garbled travelogue ever narrated. Checking our finances, we found each of us still had about $5 left of our original $25 expense budget. It wasn't noticeable at the time, but the truth is that all four of us did a lot of growing up in the 10 days of our travels.

Away with play, work beckons

My pursuit of some finer things in life, as compared to achievements at work, improved somewhat once I entered medical school. City Hospitals had two squash courts, in poor shape but usable, and I found that squash came naturally to me. Liking the sport made it easy for me to train for it, and in time I became the top player in the City Hospital group. My peak at squash came when I won a tournament at City Hospitals, soon followed by winning the Class B. Maryland State Championship.

I hadn't realized what I was getting into when I began playing squash, but its importance became clear when, years later, the Jesters of Squash invited me to join their group. Jesters is an organization formed in England, and has chapters in Ireland, The United States, Canada, South Africa, Rhodesia, Australia, and perhaps other nations originally identified with the British Empire. To become a Jester is a goal of squash players the world over. The camaraderie and good fellowship of membership continue for life, spanning all continents. Every Jester must be not merely a good player, but also a person of stature in the world of business, government or the professions. Enjoyment of squash is simply the glue that binds the individuals together as friends who play, watch, or just raise a glass together now and then. No one should wonder that I accepted the invitation of membership with tremendous satisfaction.

Meanwhile I had two years of medical school to complete. The best part of those two years was on-hands clinical activity with outpatients, and the training I received from professors teaching the University's clinical practices.

An example of this training was an incident in pediatrics, a specialty that never appealed to me. Fortunately, the University of Maryland's Professor of Pediatrics, Dr. Finkelstein, was top-notch and helped to maintain my interest in what is, after all, part of a complete medical education. This professor was a slight, intense, and upbeat teacher with emphasis on pediatric fundamentals. One of his favorite techniques was to present a sick baby to his students and develop, step by step, a scenario of the child's illness and treatment with unmistakable clarity.

One day we looked and listened as he dealt with an obviously sick baby less than two years old. When he had our attention, Dr. Finkelstein asked loudly enough for all to hear: "Mrs. Clark, when did you notice Clarissa was sick?"

The mother was almost too frightened to respond. She knew her baby was critically ill and feared to be blamed for it. "Today, I think. Yesterday, I — I'm not sure what I noticed, Doctor." Dr. Finkelstein looked at her, shot a quick glance at his students, said nothing. The mother spoke a little more confidently: "Starting yesterday, she just wouldn't take anything at all. That's why I brought her here."

Finkelstein: "Now, Mrs. Clark, we want to help your baby. So tell us, didn't you notice anything else? Didn't your girl have loose bowels?"

"Yes, sir. She was loose."

"Tell us what her bowels looked like. How often did her bowels move?"

The mother was uncertain. "They just looked loose, Doctor. You know, runny."

"And how often?"

"Oh, a lot. She did it a lot."

Finkelstein: "What does a lot mean to you, Mrs. Clark? It's important if you want your baby to live." Tears gathered in the mother's eyes. Finkelstein's voice was kind but firm. "How many times a day, Mrs. Clark?"

"Almost all the time, Doctor. I had to clean her almost all day."

"How many days? When the mother hesitated, Dr. Finkelstein probed for a more helpful answer. "Three times a day? Was it three or four? Was it as much as a week?"

The mother struggled to think of an answer. There was no point in continuing.

Dr. Finkelstein "tweaked" the skin of one arm and one leg of the child lying before us. When he released the skin, it fell back wrinkled, lifeless and dry. Even where we sat at some distance, we could see this baby was dehydrated and probably running a fever.

Now it was our turn as Finkelstein turned to the group. "What's wrong with this baby, gentlemen?" He pointed to a student who answered, "It looks like infectious diarrhea to me." Finkelstein, saying nothing, pointed to another student who said, "It could be typhoid fever, Doctor." Still saying nothing, Dr. Finkelstein pointed to another and another student who all volunteered their personal diagnoses.

Dr. Finkelstein cut off the last student before he finished with impatient, biting words. "Did I ask you to make a diagnosis, gentlemen! I asked you just to tell me what is wrong with this baby. Look at her, for heaven's sake! This child is near death. She is almost completely dehydrated. Her electrolytes are totally out of balance. If this baby is going to live, she needs, right now, a simple remedy of salt and water. And, gentlemen, she needs it NOW!"

His prepared assistants moved in as he rammed home his lesson so we would never forget it. A nurse rapidly set up a subcutaneous injection with normal saline. As the nurse then gently fed the baby small amounts of Coca Cola plus paregoric by mouth, Dr. Finkelstein swiftly injected syringes in both thighs to re-hydrate his tiny patient as quickly as possible.

Still tending to the child, Dr. Finkelstein continued: "When you leave here today, I hope you do so remembering this one thing: A nice, clear diagnosis looks good, makes you feel good." He smiled almost to himself as he added, gently, "I'm not too sure about your patients. But you can lose a patient with speculation, as some of you were guilty of doing this afternoon. While you grope for that accurate diagnosis, treat the obvious! A good doctor knows without thinking how sick a patient is from whatever cause. As often as not the indicated treatment to stabilize the patient is obvious. Do it. And don't waste time doing it."

We took notes as he ordered stool cultures, blood work, urine tests, the usuals. By the time our class end and the baby was taken away, her improvement was visible.

Alas, not all of our training was that effective. At that time there were no organized medical training programs and few full-time medical professors except for those in elite schools like Harvard, Johns Hopkins, Yale, Columbia. That handful of medical schools was, even in my undergraduate days, turning out highly specialized individuals who went on to become the bedrock of our teaching institutions around the nation. More years would go by before full-time medical professors became the norm rather than the exception.

How far medicine has come since my medical school days! I find it no exaggeration to call medical advances in the years following World War II close to a miracle. Think about it. Tuberculosis was fatal. Infantile paralysis crippled and killed or imprisoned victims in an "iron lung." Cancers raged without effective therapies. People with peptic ulcers were immobilized or submitted to mutilating surgery as a last resort. We had no truly effective treatments for prostate cancer or prostate growth; diphtheria; yellow fever; smallpox; diabetes. The list of conquered or minimized diseases goes on. We have become so medically effective that the occasional failures make news, when once we merely buried them.

I was too new and inexperienced to see at the time how our entire world of medicine was beginning to explode with new knowledge and new therapies. My problem was real and personal: graduation was at hand and a decision about my medical route had to be faced.

Fortunately I was too young to recognize how serious my decision would be, or I might have become immobilized. My love of anatomy and my clinical experience pointed me toward a career in surgery. But what I wanted and what I could manage with my limited resources suggested I was dreaming. Well, what's wrong with dreaming? I don't set boundaries on what I can, and cannot accomplish. When I checked out what could be possible, I found to my delight that a residency in surgery under Dr. Robert P. Bay at Maryland General Hospital would be as close to a guarantee of medical and financial success as this world can offer.

I emphasized Maryland General because Dr. Bay had been one of two very top physicians at The University of Maryland. The other man was Dr. Arthur Shipley. Both doctors were zealous about their medical reputations and friction between them grew to the breaking point. What the administrators of the University of Maryland Medical School did not realize was the enormous size of Dr. Bay's practice. Long before others in medicine recognized the importance of what has become known as "industrial surgery," Dr. Bay became the leader in this field. He guided the formation of the state's Worker's Compensation Commission and controlled much of the state's industrial surgical practice for years.

When Dr. Bay tired of the contention, he approached Maryland General Hospital about moving his practice there. Maryland General wasted no time in assuring Dr. Bay of his welcome. The very next day Dr. Bay brought in several dozen ambulances and took his patients, assistants, nurses, and others to Maryland General. That day, a general surgical renaissance began at Maryland General Hospital.

Would the famous Dr. Bay accept Ross Pierpont as a junior internee? It was a long shot, with one way to find the answer. Obeying my customary refusal to accept a possibility I would be turned down, I applied for the opening.

Success! Dr. Bay's acceptance meant my cherished career was now on its way to reality even though I had another year to go in medical school. Not only did I have to complete medical school, there were other problems. Internship with Dr. Bay was full time — and no pay. Unless I worked, I could not even pay for my senior year in medical school. Tuition and living expenses had gone up steadily, and my minimum need for my fourth year was a thousand dollars.

A thousand dollars loomed before me like facing an iceberg in the Atlantic Ocean. Up to this time, I had always made it, somehow, on my own. That was then. This was now, and money far beyond what I could earn. It was time to ask for help. I turned to a physician I had come to know, Dr. Harold Dix, who believed in me and was encouraging.

"I belong to the Kiwanis Club of Baltimore, and the Club has an Endowment Trust Fund," Dr. Dix said. The Fund has some money it loans to students who need help and deserve it to succeed."

"That is a perfect description of me," I blurted out. Even now I wonder how I could have been so cocksure in my remark.

"Let me look into it and I'll get back to you when I have anything to tell you," Dr. Dix said.

The passing days may not have registered with Dr. Dix, but they were unrelenting anxiety to me. I'm not sure how I managed to sleep, but the discipline of the years working my way through Pharmacy School probably weighed in. Suppose he didn't come through...if I couldn't get the money I needed, and fast — I tried to put the doubts out of my mind, but they never went away. Then one day Dr. Dix stopped me in a hospital corridor and said, "Good news, Ross. The Kiwanis does have the money in the Fund, and I checked the qualifications. I think you should be able to meet them all right."

"What should I do now?"

"Sit tight till next Thursday. The Club meets for lunch at The Emerson Hotel, and you will be my guest." With that, he hurried away to get an elevator to the operating room

If I had any real sense, the Kiwanis lunch would have terrified me. There I was, just turned 21, in a room with about 100 men who were professionals, heads of companies, bankers, or important otherwise. After lunch I met with their Trust Committee. They couldn't have been more polite, or nicer, but I knew these men were successful because they were far from fools. If they saw defects in my character, or my reason for wanting the loan, I was dead. Bury me. They wound up our meeting with a promise to give me their decision in a week.

A week! I stayed busy so I wouldn't have time to think. Then the cloud lifted. They came through with their thousand dollar loan, and my way to the junior internship was clear.

From the day I started with Dr. Bay I knew I had made the right decision. I looked forward to each day's duties, what I would learn, the medical needs of different kinds of patients. I liked the people I worked with and from all indications they liked me and my attitude toward surgery. One day, Dr. Bay met with me to discuss my status and we agreed that after my first year of Rotating Internship I would be a resident for the next two years. I had studied Pharmacy for three years. Gone to medical school for four years. Junior internship ahead for another year, a resident for two more years — would I have enough years to become an honest-to-God doctor?

Things do happen in time, and the day came when I graduated from medical school and assumed my Rotating Internship at Maryland General Hospital. I was a happy young physician eagerly looking forward to the next two years of surgical training under the eminent Dr. Bay.

That world came crashing down Christmas Eve, 1940.

Dr. Bay was at the home of Dr. Charles Reifschneider for a Christmas Eve party when he suffered a massive cerebral hemorrhage and died on the spot. His sudden death changed everything and forced me to take a new look at my medical future.

I liked and admired many of the physicians at Maryland General, but the blunt truth is that none had the reputation, surgical skill, and panache of Dr. Bay. Continuing an internship at Maryland General with Dr. Bay gone wasn't exactly a dead end, but it would do nothing for my medical stature. The closer I examined the situation, the more I knew it was time for me to move on. If I wanted to re-locate to a different residency, I had to act at once before opportunities closed down.

Writing this now, from the perspective of advanced years and in a life-situation impossible to imagine when a medical novice, it occurs to me how little we know at any given moment what the future holds for us. How little we understand that what looks wonderful today can contain the seeds of disaster. And what looks like the end of the world can hide a benefit beyond anything not even remotely anticipated. The events which turned my life upside down when I was 23 actually laid the groundwork for a medical career I had no way of imagining at the time.

One of the better residencies in Baltimore was open at Baltimore City Hospitals. This was a very large, busy, municipal hospital with many more nurses, interns, residents, and patients than I was used to. Going there would be a step down financially — from $10 a month to zero. But it was a step up surgically. My decision was no longer a question. I applied for a residency and after much back and forth obtained a third assistant surgical residency at Baltimore City Hospitals. There I remained for the following three years where things happened to me that would affect my life forever.

Chapter Five
The "Fortunes" of War

Without giving one second's thought about what I was doing, I developed habits which shape my life to this day. This was getting a pre-dawn start. As a boy with a cow to milk and pasture before going to school, or doing anything else, I had to be out of bed and chores done by seven o'clock seven days a week. Rising at 5AM became routine. This habit made a total difference between the way I learned and practiced medicine, and the ways my fellow students and associated physicians approached their careers.

Anyone who has not started each day at about five o'clock, may find it difficult to appreciate the difference a pre-dawn start can make. In the very early hours in a hospital, there is no competition for your time and attention. At Baltimore City Hospitals during my residency, no one else would be around between 5 and 6 except the night nurses. After their own long, lonely nights, they were always glad to see me welcoming a new day. When I ordered a treatment it would be followed right on through to completion with top efficiency because there were no interruptions or distractions. Starting on the floor by five o'clock, I made rounds of my patients, checked the day's activities, wrote orders, collected laboratory data, and did my clinical lab work. Most days I was able to return to my room by six o'clock and nap for an hour, then still be the first one in the dining room at seven o'clock.

A funny thing, no physician on the hospital staff, nor I, said anything about my early morning routine. In time, however, it became clear that the senior resident staff of the hospital was highly impressed by my ability, as one of the hospital's newest and youngest residents, to deliver full reports on my patients daily at 8a.m. I was proud of what I accomplished, of course, but I never made a point of it. What I did stood out for the simple reason that none of the other members of the staff were so thorough, or so up-to-the-minute on their patients' status. May I make something plain? In doing what I did, I was not necessarily smarter or better than my fellow doctors. I'm sure some of them could have taught me more than a thing or two. I was just completing my work before the others got to it. This taught me a lesson I never, ever forgot:

early achievement is a powerful way to build a reputation for ability and accomplishment whether it is deserved or not.

My early morning naps suggest a second characteristic which has helped me so much. The irregular hours of my Pharmacy School, pre-med school, and Medical School taught me to relax and sleep on a moment's notice, no matter where I happen to be. I could, and can, sleep for five minutes or an hour, in any location or situation, and wake up ready to go. I truly believe that my pre-dawn routine, and my ability to restock my energy on demand contributed as much to my eventual medical success as any other capabilities I eventually mastered.

The workloads at Baltimore City Hospital in the 40s put my early-up, sleep-when-you-can habits to a real test. This was a time when medical care was pay as you go. Health insurance for all practical purposes did not exist. No one had even thought of organizations like Blue Cross and Blue Shield. No one had invented credit cards. The only people who could pay for major medical care were the rich. When a medical disaster hit unemployed people, blue collar workers, or virtually all middle-class people, their only choice was to go into a hospital that would treat them with little or no charge. These were church-supported hospitals, some medical school hospitals, and City and County-operated hospitals. The state took care of institutions for the insane — pretty good care, too. Sanitoriums for tubercular patients and other highly contagious diseases were also funded fairly well.

All patients at Baltimore City Hospital were classified as charity patients. The cost to city taxpayers was enormous, considering the times, but those costs did not include paying the house staff. In my second year of residency, my pay consisted of meals and a room for sleep and study. Money? Zero.

During this time in my medical career, Baltimore City Hospital was one place for an aspiring physician to be. The surgical residency was, for all practical purposes, run by the resident staff. All diagnosing, surgery, and direction were managed through a pyramid system of training. We had a Chief Resident (his fifth year; that's right, fifth year); two First-Assistant Residents; four Second-Assistant Residents; six Third-Assistant Residents; six Fourth-Assistant Residents; and six surgical interns. Yes, it was quite a pyramid, and it shows very well the size and scope of surgical procedures we carried out on a constant flow of patients of all sizes, genders, ages, weights, colors, and dispositions. When someone needed an operation and couldn't pay for it, one of our resident surgeons did it!

Considering non-existent physician pay and the hours, a good question is what quality of medical care did patients receive at City Hospital during the three years I was there? In a word, excellent. Though we residents worked our behinds off without one cent of money, we did it willingly and most of the time cheerfully. No one was ever shorted for care because he or she could not pay for it. The pyramid surgical staff and a top-notch backup system delivered the care needed, where needed, and when needed.

As a Fourth-Assistant Resident, I got all the hands-on training and responsibilities I could handle. The hospital Accident Room was a non-stop cauldron of surgical activity. Every day brought automobile accidents, bullet wounds, industrial accidents, poisonings, burns, cuts, and more. When a patient needed skills, specialized diagnosis, or treatment beyond a resident's capabilities, he climbed the pyramid layer after layer of residents or even to the Chief Resident for help. When that was still not enough, we had on call a large consulting and overseer staff of accomplished surgeons and specialists in neurosurgery, urology, gynecology, orthopedics, EENT, oncology, psychiatry, and other arenas of medical care. Before I left the hospital, our visiting surgeons were members either of the University of Maryland or Johns Hopkins medical schools.

My days were full and busy, demanding a variety of skills too tedious to list. Fortunately, my affinity for anatomy made my medical life easier, but the pace and the responsibilities, added to the stress of my earlier years, demanded their due. The time came for me to pay up. One day after my early morning rounds, I was too restless to nap, and the pains in my stomach were too severe for me to ignore. I had such pains before, and not being a total medical fool I reluctantly recognized them for what they were: symptoms of a peptic ulcer. But I was Ross Pierpont, Fourth-Resident Surgeon. I was not about to let some damn fool, minor stomach pains put me out of action.

So much for the physician treating his own illness. Before I knew what had really happened to me, I was flat on my back, a patient in my own hospital. Bleeding ulcer. The Chief of Medicine became my personal physician and ordered bed rest, a bland diet, antacids, and monitoring of my stools for blood. I did as I was told, and in less than a week the bleeding stopped. X-rays of my stomach and intestines showed the ulcer had dug a "channel" and scarred the valve leading from the stomach to the intestine. Ordered to take it easier on my workloads, I submitted to a special diet in the dining room and continued to watch my stools for blood.

If you have stayed with me until now, you know damn well I was not going to take it easier. In fact, events gave me no choice but to increase both my caseload and my responsibilities.

The changes began on the morning of December 7, 1941 when the Japanese bombed Pearl Harbor. That one act, in one day, changed the lives of every living American. A nation that had been more or less drifting along in fighting a listless economy suddenly had more work than people. As men by the millions went into the Army, Navy, and Marines (there was no separate air force; the air force belonged to the Army), unemployment disappeared. Bethlehem Steel illustrates the magnitude and speed of the change. 5,000 people worked at this company at the time of Pearl Harbor. In months it built its workforce sixfold — to 30,000 — and the world's largest tidewater steel plant.

Within only a few months after Pearl Harbor, German submarines were sinking U.S. ships in sight of the Eastern seaboard, and it was a question if we could build replacement ships as fast as the Germans were sinking them. The fate of the world hung in the balance.

As the impact of the war changed Bethlehem Steel, it just as swiftly changed our world of medical care. Patients unable to pay their medical costs became patients with money to pay for medical care in hospitals that charged for their services. All medical personnel, everywhere, registered with one of the military services, and doctors and nurses were called from the hospitals to go where the Army and Navy sent them. Major medical training centers of the University of Maryland and Johns Hopkins organized hospital units from their visiting, teaching, and house staffs to be ready for the war effort.

It would be hard to exaggerate the high standards set by the Armed

Forces for medical personnel. The general attitude was that doctors and nurses were necessary but not well adapted to military discipline. Overall, it seemed, medical people were subordinate to the real job of the fighting forces, which was to drop enough bombs, and sink enough ships, and kill enough Germans and Japanese to win the war.

I was like every other doctor facing the call of the Armed Forces. All of us reported for physical examination and filled out the required forms. The Army wouldn't use Navy forms; the Navy wouldn't use Army forms, so filling out forms became quite a project. Every day, it seemed, someone I knew was called. Graduates not long out of medical school were commissioned as First Lieutenants. More experienced doctors went in usually as Captains. Some top-notch doctors were commissioned as Colonels. Dr. John King, of City Hospital, received a commission as a Colonel, and was assigned to oversee medicine at Walter Reed General Hospital in Washington, D.C.

I looked at my options and decided to ask for the Navy. It was a very practical decision. If it came to dying, I would rather go down with the ship than freeze to death in ice, snow and mud. As it turned out, it really didn't matter what I decided. The Navy didn't want me. The Army didn't care for me either. The rejections were another little lesson in the way one's life can be turned by happenings that are totally irrelevant to later events at the time.

The Navy recruiter who reviewed my application stopped when he saw I had checked a box on the form for sleepwalking. "You indicate on your application that you sleepwalk."

I felt a little silly about that, but I had to be truthful. I said, "I don't walk in my sleep very much, but my training taught me to sleep when and where I can, on demand. So sometimes I'm not completely asleep, and I walk a little."

The young Petty Officer looked at me.

I said, "What does that have to do with being a doctor in the Navy?"

This Petty Officer was tough. Goddam tough! He wanted me to know he was Mr. Tough. "Doctor, the Navy doesn't really give a damn about the way you do or don't sleep. What the Navy cares about is what would happen if you are on a battleship or aircraft carrier and you step into an open hatch in your sleep." The idea clearly did not appeal to him. (Maybe it did, now that I think about it.) "There you go, 50 feet down and end up dead or smashed up. The crew ends up in the middle of the ocean, in the middle of a war, and with no doctor."

That seemed to end it for me. I thanked him for his time and got up to leave. He said, "You're not through, Doctor. When we turn you down, you have to see if the Army wants you." He smiled a half-smile. "The Army has lower standards for induction than we have. They're right across the street."

I didn't miss the put down, but my patriotism was enough to overcome it. Lamb-like, I obeyed instructions and walked across the street to the 5th Regiment (Maryland National Guard) Armory in downtown Baltimore and approached a waiting recruiter. He greeted me with a sheaf of papers; I spent the next half-hour filling out sisters to the papers I had just filled out for the Navy, and gave them back to the Sergeant. He routinely started through the forms until he suddenly looked up at me and said, "What's this about a bleeding ulcer?"

"I had one last year," I said. "It's cured now, but I was told to come here with all my records about hospitalization, so that's what you have there."

He stared a me a moment, and the slight half-smile on his face told me he was less than charmed by my statements. "I'll have to read all of this," he said. Leaning back, he propped his feet on a countertop between us and started to read. I could only sit and watch, when he abruptly sat straight up while reading a letter in the file. It was a letter on the stationery of the top hospital of the U.S. Army, Walter Reed General Hospital, in Washington D.C. The letter to me was signed "John King, M. D., Chief of Medicine, Walter Reed General Hospital."

As most of us have learned, men in the military respect authority. The Sergeant-Recruiter had just come across authority. Instantly, his attitude changed from indifference to visible respect. "Dr. Pierpont, we have to get an X-ray of your stomach to see where this goes from here. Will you please go right down this hall to the X-ray department and come back after they're done?"

I obeyed the instructions and the Army did a complete GI series (not as in G.I. for "General Issue," the Army's common term for enlisted men, but as in gastrointestinal). Of course, the study showed my channel ulcer scar, and that was the end of my military career. I became a 4-F for the rest of the war.

I would have had it one hell of a lot easier in the Army! Physically unfit to serve in uniform, I was nonetheless qualified to resume my residency at Baltimore City Hospitals where the caseloads and responsibilities far exceeded anything I would have faced as an Army doctor. Doctors and nurses who met military standards were inducted in bunches. Those of us who remained had no choice but to take over the work of those inducted and add it to our own.

As the Armed Forces grew to exceed 10 million men and women, battle casualties were taking their deadly toll. The need for more doctors and nurses grew steadily, and every six months I was ordered to appear for re-evaluation. What would happen to me with each call I never knew before I went. My physical condition did not change, but the services lowered their physical standards. By the third year of the war, the Army had reached the bottom of the barrel and was drafting men unable to carry a pack or make normal marches. The handicapped were used to replace physically healthy men who were working as clerks, cooks, mechanics, supply personnel, and other non-combat positions. Physical requirements for doctors were also relaxed, so I never knew on reporting for re-evaluation what the outcome would be.

One thing that did not change was the routine. Each time I filled out the required forms, and each time the Navy did a GI series. They found the same channel ulcer scar and followed through by directing me to the Army. The Navy still prided itself on maintaining standards of acceptance higher than the Army's. By this time there was a rather severe shortage of X-ray film, but the Army stubbornly refused to accept the Navy's findings. So I would go through the whole process, X-rays included, all over again. The Army had its own explanation for its position, though. With the true aplomb of any true bureaucrat, they simply went their own way by saying, "We don't deal with the Navy." Case closed. Six months by six months, I would be re-classified 4-F to return to my ever-growing case-loads at City Hospital.

As life goes on, you adjust or fall by the side of the road. All of us at the hospital, and no doubt, in private practice, learned to live with the possibility of a sudden call to military service. Those of us called said their good byes and disappeared into assignments anywhere and everywhere across the country, and around the world. Those of us left to carry on as civilians worked harder and longer hours. By the third and fourth years of the War, we no longer had a pool of physicians we could call on to help us meet unexpected, or unusually demanding needs. Our shortages became so severe that Dr. Donald Hebb and I — a First-Assistant Resident Surgeon — were temporarily in charge of the hospital's entire surgical service. It has already been mentioned, but it bears repeating that throughout this crisis, Dr. Hebb and I were not only responsible for general surgery, but also for the orthopedics, gynecology, urology, and the general surgery department of the entire hospital. Why we weren't totally overwhelmed by our responsibilities can be explained only by the self-confidence and energies of youth. The military call for doctors still exceeded the supply. To meet military demands, medical schools expanded and accelerated their training periods to turn out graduates faster. The schools went to year-around teaching and what became known as the 9-9-9 month system of medical education. The four-year medical program was cut to two- and one-half years.

The residency programs of teaching hospitals were also compressed into the 9-9-9 month system as the only practicable way to crank out surgeons needed for the military services. Month after month, we lost junior visiting staff doctors as they joined units for general hospital services of the Army and Navy. The hospitals of the University of Maryland and Johns Hopkins organized units for overseas services. City Hospitals was fortunate in finding older professors of the two medical schools to replace those gone into the Armed Forces. The roll call of these older replacements is impressive. On the general surgical side, City Hospitals called on Dr. Thomas B. Aycock from the University of Maryland to become Chief of the general surgical service. Dr. Otto Brantigan came in to back him up as his assistant. Dr. Brantigan was a pioneer in chest surgery and a former Chief Resident of Baltimore City Hospital. Other physicians were recruited to cover surgical orthopedics, urology, and other specialties.

Among my other responsibilities during the war years, I was resident in charge of urology. City Hospitals had a very large flow of venereal disease patients, and before the days of penicillin such diseases could become highly complicated; syphilis at that time was often fatal. Teaching urology to medical students rotating through the hospital was an extremely active and essential part of their medical training. The hospital brought in Dr. Howard Mays, an excellent urologist from the University of Maryland, to lecture second-year students of the University's Medical School.

I assisted Dr. Mays in his classes by setting up his clinical materials to be demonstrated. These included equipment to demonstrate the treatment of urethral stricture (part-closure of the urethra) by dilation; bowgies, catheterization to permit urination before or after surgery, cystoscopic examinations, and other fairly complicated treatments for urologic diseases in both men and women. As Dr. Mays explained how urologic equipment functioned, I showed it to the students and demonstrated how it was used.

Demands on doctors' time were so severe that sometimes Dr. Mays could not clear time for his lectures, and I would take over the clinic for the day. We never formalized an understanding of this; I just filled in when needed to do so. One day, students and I were waiting for him to appear for a 2 PM class. When he did not show up by 2:10, and the students were beginning to mutter unhappily, I closed the door and started the lesson. About half-past two, I saw the door open a few inches and there was Dr. Dan Barker looking in. He listened to me for about a minute, then began trying to smile and was holding in laughter as he quietly closed the door and disappeared.

Seconds later, the door opened again, and there were Dr. Mays and Dr. Barker, both grinning as they looked in. After the class was over, I joined the two doctors in the hall. Both were still amused, and, puzzled, I said, "What's going on?"

Dr. Barker answered, "When I came on the floor from the elevator, I saw Dr. Mays pacing up and down the hall and muttering to himself. I asked him what was wrong, and he said, 'I have a class in that room, and some long-winded idiot in there must not know his time is up.' I wasn't sure what the problem was, and that's when you saw me peek in the room. I told Dr. Mays, 'That sounds like Robin in there, with your class, Dr. Mays.'"

Dr. Barker continued: "Mays said, 'Who the hell is Robin?' I said, Ross Pierpont."

The three of us paused a moment, taking in what had happened. Dr. Mays said, "Well, 'Robin,' if I can't make it on time again, at least I'll know what to expect from you."

We left it at that, and in fact I don't recall Dr. Mays ever being late for his class again. Meanwhile, teaching assignments at the hospital increased as the shortages of doctors increased. My teaching increased along with that of everyone else, but I didn't mind the extra work. Indeed, I found it satisfying. At one time, I thought seriously about staying on the staff as a full-time instructor, but it was not to be for me.

Unpredictable events. Unexpected results. These are happenings which alter one's life yet go unnoticed as not worth thinking about at the time. Had I not developed a bleeding ulcer, and a resultant scar, I certainly would have been called for military service. What would life have held for me had I gone into the Army or Navy instead of staying at Baltimore City Hospital? There is no way to know. What is certain is that my life, *without my peptic ulcer*, would have become totally different. Better? Worse? Who's to say? But one important thing I do know: Without my peptic ulcer I would not be writing this from our daughter and son-in-law's castle in northern Germany!

Chapter Six
Matrimony, Medicine, Malcontents

My junior residency at Maryland General Hospital was a turning point in my life. The sudden death of Dr. Bay had knocked all of my plans for a career in surgery into the proverbial cocked hat, but that setback was more than matched by finding the woman who was to make the personal side of my life complete.

The patriarch, financier, and Superintendent of Maryland General when I was an intern there, was a well-known Baltimorean, Milton Gatch. As was fashionable in his days, the Superintendent sponsored a spring staff dance. I hadn't planned to attend because I didn't know anyone to invite. Medical studies and long hours on the hospital floor had left me with no time or energy — not to mention the money — to look for feminine companionship, however, a fellow resident and friend, Clarence Martin, suggested that we go "stag." I welcomed the idea for a change of pace.

The dance was in full swing when we entered. I stood looking around a large hall with chandeliers providing romantic lighting, tables surrounding the dance floor, an orchestra at one end, and perhaps 50 men and women in their twenties circling and swaying to the beat of the band. It was like a scene from a Hollywood movie. By habit, I took in the scene to see how I fitted into it. The young doctors — I knew almost every one of them — would be my competition. Still almost painfully skinny at age 22, with unruly, blondish-brown hair cut short to save haircuts, and wearing my one dark suit bought off the rack by price, there wasn't much about me for a girl to write home about. But an inner confidence built from meeting and winning every challenge so far set before me was still there. At least I no longer smelled like a cow!

Clarence murmured, "I'll see you," and ambled off to see a nurse he knew. Scanning the nurses, none really caught my eye until — there! As I looked at a slim young woman I'd never seen before, something inside me went "click!" I'm sure I was staring at her, but fortunately she did not see me. Her face was so smooth and fair that coloring it with makeup would have been disgraceful. Her peaches and cream complexion and dancing blue eyes were offset by brown hair combed back making a frame of her face. An inch or so shorter than I, her body was trim and visibly feminine. The man talking to her said something that made her toss her head with a laugh, and her eyes seemed to crinkle with delight.

Then and there, none of the other women in the ballroom meant a thing to me. Unfortunately, she was popular with other embryo doctors, and I waited for the right time to meet her. When a break came in her attention, I took the opportunity to introduce myself.

She was Grace Schmidt, graduating nurse.

She accepted my invitation to dance, and as I put my arm around her waist the feeling was immensely stimulating; her flesh was yielding yet firm. She moved easily with me. I was far from a good dancer, yet, again, something clicked between us. I sensed she felt the same. Neither of us said a word but as our eyes met from time to time both knew this was more than a casual dance. We were meant to see more of each other.

And we did! Indeed we soon dated no one else, and our relationship grew from attraction and enjoying each other's company to mutual love. Ah, love! How it must sometimes wait on fortune. The best we could do was continue to see each other as often as time permitted. After Grace graduated, she left Maryland General to take a position at Woman's Hospital, a small, specialized hospital in the midst of middle-class Baltimore homes a few blocks from Maryland General. Grace did well at Woman's Hospital, rising rapidly to Senior Nurse in Obstetrics. Earning $60 a month in her new position, she paired up with another nurse from Maryland General to rent a small apartment around the corner from Woman's Hospital. The two of them managed quite well. For all of us, however, the hospitals were not just where we worked. Hospitals, patients, and fellow practitioners were our lives.

As for my fortunes, I turned blood into money. Blood for transfusions brought a hefty $15 a pint in those days, and I gave as many pints as my body could spare. I never thought of the tiny diamond ring I gave Grace when I proposed — this happened in late 1941, the months just before Pearl Harbor — but truth to tell, every 100th of a carat of it was bought with blood money. She accepted my ring and proposal and our happiness with each other at that time was immense. We were committed, but total commitment in marriage would have to wait until we could afford it. That's the way we thought in the youth of our times.

I continued to save as much money from my monthly pittance as I could. The increased military buildup that dominated events in 1941 intensified after Pearl Harbor. Following the declarations of war against Germany, Italy and Japan, the shortages of doctors and nurses created a new opportunity for Grace. A doctor with a large and very profitable practice serving the civilian work force at Edgewood Arsenal, a military base about 20 miles east of Baltimore, needed an industrial nurse. The money they offered Grace was so much more than she earned at Woman's Hospital she accepted it at once. I find it strange I do not remember, at this exact moment, exactly what Grace's new job as an industrial nurse paid her. I'll have to ask her about that. The important thing is that her increased income made it possible for us to marry.

Writing this gives me reason to look back at what I have gone through in my life, and more than a half-century of marriage to Grace. The urge to muse about attitudes toward man-woman relationships then and now is irresistible. Why did it matter so much that we marry? In our financial straits, starting a family was the last thing on our minds. We had grown so close to each other that we knew, whatever "love" is or was, that we cared deeply about each other, and wanted no one else. Being tempted by others was not even worth thinking about. I was for Grace. She was for me. Why wasn't that enough? Why didn't we just live together? We were oh, so young, and it was a tempting thought, but there was not really any question of living our individual lives until we could marry. We did not try to put our feelings about marriage into words but we understood that it would not work for us to live together without the mutual commitment formalized by marriage. Feelings come, feelings go. The physical need for each other — touching, embracing, sensing nearness, sexual completion — must be satisfied, but young though we were we knew that physical presence is not enough. Love, no matter how real, and how intensive, will wither and die without another kind of presence: the symbolic and powerful presence of the commitment contained in what, for convenience, we attempt to identify with a word. Surely it is no accident that everywhere men and women exist, and have existed, on this globe, marriage in one form or another is basic to the man-woman, and family relationship. How easy it is to confuse love with marriage. Love is quite different. It happens or doesn't happen, and when it does it can be as powerful as dynamite. Marriage is something different altogether.

In the spring of 1942, Grace and I took our vows at Grace's Lutheran church in Glyndon, MD, not far from where I grew up in Woodlawn. I can still feel the glow of my pride in Grace as we stood together to repeat the magic words. God! Was I alive that day! Whoever said all brides are beautiful could have had Grace in mind, for, trust me, she was gorgeous. All of our fellow house officers from City Hospital attended the wedding, and stayed on for a reception in the hall of the church. Whoever made the punch for the reception meant well (much later I found out the culprit was none other than the head of the laboratory at Baltimore City Hospital), but he could have turned the reception into a drunken disaster. Someone made the punch using absolute alcohol borrowed from the laboratory, some lemons and oranges borrowed from the dining room, and mixed it with ginger ale donated by the hospital soft drink supplier. It was meant as a noble (and money-saving) gesture, but what this ambitious fellow apparently ignored is that laboratory alcohol is more than twice the strength of most bar whiskeys or gin (190 proof vs. 80 or 90 proof, or less). Fortunately, someone quickly detected the strength of the punch — it should have been called "Wham!" — and diluted it to sensibility with water.

Following the reception, my brother honored us with a party in the pleasantly fashionable Charles Room at that grand old lady of a hotel, the Belvedere. As Grace and I, arm in arm, entered the room, Don Bestor, leader of the band, called out, "Begin the Beguine!" and the unforgettable music of that Cole Porter number swelled throughout the room. Of all remembrances of that party, it still brings a smile to remember getting 24 oysters on the half-shell, and giving Grace half as many. No one ever explained the reasoning for the difference.

Everyone knew we were going to New York for a week's honeymoon, and at two in the morning we drove off for New York. What people didn't know was that we doubled back to our apartment and spent the night there. Our first apartment was an adventure in itself. We had rented it before our marriage, and Grace lived in it by herself while making it habitable. It had a bedroom, a small living room, a combined kitchen-dining area, and bath. The rent was $30 a month. For furniture, we had haunted second-hand stores like Moses Zalis on Gay Street, a veritable treasure trove of other people's cast-offs. One day we triumphed by locating a second-hand refrigerator for $8 and its sister appliance, a gas stove, for $10.

We spent our honeymoon as typical "gawkers" on the New York scene. Then it was back to hospital life again. The main difference was that we now joined with other married couples with apartments in our row house at 312 Elrino Street. Our off-duty life revolved around at-home get-togethers (they were too hit-and-miss to call entertaining), impromptu bridge, and an occasional fling in the hospital's bowling alleys. Grace and Adelaide Barker became close friends as I did with Dan Barker, a prince of a fellow and darn good doctor. We literally did almost everything together at the hospital, until some humorist on the staff labeled us Judge and Robin, patterned after a lampooning cartoonist of the times.

An episode I still remember illustrates how our hospital training colored our everyday incidents. Dan and I were walking home together one night. As we passed a corner house a penned up, ferocious Doberman Pinscher leaped at us against the top of its fence and came within inches of clearing it. This had happened before, and as we hurried on Dan said, "Robin, one night that dog is going to make it over that fence, and we'll have a hell of a time getting patched up in the emergency room."

"You first!" I said. "I'll help with the patching."

To relieve the pressures of the long hours and the life-and-death responsibilities that come with surgery, we sometimes let ourselves go a little. I don't remember what got into me one day, but I took advantage of a situation to play a prank on Dan. At the time it happened, Dan had been assigned to assist in nose and throat for bronchoscopy, laryngoscopy, and gastroscopy. None of us liked this work; it was messy, usually minor, and painful for the patient. In 1942 medical practice, and for many years afterward, the only instruments available for nose and throat, bronchoscopy and laryngoscopy, were monstrous to work with. They were inflexible instruments as long as your arm, with light delivered from either end. They have been rendered obsolete by flexible, fiberoptic instruments which are virtually painless.

The doctor assisting in these procedures administered local anesthesia to lessen the pain. He then pulled the patient's head back to create a straight line for the rigid instruments to go through the mouth, down the throat through the larynx (voice box), and down into the trachea (windpipe) or past the larnyx into the esophagus — the tube carrying food to the stomach. Once the instruments were in place, the assistant had to continue holding the patient's head firmly to prevent any damaging movements. Some physicians were so slow in this procedure it could take well over an hour, exhausting the assistant's muscles in shoulders, arms and hands.

I didn't fight this work as much as some others did because my approach to surgery was always to get as much total experience as possible. In approaching nose and throat instrumentation as a challenge to be conquered, I gained a reputation of being the hospital's most skilled resident in handling the task. That reputation may have been encouraged by some doctors who didn't like this surgery, and were just as happy to let Ross Pierpont assist when the anesthesia looked tough. Spending two to four hours under anesthesia sheets pumping ether into the patient was not something to call fun. The fumes of ether were so strong at times I thought I would knock myself out, too.

Later in my career, this skill came into play more than once when I had to take over in the middle of an operation when an anesthetist, or anesthesiologist, could not handle his job. Most of these incidents were to finish an operation, however, there were times in my private practice when I used a minor skill learned as a City Hospital resident surgeon to conduct a life-saving maneuver of endoscopic intubation.

Every surgeon has his own methods, and the methods of some doctors in the operating room can drive their assistants up the wall. Discipline in the operating room is firm, so there is nothing a frustrated assistant can do except bite his tongue and bear it. This problem applied in spades to a resident from Johns Hopkins Hospital rotating through Ear, Nose and Throat at City Hospital. He was an excellent surgeon, but painstaking beyond anything reasonable. His reputation for long drawn out operations grew until he became known as Doctor One Cell, the doctor who took out tonsils one cell at a time.

One afternoon after I had my own share of annoyances and needed some comic relief, I went into the doctor's room where Dan and "cellular-one" were relaxing over a soft drink after a two-hour tonsillectomy that had worn Dan down to a frazzle. I knew about the long time of the operation, and could see from Dan's unhappy face that he was with the other doctor only because he had no choice.

Something in Dan's demeanor inspired what seemed worth a laugh at the time. In retrospect, I wouldn't do it to Dan again. Hardly! Anyway, without really thinking, I said to the Hopkins rotating resident, "Jackson, I've been thinking about your experience here for some time. I looked over the patients in the old infirmary building, and I think I found some chronic mastoids for you to do."

Dan Barker, the "Judge" of "Judge and Robin," swallowed his soft drink the wrong way and stared at me as if I had gone out of my mind. Choking prevented him from saying anything, which probably saved us all, but his face told me it was a good thing we were not alone. Nothing violent, of course, as we were good friends, but the language would have been unprintable. To saddle him with "cellular one" on mastoids was cruel and unusual punishment, however, I had committed myself and knew no way to back out of it, especially when the rotating resident jumped at the opportunity.

"Robin, you're great! When can I see them?"

I avoided looking at Dan as I replied, as light-heartedly as possible, "I think I can get them to you the day after tomorrow."

The rotating resident from Hopkins left quickly, and Dan didn't wait to pounce on me. "Ross, you miserable bastard! What the hell did I ever do to you? That man will take five to seven hours on every mastoid, with me under the dammed sheet breathing ether fumes all the time! Fifty years of mastoids and you had to bring them to Jackson today!"

"Hey, Judge, it's my duty to see that you get all of the experience City Hospitals can offer. I'm your friend!"

"With friends like you, who the hell needs enemies?"

With that, Dan stalked out of the room and left me to mull over a bit of fun turned sour. Thoughtlessness has its price. It really wasn't all that bad, though, and after several weeks, time worked its magic, and Dan finally could talk about his mastoid experiences with black humor.

(I had cut them to only two.) Of course, the whole staff learned about the episode, which became the "did you hear about?" chit-chat for the next days.

I'll never know if my friendship with Dan was to hurt him when months later a vacancy for a second-assistant residency occurred. In my judgment, and in the judgment of most of the staff, Dan was the clear choice for the spot, but the doctor in charge of the residency program, Dr. Tom Aycock, passed him over. Later events proved that Dr. Aycock also had no use for me whatsoever. Grace and I were truly sorry to see Dan and Adelaide leave Aycock and Baltimore to settle in Fairfield CT, where Dan established a practice that lasted for the next 50 years.

Upheavals in medical practice and hospital staffing increased rapidly as World War II entered its second year. Grace and I had improved our financial position by then, largely due to Grace's industrial nursing job. However, her job was with Dr. Ralph Horky at Edgewood Arsenal, miles from our apartment. A car became a necessity. We shopped until we found a used Chevy for $250. Not long after, we ran across a Plymouth sedan in good condition for $400. We sold the Chevy for $300 and for a net cost of $100 moved up in class.

The Plymouth got a real workout, too. I had taken a moonlighting job to give some overworked doctors in Aberdeen and Churchville, MD, some badly needed time off. It would be hard to exaggerate the demands on medical personnel during those times of World War II. Aberdeen Proving Ground, the Army's Ordnance base, was bursting at the seams with people. Edgewood Arsenal, the Army's Chemical Warfare branch nearby, was smaller but also struggling to cope. The demands spilled over into steel making, shipbuilding, all kinds of other industries, into restaurants, nightclubs, and more.

War is a terrible blight on humanity, yet the sheer energy expended in the wartime Baltimore of World War II was incredible. It was electricity generated by activities that went on around-the-clock, in the faces and actions of the people. It was a time never before seen in human experience, and I doubt will ever be seen again.

During the wartime build-up, I took my first job outside the hospital. It was near the Army bases in Harford County, MD, about 30 miles and an hour's drive from downtown Baltimore. Dr. Ralph Horky, a small man who was a veritable dynamo, had built medical offices in the first floor of his two-level home. Dr. Horky could barely handle the demands made on him during office hours, not to mention the heavy home visit schedule of the practice. The only time Dr. Horky had off was when he could persuade another physician in Aberdeen, about five miles away, to take over for him. This was rare because the Aberdeen physician was almost as busy as Dr. Horky.

Dr. Horky approached Grace to see if I would handle patient demands on weekends, if I was free, and any other time I could make available. I met with Dr. Horky who quickly oriented me into the details of his patient load, and asked if I would help free him for time off. He had worked out a plan in which Grace and I would move into his house while he and his family went away on vacation days. We would simply take over the house and his practice for the time he and his family were away.

What Grace and I would give up, of course, would be most if not all of our own free time in return for increased income. I knew Grace would go along with any decision that made sense, so it was a question of money. "What kind of financial arrangements do you have in mind, Ralph?" I asked.

He had his answer ready and did not hesitate. "You do the practice and keep whatever you collect."

I was stunned. Ralph Horky continued: "This is a cash practice. It will keep you busy. Depending on how good you are, you will make $400 to $500 on a weekend. Maybe more. Whatever you collect, you keep."

I was unprepared for figures like that, or for a sharing agreement so generous. It was unheard-of. Finally, I said, "Ralph, what about the expenses? Are you sure you mean you're not sharing the income after taking out expenses?"

Dr. Horky did not hesitate. "Ross, you keep what you collect. Ask Grace what I go through here, what my family goes through when I work 18 hours a day, maybe more, seven days a week except when I can convince George Jastram to give me a break. I'm not interested in your money. I need some time for myself and my family, and I'm ready to pay to get it. Ross, there's more than you alone can take care of. Talk to your friends at the hospital. We will give you and them all the work you want to take on at the same terms for everyone."

Grace and I pitched in as relief angels for Dr. Horky and money began to roll in at levels we had never seen before. We not only handled the overflow at Horky's clinic, we also began to fill in with Dr. Jastram in Aberdeen. Not only was the money terrific, the patients we saw were a welcome change from the semi-chronically ill we treated at the hospital. The variety was endless. I treated children with pediatric shots, diseases like diphtheria, measles, appendicitis, influenza, cardiac disease, virus infections, diseases of the aged, and more. If it was an illness or accident, I treated it.

The variety extended to being on call for the county coroner. One night a call came in to rush to a wreck on Route 40 near Aberdeen. On arrival, I found a car rear-ended by a truck. The accident had ruptured the gasoline tank, fire started and burned the car to a charred shell. What remained of a prominent Baltimore man was sitting bolt upright behind the wheel of the car, and burned to a crisp. It was my first experience in examining a barbecued human being — and not one I care to repeat, but it was necessary and I kept at it until I wrapped up the necessary reports about 3:30 that morning.

In the main, this kind of medicine did not have the pressure of the emergency room and the operating room. That doesn't mean there weren't other kinds of pressure. One rainy night the call came in to rush to the home of an older woman with a high fever and trouble breathing. My directions to the home were far from easy to follow in the county's rural back roads, but I had to answer the call.

Rain and low clouds made the darkness pitch black, except for the limited glow of my headlights. Rain pelting the windshield made vision even more difficult. Coming to a dirt road, I checked my directions which included a clipped warning: "Be sure you watch out for the quarry."

I turned off the paved road and drove slowly past wind-whipped trees until, suddenly, I could see nothing. The dirt road had disappeared. Where in hell was I now? Putting on the parking brake, I got out of the car and walked forward in the beam of my headlights until I saw where the dirt road made a sharp 90-degree turn to the left. Straight ahead was darkness. Stepping into the darkness carefully, I made my wa©y forward one slow step at a time until suddenly I was again looking into black space, standing on the brink of a hole so deep I could not see the bottom of it. This was the quarry my directions had warned me about! It had no barrier, nothing to warn a driver to stop where the road turned left. A moment of carelessness on this dark night would have pitched me and my car to certain death far below.

My success in treating the woman that night could not compare with the adrenal flow produced by following the lane to her home. She made it. So did I.

Medical school training constantly advises doctors to listen to their patients. My moonlighting experience proved the value of that advice again and again. On one of my turns in Dr. Jastram's office, a woman about 5 feet 7 inches and weighing at least 230 pounds described how she had suffered upper abdominal pains over a period of about 10 days. She said her pain never stopped, but was worse at some times. Then, for no reason, at other times her condition seemed to get better. I asked her to show me the exact location of the pains. She pointed to the upper right section of her very large abdomen.

"About four days ago," she said, "the pain became so bad I could hardly stand it and I vomited a lot. I was getting ready to come here to see you when all of a sudden, the pain hit me so hard I couldn't breathe and had to hold onto the toilet for about five minutes. I felt like I would die! Then all of a sudden it stopped.

"I felt such relief I laid down on my bed and went to sleep. I must have slept about four hours."

I studied her for a moment. "Was that the end of it?"

"At first it was. I was fine for two days. Then I had more cramps in the right side of my stomach — here." She pointed to her abdomen about six inches above the groin line.

What did the cramps feel like?"

"Just cramps at first. Then they got worse. Really hurt!"

"Was the hurting continuous? Or did it come and go?"

"The pain would come and go for about a day and night. Then they got so bad they were like labor pains. When I got ready to come here the other day, they got worse, terrible, and lasted a long time. Then all of a sudden they stopped."

"Have the pains come back? Is there anything else to tell me?"

all of a sudden they stopped."

"Have the pains come back? Is there anything else to tell me?"

"Oh, yes! This morning when I moved my bowels I heard something go clunk in the toilet. I looked to see if I could see anything there, and there was this lump. I fished it out and brought it in this bottle."

She put a Mason jar on the counter. It had something egg-shaped in it. I left her sitting while I took the jar out to the laboratory and washed the specimen in the sink. The object from the jar was a gallstone the size of a hen's egg. I put the gallstone on a towel and took it back to her. "This is what you passed into the toilet today, Madam. You have had a severe biliary colic with acute inflammation of the gall bladder so severe your gall bladder adhered to your gut — the duodenum. The amazing thing is that the gallstone worked its way through the wall of your gall bladder and passed into your small intestine. Then it moved down your small intestine to the lower ileum where the ileocecal valve blocked any further movement. This is why you had cramps and irregular pain on the lower right side of your abdomen. Gallstones account for about three percent of acute intestinal obstruction of the small bowel. In your case, your body tolerated the spontaneous dilation of the ileo-colic valve by the huge size of your gallstone, and just like the delivery of a baby, you had pains like labor pains when the ileum pushed your gallstone into the large intestine and your pain stopped. Today, of course, you found your gallstone in the toilet."

I have brought up this incident not just because it is somewhat unusual. It is a fine example of the marvelous powers of the human body to heal itself. This woman's very overweight body had tolerated an unusually painful and potentially dangerous series of developments, all unseen and visually undetected, to rid itself of something that was a serious pathological condition. The longer I practiced medicine, the more I saw the human body perform in ways to marvel about.

Although my work with Drs. Horky and Jastram was excellent training and paid extremely well, I was still in a way station on the route to my medical goal. They offered me a position paying $45,000 a year for my first year, to finance a home for us, and to start us in a surgical practice. It was all very flattering, and tempting, for Grace and I still lived below the poverty line. In 1943, $45,000 a year looked like a small medical training. That meant a full residency qualifying me for fellowship in the American College of Surgeons, and Diplomate of the American Board of Surgery. Grace and I often talked it over during my fourth year of residency. The offer remained on the table, but in our hearts we knew there was no way I would accept the two doctors' offer. I told them I would return after a year and would open a practice in surgery in Havre de Grace, a small town just beyond the Army's Aberdeen Proving Ground and a central point for these practices.

A bright spot in my residency at City Hospitals came as the result of my interest in the illnesses of older patients. I had become intrigued with a typical problem of aging, the lack of blood circulation in the lower extremities of the body. In extreme cases, this can lead to gangrene and amputation. If not corrected, it can cause death. An unusual aspect of this condition is that a fairly large number of the very old have no pulse in their arteries of either leg. Yet they are otherwise well and without obvious leg problems.

As an aside, the health care fight of 1994 featured a case that sheds some light not only on the problem of poor circulation, but also on some of the problems in the practice of medicine in the glare of scandal-hungry media. In this case, a doctor in Tampa, FL, was accused of cutting off the wrong leg of an elderly man. A jury awarded the patient (read lawyer) a sum I recall as several million dollars. The press pounced on the case and the verdict, but turned a blind side to the true story. This man's legs were so diseased, that both had to come off or he would die. It was only a question of which leg to amputate first. The man requested amputation of his right leg as causing more pain than his left leg. When the surgeon examined him under anesthesia, he found the left leg to be a greater threat than the right leg, and consulted with a second physician on the proper action. Exercising his professional judgment, supported by a second opinion — such dumbbells! — the doctor cut off the more diseased leg. According to the record, the patient himself was not upset by the decision. No matter; his lawyer saw a chance to make a fortune. He did. Another overlooked fact in the case was that the man's other leg had to be amputated a short time later. So much for the reputation of a competent surgeon, and the hospital where he practiced.

As a footnote to this debacle, it is worth mentioning that an immobile person confined to a wheel chair, like the man involved, will be more comfortable after amputation of both legs, rather than keep one. It sounds heartless, but pre-gangrene legs will be lost in a very short time.

My investigations of circulation problems found many old people with intact functioning of their lower extremities, but they had no effective pulse in their legs below the pulse in the groin level. Many of the patients in the worst condition had a barely detectable pulse even at the level of the main artery in the groin. I also found that the extremities of nearly everyone I examined were cooler than normal although the skin itself appeared to be normal.

About this time, the head of the hospital's peripheral vascular service was called to military service and Dr. Ferdinand Lee replaced him. Working with Dr. Lee was immensely rewarding.

After finishing his training at Johns Hopkins Medical School and Hospital, Dr. Lee taught anatomy. His classes were noted for his teaching the Socratic method. "How did you reach that decision?" he would demand from a medical student. Or, from other students: "What if things turned out not as you predicted? What are the other possibilities? What makes you sure you are right? How can you be so confident? If you are wrong, what happens to the patient?"

Dr. Lee dominated the scene wherever he appeared although he was essentially a quiet man who usually spoke in a low, cultured voice. However, his imposing stature at six feet, six inches, his well-trimmed mustache and dark probing eyes spoke more eloquently than some men's words. Part of his assurance, perhaps, was his association with some of the most influential people of Baltimore. He had married a granddaughter of the founder of the Baltimore Sunpapers, then and now one of the most potent powers in Maryland. He lived in a mansion in the northern suburbs of the city so enormous it had its own bowling lane, and must have required a crew of caretakers just to maintain it.

I became close to Dr. Lee as we probed problems in human circulation. I had, by now, become recognized as an expert in the delicate process of blocking the sympathetic nerves in the neck, thoracic, and lumbar regions. The sympathetic nerves run down the spine as a main part of the body's autonomic nervous system, and one of its functions is to contract the blood vessels. Blocking the sympathetic nerves in the neck, thoracic or lumbar regions of the spine with an injection of absolute alcohol or an anesthetic was necessary in the treatment of causalgia, phlebitis (inflammation of the veins, especially the legs), spasms of the arteries, and similar diseases of the blood vessels and the sympathetic nervous system.

Dr. Lee liked my work, and between us we decided to study the use of a new, long-lasting anesthetic named Bromsalizol in the treatment of circulation problems. To use skin temperature as a measurement of blood circulation, I designed a constant temperature room where I planned to monitor the temperature of the extremities of 24 patients in advanced years who had severe circulation problems. I explained to these patients the reason for monitoring their skin temperatures. Our goal was to evaluate the ability of the new anesthetic to block the lumbar sympathetic nerves — nerves located on the front of the spine just in the small of the back — on a long-term basis. We knew that the sympathetic nerves controlled, in various degrees, spastic influences over the blood vessels traveling through the legs. If the new anesthesia relaxed the spastic influence of those nerves, and circulation improved, the new drug could replace absolute alcohol or phenol, both of which caused problems in their own right. The new anesthesia mixed with peanut oil had no evidence of toxicity or other undesirable side-effects in clinical trials.

After briefing our patients, I inserted three needles 4 1/2 inches long beside each of three lumbar vertebrae on one side of the spine and injected five cubic centimeters of the anesthesia beside and anterior to (in front of) the vertebral body. The other side of the spine was left alone — not anesthetized. I connected a thermocouple to measure and record the temperature of each patient's foot, ankle, mid-calf, and thigh eight inches above the knee. We measured temperatures for two hours in each extremity. I repeated this process daily until no measurable difference could be detected. The skin temperature of the treated side increased on almost every patient, in comparison with the untreated side. Unfortunately, this effect lasted a maximum of only 12 days. This was not enough time for any long-term improvement in the circulation in the lower extremities, which is what we had hoped to achieve. The only use we could make of the process was to treat some diabetic patients with gangrene of the foot, where a short term increase in collateral blood supply helped healing to take place.

Our study yielded an unexpected lesson. In some cases that required permanent elimination of the nerves which control blood circulation in the lower extremities, the surgery created severe problems following Bromsalizol injection. Surgery to expose the lumbar sympathetic nerves of patients using a blunt extra-peritoneal approach was usually quite simple, but the Bromasalizol in peanut oil complicated the operation due to a sterile inflammatory reaction. Instead of a steady and flexible, or sliding, movement of tissue in the surgical area, the mildly-inflamed tissue resisted movement and without warning could crack and rupture a large lumbar vein. When this happened, blood instantly gushed into the deep hole needed for exposure in the operation, with results not difficult to imagine.

In one of my most unforgettable cases, I operated on a 70-year old woman brought to me by her daughter-in-law, who was also a floor charge nurse at the hospital. I first tried treating the condition by cutting off parts of her gangrenous feet, and injecting her sympathetic system with Bromsalizol, but this was not enough. I then operated on her to cut the sympathetic nerves. As I pushed aside the tissue which normally slid easily under my hand, I had to apply additional pressure to get it to move. Suddenly, the tissue cracked open and tore a lumbar vein from the vena cava. Blood gushed from the vein to fill the incision eight inches deep. Unless I stopped the bleeding fast, she would bleed to death almost instantly on the operating table. I did the only thing I could think of. Grabbing four heavy gauze pads, I jammed them into the hole as hard as I could. My own breath came hard as I pushed firmly on the gauze. Life or death became a matter of seconds. One minute. Two. Had the bleeding stopped? Another four minutes of pressure, then one more minute to test my patience. Finally, and very slowly I began to remove the packs of gauze knowing the next seconds could mean life or bring death. To my relief, the wound was dry. The bleeding had stopped! I gathered my strength and finished the operation successfully. Would the nurse know how close her mother came to death? The mother? For a surgeon, coagulation at the right time and in the right place can approach a miracle!

After that experience, I never used Bromsalizol when the patient's condition indicated an operation could become necessary.

Dr. Lee and I wrote up our work and to our great pleasure The Journal of Medical Sciences published it. Did I preen a little? Maybe more than a little.

The kind of experiments just described were typical of the revolution in medical care that began in the 1940s and led to advances no one dared to dream of at the time. The drug we used in our circulation studies became obsolete with the successful development of arterial bypass, and balloon dilation of the lower extremities. However, injecting the lumbar sympathetic nerves by local anesthetics, or surgical removal, still has a field of usefulness.

In a process I cannot imagine ever happening again, medical requirements became more and more strict throughout World War II and the years immediately following. As advances in medicines and techniques followed one another in rapid succession, medical requirements kept pace mainly by becoming ever more strict. Meanwhile standards for accreditation were being lowered to provide medical personnel for the armed forces. In the 1940s, medical schools had no choice but to speed up the education of doctors in both quantity and quality. The American Board of Surgery, originally set up in 1937, moved to an unheard-of, new requirement of five years of post-graduate training in surgery, followed by a strict evaluation process. After a new surgeon met the Board's qualifications for examination, he had to pass an exhaustive written examination. About one doctor in three never got past the written part. Those who did became eligible for part two. This was a practical examination conducted under the eyes of some very critical peers. Passing the practical test entitled the successful surgeon to hang a Certificate on his office wall. This is a process that can be sidetracked by subjective judgments. Human beings, and some very opinionated ones at that, conducted the Board's examinations, and these doctors were not, are not, exempt from human frailties. The human side of the surgeon's qualification process includes favoritism, prejudice, and errors of judgment. It cannot be otherwise.

From the vantage point of a doctor no longer in active practice, I can say truthfully that our American medical system, including its faults, produced some of the most remarkable advances ever recorded in the entire arena of caring for the human body. Earlier I only touched on some of those advances. In less than half a lifetime, we developed an arsenal of antibiotics which continues to grow. We developed beta blockers, calcium inhibitors, joint replacement, electron microscopy, laproroscopy, an entire field of organ transplants, coronary bypass, aorta replacement, and most recently genetic (DNA) replacement. In the days of my residency, we didn't have a vocabulary to describe such developments, much less have them available to treat the human condition.

My second year of residency at City Hospital brought yet another example of the way events which occurred without special notice altered the course of my life. World War II literally changed the medical structure of the hospital. Not only did doctors and nurses leave abruptly and in quantity, the patient mix turned upside down. Before the war, the hospital was filled by law with an enormous range of charitable patients. Not long into the war, the hospital's population had dwindled to a small group of acutely ill patients and a much larger group of chronically ill patients.

To put it kindly, the doctors who had just joined the staff to gain a broad medical experience were furious. They had responded to a recruiting brochure promising broad experience. What they received was routine care of long-term illnesses for one year and military service dead ahead. It did not take long before the new doctors gathered into an angry group of dissidents. They had signed on for complete hospital training; they wanted it now! With their futures at stake, how could anyone blame them?

Few of the senior residents joined the dissidents, but I saw problems that could only grow worse. I joined the insurgency. It was a good thing I did, because the hotheads in the group were ready to burn the house down. Long before today's age of litigation, the hotheads wanted to sue the hospital for fraudulent advertising. Some wanted to write to the American Medical Association, others to the Accreditation of Hospitals Association charging fraud, not only against the hospital but also against the national organizations to which Baltimore City Hospital belonged. I was very young and unsophisticated, but instinct told me that if any of these actions were taken, the omelet could not be unscrambled. Only God knew what the results would be, but disaster would not be too strong a word to describe them. My medical career was in peril, no doubt about it. If the dissidents discredited the hospital, and if national medical organizations were to remove all of the credits previously granted to doctors in training, I would be back at ground zero. The action would wipe out some of my credentials, cripple my right to belong to national medical organizations, and probably end my chances to complete my training.

Discreet conversation led me to some people I came to trust. One was Bob Weston, a tall, angular and amiable sort of fellow who had come to the hospital from Des Moines, IA. A Harvard Medical School graduate, he managed a position in internal medicine similar to mine in surgery.

Between us, we found Fletcher McDowell, just the person to make us an informal committee of three. Fletcher was a stabilizer. His large, round bifocal glasses gave him a bit of an owlish look, and with his rollicking laugh, he was a character right out of a Mickey Rooney movie. To top it off, the twang of his midwestern drawl identified him as a true, conservative son of Indiana. To wrap up his advantages, Fletcher was a first-year, rotating intern who thereby had the confidence of his fellow interns — the firebrands of the insurgents. We needed this doctor if there was any chance of stopping the revolution.

The case against the hospital really came down to the brochure the doctors called a fraudulent misrepresentation of Baltimore City Hospitals. That the brochure misrepresented the hospital as it had become due to the war was true. However, the brochure had been printed before all the changes took place, and in that sense the charge of fraud would not hold. It looked like an insoluble impasse. The hothead doctors saw their residency as wasting a year in a chronic care institution, followed by induction into the Armed Forces. The hospital couldn't change what had happened to it.

Money — more accurately the lack of it — aggravated the situation. As one simmering resident put it: "Besides managing a bucket of slop, we're working for nothing. Why the hell should we put up with that?"

That a storm was brewing was beyond question. Bob Weston, Fletcher McDowell and I met to see if there was any chance of heading it off. We had no trouble agreeing that something had to be done, fast, or we faced the possible loss of our residency, the need to find a new position heaven knows where, and other unknown damage to our careers. I let both doctors muse over the bleak possibility of our dead end. Then I locked in on them, eyeball to eyeball: "We do the only thing we have any chance of pulling off in this mess."

"What the hell is that?" Weston asked.

"We take the lead. At the first opportunity, quietly suggest to some of the hottest guys we need a meeting. At the meeting, we say a real organization is needed, including officers to take the lead." I paused. "Our only chance to save this situation is for us to take the lead. We have to take the lead."

They stared at me. We needed no one to tell us that I was suggesting we take on the hospital organization, and expose ourselves as the leading insurgents.

"Damnation!" Bob Weston finally muttered. "Why the hell us?"

Fletcher McDowell studied me through his bifocals. In his quiet voice, he said, "Robin, what else have you got in mind to tell us?"

"We have got to have the guts to be the officers. Bob, you're easygoing and the others like you. You ought to be President. Fletch-"

"Hold on, Ross!" Bob Weston broke in. "I haven't asked for this. I don't want to get into the middle of —"

I held up my hand to wave him down. "Bob, we're all in the middle, whether you like it or not! We're in a boat without a paddle. You don't have a choice!"

Bob let that sink in. He knew I was telling the truth. That didn't mean he had to like it. Finally he said, "OK, I'll do it, but let's have the rest of it."

"I think time is on our side. If we can buy a couple of months to let things cool down, we should be able to settle this without killing our careers. I'm not saying we sell out the others. We should go after the powers that be on all fronts, but when we get more into the present year, everyone will see that tearing down the house to get rid of the rats won't work. These guys don't have a lifetime job. They have a one year appointment. Delay action a couple of months, and their stake in finishing the year and not losing credits for their time spent will make the difference we need."

My speech sounded confident, but I wasn't sure how true it really was, but Weston and McDowell went along with me. McDowell said, "Where do you fit in? We're not going to be left hanging out to dry."

I said, "Fletch, you ought to be executive vice president. You're the man to work with all the first-year men. Me, I'll be the one in touch with the senior residents. I'll run for secretary. That way, I'll handle the correspondence."

Bob Weston wasn't sure about that. "That makes us a committee of three, and they're not going to let us run the show."

Now my homework paid off. Bob was dead right, and I was ready for him. "Right you are, Bob, m'boy! We propose a committee of five. That way we have a three-to-two majority, even if we can't convince the other two of what we need to do."

McDowell allowed himself an owlish smile. "I feel like Patrick Henry. Give me my residency or give me a five-cent cigar." I looked at him, and he said, "Forget it. Problem is, Mr. Secretary, they wouldn't trust Superintendent McMillan sitting on a pole with the pole up his ass. How do you answer that?"

I said, "Here's my idea. First, we write up a complaint that includes everything the men are mad about, but we don't hand it over to the muldoons on the Board of Welfare. We go to the top with it — to the Mayor and the Baltimore City Board of Estimates."

"Hoo—eee!" Weston exclaimed. "They'll shit their pants!"

I had struck pay dirt. "We'll ask for more money for the house staff, and relaxing the rules to admit some paying patients and get a better mix for the residents' training."

A phenomenon often encountered is that situations arise which seem to have no solution, but once an answer is found, it immediately becomes simple. We had struggled on and on with the threat of hospital destruction, with no results, but once we cut the knot, we ended up wondering what took so long. A marvelous lesson in life is that one person with a practicable plan can carry the day against a noisy unorganized majority with nothing in their favor except noise. The dictators of history have proven the point again and again. We followed our discussion by calling for a secret meeting. It had to be secret because we were putting our careers on the line.

The meeting began in disharmony and proceeded downhill from there. One young man ranted on and on until everyone tired of him. He finally realized he was making a fool of himself, which only made him madder. Others wouldn't be satisfied until they had their say, and we waited them out. The meeting was drifting by this time, but I exercised patience not particularly typical of my nature. Eventually, fatigue set in, and this was where we came in. I motioned to Bob Weston, and he called for attention. He said that I had worked up a plan to tackle our complaints and asked me to explain it. It took just a few minutes for me to cover our proposed action, and when they heard I wanted to go over the head of the hospital and directly to the Mayor and Board of Estimates, the mood changed from "to hell with it all" to "hooray!" except for the problem of Superintendent McMillan.

It was common knowledge throughout the hospital that McMillan's answer to a problem with the hospital staff was simply to dismiss it. One of his classic comments was widely known. When confronted with a probem involving hospital doctors, he snorted, "Don't bother me with house staff!" In another incident, he bellowed: "Those doctors are dime a dozen and I can get as many as I want any time!" McMillan's approach to hospital management reflected the attitudes of the men making up the Board of Welfare, which managed the hospital for Baltimore City. The saying goes that power corrupts and the Board running the hospital often demonstrated the truth of that proposition.

With the group settled down and generally receptive, I pointed out the natural tendency of national organizations to defend their own turf. If, I asked, we handed national organizations a dilemma they could resolve by cutting the throat of just one municipal hospital, suppose they did just that? What would happen to every doctor in the room? There was another possibility. If national organizations responded to our complaints, an investigator could charge the whole problem to our group. This would go on everyone's record and follow everyone for the rest of his life. They suddenly changed from a clamorous, unorganized group of young men to quietly receptive. We ended the meeting with a unanimous vote to proceed. Our next step was a written complaint to the Mayor and Board of Estimates of Baltimore City that did not mince words. Tough and to the point, we laid the blame for an intolerable situation squarely on the management of Superintendent P.J. McMillan, his staff, and the Board of Welfare.

We delivered our complaint to the Mayor's office in the fall of 1942.

All hell broke loose.

The *Baltimore News American* and *The Sunpapers* splashed the story on their front pages. The news hit the corridors of City Hospital like a fire alarm. Fellow doctors, most of them secretly applauding our resolve, didn't know whether to congratulate us or avoid us like the plague, which means anyone not in the complaint kept his distance. The lesson was not lost on me: in a situation involving risks, loyalties diminish in proportion to the risk.

The nerves of everyone involved in the protest took a daily beating before we were finally notified to appear at City Hall. None of us cared very much what we looked like entering City Hall, but I am sure the whole lot of us looked like a group of serious and very nervous young men.

The meeting room was full of people including reporters from the daily newspapers. The protesting committee sat on a bench facing the Mayor and members of the Board of Estimates. This Board included Mayor Howard Jackson, the City Comptroller, the President of the City Council, the Head of the Department of Public Works, and the City Solicitor. We were face to face with the people who ran Baltimore City.

At the other end of our bench sat Superintendent P.J. McMillan, Thomas Waxter, the head of the Board of Welfare, and members of that Board. Mayor Jackson presided over the hearing officially entitled The Case of The Committee of the House Staff of Baltimore City Hospitals versus the City Hospitals and the Board of Welfare. Mayor Jackson invited us to present our case and listened in silence while Bob Weston, summoning a marvelous act of self-assurance, read the paper stating the substance of our protest. When he sat down, the silence in the room was eerie.

Mayor Jackson invited Superintendent McMillan to respond.

A more uncomfortable man than McMillan could not be imagined. His fellow defendant, Thomas Waxter, was just as disturbed. Until this moment, they had been essentially dictators with no need to justify anything they did so they did what came to them naturally. They simply ignored everything in our written protest, plus what Bob Weston had added personally, and blamed our situation at the hospital as a result of the war.

Our protest sat on dead center. Even though Superintendent McMillan and members of the Board of Welfare had said nothing worthwhile, these men were where they sat because the political establishment — the people who were hearing our case! — had put them there. They were part of the establishment, and the war made a good excuse for everything we were objecting to. Although we were in the right, our protest was not going well. Tension filled the air as some members of the Board of Estimates shuffled some papers. From the expression on Mayor Jackson's face, he was considering how he was going to handle this. After an eternity, the Mayor said, "Mr. Waxter, Mr. McMillian, I am directing you to hold a very early meeting between the Board of Public Welfare, Baltimore City Hospital, and the House Staff Committee of Baltimore City Hospital to resolve this matter."

After Mr. Waxter and McMillan thanked the Mayor, everyone left. Two weeks later, we attended a luncheon meeting in the office of Superintendent McMillan. Facing our five-man Executive Committee of the House Staff were the Superintendent, the Chairman of the Board of Welfare, and two other members of that Board.

The luncheon began with palpable hostility and never changed for the better. Members of the Board of Welfare representing a challenged City Hospital were also under challenge, and our attempts at civility were met with icy silence. At last dessert was being served, and Mr. Waxter turned the meeting over to the hospital superintendent, Mr. McMillan.

McMillan, visibly uncomfortable, rambled on in a speech attacking what we members of the House Staff had done, and how wrongheaded we were. Finally, he said, "If you had some problems, why didn't you come to me?"

That did it. The question was just too much for me to swallow. Maybe the strain of the previous weeks had gotten to me, but for this contemptible man to ask such a question was pure gall. I broke the silence of the moment. "Mr. McMillan," I said, and caught myself. My voice was entirely too weak. Raising the volume, I resumed. "Your resident staff, to a man, faced what could easily have become a disaster — for the hospital as well as the doctors. Before we drew up our protest, a number of the residents had decided to take their protest to the American Medical Association, and to the Board of Accreditation of Hospitals. These doctors felt cheated and badly treated, and they were ready to charge this hospital with an abrogation of their contracts due to the misrepresentation in the brochure which led them to sign up. These men believe the information put out by City Hospital was a fraud."

I can still see Superintendent McMillan looking at me as if I had gone mad. He was a gray man from gray hair to gray face wearing a gray, clearly expensive, tailored suit. He looked almost the personification of the executive of the times. His normal lack of color went from gray to pinkish from the strain of the situation we both faced. I was a gawky youth about his height and half his age, wearing my House Staff whites, and I am sure my face revealed the strain I was under.

No one on the Board was shuffling papers or looking out the window now. When I said "fraud," I could have set off a fire alarm. Every eye was on me, with the pressure going up. My adrenalin level must have set a record. Now the only sound in the room was my voice.

"If your staff doctors' complaint had gone forward as planned, the situation would have gone out of control. It would have been out of your hands and out of ours. The damage to Baltimore City Hospitals, to the Board of Welfare, and not so incidentally to the doctors involved, is beyond my ability to imagine. I can only tell you it was something we had to avoid at all costs.

"When the doctors in this protest saw what their intended actions could lead to, a formal protest to the City was unanimously agreed. Unanimously sir! There was no time to waste, no middle ground to take. We saw — correctly, sir! — we had no choice but to take this matter to the highest local level, as the only way to keep it local."

McMillan's pink-tinged, gray face now turned red. His agitation was obvious as, abruptly, he raised a hand to stop me and, almost shouting, demanded: "But why didn't you come to me! Why didn't you come to see me?"

His question was aimed at the heart of our protest and had to be answered, or else our cause was lost. Why hadn't we gone to the Superintendent and the managing Board? I replied in a voice as measured as I could make it. "Mr. McMillan, I don't want you, and the members of the Board listening to this, to feel that I am speaking my own, personal thoughts. I have been asked to speak for the doctors in this protest, and these men know your reputation, and the reputation of the Board of Welfare as well. We live and work 24 hours a day under your rules. The truth, sir, is the doctors I speak for look on you as an unfeeling, arbitrary son-of-a-bitch. You believe and have said so for doctors to hear, that doctors on the house staff can be bought a dime-a-dozen. Every doctor I speak for has found out, when they get to meet you, that your reputation is the truth. You are what they call you, a son-of-a bitch."

McMillan's mouth was agape. What he had just heard, in front of his Board of Welfare, had to be beyond his belief. He stared at me almost in horror, speechless, and as if his only thought was escape. Members of his Board of Welfare looked through me, also in silence. I remember thinking he can't answer me. Maybe I should have felt sorrow for him as a man I may have damaged irreparably, but I felt nothing except the sheer challenge of the moment. The man was everything I had said, and more.

Thomas Waxter, Chairman of the Board of Welfare, realized McMillan was in no condition to reply. Knowing there was no way he, himself, could answer my statement, he met the occasion by doing what politicians do so well — straddle the issue. In a voice meant to be mollifying, he said he could understand the problems created by the country's military build-up, but also that the complaints of the house staff seemed to be justified. The he turned to the members of the Board of Welfare to confer with them briefly. The conclusion was that we could expect an improvement in our financial status, and the hospital would take up a relaxation of admission policies to attract other than chronically ill patients.

That night I told Grace what had happened and my unplanned denunciation of Superintendent McMillan. Grace's face told me I had upset her terribly, which was surely understandable. Our fate would now be determined by the outcome of the protest, and in the process I had made myself a marked man. It could not be otherwise no matter how justified my description of the Superintendent. He, and likely the other officials at the hearing, would be down on Ross Pierpont for life.

Fortunately for both Grace and me, she fully understood and accepted that I could not have done anything different and remained myself.

We had invested more than two months in lodging our protest. There was nothing more to say. We left the meeting totally unsure of our medical future. Throughout the next days we heard nothing at all from the Board of Welfare, or Superintendent McMillan. We said nothing more either, then our next checks arrived with a minor increase in pay signifying our protest had carried some weight. Admission standards were also changed to permit other than charity patients. Some members of the house staff landed positions in other hospitals and left. We had some more committee meetings but there was no fire left in them. The meetings soon stopped altogether.

The "mutiny" was over.

Had we proved you can fight City Hall? Not really. What we had proved was when your case is right and you have the guts to bring it before the American public, the power of the haughtiest of bureaucrats cannot protect them from judgment.

My run-in with Superintendent McMillan had no outward effect on my status as resident surgeon, but I knew, deep down, I had made some powerful enemies. The patient mix improved and attitudes of the staff improved with it, although the surgical staff itself continued to dwindle due to military and other departures. For the last 18 months of my residency, our staff was so short that Donald Hebb and I directed the day-to-day surgical functioning of the hospital by default. We were literally Co-Chief Residents.

Don Hebb, like Ferdinand Lee, was a bright spot of my early medical years. Hebb was a paradox. He was the absolute opposite of Dr. Lee, who physically and intellectually dominated situations he entered. Hebb was laid back, casual, soft-spoken to a fault, with absolutely no interest in power or position. He looked as he behaved, with a well-padded, five foot, eight inch frame, and blond hair that usually looked in need of a comb. The hospital was in many ways his home. At times, I thought, the hospital was even more his home than his life with a wife his intellectual equal. Medicine does that to some men.

One day Hebb came into the dining room at breakfast time and handed everyone a small cheroot called a cigarillo. "Had a baby, last night." he said in his offhand manner. We looked at him. "A boy," he said.

"Congratulations, Don," someone said, looking at his cigarillo. "Is this supposed to be a cigar?"

Hebb tossed over his shoulder as he walked away. "Small baby."

Hebb had little time for fools, or doctors who talked better surgery than they practiced. One of his assistants was a young doctor who had the bad habit of carrying his position as a resident surgeon beyond his capabilities. Hebb put up with him as a necessity, until one day in the operating room the young man went too far. Working as Hebb's assistant that day, he kept trying to cut sutures with his left hand, and mangling the job. It finally became too much for the laid-back Hebb, who said, "Bible, why don't you cut those sutures with your right hand? You are right-handed, aren't you?"

Young Dr. Bible, wounded in front of those present in the operating room, attempted to justify his left-handed technique. "Doctor, I am ambidextrous."

Hebb appeared thinking about that as he studied his incision. Without wasting a look at his assistant, he said quietly yet heard by everyone in the room. "You mean to tell me you are equally inadept with both hands.

Chuckles throughout the room finished Hebb's quiet reprimand. Young Dr. Bible said nothing, but his face reddened as he quietly cut the remaining sutures with his right hand.

In sharing hospital responsibilities with Donald Hebb, I covered an unusually large field of surgery. The hospital's expanded emergency admissions thrust me into general surgery, orthopedic surgery — this grew into a large part of my daily operations — gynecology, urology, peripheral vascular disease, some nose and throat, and even some neurosurgery. Advances in US medicine have made it impossible, today, for a resident surgeon to gain the extremes of experience I gained years ago in a relatively short time. Training like that now could be gained only in a third-world country where medical care is still relatively primitive.

But as widely as I practiced, it was not enough. By the time I had to commit myself to my last year of residency, I realized my training was excellent only as far as it went. I had gained very little experience in the major elective cases referred by general physicians. Such cases included surgery of the thyroid, surgery for peptic ulcers, biliary surgery, colon and pancreatic surgery, and other specialties. If I stayed another year at City Hospitals, my training in these important fields would be minimal. That meant I had to find a better answer to my training if I were to grow into the surgeon I was determined to become.

The situation I had to face went beyond a simple decision about my medical career. Grace and I had struggled to make a life for ourselves ever since we married. My hospital pay was still a pittance, far less than she earned. My moonlighting earned much more, but it cost us all of our free time. Grace deserved more than a move to strange surroundings, giving up her job, leaving friends and family, living once again on a resident surgeon's income. Loyal and loving as she was, would our marriage survive such enormous demands? If she were to stay in Baltimore, would our marriage survive a year's separation?

We talked things over and decided I needed to check out my options. By now the war continued to complicate my 4-F status at the hospital as it almost decimated hospital ranks of physicians. On the plus side, the situation meant I could expect to find openings in other hospitals offering the training I needed. In early 1944, I wrote to a number of the top hospitals requesting information about a senior residency appointment. Replies exceeded any possible expectations. Dr. Smith Peterson, famous for developing hip nail surgery, offered me the Orthopedic Residency at Massachusetts General Hospital. I also received offers from Columbia, Cornell, Yale, the University of Iowa, and others. Every hospital was looking for four-year advanced residents who could stand the rigors of hospital practice and had the physical stamina that residency demanded.

The word got around that I was thinking of making a change. No doubt Dr. Aycock, a daily reminder of the truth of "the Peter principle" and head of the residency program, had heard about it before I met with him to take up my final year of training. Any hope of change in the residency program to broaden my training was swallowed up by Dr. Aycock's firm conviction that his philosophy of physician training was the only philosophy of physician training. He was smart enough to avoid mentioning my part in the residents' protest, but of course he had to know it. It's almost certain that describing Superintendent McMillan's character in colorful terms before the Board of Welfare did me no favors with the administrative types.

Needing a sounding board and some top-level help, I went to Dr. Ferdinand Lee for his advice. He listened quietly, as was his manner, while I summarized the need for a decision. "You know the patient mix here, and that it leaves a lot to be desired when it comes to training in elective surgery. I've done the Chief of Surgery job, along with Don Hebb, for the past two years, but continuing to do what I've been doing for the next year isn't going to give me the training I need to be the surgeon I want to be."

Dr. Lee allowed himself a fleeting smile. He had been through it all years before. Now he appreciated what I was facing. "Ross, it's a big decision. It will make the rest of your life as a doctor, not to mention what your decision will do to your personal life. Why don't you get to the point?"

That was Dr. Lee for you. Get to the point! I pulled out the answers to my letters of inquiry. "I think I need the kind of training available only at a good university medical school. Here's what I've gotten back from schools you will know. Some of them speak of two years, I might add."

Dr. Lee reached for the responses to my inquiries and leafed through them. Instantly recognizing the letterheads, he said, "What a change from my days! You've got some top-drawer offers here. If you had told me when you were writing these schools, I would never have believed answers like these."

I laughed. "Dr. Lee, in me you're looking at the product of a peptic ulcer and opportunities created by the war. My ulcer left me with a permanent pyloric channel scar that makes me one of the few 4-F candidates who can still work a full day. The rules for induction don't allow for channel peptic ulcers, so unless they lower the standards more than they have so far, they won't call me up for military service."

Dr. Lee said, "I don't know how much you know about the University of Iowa, but it's a sleeper. The Eastern mindset tends to forget there are some real schools that aren't on the Atlantic coast. Iowa is a top residency. In fact, an old friend of mine from Hopkins is Professor of Radiology there."

I said, "I think I ought to tell you what I've been thinking about my position here. I don't want to let the hospital staff down when its so short-handed. I want to ask Dr. Aycock if he will credit my 9-9-9 credentials if I stay to teach anyone he wants me to teach for three months after the first of July, when this resident year is up."

Dr. Lee was skeptical. "What makes you think he will go for that?"

"Well, I think it is fair."

"I think it will be more than he will do for you, too."

The next morning I saw Dr. Aycock in the operating suite between operations. "Dr. Aycock," I said, "do you have a few minutes? I would like to talk with you."

Aycock didn't hesitate. "Come with me, Pierpont! He gestured toward one of the prep rooms. We went inside and I said, "Dr. Aycock, I have been thinking about my career here, and afterward."

Aycock, stiff as a board, said nothing. He had no need for a summary of my tenure at the hospital. He knew about my work with Dr. Lee, and the publication of our study in the medical journal. He knew full well the long, arduous hours Don Hebb and I spent managing the surgery staff as Senior Residents. Most of all, he certainly had no doubt about the hospital's limitations in surgical training due to the semi-chronic patient mix, but I felt I had to explain my need to move on, in spite of everything Baltimore City Hospitals had meant to me.

Dr. Aycock fidgeted impatiently as I continued to offer to stay on for three months after July 1st. The man looked from me to the windows, past me to the wall. His face began to glower, but I went on. "Dr. Aycock, I want to make this as smooth as I can, and I must also ask you to assist me with my 9-9-9 credits in case my 4-F status changes, or I cannot get the position I am looking for."

115

What power does to people! What power does especially to little people! Dr. Aycock now exercised the power of his authority to show who could do what to whom. He looked me squarely in the eye, his face flushed and angry, for no one else had dared to put his career ahead of an Aycock residency at City Hospitals. "Pierpont, what you will get is credit for the exact time you spend here: no more, no less. I am not going to change this program to suit your ambitions."

I stared at him, struck silent by his obvious anger. Dr. Aycock sucked in a deep breath as if he needed air to make his point. Almost shouting and in inexplicable anger, he declared, "You will take this Chief Residency from July 1, 1944, to June 30, 1945 or you take nothing! Is that clear, Pierpont! Have I made myself clear to you?"

It was clear, all right. Not only was Dr. Aycock clear, he had made up my mind for me. To this day I cannot say how I managed to stay in total control before Dr. Aycock's brutal response. I doubt the man was in any mood to appreciate a calm fourth-year resident, anyhow. I said in a tone so measured it almost surprised me, hearing myself: "Dr. Aycock, I guess the only thing left to be said is you'd better get yourself another boy."

With all of the confidence in basic human decency not yet drained from my youth, I foolishly tried to explain to this man too limited to understand, much less accept, that my need to move on was not a reflection on him or City Hospitals. "Dr. Aycock, I've given this hospital everything I had for four years. I hope you will give me your recommendation."

Dr. Aycock stood to leave the room before I finished the last words. He threw over his shoulder, his voice harsh and deep in his throat, "I'll give you your recommendation when the time comes, Pierpont, but it won't be a good one!"

"...But it won't be a good one!" I had no way of knowing how those words of that angry man would come back and threaten my entire career as a surgeon. But I knew enough to tell Dr. Lee about my talk with Dr. Aycock when I saw him the next day. Dr. Lee knew Dr. Aycock well, and knew what Dr. Aycock could do to me. He said, "Pierpont, don't repeat that story to anyone. It can only hurt you, and Dr. Aycock intends to hurt you. I'll get in touch with my friend at Iowa, and you get your application out to them right away."

I did as he suggested, and it turned out to be the best training decision I ever made. My position led me to work with Dr. Frank Peterson for the year July 1, 1944 to June 30, 1945, a priceless year for a budding surgeon. As for Dr. Lee's assessment of Dr. Aycock, Lee had Dr. Aycock's attitude toward me right all the way. Originally encouraged to apply by every hospital to which I had written, not one who received a later application using Dr. Aycock as a reference ever bothered to reply. I had challenged the authority of City Hospitals, won the challenge — but the total cost of Dr. Aycock's bitter enmity was yet to come.

Doctors like Dr. Aycock make up a side of medical practice the public never sees — fortunately perhaps — but are only too real to those who must work under such doctors' control. It's hard to say how Dr. Aycock got his position at Baltimore City Hospitals, but I know he was one of Dr. Shipley's favorites. Dr. Shipley was the man whose narrow-minded love of prestige had driven a far better surgeon, Dr. Robert Bay, to quit the University of Maryland Medical School and take his entire practice to Maryland General Hospital. A defensive maneuver of doctors like Shipley and Aycock is to mask any weakness they may have by driving out others if they challenge them with superior ability. Getting rid of any threat to their prestige leaves them surrounded with doctors who make them look like resident geniuses in comparison. City Hospitals' loss of Dr. Dan Barker through the Aycock process was an example of "superiority-by-denigration" at work.

Chapter Seven
Iowa: A "Side Trip" On My Journey Into Surgery

During the years I spent earning degrees in pharmacy and medicine, followed by more years of 10-and 12-hour days at City Hospitals accompanied by giving two doctors in Harford County weekends off, my goal was so powerful it never dawned on me to think I was overworked and underpaid. The truth is, I loved what I was doing. I relished what I was learning, and would not have traded a moment of it then or now. Yes, the abysmal pittance then paid to interns and resident physicians grated on me, but that was the system. I was part of the system, and I had more important problems.

We had our good times, too. Somewhere along in my City Hospitals residency, weekend parties at our modest home at 312 Elrino Street became almost a standard procedure with the resident staff and other friends. Wartime rationing of food, gasoline, meats, liquor, and other shortages made the accumulation of party-time goods a form of high art.

The orthopedic clinic was the key to party foods and beverages. I was in charge of orthopedic services for most of my years at the hospital, putting in afternoon sessions of three hours three days each week. My patients came in as a result of automobile accidents or injury in one of the nearby factories. Wartime wages were good, and my patients were either heavily insured or making good money, or both. The hospital's policy of admitting only charity patients did not apply since these were emergency cases and we could treat anyone in that category. Under the rules at the time, emergency patients were treated at no charge, and those with fractures often remained in the hospital for weeks or even months. Follow up in the orthopedic clinic was extended and very friendly. In fact, we treated orthopedic patients graciously, and they responded to us with high gratitude.

"What can we do for you?" was a common question. One group of long-term fractured leg patients insisted they wanted to do something to show their appreciation. Finally, someone said to the other patients in nearby beds, "These doctors look human. They must get together for some fun when we don't know about it. Why don't we help with things like party food and beverages?"

The offer went over big. In a few days, they came up with food stamps for ham, turkey, other meats, butter, and more. All contributions were stored in one corner of the clinic, and it was not unusual to have a ham, turkey and beef roast there. Beverage contributions to our cause included beer, gin, blended and bourbon whiskey, and various wines. Everything donated except fresh meats went into our small kitchen to await the next party. Meats were kept in the hospital refrigerators or lockers until we were ready for them. When our collections were enough for a party, the word went forth to the resident staff that the next Saturday night was party night at 312 Elrino Street.

We were young, spirits were high, and the mode of guest arrivals was part of the fun. Some rode bicycles, some drove, some walked, and some came across the roofs of adjoining houses to enter through our open bedroom window. Youthful hunger soon took its toll of the ham and turkey Grace usually cooked and decorated for such occasions. Each guest was free to choose a preferred beverage, chilled with ice donated from our generous hospital freezers.

Our friends made themselves at home on chairs, on the bed, sitting on the floor, and, if weather permitted, on the front roof. The level of music, conversation, and singing (we had a few operatic types) increased as the night wore on. Our need to "let off steam" overpowered our sense of neighborliness, and more than once unhappy neighbors called the police to complain. The police were typical of the amiable Baltimoreans of the era, and when they came we toned things down for them. We invited them to join us for a sandwich and a beer, which they accepted with pleasure. Cautioning us to keep it down a little, they left, often to return an hour or so later when enthusiasm took over for good judgment. These parties usually ended about one in the morning, and one by one the revelers drifted off except for a conscientious few who stayed to clean up the mess and restore our apartment to some semblance of order.

When we announced our decision to leave City Hospitals and go to the University of Iowa, one last shebang was in order. It was a great one, too. Indeed, I cannot recall, even now, any party we have given that matched the relaxed camaraderie of our "pick-up" parties in the company of the staff and friends at City Hospital.

Another way I escaped the stress of hospital tours was in playing squash on the long-neglected but refurbished hospital courts. I have already described my love of this sport, helped no doubt by my affinity for it. Grace learned the game with me, and together we met some of the finest men and women on the globe. Not the least of these were Ann-Elise and Bill Fitzgerald, who became U.S. Ambassador to Ireland.

Farewell to Baltimore, hello to Iowa!

I grew up a farm boy, and Iowa is farm country, but neither Grace nor I were truly prepared to pull up our Baltimore roots and move to a state a thousand miles away. We didn't say much to each other as we loaded our car for the long drive to Iowa City, but all change is troublesome, and we had no way of knowing what our lives would be like during the year ahead.

A first-class car made the first day of our trip as pleasant as narrow, twisting Route 40 permitted. Just after we had decided to take the residency in Iowa, one of the staff physicians at the hospital decided to take a sabbatical overseas. He had an excellent Oldsmobile "96," a two-door black sedan with an Olds "98" body and a six-cylinder engine. Letting it sit while he clipped his inherited bond coupons on his sabbatical made no sense, and we took it off his hands for the asking price: $650.

I had fun sitting behind the wheel of our "fancy" car, and driving from Baltimore to Iowa City in 1944 was an adventure in its own right. We drove on two-lane roads that wound through the Appalachian Mountains of Maryland and West Virginia, across the flat lands of Ohio, Indiana, and Illinois where farm led to farm and to more farms, and finally into Iowa. Where the farms left off, we passed through burgs, small towns, and cities all along the way. The roads of those times led through the heart of the cities where city traffic and traffic lights made for slow going. Every sight was a new experience for us because neither Grace nor I had ever driven west more than a few hours distance from our native East Coast. It was nothing like my trip to Niagara Falls with three other teen-age boys in what seemed a lifetime ago.

Our first stop late in the first afternoon of the journey was at the home of Jim O'Hara in Canton, Ohio. Jim and I had become friends when we were classmates in medical school. He welcomed us warmly and being the successful, expansive Irish physician he was, he rolled out the red carpet. He and his wife were proud of their large home with the gables favored at the time, and made sure we shared his pride. Telling us he would not have it any other way than for us to spend the night with them, he also had invited some of the "leading lights" of Canton to join us for dinner. Before dinner, we had a nostalgic time swapping memories and laughable events of our student years. After dinner our Irish host brought out Benedictine and Brandy and we let our batteries wind down for the night.

Somehow breakfast is never as convivial as cocktails and dinner, and we had a business-like "get up and go" meal before we hit the highway early in the morning of June 28, 1944. The rest of Ohio looked to us like the first of Ohio, field after field of winter wheat ready to be harvested, and the corn rising tall left and right. Indiana and Illinois were more of the same. If you had blindfolded us and sat us down almost anywhere along our route, we could never have told you which of the three states we were in, or which direction to go to get out of there. We crossed the headwaters of the mighty Mississippi River where Moline and Rock Island, IL join with Davenport, IA to make a three-part urban area. The main school of chiropractic, the Palmer Institute, is in Davenport, and we made a short side-trip to see what it looked like: very small, very promotional at the time.

As we left Davenport and crossed the crest of a hill late that afternoon, a fiery landscape spread before us that had no beginning and no end in any direction. The sun was a dazzling ball of fire motionless in a cloudless, blue afternoon sky. It seemed waiting for us to meet it as we crossed each sloping hill, then returned high above us as we descended the slope. The sky and the land continued until they met each other at some nameless distance. The road turned directly into the sun and suddenly we caught our breath to see a majestic cock pheasant in all its proud glory facing us smack dab in the middle of the road. The sun's glow enhanced the bird's feathery brilliance as though God had placed both sun and pheasant in a planned portrait.

We eased toward the pheasant, and I brought us both back to earth. "Well," I said to Grace, "if that is our introduction to Iowa, what can they do for an encore?"

Grace laughed. Some of our anxiety about our decision to make Iowa our home for a year started to melt. She said, "Maybe it'll just get better and better."

Her words were a perfect vision. We were entering times never anticipated, never to be repeated.

It was a long day by the time we reached Iowa City and found the Jefferson Hotel in the heart of the city. Fortunately, we were in time for dinner, so we registered and freshened up sufficiently to have supper — not dinner, in farm country — in the hotel dining room, the "Huddle." Surveying the scene of the dining room, as is my constant trait, one couple was conspicuous. The man was not just large — though he was sitting you could see he went well over six feet; and he was also about 100 pounds overweight — I judged him to hit the scales at about 300 pounds. The woman at the table with him didn't match his size, but she was in the same league. She was also more refined, limiting herself to a half-smile at his stories and comments delivered loud enough for most of the room to hear. One remark to her contained the phrase "a new resident," and I said to Grace, "Is that one of our confreres? He looks more like an undereducated, untrained, over-stuffed small town practitioner."

When I write a remark like that, I have to admit I must be something of an elitist. Who the hell was I entering Iowa as a new resident surgeon to label anyone at first glance the way I had just done? Well, I felt it. I said it, and I cannot take it back. Alas, my first impression turned out to have overstated the man's abilities. I soon found out that the overweight diner in the hotel was also joining the staff at the University of Iowa Hospital. The difference between Ross Pierpont and "Lord" Harrison, as he labeled himself, was day and night. My training was in a top medical school where competition got rid of the less capable, followed by four years of residency in which I had functioned as a Co-Chief of Surgery. "Lord" Harrison had a general practice in a small Midwestern town notable for its lack of professional competition. He was accepted by the University of Iowa Hospital because the hospital needed all the physicians it could get at the time. A Cleveland physician who personally knew the Professor of Surgery at Iowa had recommended the man. I never learned if the Cleveland doctor was told how his recommendation of "Lord" Harrison turned out, but it was not long before we learned the man did not belong in surgery. It was a good question if he even belonged in medicine.

I quickly found out that "Lord Harrison" and I were the only two new residents in a full-time surgical staff. This consisted of a Chairman, a Professor of Surgery, two assistant professors, a Chief Resident and Instructor, and other residents who had returned from general practice for additional training due to the wartime shortages. As usually happened, I was the youngest one of the group. Lord Harrison was oldest. Both of us would have to earn our places in a cohesive group of long-term Iowans. My relatively brief lifetime of fighting for survival instantly alerted me to a need to adjust. I was in a highly structured medical environment where personal relationships went a long way. My future would depend on how well, and how quickly, I could fit myself into a medical world where Grace and I were strangers.

This world was new to me on two fronts. The first was medical, where I had to fit into a staff pyramid built around seven years of surgical residency. The Iowa staff had a background in surgery that was completely foreign to me. I was trained in a city where 14 approved surgical residencies served a Maryland population of 2.5 million. The State of Iowa had just one approved surgical residency — the one at the University of Iowa — serving nearly twice the Maryland population. The State of Maryland supported the University of Maryland with $250,000 a year. The State of Iowa supported the University of Iowa with more than 40 times that much money. In Maryland, people came to local hospitals for their medical care; the University of Iowa had a regular fleet of ambulances that covered the state to bring complicated cases to the hospital in Iowa City. Because the hospital was organized to concentrate on major surgery, it did not admit patients from elsewhere in the state who needed minor or routine surgery. An exception was made for patients in Iowa City itself. Third, fourth and fifth assistant residents and surgical interns got all the training in hernias, varicose veins, hemorrhoids, and tonsillectomies they needed from Iowa City patients. During my year there, it was routine to have six or eight radical breast procedures, four or five gastric resections, three or four colon resections, three to five thyroid operations, two or three parotidectomies, plus a virtual spectrum of other pathology cases taking place at any one time. The training in major surgery I would gain during my 12 months in Iowa was almost staggering. This one hospital offered as much major surgical pathology as was spread across Baltimore's 14 approved residencies at any one time.

For someone who lived, breathed, and slept surgery as I did, this place was a surgical heaven on earth. Dr. Ferdinand Lee had been absolutely right in recommending Iowa. I wasted no time in going to see Dr. Dabney Kerr, Chairman of Radiology, and Dr. Lee's friend, to thank him for vouching for me. Later events were to prove that if their recommendations hadn't been forthcoming, I would never have been accepted.

Meanwhile, I had yet to live up to my friend's recommendations. In the days — not weeks — ahead, I had to prove my professional capabilities. After that, I had to find a niche in the staff pyramid to make sure I got the cases in major surgery I was in Iowa to receive. My hands-on experience was good, but my knowledge of procedures as written in medical literature left much to be desired. I did not wait another day to spend every waking hour I could in the library studying the latest innovations in the procedures I wanted to do.

Fortunately, I now had free time I had never known in Baltimore. I gave up my "residency call time" to juniors on the staff, which they appreciated. I had done three full years of "residency call" surgery, with senior staff responsibilities for two of those years. I had nothing to learn by taking those kinds of cases. In actuality, the thoroughness of my training in that category of surgery was far more extensive than any of my fellows could get even in the Iowa arena.

By the end of my first month, my "homework" paid off. Participating in staff meetings and instruction periods, and evaluating my mental preparation as objectively as I could, I found I had forged ahead of the other residents in knowledge of the procedures we were to perform. The teaching was outstanding. Every night we met with Dr. Peterson or Dr. Dulin, and everyone had his cards of patients in hand ready for discussion. I looked forward to these sessions eagerly. They were spirited, open, and straightforward. Deficiencies were uncovered and examined with no holds barred. Tender sensibilities were not allowed to interfere with free and frank criticisms and recommendations.

At the close of our nightly sessions, Dr. Peterson or Dr. Dulin posted the assignments for the next day's surgery. By the end of a few weeks, it became obvious that the choice assignments were going to the doctors at the top of the pyramid. I was not in their position. I was perched most uncomfortably on the horns of a dilemma. If I did nothing, I would fall far short of finishing the training in major surgery I had journeyed to Iowa to get. My year would come to an end without getting my hands on the gastric, colon, thyroid, peptic ulcer, and radical breast surgery I had missed in my Baltimore City Hospitals training.

If, on the other hand, I pressed for some of the assignments now going to the "regulars" on the staff, I risked not just a rejection, but also the anger of others on the staff, and possibly the disfavor of the department chiefs. I confided my analysis of the situation to Grace, and as always she was ready to support me in whatever action I chose.

I hate indecision. I would much rather do something wrong, and act to correct it than to twist on the horns of a dilemma. Somewhere I had heard about the two men watching a dog twist uncomfortably and whine as it lay on the porch. Finally, one man asked the dog's owner, "What's your dog whining about?" Replied the dog's owner, "Oh, he's a-layin' on a burr or a nail or something."

"But why doesn't he get off it?"

The dog's owner eyed the animal a moment. "It don't hurt him enough yet."

The "burr" I sat on hurt enough to get off it one way or another. The decision made, I gathered the records of my surgical cases at Baltimore City Hospitals and went to see Dr. Frank Peterson. Not knowing what to expect, I quickly found myself conferring with a total gentleman as well as a topnotch surgeon.

We chatted briefly about what had gone on in the hospital since I had arrived, and then he listened courteously as I explained the reason for my visit. I told him I had applied to the hospital to get training I had to obtain in order to meet my surgical goal. I laid my experience before him, including its strengths and what was still missing. "Dr. Peterson," I said to wrap up my case, "I live up to my commitments, and I will do so here. You can count on it. I came to you now to tell you that if I continue on my present course, I am going to waste my year here, and no doubt miss a very great opportunity awaiting me back in Baltimore. I already know the kinds of surgery I am doing here. I need the kinds of cases I am not getting so far."

Dr. Peterson said, "Ross, we are in difficult times. I have watched you and know from your participation in the evening sessions that you have a great deal of experience. I also know you have been working with Ed Besser at Oakdale. Bob Hayne has told me about your expertise with sympathetic surgery and injections."

Dr. Peterson knew more about me than I realized. His reference to Dr. Hayne was about my experiments with Dr. Ferdinand Lee in Baltimore to relieve vascular spasms of the blood vessel system in the lower legs and feet. Apparently Hayne had also told him I had extensive experience in surgery of the thoracic sympathetic nervous system for hypertension. Neither of these were the usual areas of resident surgeon's expertise. Oakdale was a tuberculosis hospital about eight miles from the University of Iowa hospital. One day I had been talking with Dr. Besser, Chief Resident and Instructor, about my experience at the tuberculosis sanitarium in Baltimore City Hospitals, and this triggered an idea of Dr. Besser. Oakdale had some special problems in areas of our expertise, and for no particular reason we decided to pitch in to see if we could help. "Cast thy bread upon the waters..." as the old saying goes.

Both of us had paused to arrange our thoughts, and I sat waiting to see what would come next. It was only a moment before Dr. Peterson said, "I like the way you handle yourself. I have no problem understanding your ambition. If you decide you have to leave here to get what you need, I will help you any way I can."

Oh boy! I thought. I'm leaving with a can tied to my tail!

Dr. Peterson took a drink of the ice water he favored. I waited for the kiss of death. He said, "But if you really would like to stay with us, and I hope you do, write down those procedures you need to do to complete your training. I will see to it that you get enough of them to finish the job you've set for yourself."

What a turnaround! I knew what I had just heard. I knew it was everything I had come to Dr. Peterson hoping to hear, but it was said so casually, with no ifs, buts and ands, that I had trouble believing it was all true. I looked at Dr. Peterson and am sure he saw on my face the satisfaction I now felt. What a man! What a difference between a true gentleman and a horse's ass like Dr. Aycock! Never have I been more proud of my medical profession than I was at that moment.

"Dr. Peterson," I said, "you are more than generous to me. I know I am asking a lot, and I promise I will do my best while I am here. I'm glad to say Grace and I like living here, and I like everyone here at the hospital. It's a great place for me, and offers me everything I need. If I ever cause a problem, please tell me and what I can do to change it."

Dr. Peterson smiled. "Good decision, Ross. And no problem. Thank you for coming in."

I left Dr. Peterson and the hospital on cloud nine and met Grace at home still up in the clouds. Reality came when two days later at the regular evening session when Dr. Peterson assigned me surgery for a duodenal ulcer. Adrenalin spurted in me with the news. Others in the room stirred as the significance of the assignment sank in. The barbarian had climbed aloft the "regulars'" pyramid. No one dared to question Dr. Peterson, and the meeting broke up with no one saying a word to me.

Fortunately for me, the operation went very well. While I am sure no one wanted me to fall on my face, my success created a whole new order of things, and the unrest of the "regulars" was in the air. The most unhappy fellow of the staff was none other than Bob Bartels, an assistant professor in the department. Bartels didn't say anything, but his annoyance with me was anything but a secret.

One day later, I was in my fifth floor office when Dr. Poole and Dr. Mikelson came in together. Poole got to the point without introductory remarks. "Pierpont, we have been here a long time and are old Iowa alumnus." (Alumni? I thought.) "Frankly, we don't like you distorting a system which has worked very well for a lot of years before you came along. You took a gastric resection ahead of Ed Besser. He's in his seventh year here!"

Mikelson joined the dialogue. "Yes, Ross, I feel the same way, and I know Obie does too." Obie was a favorite nickname for Bill O'Brien.

I stood up so we were all on the same level. "I can guess how everyone feels," I said. "But I have to tell you, I didn't come to Iowa to make friends. I came here to complete a surgical training which is much broader in experience than any you have to offer. I don't want to get in anyone's way, and if I make friends, that's fine. But if I don't make friends, forget it. Making friends won't make me the complete surgeon I intend to be, and what I came here for."

The two doctors looked at me. They were not ready to hear what I was saying. "I did what any of you can do. Take your records to Dr. Peterson as I did. Give him a chance to help you or move you. That is all I did. Dr. Peterson is a man of honor and so am I. We have agreed on my future here, and I am going to hold up my end of the bargain. I am sure he fully intends to do the same. Now if you want to make something more of this, do so, but I will tell you this: I will defend myself and my record against anyone and all of you with no holds barred! Is that clear?"

Mikelson turned to Poole. "Harold, I guess maybe we misunderstood. I have nothing more." Unexpectedly, he extended his hand to me. I shook it. Poole would have no part of such courtesy. He made some sort of disgusting grunt, turned and left.

I had no desire to become a lighting rod in Iowa's medical politics. I also knew when I went to see Dr. Peterson I would disrupt the system, if successful, and a price would have to be paid. Things came to a head a day later when I was in Dr. Tidricks's office with Ed Besser.

Tidrick took the opportunity to negotiate. "Pierpont, you know you have caused some problems around here. You've got Bob Bartels really upset about the change in assignments."

What Tidrick was asking for, indirectly, was for me to give up my position in major surgery cases — to reverse myself. I looked at him; he really didn't know what he was asking. I said, "Look, Bob, this is between Dr. Peterson and me. If Bartels has a problem with me, why send you to tell me?"

Tidrick, now embarrassed, got a little pink in the face. "Now, look, Pierpont. Bartels has been here a long time" (by inference, I had not) "and he feels he is responsible. I —"

I interrupted. "Bob, Bartels isn't training here because he loves this place. He is here because he is dodging the draft on a 'necessary assignment basis." Tidrick's face got pinker. I had dared to say what everyone knew, but everyone was too polite to acknowledge: not a nice way to win a popularity contest. "Let's face facts, and I have given you the facts. If he wants to discuss these ramifications, I'm ready."

Tidrick raised his finger across his lips to indicate silence. Bartels, he knew, was in the adjacent room. I also knew he was there, too. That's why I had spoken more loudly than necessary. The three of us collected our thoughts a moment, Dr. Besser gave a little cough, and the three of us left the room in silence.

Medical politics is a world of its own. As in any profession, medicine has fakes, incompetents, doctors who get by on the strength of their access to power. But doctors also respect merit. My position had merit, with the result that the disturbance in the staff's pyramid power structure I had caused settled down into accepted daily routines. The sign of peace came Monday after our Sunday ritual of complete ward inspection of cases. "Lord" Harrison had two cases and both were disasters.

The first case of his we saw was a radical breast procedure with a severe mixed streptococcus infection of the entire wound. The infection had caused a massive loss of skin flaps. Harrison's second case was a hemorrhoidectomy in which he had virtually sealed off the man's anus. The aperture Harrison had left open would accommodate nothing larger than a pencil — and a small one at that. I looked at Dr. Peterson, whose face bordered on apoplexy as the patient spread his buttocks and the gathered staff stared at the tiny anal orifice.

Harrison knew he was in trouble and tried to cover. His beefy face red and damp with sweat, he started to say, "Well, sometimes we get one of these solid, scarring healers, and —"

Dr. Peterson cut him short. "Schedule this man for tomorrow. We'll have to divide that scar tissue and dilate that anus and keep it dilated." Looking at the flustered Harrison, he almost growled: "I'll be there!"

At the end of rounds, we stopped by the cafeteria for coffee. Harrison's bulk was conspicuous by its absence; he had gone with Dr. Peterson for a conference. It was a somber group until Tidrick broke the silence. "Harrison is a hell of a problem. He is cocky and confident and gets his ass into one problem after another." He realized his remark had a double meaning and laughed. "Should'a been his anus, not the one of that poor soul he cut up so bad."

Ed Besser said, "I'll bet Dr. Peterson would love to give that Cleveland doctor who recommended Harrison a piece of his mind. The man should have stayed in general practice in Cleveland. He'll never make a surgeon."

Tidrick couldn't resist a chuckle. "Tell you what, though. He and 'Lady' Harrison know how to live. They had Peg and me over to their house for dinner the other night, and Harrison almost never made it through dinner. 'Lady' Harrison had cooked a full course dinner, with cocktails b'fore dinner, and white wine with the fish. His Lordship had enough white wine to drown the fish, then came a great rare rib roast of beef with a Chambertain red. His Lordship downed about a bottle of that. Then we had champagne with desert. By this time Harrison couldn't stop talking, but it was hard t' tell what he was saying half the time."

Tidrick's laconic description of the evening continued, and ultimately became a hospital classic. Tidrick had a Will Rogers sort of twang which added a nice touch to his narrative.

"After about the 'Lord's' 15th glass — well, now, no one keeps count of a 'Lord's' beverages — could ha' been the 16th or 17th, the 'Lord's' 300 pounds a' fat and muscle, mostly fat, of course, sort of oozed down into his chair: all over that chair, as a matter a' fact. 'Lady' Harrison didn't blink an eye, went on as though we weren't there, as a matter a' fact, for she had put her 'Lord' to bed so many times before.

"The 'Lord' finally tried to get up, but didn't make it. He didn't actually fall down, he sort of oozed to the floor like a ship sinks slowly to the bottom of the sea. I looked at 'Lady' Harrison, and said, 'Looks like his "Lordship" is ready for bed. Shall we try it?

"Harrison looked up at us and struggled to get up, but never made it. I was hoping 'Lady' Harrison had experience and a better idea, but there was nothing else to do but heave Harrison upright. I got on one side, 'Lady' Harrison got on the other, and Peg sort of helped in back." We began to laugh as we envisioned the scene of the three of them poised around Harrison's 300 pounds of dead weight. Tidrick continued: "On a count of three, up-see-daisy! I said, looking at 'Lady' Harrison. She nodded, smiling a very nice and thankful smile at me, a gracious lady! I counted to three and we heaved. Heave ho! An' a bottle a' rum! We hadn't moved him at all! I tapped Harrison on his shoulder to get his attention and said, 'Lord' Harrison, you gotta help. Now when I count three, and we lift you up, you get up! Hear me? Harrison grunted, opened one eye and nodded his agreement. This time he made it to his knees, then another heave ho! and we got him on his feet. Then we steered and pushed and held on for dear life until we got him bedside. There he fell on the bed, fully clothed, not making a sound except his heavy breathing. My back still hurts!"

Somehow we felt a little closer listening to Tidrick and talking about the Harrison debacle, but I didn't expect Tidrick to drop in on me the next morning. His manner was open and friendly when he came through the door and he grinned as he said, "Pierpont, you are a lucky son-of-a-gun. What saved the day for you with the staff was 'Lord' Harrison's surgery we saw yesterday. Compared to him, you're a damn genius!"

I took the remark in the spirit it was offered, but it touched me and I muttered something stupid like, "C'est la guerre, Doctor. C'est la guerre."

Thinking of Tidricks' reference to 'Lord' Harrison brings up some of the memorable aspects of my year in Iowa. The Harrisons and Pierponts both stayed in rented quarters during our year there; however, the Harrisons rented one of the "big houses" in the city. Not to spare expense for the year, they brought in their furniture from Cleveland. Grace and I found a first-floor apartment in a house owned by two of the nicest people we met in Iowa. The husband of this couple was a smiling, happy-go-lucky type, the stock room clerk in the Chemistry Department of the University, and an entrepreneur. After we moved into their home, we found that they had given up their first-floor bedroom, living room, dining room, and kitchen in return for our rent of $150 per month fully furnished. The adjustment for all turned out very well, and Grace and I could not have wanted more. We had never experienced life in a city that revolved around a college, and we fell into its daily activities as if born to them. The reputation of Midwesterners for friendliness was evident every day, although I suspect our Eastern speech and manners made us as much an "experience" for them as they were to us. Although Grace had a degree in nursing, and was in fact a senior RN, she had never been to college. She enrolled for the year and took a full college credit course. She also took up tennis and swimming, in the course of it becoming one of the best-looking "co-eds" on campus, with a figure that was the envy of many younger women. With my career on track at the hospital, and our daily life relaxed and pleasant, who could have wanted more?

This return by memory to my year in Iowa once again brings out the dramatic advances in medical practice over the last half-century. Innovations in methods and materials have driven surgery into inter-dependent areas. No one had heard of antibiotics before my days of residency. I well remember receiving my first test tubes of something new called "penicillin." My first dosages came in 10,000 units to be reconstituted with saline for intravenous injection. 10,000 units! Sounded like a lot then, and it was, but today surgeons daily inject millions of units into the muscle or a vein as a simple prophylactic against infection or as a routine treatment.

Anesthesia is such a surgical necessity it has gone from a blow on the head, inebriation, and gas to a selection of methods. Today's anesthesias permit cooling, removal and recirculation of blood which in turn make possible the most precarious brain, cardiac and transplant surgery on a patient who is in many respects temporarily dead.

In Iowa, we were still in the era of mechanical surgery. Technical performance dominated surgical literature. The giants of the times were leaders of surgical clinics and medical groups. Frank Leahy of Boston and George Crile at the Cleveland Clinic led in thyroid surgery. Owen Wangensteen at the University of Minnesota and Allen Whipple at Columbia Presbyterian in New York dominated pancreatic cancer and resection, a procedure still known as a "Whipple."

The grand leaders of clinical activity were the brothers Mayo, founders of the Mayo Clinic in Rochester, MN. They "owned" the domain of colon surgery.

Our evening meetings to discuss the day's and tomorrow's surgery in Iowa were totally dominated by techniques developed by these men. They became "star performers" through video and televised presentations of their "wet" clinics — a term meaning showing actual operations as they took place.

I still look at the roll call of clinical greats with pride, and with even with awe. How many lives have these giants saved through the years following them? How many lives have been made worth living, not just saved, by their vision, skill, and ability to transfer their learning to thousands of other surgeons in every country of the world? In my mind, nothing like the past half-century has ever happened in medicine before, and I cannot conceive it ever happening again.

Chapter Eight
Iowa: Stay Or Go?

Pundits and sportswriters like to say good luck is better than good ability any time. I had my share of good luck in my year at Iowa. I gained respect for Dr. Peterson daily. Events were to prove my association with this gentleman and physician was one of the luckiest events of my life. Thanks to his help in assigning the kinds of cases I needed, my learning curve in surgery went almost straight up, but my learning in two other critical areas had a long way to go. I had no idea, for example, that medical politics played a role in gaining acceptance by the American Board of Surgery, and by the American College of Surgeons. Membership in both organizations is essential to a successful surgical career. Another area that needed strengthening was surgical pathology. Without better knowledge of surgical pathology, acceptance in professional organizations would be unlikely or impossible.

Luck came my way when Professor of Pathology Harry Pratt developed an abbreviated course in surgical pathology at the University. He wanted some "guinea pigs" to test its value, such as three or four interns and/or resident surgeons. The opportunity was too great for me to ignore. I checked the possibilities and found two members of the Urology resident group who were highly interested in the course. One was Oscar Carter, of the Nashville, Tennessee country music Carters. Oscar was one of the most living-within-himself persons I have ever met. Polite to a fault, and an adoring husband, he was also dedicated to making a name for himself in urology accompanied by a personal fortune.

The second pathology candidate was Ollie Sarff, a physician of some 50 years of age who was changing from a general practice to urologist. He was also a man who was not about to let his age get into the way of pursuing women. To put it bluntly, Ollie was a rogue. More than once I heard an attractive nurse, aide or other female utter a sound in disgust from the food line in the cafeteria. A glance at the line showed that the sound always came from a woman ahead of Ollie who had been pinched or otherwise "approached" as Ollie demonstrated his appreciation of the female form ahead of him. After the victim had escaped and Ollie joined us, he invariably beamed his mischievous grin and answered our unspoken criticism: "Just checking, fellows. Pays to check. Gotta make calls if you want to get results!"

While few if any of us appreciated Ollie's technique, the word got around the hospital that his advances did not always fall on unappreciative women. I have to smile as I recall, today, what he got away with. In a hospital today, any man who tried even one of Ollie's stunts would be disciplined or dismissed before being on staff a week.

The three of us enrolled in Dr. Pratt's new six-week course for two hours three evenings a week. The practical examination at the end of the course was thorough, and demonstrated that Dr. Pratt's teachings in pathology were excellent. Everyone involved was enthusiastic about the results, to the point that the course became an elective and continued its success long after I had left.

Not long after I completed Dr. Pratt's pathology course, I received an unexpected call to see Dr. Peterson in his office. Wondering what was up, I promptly obeyed the call. We hadn't talked more than a minute or two before I realized Dr. Peterson had recognized my lack of experience in medical politics. How could it be otherwise? A doctor my age is not the most sophisticated guy in the hospital. "Now that you have training in surgical pathology on your record," he said, "it would be a good idea for you to write the American Board of Surgery with a list of your training, and a request about eligibility for Board qualification for an examination. While you're at it, you also ought to apply for a Junior Fellowship in the American College of Surgeons."

The suggestions almost stunned me. Of course I knew about the two professional organizations, and their importance. I also knew that many aspiring doctors fail even to win an examination, much less meet the Board's qualifications for acceptance. I hadn't thought I was ready for this move even though I had spent my last 12 years in pharmacy school, medical school, as an intern, and as a resident. At last I was getting somewhere!

I could not have appreciated Dr. Peterson's interest and help more, and I told him so. I had no way of knowing, then, that his help and advice would one day stand between me and surgical oblivion.

The American College of Surgeons and the American Board of Surgery responded to my request for information, saying my training was satisfactory, The Board warned, however, that eligibility for Board examination would require me to practice surgery exclusively following my year at Iowa. The reason for restricting the physician's practice to surgery exclusively is to assure that he, or she, is not distracted into any other activity. It is an all-or-nothing situation for a doctor seeking Board certification.

The response from the Board of Surgery buoyed my spirits. Then came news that I was accepted for a Junior Fellowship in the American College of Surgeons subject to an interview with the Iowa College Chapter of practicing surgeons, members of the college. The interview would be in Davenport, on a weekend.

Grace went with me to Davenport, where we found the office designated for my interview. The meeting turned out to be somewhat strange. Five general surgeons asked me a few questions about medical fundamentals, then the questions suddenly turned to medical practices in Baltimore. All five doctors were fascinated that a single city, Baltimore, had 14 approved residencies. The questions seemed irrelevant to my surgical qualifications, but continued on the same track. Abruptly, one questioner got to the focus of the panel's interest. "Dr. Pierpont, are you familiar with the College position on fee-splitting?"

"Yes, sir," I said. "Everyone in Baltimore was very strict about that. It isn't done at all."

"Very good," said my interviewer, "but what do you do in Baltimore about assistance in operations?"

"There are so many residents and intern staff, there are more than enough assistants."

"But what about the hospitals that do not have residents in surgery? What happens with them?"

I answered, "I am not very familiar with those institutions. The only ones I know utilize a pool of assistants, or the referring physicians who send their own bills for the assistants. To the best of my knowledge, there is no division of fees."

The interview continued on a very amiable tone, and I left with the impression they would recommend my acceptance to the Junior group of the American College of Surgeons. When I returned to the hospital, Dr. Peterson called me in to ask what had happened at the interview. I summarized the entire meeting and as I did so a slight smile broke his normal composure. Then he began to laugh in what, for this gentle man, was an uproar.

"Ross," he said, still chuckling, "I know every one of those doctors very well. Every last man of them is splitting his fee right down the middle with the physicians who refer patients to them." He paused, seeing he had caught me a little off-guard with his remark. "I would like to have been in that room after you left. Many of those men have to negotiate with the referring physician while he still has the patient in his office, or outside the surgeon's office in his car. It's a 50-50 split for the surgeon, at best!"

"They talked about almost nothing else but our system and how we didn't split any fees. Now that I think of it, none of them said anything about how they handle the problem of assistants at surgery or fee-splitting."

Dr. Peterson laughed. "I'm sure they wouldn't go into it with you, Ross, but fee-splitting is routine in Davenport, and many other parts of the Midwest. It's ironic, really, because the American College of Surgeons is located in Chicago, and that city is a hotbed of the problem."

There wasn't much more to be said, and my impression of the interview turned out to be right. I was accepted into the Junior group for progression to the American College of Surgeons.

Days then followed days, with a steady progression of my training in major surgery. One incident in my training provides a sidelight into parts of surgical practice few non-surgeons ever see. I was operating on a woman who had a mixed tumor of the parotid salivary gland on the left side of her face. I would not know if the tumor was totally benign, or partly malignant, until it was removed and examined by a pathologist. This is a bloody, sensitive, and extremely tedious operation that involves the 7th cranial nerve. This nerve comes out of the skull at its base, and divides into 5 branches which lie close the parotid gland and between its superficial and deep lobes, where it supplies the enervation of the middle of the face. If I cut or otherwise injured this nerve, my patient would have permanent facial paralysis of the left side of her face. That is problem enough, but minor pulling, pushing, or handling the facial nerve can cause temporary paralysis or weakness of the facial muscles. In some cases, such damage may also remain permanent. Advanced surgical techniques now make it possible to correct the paralysis by nerve graft, but a graft also has a serious chance of not functioning completely.

To remove the tumor in my patient, I first had to identify the facial nerve and its path. Following the standard procedure in 1945, I cut through the skin parallel to the ear, down to the neck at the hinge of the jawbone, then forward to near the midline of the neck. I then lifted the facial skin up over the face nearly to the nose. The next step was careful dissection of the superficial muscle just below the lower jaw which revealed the branch of the facial nerve I needed to see. Gentle movement of this facial nerve caused her lip to twitch. Working very carefully, I traced the nerve back through the parotid, carefully removed the parotid and the tumor, and traced the branches of the nerve back to the trunk where it emerges from the skull. The objective of this operation is to remove all of the tumor and superficial gland while preserving as many facial nerve branches as possible. I sent the removed tissues to the pathologist for immediate diagnosis of potential malignancy. If the tumor and superficial gland were diagnosed as benign, my next step would be to clean up any suspicious areas of the parotid and close the wound.

Dr. Mahlen Prickett, an older physician formerly in general practice in Ball Knob, Arkansas, administered the anesthesia for the operation. His goal in Iowa was to specialize in anesthesia sufficient to avoid returning to Ball Knob. As I had concentrated on my patient, I noticed Mahlen was peering up over the sheet to watch my hands, sometimes shaking his head and chuckling softly to himself. While waiting for the pathologist's report, I relaxed a little. Looking at him, I said, "Prickett, what the hell were you shaking your head about while I was operating?"

There, in the middle of a tedious, bloody operation, something Prickett had on his mind made him break into outright laughter. He shook his head and said, "Pierpont, I remembered one of my cases watching you, and I have to tell you you're the best I've seen do that." He paused, followed up his thought. "'Course, I haven't seen all that much."

"Thanks for the left-handed compliment —"

"Oh, I didn't mean it that way. I mean, I really admire what you're doing."

"Why? It's nothing new or unusual. Just tedious and difficult."

"That's all? If you knew what happened to me in Ball Knob, you wouldn't think that's all, and you'd know what I remembered to make me laugh. I was all they had in Ball Knob, a one-man doctor of everything, and I had one year of training in any kind of surgery before I came here. One day a very pretty young woman — she was 27 years old — came in my office to show me a lump on the left side of her face she said was hurtin' her." Prickett paused to check his anesthesia equipment and the status of my patient.

"I examined her and told her it was a sebaceous cyst and if she'd come in the next morning before I opened for office hours, I'd remove it. People started coming into my office by eight o'clock when I was there. She came in first thing the next morning, and I laid out my small set of operating instruments to take out what I thought was a sebaceous cyst." Prickett allowed himself a deep, soulful sigh. "I no more than made a small incision before I saw this lump was different than any sebaceous cyst I had ever seen or operated on. No question it was attached to deeper tissue. She was bleedin' a lot — just like this one." He motioned to my unconscious patient." I was in trouble, only thing I didn't know was how much. I began to sweat. I made the incision larger, but not too much. This went on for two, maybe three hours before I had enough nerve to cut off what I had dissected and sew over the bleeding parotid gland.

"I guess my patient's tumor was benign, so I immediately began to close the wound" Prickett continued. "I knew I had to get out of this woman's face before I did real damage, but I still didn't know what I had found either. All I could do was sew up her face and send her home. By this time my waiting room was empty, 35 patients had given up on me and gone for the day."

"Was that the end of it?"

"No," Prickett said. He sighed and his memory of the episode brought a tiny grin across his face. "Since I didn't know what she had, I sent the specimen to a path lab in Little Rock. It came back, thank God, a benign mixed tumor of the parotid gland like you are working on today."

"OK, was that the end of it?"

"Wa,al," Prickett replied in his Arkansas drawl, "I paid twenty dollars and the postage to get the report. That was how I found out I'd operated on a mixed tumor of the parotid. I read up on everything about it I could get my hands on and told the woman we had to watch out for recurrence. Of course she had no money to pay me, not even my twenty dollars."

I looked at him. "What did you charge her?"

"Wa,al, she brought me in two chickens and a bag'a potatoes. She said she'd bring me more, but she never did. Now, Pierpont, you see why watching you lay out that nerve system, and seeing what I had tried to do which I never should'a done, as ignorant as I was, I couldn't help living through everything that happened that morning all over again. Includin' the 35 patients who walked out on me! It's not funny, but it does scratch my Arkansas funny bone a mite."

I looked at this physician learning anesthesia at age 40 to escape from his two-chickens-and-potatoes practice in Ball Knob and shook my head. "Prickett," I said, "I not only understand why you were shaking your head, I think I understand why you are becoming a damn good anesthetist."

"Coming from you, that's a real compliment," Prickett said. He was beaming as he completed his part of the operation and left the room.

* * *

Life when Grace and I grew up as children in the countryside near Baltimore was far too demanding to encourage frivolity. Out of habit, we stayed busy on many fronts in Iowa. As I focused most of my waking hours on surgery, Grace busied herself at the State University of Iowa learning French, English, mathematics, music, art — and tennis. Life outside the hospital and the classroom also had many attractions unique to the region, and we thoroughly enjoyed them. The university had a full concert orchestra, and we never missed a concert. We attended football games at the stadium and basketball games at the field house.

Activities like that in a small college town have a focus not present in large eastern cities. Local people usually fill sports and cultural facilities to capacity, and getting the most desirable tickets can become a career. One day the subject of tickets to basketball games came up during a conversation with our enterprising landlord, Homer Hall. "You know, Doc," Homer said, "I have a way to get into the games and don't need any tickets, if you want to go some time."

"How's that?"

Homer laughed as he anticipated his answer. "Doc, I've got a great big pipe wrench. So when there's a game I want to see I put on my work-hauls and go to a gate and say to the ticket taker, 'Where do they need the plumber?' The guy on the gate looks at me and doesn't know what I'm talkin' about so he says, 'Go 'round there to the main office and ask 'em.' I tell him thanks and go to the men's room and stash the wrench and change my clothes and then I go watch the game."

"Homer, you're a bad man!" I said, laughing. His offer was not my way of doing things.

My love of squash came into good use during my training in Iowa. The Iowa Sea Hawks branch of the Navy was stationed at Iowa City — for reasons only the Navy could ever know; there's no large body of water in a hundred miles. Anyway, the Sea Hawks used the University of Iowa squash courts. Dr. Peterson was a good friend of the Admiral in command of the Sea Hawks and known to be a member of the Naval Executive Group. During a break in one of our evening review and scheduling sessions, I mentioned something about playing squash to one of my associates, and Dr. Peterson heard me.

"Ross, did I hear you say you play squash?"

"Yes, sir."

"Are you any good at it?"

"I think so. I won the Class B singles championship of Maryland once."

Dr. Peterson was so delighted he almost glowed. "Marvelous, marvelous! I'm going to challenge the Admiral in command of the Sea Hawks to a match with you." He paused to look at me. "Is that OK with you?"

The challenge was right down my alley, and I didn't hesitate. "Sure. I've never seen the Admiral play, and he's good. But I have played some of the Sea Hawks and never lost to any of them.. Barney Pool, the National Football League player, is the best and roughest I ever played from their gang." I paused then felt compelled to add, "I beat him, too."

Dr. Peterson added a smile to his glow. "The Admiral is the champion of the base and proud of it. He's never had anyone here who can beat him." His face still beamed but became serious as he looked me in the eye. "I want you to beat him. And I am going to bet him you will win the match!"

"OK by me," I said,

A few days later Dr. Peterson told me the match was set up for two out of three matches with 5-set championship rules. As my luck would have it, I was in unusually good form the day of the match. After I beat the Admiral with two straight wins and three games to none, we sat down in one corner of the court, and he said, "Ross, Pete was right. You are the best squash player out here, and now, dammit, you've cost me the best dinner in town with your boss. Congratulations on a really good, solid game!"

We went in to shower, and for no good reason the Admiral began to chuckle as we dressed. "I'll take the son-of-a-gun to dinner at the officers mess. He didn't specify the restaurant!"

My first and only winter in Iowa brought new experiences. One day in November, Homer and Jenny Hall joined Grace and me for a cocktail in the living room we now rented from them. During a lull in the conversation, Homer spoke in his go-getter voice as clipped as his stature. "Ross," he said, "I am going rabbit hunting Saturday. Would you like to come along?"

I had never thought about hunting wild rabbits since my boyhood days when I'd roamed the farms around our home in the Woodlawn countryside. Almost every boy I grew up with hunted squirrels or rabbits, or game birds in the more remote fields or woods. Homer's idea offered a change of pace I could really use. I said, "I'd like to, Homer, but I am not a good hunter or a good shot. I don't think I ever hit a rabbit when I was a boy growing up near Baltimore."

"No matter," said Homer firmly. "I will shoot enough for both of us."

Jenny voiced her pride in Homer's hunting ability. "He sure can do that, Doc. We froze at least 50 rabbits last year, and we must have eaten fresh, or given away, at least 50 more."

Though Grace and I were brought up around raising and butchering livestock from chickens to hogs to steers, I wasn't sure the idea of cooking lots of rabbits for our dinner appealed to Grace. Without a glance at me, she said, "Jenny, that's a lot of rabbits. Do you eat that many every year?"

Jenny replied, "Yes, we sure do. We freeze them for meat the year 'round, and eat 'em fresh, too. Of course, we give a lot away, too."

The snows came and came that week. Saturday it was eight inches deep, and we had no hunting dogs. I always get up around 5 AM, so I was awake when Homer came to the door. I said, "Morning, Homer. Looks like we have to pass up the hunt with all this snow."

Homer laughed. "Snow's no problem. I know just where to go."

So a-hunting we went. Homer drove us to a deserted area. We walked the snow-covered field to a frozen stream surrounded by a growth of bare, variegated trees, brush, and very rough ground. We hadn't taken a dozen steps along the banks of the frozen creek before three startled rabbits jumped from the underbrush and dashed their zigzag courses for cover. Homer's shotgun roared twice. Two rabbits. I fired twice. I might as well have shot blanks.

On we went down the stream banks. As we reached the end of the gulch, we had downed an even dozen rabbits. The score was Homer 11, Pierpont 1. Homer led the way to higher ground covered with dense underbrush and obviously the home of uncounted rabbits. Trampling around roused the rabbits from their haven and out into the open. Homer's gun was deadly accurate, and I improved a little; 15 more rabbits went into the snow which kept them colder than a refrigerator. It was now late morning, and Homer said, "Ross, I've got work waiting on me at the lab this afternoon, so if it's all the same to you I'd like to call it a day."

I'd had enough a half-hour earlier, but didn't want to call off the hunt until Homer was ready to end it. Now, Homer's invitation to head back home was welcome. We had more rabbits than I'd ever seen in one place before. "Fine by me, Homer! I would never hunt this many rabbits in a year at home."

At the house, I watched as Homer dressed the rabbits to be frozen or soaked in saltwater for 24 hours. Homer gave me two dressed rabbits for soaking, and the next day Grace made a rabbit potpie. The other one we deep-fried, tasting much like fresh spring chicken. In our urbanized, supermarketed society far removed from the hard-scrabble lives of our grandparents, how little we understand what they had to learn to survive off the land.

My huntsmanship days in Iowa recurred on a drive to the already-famous Mayo Clinic in Rochester, Minnesota. I offered to take Ed Besser and Evelyn Harness, a dermatology resident, to the clinic in my "Oldsmobile 96," the bargain I had negotiated from my fellow house officer at Baltimore City Hospitals, and it gave me an aura of affluence I didn't deserve. Of course, no one knew the truth; they saw only our powerful automobile.

Somehow, either Ed or I - it was probably Ed — suggested we go pheasant hunting on the way back from Rochester. It seemed like a nice break in a routine trip, so Ed brought along his shotgun, and I borrowed one from Homer Hall. As we drove through northern Iowa, then into southern Minnesota, the early morning sun lit up the gorgeous finery of a dozen or more cock pheasants by the roadside. Others were visible farther in the fields. Some trusting souls perched atop fence rails.

The instinct of animals to learn hunting regulations is phenomenal; every hunter is amazed by it. In Minnesota, the season did not open until 9 AM the day of our trip. I promise you that while I never saw a pheasant wearing a watch, those birds would disappear into the brush within seconds after 9:00 AM. As I drove and saw the pheasants watching us pass by, it was too much.

"Ed," I said, "our chances of bagging one of these critters would be tremendously enhanced if we were to find a way to overcome one now instead of waiting until the drive back."

Ed thought a second. "I think you have something in mind, Dr. Pierpont. What is it?"

"If you change places with Evelyn, and Evelyn doesn't mind, you could get your shotgun out of the trunk and put it down on the floor in the back seat with the breech open." I waited momentarily for Ed to follow my thought. "Now, we've seen all kinds of pheasants stare at us as if they own the fields and we don't mean a thing to them. Suppose we get to a lonely stretch of road, and there you see a pheasant perched on a fence rail. I could ease to a stop and you could nail him right out of the back window."

Ed chewed on the idea for a minute. "I think you're crazy, but stop the car. Let's get ready and see what happens. Ok with you, Evelyn?"

Evelyn was along for the ride. If two full-fledged physicians were ready to shoot a pheasant out of a car window, she had no real reason to object. I stopped the car, and Ed got his gun and changed places with Evelyn. We rode along for about 15 minutes, not a pheasant to be seen, and it wasn't even nine o'clock! The road had been almost deserted in both directions as we drove. Then I slowed down and motioned to Ed to look. There ahead, sitting on a fence rail, was a magnificent pheasant on the driver's side of the road. Ed lowered his rear window and raised his shotgun as I eased the car to a full stop.

BAMMM! There is absolutely no way to describe the powerful blast of a 12-gauge shotgun going off inside an automobile. It hurt! My ears rang for hours. At least the shot was accurate and the pheasant fell backwards off the fence rail. Now it was time to move.

I said, "Ed, get over there and get your bird —"

"My bird!" Ed exclaimed. "It was your idea!"

I chose to ignore his response. " I'll drive down the road, turn around and pick you up like a hitch-hiker on the way back. Let's go!"

Ed had no choice but to jump out. Evelyn sat in silence, probably still half-deafened, as I drove ahead about a mile. When I turned the car around to head back for Ed, she finally exclaimed, "You two guys have to be crazy!"

"Goes with the territory!" I replied. All at once, it seemed, the road which had been empty when Ed shot the pheasant seemed to fill with cars going in both directions. I thought I would not be able to stop and pick up Ed, but there he waited beside the road clearly anticipating his pickup. The sight of Ed, always fastidious in every way, but now wearing a slightly anxious expression on his face and a trench coat with a mysterious bulge where no bulge belonged, was too much. Evelyn burst into laughter and I joined her. I stopped to let Ed in, and cars passed us without incident. Once inside, Ed saw the incongruity of the situation and began to laugh, too. Although our hunting innovation was successful, I must add that shotgunning pheasants from the back seat of a car is not a recommended way to out-smart the birds.

Arriving at the Mayo Clinic, we spent the rest of our day with the Clinic's Dr. Harry Smith, the head of colon and rectal surgery. At the time we were there, he was working closely with a professor of anesthesia, Dr. Lundy, who was perfecting caudal anesthesia. This is a technique of injection outside the spinal cord to numb a nearby, local area.

Dr. Smith's patient was a woman in the "over the barrel" position enabling Dr. Smith to perform a hemorrhoidectomy. She had been given the new caudal anesthesia, so she was awake. Recognizing our presence, she turned her head and said, "You would never guess my reason for coming was to have my throat looked at!"

The reputation for thoroughness at the Mayo Clinics is well deserved. Anyone entering the Clinic gets a going-over from one end to the other, nothing left out. The Clinic's rule is that you will never know what you will find until you look.

Not once in my year in Iowa was I let down medically after I got straightened out on surgery assignments. No surgeon at any age ever had a more thorough, more complete year of surgical training than I received while there. Nothing in my experience prepared me for the day when I ended a tour of duty to receive word that Dr. Peterson wanted to see me in his office.

When I entered the room, he stood up and to greet me and said, "Please sit down, Ross."

It was clear he had something important on his mind, and I was mildly apprehensive although everything, I thought, had been going well. "Ross," Dr. Peterson said, "I see and train a lot of doctors. Some have what it takes to be very good. Then again, some don't." He allowed himself a slight smile, and I suspect both of us thought of "Lord" Harrison. Dr. Peterson resumed: "You are a very good surgeon now. I have no doubt you will become a superlative surgeon and a very good teacher of surgery."

The normally very direct but polite Dr. Peterson was choosing his words carefully. He put the tips of his fingers together to make a temple, glanced out the window, and turned to look deeply into my eyes. "I have decided to offer you a position on the full time surgical staff of the University of Iowa. If you wish to stay with us and teach, we would like to have you join our permanent staff."

No one who has never dedicated his waking life in the pursuit of a career in surgery can possibly imagine the sheer power of those words from a man and physician I deeply admired. Yes, I knew I was good; I pride myself in being a realist about myself as well as life itself. Now Dr. Peterson was telling me I was better than I had ever imagined myself to be — what a triumph! How it made the years of denial and study all worthwhile!

Both of us knew instinctively it was not to be. It just did not fit into the way my life was meant, somehow, to be lived. I weighed briefly how Dr. Peterson's offer compared to the tremendous opportunities back in Baltimore and Havre de Grace. Those were my roots. There, somehow, I belonged. I said, "Dr. Peterson, there is no way in the world I can tell you how grateful I am about this wonderful offer. I like this place. I admire the people, the teaching, the surgical opportunities, and more, but I am not independently wealthy. In fact, I am in debt. Would you give me a couple of days to sort out my thoughts and get back to you?"

"Of course, Ross, of course. Take your time. I understand what you must be thinking. Just let me know as soon as you feel you can."

I walked on air as I left Dr. Peterson that day. It was a "high" new to me, never, really, to be experienced again. Realities clouded the euphoria, however. A full-time surgeon at the University was paid a starting salary of $6,500. With all the years I had invested in my training, and with my obligations to Grace as well as myself, I had to earn more money than that. From the purely economic point of view, not the medical one, the decision to return to Baltimore was the only practical one. Grace, as always, respected my thinking and while she had thoroughly enjoyed our time in Iowa was glad to think of returning "home."

I sought out Dr. Peterson and again expressed my appreciation for his generosity in helping me along the way, and the magnificence of his offer. He was not surprised, and indeed seemed prepared because he said, "Ross, you have always played the game straight down the line — hard and honest. That is one of the reasons I offered you a full-time position here. I feel you offer us a new dimension." I started to say something, but he raised a hand. "As I said before, you have what it takes to make a good, maybe a great surgeon. I have no doubt you will go far whatever you do when you leave here. I will be sorry to see you go."

For a couple of "hard-bitten" surgeons, we were both a bit emotional. Dr. Peterson spoke again. "Let me wish you all the best of luck and allow me to offer a bit of advice. When you leave here, you are going into a tough competitive world — much more competitive than people not in our profession ever recognize or know about. Just remember one thing as you go: There will be people who like you and are on your side. There will be people who can't stand what you are or how you think, and they will be against you all the way. That's just the way it is, and no one is going to change it. So if 51% of the people are on your side, and the other 49% are against you, forget it. You will be a success and to hell with the 49%. If it ever shifts the other way, look out. Now, one more thing before you go. If I can ever help you in any way, please feel free to call on me."

What a man! What a physician! And, as events were to prove, what a friend! I left him feeling real sadness, a real loss. Life lets us meet so few great ones. I had met one who stood at the top of the list.

With regrets and anticipations, we left Iowa, and Dr. Peterson, for Baltimore on July 1, 1945.

Chapter 9
A Forgotten Enemy Does His Best To Destroy Me

Baltimore at the time Grace and I returned to it was the largest city in the Mid-Atlantic region. Much larger and more genteel than Washington in that era, the city dominated the state's economy and political structure. Charles Street was the fashion street of the region, and its boutiques attracted the well-to-do from Washington as well as Baltimore itself. The Baltimore Cotillion was the social event of the year when debutantes made their entrance into adult Baltimore society official.

Yes, this was a time of debutantes "coming out" in a very formal ball!

The city was an amalgamation of neighborhoods. The Irish had their niche in northeast Baltimore. The Jews had migrated from their original neighborhood where they had settled as immigrants from the ships bringing them from Germany, Russia, and other European nations, and now lived in "the Golden Ghetto" of northwest Baltimore. Italians and east Europeans favored southeast Baltimore where they faithfully scrubbed their white marble steps and painted window screens with fastidious cleanliness. Most of Baltimore's numerous blacks were clustered in the west side of the city with Pennsylvania Avenue as their "main street." People known as "old money" built their mansions in an enclave called Guilford in the absolute heart of the city, in Homeland in the north, and in the horse farm exurbs in Baltimore County.

The neighborhood atmosphere of the city gave it not only a sense of "clubbiness," but also a sense of mutual helpfulness. Because Baltimore's people grew up knowing one another, there was neighborliness about the city, which was often noticed by newcomers. The courtesy of Baltimore's policemen and the operators of streetcars was almost universal. The people and the times were so distinctive that a local newspaperman wrote a book about its people entitled "The Amiable Baltimoreans." Perhaps nothing illustrates the quality of this bygone era better than the then-practice of selling Sunday newspapers on the honor system. Each Saturday night, stacks of Sunday newspapers were put on the busiest street corners for revelers who could buy one just by picking it up and putting some money on the top paper. Later, the newsboys would come by and collect their money. If anyone took a paper without paying, of if anyone stole money left on the top paper, it was so rare it did not stop the practice until the city declined not too many years later.

I think about what is happening to us, and it makes me a little sad.

As this word-picture suggests. Grace and I had a fondness for Baltimore-of-the-forties that became a prime factor in deciding what we would do after returning to our old apartment on Elrino Street early July, 1945. We had kept in touch with our former employers in Hartford County. Dr. Ralph Horky, and Dr. George Jastram. They now offered to help us establish my surgical practice in Havre de Grace. This small town had just opened a new hospital with no physician in the area limited to the practice of surgery. The opportunity for a new surgeon to set up there had tremendous appeal, especially for anyone who likes small town life. Both Grace and I knew the advantages of small town life; we had grown up and gone to school in small towns. But Grace yearned for the cosmopolitan life offered only by a city as big as Baltimore - the opera, the symphony, first class motion picture theaters, The Baltimore Museum of Art and the The Walters Art Gallery. We hadn't come back to Baltimore from Iowa, where life was delightful, to give up the amenities of metropolitan living and contacts with our families, friends, and professional associates from my residency days.

A different opportunity came from one of Dr. Bay's early residents, Dr. Charles Relfschneider. Dr. Bay was the physician I admired and joined at Maryland General Hospital as an intern - a career setback when he died very shortly thereafter. Dr. Relfschneider had acquired a large part of Dr. Bay's practice and made it much larger. Like Dr. Bay, Dr. Relfschneider was a leader in providing medical care required by workman's compensation laws. At the time we talked about a mutual arrangement, he had a practice larger than he could properly manage. Part of his problem was his younger brother, who had pioneered in the relatively new field of anesthesiology. He had been called up by the Army, and was no longer of any help in Dr. Relfschneider's clinic in downtown Baltimore.

It takes only two words to describe the attractiveness of surgery in an industrial clinic: security and money. If I joined the clinic, my income would be, for all practical purposes, guaranteed, both in amount and duration. The offer from Dr. Relfschneider included a small salary, office space and secretarial service at no charge, plus time for developing my independent surgical practice in an extremely desirable part of Baltimore City. Any income from my own practice would be mine 100%.

This is the kind of thinking that goes on "behind the scenes," and which non-doctors have no way of knowing.

It was decision time. If you have followed my narrative, you would know by now that I cannot tolerate indecision. (Well, think about it. Do you want a surgeon deliberating about what comes next while standing over you on the operating table?) Grace and I went over our options. As far as Grace was concerned, the river town opportunity was out. But I had looked at the possibilities from a different angle. I said, "I know we aren't going to live in a small town like Havre de Grace, Grace" - I pronounced the town's name incorrectly, the way it is spelled, then couldn't resist adding an extra "Grace." (The correct pronunciation, not liked by those who actually live there, rhymes, of course, with "haw.")

"But I've been thinking," I continued as she looked at me a bit anxious about my next ideas. "If we play our choices right, we can have our cake and eat it, too." My pause was wasted. Grace was used to listening to me; she simply waited for what was coming. "You've got to keep an open mind on this."

"It's open."

"If we take the job with Dr. Charley in Baltimore, he has to stay flexible. He needs to keep his options open for the time when his brother comes back, which I have no trouble with. What we have to realize is, his interest in bringing his brother back into that practice probably means I would have to go." My mind took me back to my meeting with Dr. Relfschneider and my contact with his secretary. I had to laugh. "There's one thing I know for sure! That old maid secretary of his resents anyone else sitting behind Herb Relfschneider's desk. That woman is absolutely in love with Herb's memory! She's so possessive you could cut her jealousy with a blunt scalpel. Of course, the fact that Herb is married doesn't count."

"Are you saying she could make trouble for you - or make your life miserable there?"

"No. Not at all. Grace, If I've learned anything the hard way, it's to do my job and what people think about me is their problem. In any case, I'll do my job and hold on to the money. But the point is, the flexibility Dr. Charley wants may give us the flexibility we need. Think about it a minute," I continued as Grace listened patiently. "Dr. Charley wants help but not full time help. Havre de Grace with the new Route 40 is less than an hour from here. Why couldn't I have an office in both places?"

Grace learned long ago to catch on with no need from my help, and has supported me through long years of longer and longer hours. But the sheer notion of a new doctor opening two offices without a single patient was more than she was ready to accept.

"Ross, have you been keeping something from me? Have we become independently wealthy? Or am I missing something?"

Just talking about my idea, once so novel, now sold me on it. "The cost to start my practice with Dr. Charley is zero. Whatever I make on my own, I keep. I can handle any load he gives me, and patients of my own, by scheduling office hours three days a week. I would keep office hours in Havre de Grace three days a week, too. I can use referring doctors to handle post-op care. Grace, it's a breeze!" I ended triumphantly.

"What about the expenses in Havre de Grace? Who pays them?"

"I'll need only a small office - in that town, the rent won't be more than $30 to $40 a month. I'll bring that in the first day I'm there. Our car is still in good shape, so that's no big expense." I had reached the point to throw in the final pitch. "You would be in this, too. You would be my nurse for the Havre de Grace office, and handle the books and records for both places." I couldn't resist a bit of teasing. "Of course, you would have to work for nothing to start. Then I'd pay you what you're worth."

Grace laughed. "You'll never afford to pay me what I'm worth."

"For your office work, I will!"

She laughed again before she became thoughtful. "Have you thought about difficult cases, and post-op complications?" She stopped short, staring at me. "Of course you have! OK, what about them?"

"We would send or bring them to Baltimore. We have the house staff at Maryland General for support, and I will be at both places. Most complicated cases in the county have been brought to a Baltimore hospital anyway."

"It's a good thing we are used to long hours. Because if I know you, the only time I'll see you is about midnight and for breakfast. Do you suppose you could spare me Sundays?"

"Every Sunday, and Saturday afternoons, too! You'll see."

And she did see. We rented a nice office in Havre de Grace from a long-time resident of the town, a widow who had good use for the rent money. My practice took off the day I opened the two offices, and we never had time to look back.

That office in Havre de Grace was another example of good luck being almost as important as being a good doctor when it comes to a success in medicine. This part of rural Maryland was dotted with very small towns that make the area sound like a transplant from England: Fork, Fallston, Port Deposit, Perryville, Elkton (famous for same-day marriages at the time), Edgewood Arsenal, Aberdeen, Bel Air, plus, for a difference, Havre de Grace itself. The main source of my patients was the nearby highways. From Washington to Baltimore, then to Wilmington, Delaware, to Philadelphia and on to New York and New England, motorists had a choice: Route 1 or Route 40 through the middle of Harford County, Maryland. The consequences of the constant, heavy traffic on those two roads were predictable: frequent, often extremely severe auto and truck accidents. My advanced training and surgical expertise soon became well known, and my emergency services soared. Soaring is the only word for it.

In any given week, I scheduled my first surgery daily at 7:30 a.m. – if not at Havre de Grace, then in Baltimore. I alternated the days working in Havre de Grace Monday, Wednesday, and Friday, and devoted the other days of the week, including Saturday, to Baltimore. As my patients' conditions required, I made rounds to see them before going to the operating room before my first 7:30 a.m. operation. My practice quickly grew to the point I expanded my hospital privileges beyond my base at Maryland General to Franklin Square, Church Home Hospital, Greater Baltimore Medical, University of Maryland Hospital, and Union Memorial Hospital. The time I had to spend just to travel from one hospital to another was sheer waste, and that bothered me. But there was no other way to manage my cases. At the time, there was a shortage of hosptial beds, and individual patients and their doctors had preferences I had to follow.

After morning rounds and surgery were completed, I spent my afternoons caring for my own patients, or patients of Dr. Relfschneider in the office he had turned over to me in his downtown Baltimore location. When it became clear my practice was on solid grounds financially, we bought the very first home of our lives in the Mayfield section of Baltimore. It was a huge, three-story, semi-detached home, and we enjoyed every moment of buying what we needed to furnish it. However, it wasn't such a thrill to go from $38 a month in housing costs to first mortgage payments several times our former rent. For the first time in our lives, we had to think about things like interest rates, property assessments and resulting real estate taxes. Fortunately, my income now had become more than adequate, so we even bought a car no one else had owned before - a new car! We also began to blossom a little socially by joining the Hillendale Country Club where we played golf and went to weekend dances as often as time allowed.

Just as life seemed great and getting better, the American Board of Surgery delivered a crushing blow. The Board rejected my application to take the examination necessary for certification and membership. My feelings as I read the letter of rejection over and over, as if it were impossible to understand what it meant, were a tumult of disbelief, anger, the crushing pain of rejection, and fear of what rejection would do to me as a physician. It could destroy me.

The letter of rejection was carefully worded in doublespeak. It gave no real reason for refusing to let me take the Board's examination. There was none. I was completely familiar with the Board's requirements, which was my main reason for spending a year at the University of Iowa. I had met every specification. Dr. Peterson, Chief of Surgery at the University of Iowa, had coached me in drafting my 1944 letter to the Board in which I asked the Board to state further activities I needed to qualify for examination and membership. The Board's reply was, basically, that my training was satisfactory and that I would have to restrict my practice to surgery. I had done so. I had been offered a full-time position on the University of Iowa surgical staff. I had finished a term of service with Dr. Charles Relfschneider, a charter member of the American Board of Surgery. I had joined Dr. Otto Brantigan, Professor of Surgical Anatomy at the University Of Maryland Medical School as an instructor in anatomy. Dr. Brantigan was also a member of the American Board of Surgery. To be sure of timeliness in taking the examination in the fall of 1948, I had sent my application to the Board six months ahead of time.

After all my years devoted full time in preparation, after all my years of single-minded training and living like one of the most impoverished persons in America - rejection! I am not describing accreditation. Not at all. I describe taking an examination for accreditation. I detested the paper I held before me, hating the thought of having to tell Grace what was being done to us. I had no illusions about the consequences of the Board's rejection. At that time it was enough to stop Ross Pierpont, M.D. in my tracks. If that removed me from my practice of surgery altogether, that result would be "unfortunate" but "necessary" as far as the Board was concerned. Whoever had it in for me would be smiling like a Cheshire cat at knocking me down.

What brought me to think "someone" had it in for me? The only possible explanation of the Board's action was that someone - or someones — had specifically opposed my taking the examination. But who was it? If I were to avoid a fatal mistake, I had to examine my position coolly, calmly, objectively. I made a conscious effort to purge anger and pain from my mind in order to see exactly where I stood. The discipline learned as I grew up now came to my aid. I had made my own way ever since I was an eight-year old, skinny kid wearing knee pants. I had worked my way through four years of college, through pharmacy school, medical school, and five years of residency under workloads that demanded all my strength. Hard knocks had instilled me with a sort of "sixth sense" about favoritism and one-upmanship in the world at large, and the medical world in particular. Before the American Board of Surgery was founded in 1937, surgical recognition was informal. Approvals were usually granted at local levels through a decision of an older colleague. In Baltimore, The Johns Hopkins Hospital and the University of Maryland had carried the weight of authority for acceptance. Doctors passed over in this hit-or-miss situation were often resentful, and with just cause in many cases. It was really an "old boy" situation. In the early years of the American Board of Surgery, surgeons could be certified upon nothing more than a recommendation of the Board's founders, a practice all too often rooted in personalities and sometimes rank favoritism.

New medicines, and new techniques known by younger surgeons, or quickly adopted by them as they were authorized, worked to create an undertone of envy, and sometimes jealousy, within Baltimore's "old bulls" in surgery. I had more than just instinct to tell me that many of the "old bulls" were keenly aware of my growing practice and viewed my progress with less than an approving eye. Some of these surgeons were very good, some average, and of course some were just getting by on friendships and powerful contacts. All of these doctors prided themselves on maintaining personal relationships with their patients and the general practice physicians (now called primary care physicians) who referred patients to them when an operation was indicated. A new and very active surgeon offering the latest in surgical care, as I did, constituted a negative comparison, not to mention a threat to a system that kept many surgeons comfortable.

Were some of the "old bulls" behind the Board's rejection of my application. If so, what could I do about it? Or them?

The answer to both questions was simple: not much. I thought about all of the surgeons I had come in contact with, or who knew me by reputation. Being strictly objective, I could not think of a single doctor in Harford County who would oppose my membership. In Baltimore, who? The Superintendent of Baltimore City Hospitals whom I had badly embarrassed immediately came to mind. But he was not an element in the Board's procedures. Working on through the names brought me down to one man: Dr. Thomas Aycock. His threat when I resigned to go to Iowa and told him he would have to "get himself another boy" rang loud and clear: "I'll give you a recommendation. But it won't be a good one!"

If I were wrong about my conviction that Dr. Aycock was the guiding force behind my rejection, if it really were someone else, I was doomed. In a strange sort of way, I had a feeling of relief. Dr. Aycock had always been a submerged threat to my medical career after I left Baltimore City Hospitals. I thought back to the medical schools which had first welcomed my application, then ignored me, after I gave Dr. Aycock as my chief reference. I thought about Dr. Peterson's warnings in Iowa, and Dr. Lee's advice when I told him about Dr. Aycock's threat. At least and at last, the game was drawing to its end. I could not be wrong in identifying Dr. Aycock as my mortal enemy. Now my job was to beat Dr. Aycock at his own game. Unfortunately, the man held all the weapons and I was unarmed.

As I write this, looking back, it seems almost absurd, perhaps even foolhardy, for me to have no doubt I would, somehow, succeed in the long run. But the main lesson of my past was never give up. Never! Persistence can win when nothing else is possible. A new confidence buoyed my spirits, and I set upon an immediate course of action.

I approached Dr. Otto Brantigan in the dissecting room at the University of Maryland Medical School. I had all of my credentials with me, plus the letter of rejection from the American Board of Surgery. My grim face must have revealed the seriousness of coming to see him, and he looked from me to my papers. "What's the matter, Ross?"

I handed him the Board's letter which he took in almost at a glance. "Doesn't give you any reason for turning you down, does it? That could kill you. What are you planning to do?"

"You know the Board relies on Chiefs of Surgery at the hospitals where training has taken place. I trained at only two places: Baltimore City Hospitals under Dr. Aycock, and under Dr. Peterson at the University of Iowa. Dr. Peterson said to me that I had what it takes to become a great surgeon, and offered me a full-time position. I don't think anyone can have a better recommendation than that. But Aycock became furious when I left after four years to go to Iowa and told me - these were his words, I still remember them: 'I'll recommend you, but it won't be a good recommendation.' I am convinced that the Board reached Aycock about my application, and he did exactly what he said he would do: give me a bad recommendation. I have reason to believe he followed through on his threat when I applied for residency at leading medical schools. Not one of them bothered to respond to my application after I named Dr. Aycock as Chief of Surgery during my four years at City Hospitals."

Dr. Brantigan whistled. "Makes sense, Ross. But it won't be easy to get the Board to reverse course once they have turned you down -- assuming Dr. Aycock is behind it."

"Otto, nothing in my whole life has been easy, starting when my father died when I was three. I have to believe the truth will win for me. The truth is in my letters to the Board of Surgery spelling out exactly what I have done since leaving Iowa. The truth is, I have satisfied every requirement they gave me. I have worked under you here in surgical anatomy, and with Dr. Relfschneider in surgery. I have done more than everything asked of me. I intend to see that the Board now lives up to its stated commitments."

What I was looking for was Otto's reaction to my intentions. As a member of the Board, his attitude would tell me if I was going off the deep end without a life jacket.

It was impossible to tell exactly what Otto was thinking as he heard me say I intended to challenge the Board of Surgery. What he said was encouraging though not enthusiastic. "I don't see where you have much choice, Ross. You can't just take this rebuff lying down. I think what you are saying is true, and the Board for whatever reason has reached a wrong decision. That doesn't mean they'll reverse it. So go ahead. Let me know how you make out and I'll do what I can for you." That ended our conversation and he turned to go to the dissecting room.

Grace was even more devastated by the rejection than I was. But she had gone through much with me, and it helped her to know I was in the right. We reviewed all of the credentials I had collected and considered my alternatives. To write a letter to the Board would be to waste the stamp. If I replied at all, it would only harden the Board's original decision. A telephone appeal would be equally useless. That left us with just one choice. Our only possible action with any chance of succeeding was a face-to-face meeting with the Secretary of the Board.

Decision made. Now came the question of when and how. Grace and I settled on Friday morning of the following week for both of us to go directly to the office of the Board of Surgery in Philadelphia. (At least it wasn't somewhere a thousand miles away, but distance wouldn't have stopped us either.) Why both of us? One reason was our sharing the problem. The other was instinct that told me Grace's presence would help make a difference. Instinct also told me that just as I knew it would be useless to write a letter or make a telephone call, trying to make an appointment with the Secretary would be a kiss of death. Board of Surgery procedures were like so many other procedures in medical politics:

defend the status quo. Stay away from arguments; you might lose. Play for delay until the problem dies a natural death.

We would arrive at the Board unannounced, unexpected, and take it from there. Our intentions demonstrated a generous allotment of brass balls, but it was the only way to go.

We arose early for our Friday trip. Grace put on a dignified and tasteful dress. I put on a businesslike dark suit. We made an effort at breakfast, and attempted some light talk, but neither of us had any real interest in food or conversation. About 6 o'clock that morning we drove out of Baltimore to be sure of arriving at the Board's office when it opened at 9 a.m. Our timing was good and we opened the door of the Board's offices on the 15th floor in one of Philadelphia's skyscraper buildings at exactly 8:45 a.m. I introduced Grace and myself to a young, red-haired secretary who was visibly set back by the entrance of an unannounced young man and woman who appeared to be of some substance. I was 30 at the time, now parting my normal length, brownish-blonde hair on one side. I had filled out considerably from my skinny, tow-head days, and both Grace and I were normal weight and size, except for my neck. I have an unusually short neck so my head sits close on my shoulders.

Training had taught me how to gain and hold eye contact, and I used it when identifying us. Speaking in level, everyday tones to the young secretary, I still left no doubt about my confidence in being there. The young lady was annoyed to think anyone would expect to see anyone at the Board without an appointment. I told her we had come to speak to Dr. Stewart Rodman (secretary of the Board) on extremely important business. "I simply did not have the time," I said, "to make an appointment."

The girl, full of authority, smiled a knowing smile. "I'm sorry, Dr. Pierpont. All of our time has been scheduled for today. Dr. Rodman never sees anyone without an appointment."

"I understand, and I hope you understand this is so important to me and my wife that we had no choice but to come without an appointment. We will just wait for an opening."

Redhead did not believe what she was hearing. No longer polite, she clipped out her response. "I have told you we never see anyone without an appointment."

"Thank you, I appreciate it. But we will still wait."

We found two unoccupied chairs and sat down. Fifteen minutes went by in silence. Redhead's annoyance showed in her angry glances at us, and a bit of color appeared in her pale cheeks. We watched and waited as six people entered and were sent away by Redhead because they had no appointment. She wasn't kidding.

We just sat there and said nothing. Noon came. Grace went out and brought back sandwiches and a soda pop for our lunch. Young Redhead stared in total disbelief as we calmly sat in the waiting room and ate our sandwiches, but she chose to ignore us.

The afternoon wore on. I had no way to be sure Dr. Rodman was in his office. Not a door opened. Not a sound emerged. About 2:30 that afternoon, Redhead could ignore our presence no longer. She got up from her place behind her desk and came to stand directly before us. "It's no use, Dr. Pierpont. You may as well go home and not waste any more time here. I told you Dr. Rodman never sees anyone without an appointment."

"Thank you, miss. But we don't mind waiting."

She started to answer me, thought better of it, and turned on her heels and stalked away. Her unhappiness with us was now total. About an hour went by, and this time she spoke from behind her desk. "I've told you several times we don't see anyone without an appointment. Won't you please go?"

I smiled my friendliest smile and said very gently: "I understand your position. I hope you understand ours. We'll wait."

It drew close to closing time. I glanced at the clock on the wall as Redhead once more came by at 4:45 to say, "Dr. Rodman will not see you. I really would appreciate it if you will go."

"Well," I said, "I came here to see him, and I intend to see him. He is in that corner office, and the stairway and elevator are outside the office door. When he comes out, I will be here with my wife. We will see him then."

With an unladylike snort to show her disgust, she turned and walked to one of the closed doors, opened it and disappeared. Time became our enemy. It seemed like forever, and I felt tension mounting inside me. As abruptly as Redhead had disappeared, she reappeared and approached us grimfaced. "Dr. Rodman will see you now!"

Grace and I got up at once and I replied, "Thank you so much for putting up with us all day. I know what you have been through." Grace beside me, we entered Dr. Rodman's impressive office. Sitting behind a very large desk with two or three fairly thick files on it when we entered, he got up to acknowledge our presence. He was a medium-size man somewhere in his fifties I assumed, with thinning, graying hair combed to the side. He impressed me as having what could be called "a patrician look," the appearance of someone with advanced learning, confident in what he does and enjoying doing it. Gray-green eyes went from me to Grace and back to me as he sat down and left us to stand. "Well, what brings you here today, Dr. Pierpont?"

I had had plenty of time to rehearse my statement and I wasted no time in delivering it. "Dr. Rodman, I am not going to beat around the bush. I am here because I have pointed my entire career of more than a dozen years of training toward a successful surgical career. I intend to follow the rules, and I have done so."

I held out the records of my medical training for him to see. My career, my life, on the line, I did not back off from getting to the point with total conviction I was in the right. "These records prove I am ready to take the Board of Surgery examination and successfully complete it. I have followed your directions to the letter and have done more than asked in your letter to me when I was in Iowa. I intend to take the Board exams."

Dr. Rodman was careful though courteous in his reply. "Dr. Pierpont, I'll be frank with you, especially in consideration of your determination to state your case." He glanced from me to Grace, standing beside me, who I knew without looking was watching him intensely. I did not take my eyes off Dr. Rodman. Grace said nothing. "It is in the opinion of some of our people who know you that you need more training in surgery. We can't know everyone so we have to take the advice of Board members who know each candidate best."

This was the moment of truth. All I had worked for came down to this moment. I laid copies of all correspondence up to and including my full year in Iowa on the desk. One of those letters was written by the man now watching me — *Dr. Rodman now saw his own letter advising what I should do to complete my surgical training.*

"Dr. Rodman, here is complete evidence that I not only complied with everything you had in your requirements, I went much further than you requested. During the past couple of years, I have worked in direct daily relationship with two American Board of Surgery members, Dr. Otto Brantigan and Dr. Charles Relfschneider. Besides that, I have done nothing but referred surgery in my practice. As far as I can see, I am in total compliance with your letter and a great deal more."

Dr. Rodman was clearly trying to get a handle on my presentation to this point. I took advantage of his silence to press on knowing I was approaching the decisive point of the meeting. "Dr. Rodman, you have been frank. Allow me to be the same. You have in your possession, following the rules, two letters of recommendation from my chiefs. One is from Dr. Frank Peterson, Professor and Chairman of the Department of Surgery at the University of Iowa, who offered me a full-time position on his staff as surgeon and instructor. You also have a letter from Dr. Thomas B. Aycock, Chief of Surgery of Baltimore City Hospitals.

"In addition to offering me a staff position," I said, "Dr. Peterson told me I had what it takes to become a fine surgeon. He also told me if I ever needed help to call on him. If, sir, you will dial him at Iowa City, at my expense, he will confirm everything I have just told you."

I had Dr. Rodman's total attention. It was time to play my make-or-break card. "The letter you have from Dr. Aycock is from a deteriorating alcoholic in charge of a deteriorating service in surgery at Baltimore City Hospitals." Dr. Rodman's eyes widened telling me I had hit a hot button. "Dr. Aycock promised me, when I resigned from City Hospitals to accept a residency I needed to complete my training in major surgery that any recommendation about me would be a bad one. He has, I am sure, lived up to his threat."

Dr. Rodman eased a bit in his chair as I drove ahead. "I don't ask you to take my word for anything I have said. Please come to Baltimore at any date you choose, at my expense, and we will take a look at Baltimore City Hospitals' surgical situation, with or without Dr. Aycock. You will see for yourself that everything I have just told you is the truth. Dr. Otto Brantigan at the University of Maryland and a Board member will also back up everything I have said."

Dr. Rodman continued to listen in silence as he waited for me to finish. "I realize how painful this is for everyone involved, but my training of more than 12 years, and my future as a physician, have been put on the line by Dr. Aycock. I will continue through every avenue open to me to prove my case and gain examination and membership in the Board of Surgery. I hope you understand why I cannot accept anything less."

Not a sound was to be heard. Dr. Rodman picked up a batch of papers in one of the files before him and scanned them briefly. We waited. At last he looked from the papers to me. Whatever he had seen in the papers changed his demeanor. His voice was low, thoughtful as he said, "Please sit down, Dr. and Mrs. Pierpont." We sat down. "I want to thank you for coming here today." Oh no! I thought, here comes the put-down. Rodman spoke into my hasty reaction. "I am very pleased that you managed to outlast my secretary – not many do. Your persistence helps to support what you have just told me, but I hope you understand we can't know every doctor who applies. I have no choice but to take the word of my close contact Board member who has trained the applicant."

Then he paused for a reason I'll never know, to leave me hanging by my fingernails. Turning to stare momentarily out the 15th floor window, he seemed to be thinking about what he intended to say to us. What he did say was something I had never expected to hear on that momentous afternoon. "We made a mistake. No question about it, we erred in your case and I want to apologize to you for the error."

It took only a moment for what I heard to sink in. My relief was so intense it had to be obvious, and I dared not look at Grace for fear it might break the spell. Dr. Rodman continued, "I have the authority to recommend to other Board members that an error has been made in your case. I will recommend you for examination. There is no question you have met all qualifications for the examination and I am sure you will be allowed to take it."

There it was, and I still had trouble believing it! We had won! The magic words were far more than we had dare to hope for when we began our trip nearly 12 hours earlier that day. Now Dr. Rodman had said all he intended to say to me, so my youthful exuberance — took over. "I beg your pardon, Dr. Rodman — but when will I know?"

My eagerness broke the tension and Dr. Rodman leaned back in his chair and laughed a gentle laugh. "You don't quit easily, do you? But

I don't blame you for asking. I'd be skeptical, too, but it is too late to change the decision for the next exam. Everything has gone out."

"Fine with me, Dr. Rodman. But when will I know?"

Dr. Rodman chuckled again. "I'll have an answer in your hands in 30 days. You will take the next examination in Baltimore. Is that OK?"

"Absolutely! Yes, sir! You've done more than I had dared to hope." I was smiling, and meant well, but it had to be a weak effort. I was too drained to laugh.

Dr. Rodman signaled our meeting was over by standing up. We turned to leave now knowing our situation had changed from "won't you please leave?" to mutual trust and good feelings. In an unexpected gesture of cordiality, Dr. Rodman came around his desk and placed a fatherly hand on my young shoulder. "Good luck to you."

As we passed through the waiting room, Redhead was closing down her desk. The sun shining through the skyscraper window behind her was now setting on the horizon. I shouldn't have said what I said to her, but we had gone through a rough day and she had not made our ordeal any easier. "Thank you, Miss Kelly. We appreciate all you have done for us today."

Yes, it was sarcasm, and looking back I can't say I am proud of it. Blame it on the daylong stress.

What a difference it was driving back to Baltimore in comparison with the gut-wrenching doubts we had driving up to Philadelphia! We were virtual chatterboxes. Somewhere during that trip home, the sudden and total change in Dr. Rodman's attitude struck me. "Grace, something Dr. Rodman saw in my file made him change his mind 180 degrees almost instantly. What do you suppose he saw?"

Grace thought a moment. "I don't know. But he went from 'What are you doing here?' to 'We have made a mistake and I apologize for it.' It couldn't have been something from Dr. Peterson or some others. He saw something else that said there was a mistake."

I mulled over the possibilities. What the devil had he seen? My file with the Board covered years and contained a large number of records. None of them, nor the letter Dr. Peterson had sent, would have been enough to make the Board's secretary reverse the decision to reject my application. Only one explanation made sense. Dr. Rodman had re-read

Dr. Aycock's letter. That letter had to be so full of exaggerated statements contradicting everything else in my record the venom behind it was unmistakable. Dr. Aycock's desire to bring me down was so extreme he had gone too far. He had ruined his own case! I never found out the truth, of course. But to this day I think my analysis of Dr. Rodman's turnaround is correct.

The 30-day wait passed and the letter finally came authorizing my examination in Baltimore at the next session. From then on, procedures became routine. Passing the written part of the examination was easy. Next came the practical examination at Johns Hopkins Hospital. Doctors being examined were handed the work-ups of patients with observation of the care and the results. Each doctor then appeared before two examiners to respond to questions about the case.

One of my designated patients was a peripheral vascular case of advanced hardening of the arteries in her legs. When I looked over the work-up I had to laugh. I was being questioned in the area of my greatest expertise, developed when I worked with Dr. Ferdinand Lee at my would-be Waterloo - City Hospitals! Next, also a surprise, was a Board member assigned to examine me: none other than Dr. Stewart Rodman! When I appeared before my examiners, Dr. Rodman took the lead: "Give us your summation of the nature of this case, and any critique you may have about the management of it."

The situation was almost a replay of our evening sessions at the University of Iowa when we reviewed the day's cases and scheduled the next day's work. My answer to Dr. Rodman and his fellow examiner brought out the unusually thorough experience I had gained in treating people for such conditions at Baltimore City Hospitals. My work with Dr. Lee in treating lumbar sympathetic nerve block, lumbar sympathectomy, and bromsalizol had to be little known to my examiners. I critiqued the management of the case with reference to the condition of the "envelope" (skin) of both extremities, and superficial excoriation and superficial gangrene and the necessary treatment.

Dr. Rodman looked at Dr. George Stewart of St. Agnes Hospital, my other examiner. "Do we have any more questions for this doctor?"

Dr. Stewart shook his head. "No. That is enough for me."

I thanked both doctors and got up to leave. Dr. Rodman came

forward to pat me on the back much as he had in Philadelphia. Winking, he said, "Good to see you. You're doing all right."

It was only a few weeks until my acceptance by the Board of Surgery was official. The announcement also confirmed the depth of irrational ill-will Dr. Aycock bore toward me. One day I saw one of my former associates at City Hospitals, Dr. Henry Rigdon. Henry had become a "star" of Dr. Aycock and the two were very friendly. "I guess it's no surprise to you that your acceptance by the 'A.B.S.' hit Dr. Aycock where it hurts," Henry said.

I shook my head, no longer particularly interested in my would-be nemesis, and why he should hurt because of my success. I just could not understand why Dr. Aycock had such a consuming need to ruin me. Why does anyone ever need to ruin another human being? I had served Dr. Aycock and City Hospitals surgical department without reservation for four years. I had even become a de facto co-chief with Donald Hebb when we both worked up to 72 hours six days a week, for less than $50 a month. Did Dr. Aycock need to "put me down" because he saw me as some sort of threat to his superior position? Had my work and research published with Dr. Lee made him look bad by comparison? Or was it nothing more than a clash of personalities? I had no answer for such questions, so I simply responded to Henry Rigdon: "I know the man despises me, but never really knew why. I've never been able to understand why he would try to destroy me professionally. I'm a good surgeon, and he knows it."

Henry Rigdon, Dr. Aycock's "star," said: "Ross, it's one of those things in medicine. The day he found out you had been accepted he charged out of the hospital and we didn't see him for another day. I think he hit the bottle pretty hard for the next several days, too."

The Aycock vendetta had yet to run its course. News that Dr. Donald Hebb and I had successfully completed our examinations and were accepted by the American Board of Surgery was announced in medical journals, and Henry Rigdon saw it. A few days later, we saw each other and he told me he had clipped the article and showed it to Dr. Aycock at a cocktail party that evening. "He was incredible!" Henry said. "It was like a personal insult. As he read the article, I thought he'd burst a blood vessel! You know he's had a problem with booze, and I guess your acceptance gave him a reason to really tie one on. I don't know, but he almost had to be carried out of the party."

A few days after this conversation, Dr. Aycock had a massive cerebral hemorrhage and died without ever regaining consciousness.

Now that the man was forever gone from my life, I found to my surprise I had no rancor toward him. His was a tragic end to what was, in truth, a tragic career. I had never heard of the Peter Principle in those years, but I had no problems in recognizing that Dr. Aycock was an almost perfect example of the person promoted beyond his or her capabilities. Dr. Aycock, disregarding his professional failings, was an intelligent man. In fact, his intelligence was his undoing, for it enabled him to see his deficiencies in comparison with his peers - to know he occupied a position he was too small to fill. Along my way through life, I met more doctors like that than I want to think about. The saddest cases were in surgery, where a lack of ability cannot remain hidden. As a result, the profession includes surgeons who excel, surgeons who know their limitations and do not try to exceed them, and surgeons who unhappily practice the art of survival in supporting themselves. As the troubled soul of Dr. Aycock was put to rest, I reflected on my own good luck and my object lesson in power politics. I hadn't learned enough, however. The time would come in my pursuit of excellence in surgery when I would find how little I knew about the role of power in other walks of life.

Chapter Ten
No Time To Smell The Roses

My idea of dividing my practice between Havre de Grace and downtown Baltimore could not have worked better. In fact it began to work too well. My patient load grew so large I needed larger facilities in both places. We solved our Baltimore space problem by buying one of Baltimore's huge, three-story townhouses just off Mt. Vernon Place, named for the nation's first monument in honor of George Washington. This had offices on the first and lower floors, and four apartments on the upper levels. I had always looked at a partnership type of practice as the best of all medical worlds, because working closely with other doctors exposes you to different ideas - keeps you up to date on new techniques and experiences. I invited old friend and fellow resident at City Hospitals, Dr. Donald Hebb, to join me, and he agreed. We had an ideal relationship as, between us, we covered both Baltimore and Havre de Grace for a number of years.

Compared to Baltimore, my practice in Havre de Grace exploded. We built three different buildings for this practice, large enough for seven physicians at any one time. What I was doing in surgery was not going unnoticed - not by other physicians in Harford County, and most certainly not by some of the profession's local leaders in Baltimore City. Comments physicians made to one another both in their practices and socially got back to me, and spoke of envy.

Out of sheer necessity at Havre de Grace, several of us got together and reorganized the structure of the staff at the community's hospital, Harford Memorial. This included a new though small house staff in which I became Chief of Surgery. We instituted rules to guide our surgical practices that ended indiscriminate abortions, codified the surgeon's and assistant's responsibilities, and in general tolerated no slippage or nonsense in patient care.

Word gets around in medicine as in anything else, and it was not long before Harford Memorial earned a reputation for excellence. Our success reached the Board of Trustees at the hospital in Elkton, Maryland. After putting up with surgical problems at the hospital for years, the trustees decided improvement was past due. It was flattering for them to call me in to discuss their problem, and I was glad to meet them. Our meeting was both friendly and productive. Their problems were the same ones I had seen so many other time, in so many other hospitals, that analyzing them and outlining what needed to be done took less than an hour. I don't mean that to sound egotistical, because it was nothing really to be proud of. I only had to summarize what I had seen, and what I had done, including Harford Memorial.

It must have appeared obvious to the Elkton trustees, too, because they promptly asked if I would take on the job of bringing their surgical department up to acceptable standards. To say the offer surprised me would be lying, yet I had not gone to the meeting in search of more work. Far from it! I had been spreading myself too thin for some years, and it was taking its toll on Grace as well as me. In addition to my personal practice and managing two sets of offices, I was teaching surgical anatomy at the University of Maryland Medical School and supervising the teaching section of the residency program at Maryland General Hospital. Only a fool would ignore the fact that this was overdoing things, and I lay no claim to being a fool. That said, the compulsive behavior of a race horse answering the starting bell, and my basic desire to be helpful told me not to turn down the offer. I also knew I could not accept it outright, either. I therefore accepted their offer with the qualification that we would have to meet again to work out timing and other details.

Improvements in our personal lives kept pace with the improvements in my medical life, but not before I came within an inch - literally! - of killing myself. As just mentioned, I recognized that keeping up with the demands of my total practice was pushing me to the limit. But I did not realize that I had reached a point of total exhaustion until one afternoon I was called to respond to an emergency at Havre de Grace. I dropped everything, hurried to my car, and headed at top speed to the hospital, 33 miles away. Knowing the urgency of the victim's condition, not thinking about my speed, and reflecting on what I would find at the hospital when I got there I suddenly blinked and shook my head because my vision had totally clouded. The road ahead had disappeared so that all I saw through the windshield was dark gray, flat space. Again shaking my head and dimly recognizing I was half-asleep at the wheel, I saw I was looking at the huge gray back of a tractor-trailer. The hood ornament of my car was about to nose underneath the body of the trailer!

Shock struck me as suddenly as if I had slammed into the truck. I hit my brakes and pulled my car off the road where I sat almost frozen with terror. How close! Was I spared because I had something in life yet to do? Or was it just plain, dumb luck? In spite of everything, maybe in relief, I had to laugh a jittery laugh. Luck, they say, beats ability any time. After sitting there a while, I bounced back enough to resume the trip to the hospital where I would soon be operating on a real victim of the highway. How easily it could have been me on the operating table or a slab in the morgue. As I drove, I made up my mind I had two choices I could cut back on my work to get more rest. Or I could get someone to drive me between the office and hospitals so I could rest on the way, and not threaten the lives of others along with my own.

I spared Grace the fright of my near-accident; she didn't need to hear I had nearly made her a widow. Nor did I have to tell her I was about worn out. That evening I casually brought up my two options and she wasted no time pointing out what my schedule was doing to both of us. She agreed that hiring a driver made more sense than trying to limit my practice enough to make a real difference. Both of us probably knew the idea I would cut down on my work to any real degree would never really happen.

Decision made, the next step was to find a driver. Hiring a good, reliable driver may appear easy but I assure you it is often frustrating. I finally hired one who drove well enough but he drove me frantic waiting for him to show up on time. Sometimes it was a question of if he would show up at all. During the time I was putting up with this driver's behavior, Grace and I went out one night to have dinner with old friends. We met at the club where we played golf on some weekends and had the usual male-female chitchat during the meal. Later that evening, my driver problem, not far down in my subconscious, made it to my conscious during a lull in the conversation. Launching into a lament about my driver's unreliability, I didn't notice the club's chef approach to wish us a good evening. I interrupted describing my driver problem to exchange pleasantries with him and he excused himself to return to the kitchen.

Not much later that evening I found the chef's brief visit would lead to a perfect answer to my driver problem for the rest of my life.

After dinner, the four of us relaxed listening to another old friend, Ferd Kadan, play favorite tunes of that era on the club piano. As applause ended one song, I noticed Owen, the club chef, standing to one side and clearly looking to gain my attention. I beckoned for him to come near, and said, "Owen, are you looking for me?"

"Dr. Pierpont, I believe I overheard you saying you are looking for a driver. Do you want someone full time?"

"Yes, Owen, I sure do."

"Do you remember Charles Shipley, our new waiter here, Doctor?"

I thought a second. "I think so, Owen. Is he the one around 25 or so?"

"Yes, sir. Charlie would make an excellent driver for you, though I hate to see him go. His dad was Shipley the Caterer. He catered the Bachelor Cotillion, all the coming-out parties, the governors' receptions - all that kind of stuff. Charlie couldn't keep the catering business going, but he's a grand fellow. If you're interested, I'll tell him to see you."

"Tell him right now!"

I hired Charles on the spot and this was the start of a 33-year relationship with one of the finest men it has been my pleasure to know. Our days together became almost ritual. Promptly at 6:30 every working day Charles picked me up at our house and I got into the back seat with a blanket and pillows. I would read briefly or nap while Charles drove me to my offices at Havre de Grace three days of the week. When I felt the car bounce over the old rail bridge just outside Havre de Grace, it was my wake-up call. I tightened my tie, turned on my energy, put on my white coat and started rounds or began to operate by 7:30.

By 1:00 or 1:30, I wrapped up work in Havre de Grace and hit the back seat of the car for another nap back to my Baltimore practice. Working my way through college, I had developed an ability to drop off to sleep on a moment's notice. I could, and can, put myself to sleep on call, any time, any place, and under almost any circumstances. Some naps may be a few minutes, some may be long, but all revive my energies. This napping ability has kept me going through 10- and 12-hour days all the years of my surgical practice.

Never one to sit around idly in my presence, Charles became a virtual paramedic. He could take off and put on casts and run the usual setups for minor surgery along with another of the dependable, competent in our organization, Helen Jenkins. Maybe my activity was contagious; I don't know, but Charles didn't close out his day when he dropped me off. He became the top orderly and general man-about-you-asked-for-it at North Charles General Hospital where he worked the 3 to 11 night shift. Later, he became Head Attendant at Montebello Hospital. He put every one of his seven children through college and graduate schools, where they earned MA's, MS's. and at least one Ph.D. The Shipley family, with Charles its head, became a scion of Baltimore's black society, and I like to think I had a helping hand in that family's outstanding success. As I write this, Charles is on dialysis for end-stage kidney failure, but he hasn't lost his luminous smile and his ability to enjoy the life remaining -- yes, even on dialysis!

About this time in our lives, Grace and I had Christine, our only child. When Christine reached age three, our lives were so busy we decided to simplify things by hiring full-time, all-around help. Again, Pierpont good luck exceeded ability as we lucked into Elaine Cole, who came as close to being family as you can get without being born there. Sometimes, it seemed to me, Christine would rather confide in Elaine, or ask Elaine for her help, before she would come to her mother or me. When, many years later, Christine was married and living with her family and children in Germany, we called to tell her Elaine was dying. Christine caught the first plane to Baltimore. We met her at the airport and went together to the nursing home where we found Elaine semiconscious. Christine said, "Elaine, I've come from Germany just to see you."

Elaine did not respond. Saying no more, Christine took Elaine's cold hands into hers and clasped them together and began to speak gently to her. Elaine never opened her eyes, but Christine talked on stroking the woman's hands as we stood watching in a silent tableaux. At last, a faint smile creased the tired, spent face of our friend and we knew she understood. Christine looked up to us tearfully as Elaine finally showed her love through a weak, trembling clutch of Christine's fingers. We stayed until Christine was ready to leave, and as we left we knew we had just said goodbye to a friend of more than 33 years. Only days later, word came that Elaine had, indeed, left us forever. Our sadness at her funeral in a cemetery I had walked past as a boy 68 years earlier was mellowed by knowing of so many, many good years we had shared together.

I had become a Junior Member of the American College of Surgeons at the time I left Iowa in 1945, but I hadn't followed through on joining the College because I was too busy meeting the demands of my profession while starting and building my practice "from scratch." Anyway, the College in the late 40's lacked the prestige of the American Board of Surgery, to which I already belonged. I started thinking, in 1953, I really should join the College, and decided to file my application. I filled out the application thinking acceptance from Junior to "full-fledged" would be routine.

How wrong I was! I knew the College had started a program to enhance its professional image by making admission a symbol of professional prestige. I also knew some of the "old bulls" of American surgery dominated College leadership. These doctors had never earned membership into the College; they had been "grandfathered" into membership by virtue of belonging to the more prominent American Board of Surgery. The College when first formed had no way to evaluate achievement in medical school, and did not require examination by one's surgical peers. The blunt truth was that the College was originally more social than medical. Knowing all this, I had absolutely no reason to believe I would have any trouble with acceptance.

The day I opened the letter rejecting my application for membership in The American College of Surgeons is burned into my memory forever. I sat there, reading the letter once, twice, three times. It could not be! I was not only a Junior Member of the College, I was a Diplomate of the American Board of Surgery. I was fully established in my own practice with privileges in a number of hospitals. I was teaching surgical anatomy at the University of Maryland Medical School. I was Chief of Surgery in, not one, but two hospitals. I had been asked to reorganize the surgery department at Elkton Hospital.

What kind of credentials does the College of Surgeons expect? A letter from Christ! Who the hell are these people, anyhow?

My wrath and indignation subsided and reality returned. Slow down, Ross. What is this really all about? What can possibly explain the decision of the College committees to turn you down? It didn't just happen. My credentials are too good for that. Someone, somewhere, is behind this; who can it be? And why would that someone, or someones, want to kick me in the teeth? Why?

I read the letter again, and this phrase stood out: The committees consider "relationship to his confreres..." The rest was boilerplate. The basis for my rejection was my relationship with other Baltimore surgeons. What I had done that soured my relationship with Baltimore area surgeons had no basis in surgery at all. It is not false pride to say I was a better surgeon than 85% of the College's membership in Maryland. My record and reputation would easily prove it. Once I had put the professional question out of the way, that left personal relationships. I had been rejected purely on personal grounds.

Whom had I affected to the point he acted to bar me from the College of Surgeons? I no more asked myself that question than it was like deja vu – what had happened to me at the American Board of Surgery. I shifted mental gears, stopped thinking this can't be happening to me, and began asking myself: What am I going to do about this? Unless I planned to roll over and play dead, I had to put before the College a case they could not ignore, and most certainly could not refuse. Anything less would only bury my application in concrete forever.

How could I develop a response that would be irresistible? My knowledge of medical organizations helped to answer the question. The one thing the American College of Surgeons could never let happen was public confrontation and exposure of membership based on personalities rather than professional qualification. The smell of favoritism would reach to heaven. I had shown the power of exposure when I took my case to the American Board of Surgery. Now I had to convince the Board of the College of Surgeons I would open the oaken doors of the committee room and bring the members of the Board out into daylight. There they would face charges of rank favoritism and prejudice in denying my Fellowship.

To prove damages to me personally and financially, I needed more than just my personal analysis. I needed facts. These came in the form of an unexpected, but not surprising, telephone call. The Chairman of the Board of Trustees of Elkton Hospital called to ask if it was true that I had applied for a Fellowship in the College of Surgeons and had been rejected. I answered it was indeed true, for the time being, but at this point I could say no more. I asked how he had heard about my rejection, and he replied that the surgeon in charge at Elkton Hospital, a Fellow of the College, had been told of my rejection and had passed the information on to him.

The Chairman then said, with considerable embarrassment, that under the circumstances he had no choice but to cancel the hospital's offer for me to reorganize their surgery department. I said I understood and we ended the call on that note. The cancellation gave me a lot to think about. In one respect, the withdrawn offer came as a relief. To do the Elkton job right would take more time than I really had available, and in all likelihood I would have been forced to delay the reorganization indefinitely or even bow out of it. At the same time, the College rejection of my Fellowship was costing me an offer worth not only increased professional stature but several million dollars in fees over a number of years.

Bingo! Half of my case was in hand. The other half of my case was to identify my unknown enemy, or enemies. One by one, I went through the possibilities. Dr. Aycock again? No; he had learned his lesson when I exposed his irrationality with the Board of Surgery. Another unjustified attack on me would cost him more than he could take. The trail still led back, if not to Dr. Aycock, then to my role in taking the complaint of City Hospitals' residents public. It led to my success, at considerable cost in professional relationships, in reforming Harford Memorial. Somewhere in Baltimore's medical hierarchy there was a physician – or physicians – who wanted my career stopped in its tracks. Why? I had not harmed a single doctor in active practice. The only answer that made sense was that some doctor, so far unknown, saw me and my admission to the College of Surgeons as a threat to the status quo in Baltimore surgery. (To be honest about it, the unknown doctor was probably right.)

Who was the unidentified doctor - or doctors? Whoever he was, he had to be a leader in opposing changes and improvements in surgery.

Men who had spent their lives using familiar techniques saw younger surgeons using new medicines and techniques as undermining their status in the profession. Admitting Ross Pierpont to Fellowship in the American College of Surgeons would amount to acceptance, even approval. Stopping Ross Pierpont would show the youngsters, like those I was training at Maryland General Hospital, that the "old bulls" had to be reckoned with. Bringing me down would send a message to other young surgeons that the alternative to "going along" was to stay out.

Next came the hard part. Identifying my invisible enemy. Fortunately, the list of probables was relatively short. Day followed day, indirect question followed indirect question to find out who was active, who was inactive, in the College of Surgeons. Who, to put the question more directly, belonged to the Aycock-Shipley "old guard?" As I narrowed the field one by one it left me with only one doctor. At first, I could not accept the name my inquiries had identified. The man I tagged as my chief suspect was the last man I would normally suspect. He was a fine family surgeon with a reputation totally beyond reproach. He as a constant churchgoer and a truly Christian gentleman of the old school. His power came from his position as interim head of University Hospital, as well as Acting Chairman of the hospital's surgical department. If this man had opposed me at the College of Surgeons, no wonder the Board had turned me down.

The trail led to Dr. Edwards, Christian gentleman or no, so I had to follow where it took me. I called Dr. Edwards to set up an appointment. He refused to take my call, nor would he take my number and return my calls. Strange! To ignore a fellow doctor just isn't done. I was on the right track. My next step was to ask his secretary to make an appointment for me. She refused. Persisting on the telephone brought only her lame explanation: "I am very sorry, but Dr. Edwards is too busy to see you."

Too busy! Nonsense. One doctor does something like that to another doctor only for good reason, and by now I was sure I knew Dr. Edwards' reason. If I had done what I was now sure he had done, I wouldn't want to see my victim either. (I would, however.)

Convinced that Dr. Edwards was the key to my rejection, and ultimate acceptance, I had no choice but to confront him in person and state where his action would take the two of us. My strategy was the same as when I went to the Board of Surgery in Philadelphia: make it impossible for Dr. Edwards to avoid seeing me.

I obtained surgical posters from University Hospital and selected a date when Dr. Edwards would be in the operating room. I blocked out that day and seated myself in the corridor the man had to come through after finishing the day. Calculations correct, I was ready for him as his gray, distinguished head appeared in the corridor where I sat waiting. This particular corridor is very wide, almost like a small plaza. I strode across the corridor to meet him face to face. He stopped in mid-stride, his face tightening. He was clearly concerned and surprised as he recognized me.

"Hello, Dr. Edwards. I need to see you."

Dr. Edwards looked quickly around the corridor, realizing from the tone of my voice, and my body language, I was in no mood to be denied. Give the man credit; he knew his choices and said in a low voice, "Come into the Board room."

I walked right behind him into the Board Room, where we sat down in silence. I moved my chair to make sure we were looking at each other face-to-face. I waited for him to speak, and he did: "What do you want?"

I paused a second or two to let the significance of my presence sink in. Then I said in very quiet, deliberate tone: "Dr. Edwards, what have you got against me?"

The directness of my question left him staring. He was not prepared for what I represented. Strangely, I felt a tinge of sympathy for him because I respected the man's basic decency. None of that deterred me from what I had to do. "Dr. Edwards, I have known you as you have known me since I was a resident taking care of your patients at Maryland General Hospital. Do you remember how you were very strong, then, in your endorsement of my work, even praising my abilities? Now, for no reason known to me, you have blocked my Fellowship in the American College of Surgeons. Why have you done this to me?"

Unable to deny his action, Dr. Edwards took his only defense. "Pierpont, you can't prove I have done anything like that!"

My eyes locked almost unblinking upon his while I formed my

response. Of course I had no actual proof he had blocked my application. In those days, the College was a "good old boys' club." What they did, they did behind closed doors. It would have been a breach of College etiquette for anyone to disclose what went on behind those doors. Obviously, I was not a member of the "club," and the surgeons who ran the college had appraised me correctly. I had zero patience for secrecy, favoritism, and protecting a surgeon's reputation on the basis of friendship. My view of surgery was as I had described it to others in Iowa years earlier. Friendship is fine, desirable, and if we can be friends I would like that. However, I will not let friendship stand in the way when it comes to the best practice of surgery and the best care of patients. I was ready, willing, and able to back my stand in a court of law if it ever came to that. It was unthinkable for me to look aside while well-meaning but misguided physicians block me, or any properly qualified physician, in his career.

"Dr. Edwards, I have always respected you as a devout Christian and a gentleman. I hold a bible before you. If you will put your hand on this bible and swear before God that you have had nothing to do with blocking my Fellowship in the American College of Surgeons, I will believe you and say no more. Will you do that?"

I had trapped Dr. Edwards and he knew it. His fine, patrician face hardened and he stared at me as if I had gone mad. He attempted an answer, but it was so disjointed he stopped before finishing. I watched. Waited. Neither of us spoke for what seemed a long time, but was probably two or three minutes.

"Pierpont, you have no right to speak to me this way. You have no right!"

"No right, Dr. Edwards? Perhaps so, but neither does anyone, not you or anyone else, have the right to try to ruin me as a surgeon. You, Dr. Edwards, have no right to block my Fellowship in the American College of Surgeons without reason. Now I see that you are not willing to swear as a Christian you have had no part in all of this. So I have to believe I am correct. Not only do I believe you have acted against me without reason, you are giving me no choice but to do everything necessary to get what is rightly mine."

Dr. Edwards could not stop looking at me. All he wanted to do was to get away from me, to get out of the room, but he was frozen in silence. Again, I felt a strange tinge of pity for him. I doubt he had ever done anything in his life as he had done to me, and now I made him face a streak of meanness he never knew he had. The bible I still held between us accused him in ways I never could.

I broke the silence. "Why have you done this to me, Dr. Edwards?"

He was not a man to lie about his action; he couldn't. "Pierpont, you are different from other people. You have your own ideas and want people to believe them. You want to practice medicine your own way without thinking what it means to doctors who have put in many years ahead of you."

It was "old bull" reasoning, pure and simple. I said, "Do you really believe what you have just said, Dr. Edwards? You have just indicted everything this country stands for! You, and men like you, are forgetting that freedom is what it's all about - freedom to do new things, freedom to go as far and as high as a man can go. Are you ready to say my ideas should be blocked just because they are not like yours?"

"No. No, I guess that's not what I meant." I gave him time to collect his thoughts. He seemed to come to terms with his situation as he asked, "What is it you want me to do?"

There was no need to be vindictive. "Dr. Edwards, I want you to retract in writing any derogatory information about me you have given to the American College of Surgeons. I also want your unwavering support of my Fellowship in the College, and I want it now. If you refuse this, or fail to do as I ask, I intend to hold you fully responsible."

"Hold on, Pierpont! I'm not sure I can do anything like that."

"What you will or won't do is up to you Dr. Edwards, but I must tell you that if you fail me now I will sue you in public court for all you have and everything else you will earn."

I was young, but Dr. Edwards looked at me knowing I fully intended to do exactly what I had just said. Nor did I have to tell him what would happen to his standing in the medical profession if I acted against him and the American College of Surgeons in a court of law. Could he have visualized his entire life slipping away due to an ill-considered action he had not appreciated at the time he did it? I said, neither raising nor lowering my voice: "I apologize for having to speak to you so abruptly, but you have put my life and livelihood, and my family's future, at stake. Your action, if not reversed, will ruin my reputation and ultimately my practice. Thanks to your action, I have already suffered the loss of an offer worth several million dollars, and prestige. You know that my word has always been good, and my intentions are plain. I wait to see if your word is as good as mine. Thank you for meeting with me."

I left.

Exactly what Dr. Edwards did with the American College of Surgeons I have no way of knowing. I only know that the letter of rejection was withdrawn, and I became a Fellow of the College. This was not an action I took pride in, but it was the only way, and the honest way.

The episode was one of the lowest points in more than 50 years as a surgeon. I suspect I felt more shame than did Dr. Edwards, for I had put doctors above the dark side of human nature as a student, intern, resident, and fellow physician. Now I felt stained by an action to be explained only by such words as envy, spite, and unthinking malice. I had studied under Dr. Edwards, had put him on a pedestal I wanted to climb upon, too. My models had feet worse than clay. I had to admit that many doctors I had admired were in eminent positions within a great profession not because they were dedicated to their profession, and not because they were the best qualified. Sadly, so very sadly, I found many had reached eminence through an understanding of power relationships, and their ability to "play the game." It was a crushing experience to find not only that doctors like Dr. Edwards, whom I had so long admired, had feet of clay, but also that their clay was the very material used to climb upon the pedestal I had erected for them.

With mud on my ideals, I became determined more than ever to guide my practice of medicine with total honesty. How many times was I to find how difficult this was to do, when it became necessary to tell patients, or their families, messages they did not want to hear. Yet, in the long run, the honest way is the easiest way.

That determination followed me as I began to participate in government politics. Government is where the ultimate power is, power I saw changing medicine in totally wrong ways. Power, someone is supposed to have said, is the ultimate aphrodisiac, but I would not know about that. I do know that it takes power to get almost anything done in any arena of human existence. As time passed, I began to watch the politics of Baltimore and Maryland and saw an opportunity to serve in ways beyond medicine. It was to prove a learning experience which would be hard – and expensive. Well, it has always been that way for me.

Chapter Eleven
The Birth of "The Blues"...Political Control of Medical Care

In my professional life in the 1960s, I rode a tiger. The more my practice in Baltimore and Havre de Grace expanded, the more it grew. The kind of practice I had in the 60s could never happen today. To cope with a constantly growing flow of patients, I considered taking in partners. I could do this in different ways, such as the arrangement I had with Dr. Relfschneider, where I supported his practice in return for free office space and secretarial help. I had already brought the laid back, very competent Donald Hebb into my downtown Baltimore offices. The two of us took in younger men to back us up on an as-needed basis, but my two-city practice needed more than part-time assistance. The obvious solution was to form professional partnerships.

Unfortunately, partnerships and medicine do not often go well together — especially partners in surgery. My descriptions of encounters at the University of Iowa, and the almost inexplicable attitude of Dr. Edwards, provide some insight into the role of human ego in the practice of surgery. Those events are only the "tip of the iceberg." The truth is, a surgeon who lacks a powerful ego isn't going to amount to much. On the other hand, powerful egos do not usually make the most pleasant people to live with or work with. I remember as if it were an hour ago, the way Dr. John Dulin described the personality of a surgeon to us, a gangling group of young residents in Iowa City:

"If you are not prepared when you open the abdomen to confront the horns of the devil rising to meet you, and if you are not ready to grab Lucifer by the horns and dash him to the floor, and go on with your job, you don't belong in surgery! You always need to be ready for anything! You have to have the guts to climb over the problem and the ability to do the job you came for." Looking around at his dumbstruck audience of embryonic surgeons, he chuckled, as his way of nailing down his point. "You are not operating for the devil! He is just in the way. Throw the damn devil on the floor and get on with your work!"

How, why, did Dr. Dulin create his fantasy of seeing "Lucifer" in the human abdomen lying open under the surgeon's knife? Why does the picture of Dr. Dulin describing the devil in an abdomen live in my memory as a vivid image after so many years? He made his point: No matter what, who, or when something comes up that could interfere with your operation, destroy it! Let nothing interfere!

I have opened so many abdomens, in so many sizes, skinny ones and fat-encrusted ones of all ages, and in different stages of infection and disruption over so long a time, it is now hard for me to recall the icy grip of fear that races down the spine the first seconds of the first time you cut open a living person and look into the blood and unprotected organs. The new surgeon can find himself staring at his handiwork, thinking: what must I do next? Am I doing this right? Sudden doubts can challenge his ability to do the job he has vowed to do, but he cannot succeed if he doubts. The presence of fear is the presence of failure. He must not only know what he is doing, he must know that he knows what he is doing.

The very nature of practicing surgery develops human qualities unique to the human species. To put it bluntly, the surgeon becomes an autocrat — an absolute ruler of his domain. In the operating room, the surgeon does not request. He commands in a single word. People obey instantly and without question. Attitudes toward people, and behaviors which are accepted in the operating room, naturally carry over into the surgeon's personality. The effect on the doctor's private life often leads to less than happy consequences. In my life, I was incredibly fortunate by marrying a trained nurse who understood my personality and, thank God, is still able to put up with it.

My training as a surgeon, my recognition of the ego problem, and seeing more than one partnership hit the rocks, carried over into my plans for taking on partners. Developing partnerships had risks for both sides of the partnership. Ambitions run high in younger surgeons who encounter seniority and longevity which can shunt them into the least rewarding activities of the practice. As I considered my options, I decided the first need was to weed out doctors who would not fit into our methods and medical philosophy. When I talked things over with prospective partners, I issued a blunt-ax warning that went like this:

If you are a person interested in working with associates you respect, the stability and savings in effort that come with the combined activity of the partnership, time off with confidence your patients are covered, and the protection of insurance, pensions, and earned ownership in real estate, but at the same time think you are doing 90% of the work while you get only 10% of the pay, a partnership with our group is a real possibility.

Many doctors liked the first half of the partnership arrangement, but foundered on the way the money was to be divided.

A lesser but critical problem in medical partnerships is the spouse relationship. To get a half-dozen or more medical egos to work in harmony under conditions where differences of opinion are not just frequent, but continuous, almost contradicts itself. If spouse differences get into the relationships, it is a recipe for disaster. All of our partnerships were men. All partners' wives had ideas of their own. My technique of managing this problem was dictatorial, absolute, and it worked. No wife had any input or rights in our partnerships. They would not take part in any business relationship. Moreover, the physical set-up of the offices was sacrosanct. No spouse could suggest or participate in the arrangement of the furniture or decorations. These edicts applied in full to Grace Pierpont as well as all other wives.

The reaction of wives to my rules is easy to imagine. Many of them were strong-willed women with strong ideas of what their husbands' environment should be like, but their resentment of my dictates confirmed my point. Once the nose of that camel gets under the partnership tent, there goes the tent. I have seen all too many fine associations broken up for no reason other than wife interference. Of course my rules were harsh, but our surgical partnerships in Havre de Grace and the ultimate Pierpont, Hebb and Finnegan partnerships in Baltimore were among the longest and most successful surgical arrangements in the state of Maryland. All doctors who worked in my partnerships did well professionally and financially.

One of my necessary but unrewarding tasks in the partnerships was managing the business end of things. I hired, fired, worked out personal differences, made decisions about pensions, insurance, profit-sharing, and legal matters. I held meetings in which we set up our fee schedules for individual doctors and the partnerships. In all of these troublesome but essential details, my experience in managing finances from age eight, and negotiating the shoals of professional jealousies smoothed the way. My partners, and others familiar with the scope of the partnerships, complimented me from time to time on how we got along. The compliments were nice to hear, of course, but somehow I was rather neutral about them. I felt I was only doing what was necessary and expected of me. I did nothing special to earn compliments, nor did I expect gratitude. I learned long ago that if thank-yous and gratitude in a business arrangement are expected, look for disappointment as the result.

One of my first partners was Dr. William Brendle, formerly one of my residents at Maryland General Hospital. He not only joined me full-time at Havre de Grace, he and his wife also moved into the second floor of our clinic building. At that time, we had a two-story surgical building within three minutes walking distance to the emergency room of Harford Memorial Hospital. The clinic's facilities were compact and efficient. The waiting room accommodated 25 patients. Dr. Brendle and I had dual desks in a large consultation office adjoining two examination rooms, a large treatment room, and an X-ray/dark room facility.

Dr. Alfred Grigolict, a most gregarious physician of German descent, joined us. His presence, though welcome, made it necessary to expand the medical facilities to the second floor. Dr. Brendle was doing well, and the Brendles bought a house nearby and moved into it. We had no more than remodeled the upper floor than we found our space once again inadequate. I found a building for sale near our clinic and bought it. The two buildings looked ample for our practice at the time, and even provided room for a physical therapy facility under a very fine young therapist, Habern Freeman — a man destined to play a different and important role in my life.

While we were setting up in our newly-acquired building, an optometrist bought a large building directly across the street from the emergency room of Harford Memorial. He built a one-story motel and optometry facility a half-block long on the site, with parking in front. I watched the building take shape enviously because I saw the practice growing beyond the building we had just occupied. Suddenly an unexpected opportunity presented itself. The optometrist fell seriously ill, soon died, and his building went on the market. We lost no time buying the building which we took down to its bare walls and completely renovated. As soon as this work was completed, we moved our surgical clinic there.

Remodeling the building to meet our special needs tested our imagination. The main entrance had been a covered entry to a 10-room motel leading into a long hall. We widened and enclosed the hall to create business offices. The large adjoining areas became consultation rooms with adjoining treatment and examination rooms. We used a core area to provide space for an X-ray and dark room, and an outpatient operating room. We used other rooms for a lounge, kitchen and resting area for the staff. The last four rooms were turned into a modern, fully equipped physical therapy facility under Habern Freeman. Our new waiting room was able to accommodate 40 persons, with overflow space capable of handling another 10 patients if necessary. To make the facility complete, we rented space for a full pharmacy in the west end of the building.

Before moving into our new facilities, Dr. Brendle, Dr. Grigolict, and I had handled all of the fractures and bone problems. We called in orthopedic specialists on an as-needed basis. Our added capabilities enabled us to bring on staff Dr. Henry Kwak, one of my former surgical residents at Maryland General Hospital, and two orthopedists, Dr. John Im and Dr. Jin Rhee. With four general surgeons, including one fully qualified in thoracic and vascular surgery, two orthopedic surgeons, a physical therapist, and a pharmacy on the premises, we offered what amounted to a mini-surgical hospital for outpatient care and inpatient hospital care.

Out of perhaps mistaken altruism or inability to foresee coming events in medical care, we grew the practice in ways that dug a financial hole for ourselves. Our medical philosophy in those days was completely uncomplicated. We charged patients what they could afford. Often, this meant reduced charges and sometimes no payment at all. No one was ever turned away from our practice whether in Baltimore or Havre de Grace due to inability to pay. Our fee schedule "profiles" were always among the lowest in the state.

In doing what we thought was the right, humane way to practice medicine, we failed to anticipate the pricing of medical care by insurance companies and government bureaucrats. Instead of doctors charging what they considered fair and just, based on intimate knowledge of the patient's ability to pay, the insurance companies and government agencies sprung the financial trap we had innocently set. They sent us fee schedules telling us what to charge to the penny based on our "fee profile," a summary of fees charged for various services over past years. Our humanity and generosity over the years now cost us dearly. I watched residents I had personally trained go into practice and establish "profiles" twice as high as those in effect at our surgical clinic.

As arguments over the costs and availability of medical care continue to consume hours of debate and tons of printers' ink, let me register some thoughts on the subject from personal experience and private research.

In the mid-forties and fifties following World War II, and the resumption of private practice by physicians released from the military, the introduction of new medicines and technical equipment virtually exploded. Expenses kept pace, inflation took an additional toll, and responsible physicians became concerned over medical costs. Who, we asked each other, is going to pay for increasingly sophisticated care which saves and prolongs life? No one seemed aware that the process of adding several years to seniors' lives also brought additional costs for treating health problems which accompany added years.

At this time it was against the law for physicians to incorporate. Not that it mattered too much because physicians seem born with their heads in the sand when it comes to legal questions, political questions, or anything else subject to dispute. Two Maryland medical groups, the Medical and Chiurgical Faculty of Maryland ("Med-chi") and the Baltimore City Medical Society, met for formal discussions of the growing problem. Every legal restriction real and imagined was put on the table before some of the most legally inept people you'll ever meet. This was before the explosion of malpractice suits, of course!

The outcome of these discussions was the formation of an insurance organization *to be run by practicing physicians to serve the public at large, but primarily to take care of the problem of people in need of medical care and unable to pay for it.* We devised two plans: Plan A was to cover people unable to pay the total cost of their care. Plan B was a medical insurance system for people able to pay for their care. Money to pay the expenses of these new insurance companies (eventually Blue Cross and Blue Shield) was to come from contributions from the collected fees of the program. For example, my fee for removing an appendix was $75 under Plan A. Of this amount, $25 was to go toward funding the program. Fools that we were, we believed it when told the fees would be accumulated and accounted for, and then when the program reached sound financial footing, our contributions would be returned. As may be guessed, I never saw a cent of my contributions.

Thus, hallelujah! it was the birth of the Blues in Maryland! Blue Cross was to cover hospital costs. Blue Shield was to cover physician/dentist costs. It was a noble effort, and the start of controlling doctor-patient relationships by insurance statisticians and Chief Financial Officers, soon to be aided and abetted by government bureaucrats. From those beginnings born in naivete grew the behemoth of medical and health care that spread across the nation. Chief managers of these systems rack up annual salaries into the high six figures, and even beyond the million-dollar mark! Underlings are rewarded in proportion. Net result: obscene overhead.

As I watched the Blues become more and more powerful, it became clear to me that the public (spelled political representatives) was going to become a big player in our fast-changing medical system. There was no alternative. If I were to have any influence over whatever was finally to emerge, I had to learn the political game. Why me? In spite of the hard knocks of my early life, in spite of the demands of my profession on my time, I saw things going wrong, and I wanted to stop them before it was too late. I wanted to give back to others some of what so many others had given to me. In hindsight, an awful lot of what I attempted was a terrible waste of my time and money. I guess I just wanted to help. You may find that what I am attempting even now will fall in the same hole, but we shall see.

I tested the waters of organized politics as a lifelong Democrat. My political orientation came mainly from our family's response to the Civil War. Mother's family of Zimmerman's favored the Southern cause, and therefore was against Republicans then in power. Father's family of Pierponts split their loyalties, but most were loyal to the Union. My maternal grandfather, Billy Zimmerman, became a Democrat-judge of the Orphans' Court of Baltimore County. When my father died and I was eight, our family's Southern sympathies registered with me and becoming a Democrat was a natural outcome. It didn't hurt that Maryland was about three to one Democrat, and the ratio in the Baltimore area was even higher, when I became interested in the workings of political parties.

Following my training to head for the top, I found Maryland to be run politically by Governor William Preston Lane, H.C. "Curly" Byrd, President of the University of Maryland and influential far beyond the campus boundaries, and George P. Mahoney. A lesser light at the time was the state's Comptroller, Millard Tawes from Maryland's "backward" and relatively isolated Eastern Shore. Political campaigns cost money, and the pockets of Maryland political leaders were always empty. The theory seemed to be that being Governor of the state was a privilege, and anyone who wanted the office should bring his own money. As incredible as it may seem today, Governor Lane's salary was $4,500 per year. Well, he also got a mansion to live in and a chauffeured car. When Spiro Agnew won the office in 1966, the Governor's salary jumped three-fold — to a magnanimous $15,000 per year. On this salary, the man was supposed to educate two college-age children, pay his living expenses, and save money for retirement years. Other elected officials, though not upper echelon state employees, were paid on a comparable schedule.

It was a system ripe for payoffs. I, for one, was not surprised to learn that our governors had "bag men" who collected money in return for nearly all appointments, from judge down to liquor establishment inspector. The ability to raise money occupied everyone, leading to a large amount of patronage appointments at the Governor's disposal. Jobs dispensed at the Governor's pleasure (which in turn created favors for members of the Legislature) paid much more than the Governor received. Those involved rationalized the system by assuming that paying for an appointment was a fair return for the favor, and besides the money paid didn't come from the taxpayers' pockets: not directly, at least.

Every year, the Governor and his staff doled out appointments which went to the Legislature in what became known as "the green bag." The man who put together the deals for the appointments became known as — what else! — "the bag man." The power of the bag man was something to reckon with. He was almost invariably a highly intelligent man thoroughly familiar with the people needed to get things done in Maryland. The bag man was the essential link between the men who controlled the Legislature, the state's cabinet officers, and the Governor. Key traits of bag men were their ability to keep secrets, to reach the Governor privately at all times, and keep their word no matter what. Everything was done on a handshake, and one insider told the truth when he confided: "The bag man is more important to me than the Governor. He gets things done for me."

I suppose I should have been horrified to learn Maryland's political system, but it was a fact of life I would either learn to deal with, or walk away from. Power has its own fascination, and meeting with the power brokers of the political system and I found it intriguing to see what it took to play the game. I quickly learned that even minor fundraising and providing grassroots support to political leaders — bosses, if you like — opened doors. It is somewhat amusing, looking back, to see how powerful the old-time bosses were. In Baltimore, the Sun's cartoonist Yardley, identified the city's Jewish political boss, Jack Pollack, as "1/6 boss," meaning he controlled a sixth of the city's votes. There were other political machines, too. Coggins/O'Malley ruled the Irish northeast with an iron fist until ousted by Hugo Rucitti's upstarts under David Preller and Old Joe/Young Joe Curran (now Attorney General of Maryland). Tommy the Elder D'Alesandro dominated the Italian vote. The southeast had its Stonewall Club run by "Soft Shoes" Harry McGuirk, and so it went. Now of course, that system has broken into pieces.

Before the old system fell apart, the state's genial and competent Comptroller, Millard Tawes, used it in 1960 to win the Governor's mansion where he stayed for eight years. Tawes was a true gentleman, and made a good governor. As an example of the needs of the times, this otherwise honorable man felt it necessary to meet Jack Pollack, 1/6th boss of Baltimore, in a Baltimore hotel room to make a deal for the votes Pollack could deliver in the Democratic primary. Winning the primary was all that mattered to Tawes, because in Democratic Maryland the winner of the primary with rare exceptions was a shoo-in for Governor. What Tawes did not know was that Pollack was wired for sound and recorded their deal. Later, Tawes refused to meet Pollack's demands, and in revenge Pollack played his tape in public. What saved Tawes from potential destruction was that Pollack's recording was so garbled Tawes was able to deny its authenticity and get away with it.

The sixties when Tawes was Governor, and I was learning the political verities, were times of a sea change in medical care. *The only question in health care was when, not if, the Democrats in control of both Congress and the White House would take advantage of the political opportunities generated by the medical care situation.* The Blues were taking care of those who could pay their premiums — or have the premiums paid for them by their employers, but what about the millions of potential voters who were unable, or unwilling, to pay for their care? President Lyndon Johnson had not spent a lifetime in politics with blinders on. He saw an opportunity to corral the loyalties of literally millions of voters, the elderly and the poor, by creating a new system of medical care. He waited only for the brass ring to come around to where he could grab it.

I had no way of knowing what form Federal intervention would take, but I saw it coming one way or another. I still loved and lived medicine, and the thought of people who never saw me, never saw my patients, not really giving a tinker's dam about me or my patients, would have the power to prescribe what I could and could not do, almost drove me to distraction. I became close to a fanatic on the subject (and still am). I bored fellow doctors to the point they ignored me. Only one word could describe the attitude of organized medical groups from the American Boards and Colleges down to the state and local medical associations and their individual members: inertia!

I could interest no one in the problem. Few wanted to get involved. The mere idea of sullying their disinfected hands with political action made them psychologically unfit. I cannot say how many times, in how many meetings, I warned them the choice was to take control of medical and health care as medical professionals, or watch the politicians take control of us. It was the same sad story whether it was a state chapter of the American College of Surgeons, with national figures in attendance, or discussions in informal settings. Scientific and professional discussions were welcomed, but when I raised questions of public policy and medicine, those in control would counter with legal warnings: If doctors and their professional associations got into the political arena, we would almost surely lose our associations' non-profit tax position. Hearing that, doctors' faces would tighten and necks stiffen. Sit down, Ross. Next subject.

In 1962 and 1964, the political juggernaught gained momentum. Candidates in those years knew they had a hot issue, an emotional issue, and they played it to the hilt: Doctors were rich and getting richer while the poor and the elderly suffered their illnesses and accidents without care. Inevitably, the millions on Social Security saw a new way to insulate themselves from medical risks. They became an enormous lobbying and voting force uttering the cry, "We need help!"

The tide rose. It became obvious that the Federal government in the person of President Lyndon Johnson was going to push for some kind of care that would improve the condition of the impoverished, the medically indigent, and the elderly — specifically people on Social Security. The only question in my mind was the form this new system of medical care would take. I have always supported the concept that no one should be deprived of medical care due to inability to pay. Every doctor in my partnerships practiced that philosophy every day. My idea was simple. If medical care were set up to meet the needs of the indigent, as we practiced it on our own, it could be expanded into a full-fledged system of care *managed by local physicians and provider groups for the best deal for the patients, the medical professionals providing the care, and the taxpayers.*

I am not a fool and I knew that poking my finger in the dike would not stop the flood. But the dike was there. The flood pressed against it, and my nature impelled me to do what I could. Using my contact with Governor Tawes, I urged him to stop the passage of proposed legislation that would end American medical care, which was leading the world. Well do I also remember trying again and again to get Senator Daniel Brewster and Senator Joseph Tydings to resist participating in the medical fraud on the public known as Title 18, Medicare, and Title 19, Medicaid. With them I pulled no punches. This legislation, I said, was created in haste, badly flawed, and expensive beyond anyone's comprehension. It promised more than it could deliver, even if the program was fully funded, which it was not.

To corral Dan Brewster and sit him down long enough and sober enough to understand my argument took some doing. Gov. Tawes interceded with Sen. Brewster, and I went to his home to brief him on the implications of the medical legislation then under consideration. It took me less than 10 minutes to realize our meeting was going absolutely nowhere, so I smiled and said I had an idea.

"Dan, we aren't getting anywhere in this. Let's have a debate. Right here and now. Now we both respect money, so let's make the debate worthwhile. We each put up $1,000, making a pot of $2,000. Winner takes all."

Sen. Brewster had class. He looked at me, grinned and said nothing.

"Your wife is here. Let Carole be the judge. If she says I win, I win. If she says you win, you win." The novelty of a private debate with a $2,000 prize had Carole smiling now. I said, "We will each speak for five minutes on our side of the medical care legislation. After that, we'll go at one another for two minutes for three rounds, and a formal wrap up of two minutes." Dan and Carole were with me so far, so I played a trump. "That's the rules except for one thing."

Danny Brewster, puzzled, stopped smiling. "What else?"

"You can take either for or against the legislation, and I'll take the side you don't want. For $1,000 each. Carole, are you willing to be the judge?"

"Why not?" Carole said.

The Senator did me the courtesy of thinking it over, but it was all a charade. He couldn't take either side of the debate and expose he was a total ignoramus on the medical care legislation Lyndon Johnson proposed. I left Brewster's house knowing my finger was no longer in the dike. When the time came in 1965 to vote on Medicare/Medicaid, both Maryland senators voted yes.

Nothing in "The Great Society" programs of the Johnson Administration, including Vietnam, has cost the United States more than Johnson's Medicare/Medicaid. Like all Federal government programs, the legislation of 1965 was only the beginning of a political structure with a life of its own. Its appetite had no bounds then, has no bounds now. The ultimate goal was, and is, to take over the nation's health care system in its entirety. The Clinton health care program, drawn up in secrecy without a dime's worth of consultation with the medical profession, was the politician's system for managing one of the most complex and sensitive relationships of human life. Politicians know what it means to control one-seventh of the nation's economy, and they will never rest until they have all that money at their disposal.

Only those involved directly in medical care know the broken promises of Medicare/Medicaid. How many people know that the Federal government in 1965 used its full faith and credit to promise doctors "usual and customary fees?" And that this promise was broken from day one? Only a handful! Over-promised and under-funded Medicare/Medicaid never could pay the legislated fees. To get around the obligation, bureaucrats in State and Federal governments, and in insurance companies, have constructed elaborate screening processes which turn medical decision-making over to government and insurance employees. Regulatory bureaucracies are reducing doctors to delivering care dictated in a distant office, rather than the care determined in consultation between doctor and patient. Is anyone so foolish as to believe the purpose of myriad rules and regulations is to improve medical care? The ruling principle of Medicare/Medicaid regulations is to minimize payments to doctors and medical facilities. The guiding principle of insurance companies' regulations is to minimize costs and increase profits.

What is the net result of these monumental efforts to cut the costs of medical care in the United States? Thanks to mountains of paperwork and strangling legal problems, we have reached all-time highs in medical costs. My best estimate of those costs is 15-16% of the nation's total production of goods and services! From the start of Federal intervention into medical care in 1965 to today, we have funneled trillions of dollars into a system that has not worked. It can never work as it now exists. One unintended consequence of the current system is that high costs combined with reduced compensation have made it virtually impossible for a new physician to build a private practice.

Experience in my adult life as a physician, a Chief of Surgery in a major Baltimore hospital, and the owner-operator of multi-service clinics, has shown me beyond serious question what it takes to deliver medical care from the physician's side. That is only part of the problem. To learn the entire spectrum of patient needs, how to fund a workable medical care system, and to manage it, I studied our pre-Medicare and Medicaid-era system in detail. I investigated medical care in other countries. I will present my findings as recommendations for universal medical care as an Appendix to this book. Here let me add only this: I am confident I have developed a system for the United States which will (1) provide high quality medical care pre-birth to burial, and (2) reduce the cost of such care from about 15-16% to no more than 9-10% of our Gross National Product.

Reductions in the costs of Medicare/Medicaid of that magnitude will go far toward reducing the national deficit.

Will the medical system I recommend do what I say it will? Seeking an answer, I look back at my efforts to arouse the medical profession to meet the threats to its independence in the fifties and sixties. No one wanted to listen, much less act! I look back to the lone fight I waged against the passage of Medicare/Medicaid when I was a novice in politics. I was Cassandra, with her fate. I look, now, upon the two political parties struggling to fix a medical structure being held together by good intentions, incredible amounts of borrowed money, and promises of improvement. Politicians make great speeches about medical care of maximum quality at affordable cost, but that is not their criteria. *Men and women in both political parties take stands on medical care according to their estimates of what will win them, or cost them, the most votes!*

To paraphrase Patrick Henry, if that be cynicism, make the most of it! Cynicism in this situation is more than deserved. The parties in and out of power now have little choice in the matter. They face enormous pressure from an army of employees who stand to keep or lose their Medicare/Medicaid jobs. They face the pressure of organizations like the AARP and its millions of voters/members. They are lobbied by executives of powerful HMOs and insurance companies driven by a need to focus on the bottom line of the medical care balance sheet. Those who run HMOs and insurance companies look for millions of dollars in insurance premium profits, and they had better be there. Tort lawyers laugh all the way from the courtrooms to their banks.

What good can be said about a medical system that rewards doctors according to their record of minimizing patient costs? What can be said about doctors who willingly go along with a mercenary system which forces them to prescribe care according to published directives from the main office? Unless the medical profession finds a way to regain its professional independence, doctors and patients alike will slide down the slippery slopes of managed medical care into personal disasters.

Chapter Twelve
Medical Myopia And F.M.Gs.

Today's crisis in medical care in the US didn't just happen. Doctors in charge of medical education and monitoring the performance of fellow physicians have miscalculated medical needs and resources for nearly a half-century. Their combination of overconfidence, myopic self-interest, and mismanagement has led the nation into its current medical morass. Is it not incredible that this nation possesses medical capabilities which are the envy of the world, yet almost everyone wants our system to change? Public confidence in the medical profession has dropped so low that Hillary Clinton turned to everyone but doctors in drawing up her national health plan. The failure of her plan had nothing to do with medical incompetence. It had everything to do with the inability of medical professionals to manage their profession. It had everything to do with Hillary's socialist ideas of medical care.

Who has set the standards of US medical practice? There is an informal yet enormously powerful arrangement that grew between the faculties of the large medical schools and Board Members of associations like The American Medical Association, the American College of Surgeons, and the Association of American Medical Colleges. Looking at the actions and policies of these individuals over the past 50 years illustrates the truth of Lord Acton's famous observation: "power corrupts."

The kindest way to describe the management of medical care in the US is to praise the outstanding performance of medical scientists while condemning the almost incredible shortcomings of physicians in their public and political actions. American medical science has developed medicines, equipment and techniques which have revolutionized medical care defying imagination, yet, the medical profession suffers a fall in public esteem so serious it deserves the term disastrous. Doctors have allowed themselves to be labeled "providers?. Am I Dr. Pierpont No, I am Provider Ross Pierpont. Physicians have themselves to blame for their current distress and fears for their futures.

A classic example of medical management myopia is our involvement with Foreign Medical Graduates (FMGs). Through more than 40 years, FMGs have flooded the medical profession of the United

States. The original idea of the policy makers was to bring FMGs here to complete their medical education and upgrade their techniques. They were then to return to their homelands and provide the people there with vitally needed medical attention. Grand idea! As with so many grand ideas, this one has been subverted in its execution.

What happens is that FMGs come here by the thousands. They complete their medical training — and stay. *As this is written, more than 40% of all physicians now practicing in the United States came here as FMGs.* Meanwhile, the faculties of US medical schools turn away qualified American applicants because, the medical faculties say, we have a surplus of doctors. You may want to read this paragraph again to make sure you read it correctly.

This situation is not just an example of medical myopia. It is also an example of the self-serving arrogance that has contributed to the influx of FMGs. To understand the origins of our FMG situation, nothing beats a look at the prestigious Yale School of Medicine and how it approached its responsibilities in medical education.

As the United States built up its Armed Forces in the years before we entered World War II, it was obvious to everyone in the medical field that we needed more doctors. Responding to the obvious, The Association of American Medical Colleges asked US medical schools to increase their student bodies to meet the future needs. Yale University's Medical School was one of the schools asked to help meet the need by increasing the number of its medical students. At the time of the request, Yale graduated 72 MDs a year. The Yale Senate of the Faculty roared its outrage over this request. Announcing that academic and learning standards would suffer by adding any more students, the high-minded physicians teaching medicine at Yale warned they would strike if it took such action to prevent "overloading" the student body.

How many students was Yale asked to add to its medical student body? Six! A total of 78!

That's right, six more medical students at Yale would overload the student body.

As medical myopia distorted US medical school policies during the military build-up of World War II, the demand for doctors created pressures that could not be ignored. Our shortage of physicians went from serious to critical. We literally "scraped the bottom of the barrel." If a retired doctor could still walk, he went back to work. While we struggled with shortages, European medical training hit bottom. It then stayed there as the German Army occupied France, eastern Europe, and the Netherlands. England's normally excellent medical education sank beneath a war effort that gobbled up every available resource — and then some.

American medical schools finally moved rapidly to graduate more physicians by speeding up their training. It was not enough. The end of World War II returned medical school curricula to "normal," while at the same time ushering in explosive advances in medical knowledge and treatment at the same time. Radical advances transformed the nature of medical care almost overnight so that more doctors were needed than ever before.

Just as nature abhors a vacuum, Foreign Medical Graduates responded in droves to the vacuum in American medical care.

To explore our situation with FMGs is to tread into a minefield. The risk is to find oneself blown up. Some may read what follows as the ranting of an anti-foreigner bigot. If so, the ranting is in the minds of the beholder. Truths are not bigotry. Let me add very quickly, however, that tens of thousands of FMGs from almost every nation on the globe cannot be seen as some sort of homogenous group. To the contrary, they differ enormously in their basic education, and their medical educations. They have different human values inherited from widely varying cultures. They even have different attitudes toward humanity itself. How could it be otherwise for a doctor brought up in a culture where disease and death end lives often and early? The differences in the medical competence of our FMGs are equally broad and wide. A good example of the levels of education FMGs brought with them is a group I worked with one year at Maryland General Hospital. These graduates came to the United States from a graduating class of 2,500 at the University of Santo Thomas in the Philippine Islands. All of their education had been conducted in Spanish, under a faculty about one-tenth the size of the medical faculty at Yale. To appreciate some of the differences between the medical education of a typical Santo Thomas graduate and a typical Yale graduate, recall that Yale refused to add six students to its medical school student body.

My goal here is to examine the impact of FMGs as found in our situation at Maryland General Hospital in 1946, and as it continues to affect American medical care today. FMGs contributed, and continue to contribute, essential and very valuable services to our medical system. But their contributions must not obscure problems so obvious that ignoring them serves no one — not the FMG physician, not Americans who daily entrust their health to the FMG physician, and not Americans refused entry into medical school because "we already have too many physicians."

In 1946, the year after World War II came to an end, the aspiring Dr. Pierpont had reached the grand old age of 30. That is the year I took over resident training at Maryland General Hospital. Looking at my action from the perspective gained through another 40 years experience, I can see how youth — and inexperience! — encourages some of us to take on challenges that would turn away someone with enough experience to appreciate the risks, but being 30 allowed me to charge ahead not bothered that the only experience I had in managing resident training was when I was a senior resident myself at Baltimore City Hospitals.

What possessed me to assume such serious responsibilities when I was still so new in my profession without compensation worth thinking about? I never thought about my motivation at the time. I just wanted to do it. Maybe it was ego — a feeling I had mastered surgical techniques I wanted to impart to others. Maybe it was also a feeling I wanted Maryland General to return to the eminence I saw when I trained there. The hospital had been one of five original medical schools in Baltimore during the years the city was still developing its international reputation for innovations and excellence. It had a long history in residence training led by the top-notch surgeon, Dr. Bay. His sudden death created a vacuum of surgical leadership never filled. It is not egotistical to say I was warmly welcomed by a staff that consisted, quite bluntly, of doctors in need of additional training. It was a struggle for some of them to keep up their teaching activity and maintain the credentials needed to continue the hospital's residency approval.

Although I took on my responsibilities of resident training in youthful confidence, what I encountered at Maryland General should have scared me into immediate retreat. Was I too dumb to give up or too proud? I can't say which even in retrospect. No, it was almost like a dare, and I responded like a race horse to a starter's bell. The dominant problem facing Maryland General, and me, was training a group of residents, almost all of them Foreign Medical Graduates, to meet the minimum standards expected at a residency-accredited hospital. As I took up the problem, I knew next to nothing about the foreign residents' medical education, but I soon learned that the training of many ranked from mediocre to questionable. To make the situation almost frightening, nearly every one of the residents could not communicate in English. Whether listening, speaking, reading, or writing, more than half of the time it was a question whether we understood them, or if they understood us. The impact of such tenuous communication between doctor and patient is easy to imagine.

Is "frightening" too strong to describe a situation with the hospital's surgical staff dominated by Foreign Medical Graduates deficient in spoken and written English? I faced the fact that these young doctors were dealing with sick people's bodies — peoples' lives! Every one had authority to cut people open and remove or correct diseased body parts. As the physician in charge of them, and therefore responsible for their actions or inactions, I walked a slippery slope seven days of every week. Had today's threats of malpractice with their costs and consequences of even unsuccessful suits existed at that time, my attempts to train foreign residents in surgery would have lasted no longer than the time needed to write my resignation.

Learning to communicate in English with each other, and our patients, was a problem that had to be resolved before anything else could be accomplished. I lost no time in bringing the matter before a meeting of the visiting attending staff. Some doctors came still wearing their white gowns. Others wore business suits as proper as any downtown banker. As I took the floor to describe our problems, we took each other's measure, for all knew this was to be a discussion of FMG problems. I looked into face after face that could not hide the staff doctors' concerns.

About 20 in all, they sat in silence waiting for me to begin. I let them stew for a minute or two, then said: "Every one of you must understand, if you don't already, that you are directly responsible for the actions of our house staff with your patients." Some murmured; some shifted in their chairs. "I know you doctors well enough to know you have on your hands a staff completely different from residents you are accustomed to working with. A lot of these residents simply do not understand everyday English, much less the English we use to explain our thinking, or discuss complicated subjects. Gentlemen, they do not understand! How can you expect them to get a medical history that means a damn when they don't know what the patient is trying to tell them? Their histories are not just useless, they're misleading! They can be dangerous. As to their medical training, to a man they're at best on the level of our third-year students."

I paused for emphasis. "One more thing you'd better think about. When they say yes to you, they may actually be saying the opposite — no!"

Not one doctor in the meeting was ready to accept what they had just heard. Some showed instant anger. What I had said challenged the status quo, and medical training, in following "standard procedures," tends to shore up, not destroy, the status quo. Dr. Phil Emerson, one of the more respected physicians on the staff, summed up the general feeling: "Ross, you have made out our entire hospital staff to be a bunch of incompetent nitwits. I know the residents I work with, and yes, they have some language problems, but we get the job done. I don't like the way you are criticizing these young men. I don't like it at all."

Thank God City Hospitals and Iowa City Hospital had taught me well to expect criticism and let it roll right over me, never to show outwardly it troubled me at all. The fact was, it didn't matter what Dr. Emerson thought of me! Or what the staff thought of me. Only two things counted: was I right? And a job that had to be done. Careful and thorough thought of our problems before stating them had persuaded me I was absolutely right about the FMGs. I also meant to see our job not just done; it would be done well. I rapidly scanned the eyes of every doctor before I said, "Gentlemen, Phil Emerson may be right. You can agree with him, or with me, that we have a big, complicated job to do. That job is to make these raw residents into good, useful doctors and full participants in our society. Every doctor in this room knows, deep in his heart, that these foreign residents have a long way to go. Their first step

Meet my courageous mother, Ethel Zimmerman Pierpont with her sons, (left to right) me, Roger, Edwin and Philip.

My father, Edwin I. Pierpont, who died when I was 3 years old.

Mother, Ethel Celeste Zimmerman Pierpont, in her beautiful bridal gown.

My oldest brother, Roger L. Pierpont, U.S. Army Lt. Colonel (World War II), served as an entomologist who deloused whorehouses in Naples, Italy to protect American troops from typhus.

My wife Grace's mother, Bessie Mae Moser Schmidt.

Louis Alvin Schmidt, Grace's father, in front of his favorite car in 1959.

E. Scott. Dance (left) and William Zimmerman (grandfather) were the last two Confederates in Baltimore County Company.

Grandfather Zimmerman, judge of the Orphans Court in Baltimore County, shown here with Philip, his son, and my uncle. They are standing on the front porch of the Zimmerman homeplace.

Zimmerman homeplace is where Ethel Zimmerman (mother) lived with her six brothers and three sisters.

In 1917, I was born in this house at 6712 Windsor Mill Road, Woodlawn, Maryland.

The Zimmermans and Sauters helped the settlers build a road in Oregon at the turn of 20th century. The Zimmermans were active in developing machinery for logging the forests of our Pacific Northwest.

Glenham Konigen Cornelia, my thoroughbred Holstein heifer stands serenely beside both Edwin and me. Money earned from milking Cornelia and Sookie (another milkcow) twice a day paid my way through school.

The Union News headquarters building still stands in Towson, MD. My sale of 30 subscriptions to the Union News gave me the choice of a bicycle or a Holstein heifer. I took Cornelia!

One of the happiest days of my life...here with my beautiful bride, Grace Schmidt Pierpont, February 21, 1942.

A photograph taken as I was inducted into the American College of Surgeons.

My wife, Grace, as she appeared when we were married. A local newspaper referred to her as "one of the most beautiful women in Maryland". Sometimes newspapers tell the truth!

These are our five homes:

1942-46. 312 Elrino St. East Baltimore. Paid $38.00 month rent.

1953-58. 3301 Norman Ave. Mayfield. Grace bought this house at auction for $29,500.

1958-66. 5412 Purlington Way Homeland. Paid $42,000

1947-53. 3309 Crossland Ave. Clifton Park. Christine was born while living here. Paid $15,500 for the house.

1966-97. 5602 Enderly Rd. Homeland. Paid $66,000

The two most important women in my life. Grace and our daughter, Christine, who was 18 months at the time of this picture.

Celebrating with the nurses from Maryland General Hospital where Grace earned her R.N.

My daughter's, Christine Celeste Pierpont, high school graduation photo from Roland Park Cross Country School.

My daughter, Christine, saying goodbye to us in Baltimore and looking ahead into life as Christine Celeste Pierpont von Klencke, Mistress of Schloss Haemelschenburg near Hanover, Germany.

My daughter, Christine, and I as we looked during my first birthday party at her home in Schloss Haemelschenburg. The castle is shown on the next 2 pages.

Pierpont's long time friends and working personnel, Elaine Cole and Charles Shipley at Christine's reception.

Haemelschenburg Castle, the home of Christine, her husband, Lippold von Klencke, and our four grandchildren.

Another view of the castle. From the road you can see the moat, gate, bridge. The Weserrenaissance Haemelschenburg's public museum is on the first floor. The family lives on the second. There are no elevators!

The Pierpont family in Haemelschenburg
The 17th Century castle in northern Germany, shown above, is the home of daughter Christine, top left, son-in-law Lippold von Klencke, and four grand-children: Anna, Ludolf, Henry, and Celeste. In the middle row, left to right, are Grace and Ross Pierpont with mother-in-law Viktoria von Klencke.

V for Victory as I cast my vote in 1966.

At the time of this campaign, I was also the physician for Baltimore's ice hockey team thus the hockey sticks in our campaign car. Grace and I are riding in a parade in Montgomery county.

It was an honor to support President Ronald Reagan in 1984.

Grace Pierpont congratulates President George Bush as I look on.

In 1998, I was the GOP nominee for the U.S. Senate. Beside me stands Ellen R. Sauerbrey. She lost the Maryland governorship to Parris Glendenning that year in a razor-thin vote count reviewed in Chapter 23.

In 1999, Ray Krul, long time friend and supporter, and I met with Lt. Governor Joseph Rogers of Colorado.

George Russell was my attorney during the Buscemi drug indictment case in 1971.

Late Vice President Spiro "Ted" Agnew, here with his wife, Judywere friends "done in" by Maryland politics. Ted would have become President replacing Nixon had he not been forced to resign.

We kick off our bid for U.S. Senate from our headquarters in Baltimore.

I have just won a major primary with Grace at my side.

I supported Senator Joseph Tydings (left) and Daniel B. Brewster as Democrat friends. After Tydings betrayed me, he later sought my friendship and support.

In 1966, I ran for Governor with Archie Williams for Comptroller of Maryland, the first African American to run statewide.

What a night! The late Baltimore City Comptroller Hyman A. Pressman speaks on my behalf.

Exchanging views with U.S. Senator Bill Frist of Tennessee.

My oldest granddaughter, Anna Elisabeth von Klencke, joined Grace and me at a Baltimore Opera during a 1997 visit.

Panelists at the University of Maryland US Health Care Symposium on May 29,1999. (left to right) Graf Mathias von der Schulenburg of the University of Hanover, Germany; Joseph Santos, Congressional Budget Health Case officer; Dr. Pierpont; Former Governor and now Maryland Comptroller, William Donald Schaefer and Nelson Sabatini, Former Maryland Secretary of Health and Mental Hygiene.

along the way is to learn the English language."

The tension in the room seemed to soften. I said, "If you want to manage the residents treating your patients your way, fine; however, I am going to teach them how to do histories, physicals, and the rudiments of patient care. I have had the hospital enroll them into night school for training and speaking English. If you want to help me make real doctors of our crew, I will really appreciate it. So will the residents you encourage and help. That says it for me. Now, are there any more questions?"

Doctors glanced at each other, some shrugging away any comment. In silence, they got up and left. Dr. Pierpont had won yet another popularity contest.

Popularity be damned. I had accepted the responsibility. It was up to me to call the shots. I immediately scheduled a two-hour review with the house staff every weekday evening from 5-7 PM. No matter how hard our workdays, and late dinners, hello, the staff doctors made the reviews faithfully every day. I began to feel proud of them.

It was a beginning, but as day followed day, progress seemed so meager our efforts appeared worthless. Every doctor working with me had a full load in his daily practice, and coping with the constant misunderstandings between the visiting staff and the residents took its toll on patience and energies. Fortunately, Dr. Bill Lumpkin pitched in to help me on a daily basis. One or two other conscientious physicians also came on board when they could. Five to 7, night after night, one by one, we reviewed medical histories and physical examinations until we had corrected and completed every one. Working one-on-one with residents, we answered their questions about patient care. We taught modalities of intravenous therapy, catheterization, laboratory workups, and all the rest that goes into total medical attention. There were many nights when I came home late and Grace saw the strain and none too gently asked why I was killing myself — not to mention neglecting her. I could not answer her. I had no answer.

I think those of us on the house staff were the most amazed persons in the process when we realized that after two months we had a reasonably functioning, reasonably responsible house staff. Even more amazing, now that I think about it, was that we avoided any real catastrophes!

The closeness of the experience helped us to understand each other better — not just in language, but as the different kinds of human beings we were. As we got to know each other better, we gained mutual respect for the cultural and ethnic differences built into our varied personalities. The biggest change in my relationships came in the area of the truth. My life has been based on total respect for the truth, total disdain for anyone who abuses the truth. In my first work with the FMGs, I found I could never get a straight answer to a straight question. The damn men were lying to me! If they were not lying, they were giving me an answer so jumbled it could be interpreted a half-dozen ways. All I asked from the young doctors was: "Say it like it is." What I got was garbage!

I am not a patient fellow, and I am quite sure my anger with the FMGs was only too plain. "Why the hell can't you tell me the truth?" I exploded more than once. Gradually, I learned that men who were apparently lying to me were in fact responding as their cultures had taught them to respond. It had nothing to do with truth or falsehood. As children in some countries, they learned to interpret a question in terms of the response the questioner wanted to hear. That is the answer they gave. Any other answer brought punishment. I was told, and found it possible to believe, that some of their fellow countrymen who unashamedly told the truth disappeared and were never seen again. Bending the truth to suit the questioner's desires, and even outright duplicity, became second nature.

Once we got on track with the FMGs and mutual understanding increased, the quality of hospital care and staff interactions became relatively smooth. By the mid-fifties, we had advanced to the point of bringing on additional house staff. I found new pleasure in working with surgeons like Dr. Tom Flotte, from the University of Michigan, and Dr. Robert Buxton, who later took the chair of surgery at the University of Maryland. Dr. Flotte was a prime technician in vascular surgery, and a top-notch recruiter to boot. Together, we ran the surgical services at Maryland General. Dr. Flotte became Chief of Surgery in teaching and training, and the head of vascular surgery. I became Chief of Surgery in charge of visiting staff and the head of General Surgery. A real coup occured when Dr. Warfield Fisor completed his assignments as head of surgery at the Johns Hopkins Hospital, and Chairman of the American Board of Surgery. He saw the caliber of our services and joined us as

Chief of Maryland General's Surgical Department.

My "blood, sweat and tears" paid off!

Throughout years of advances in medicine never to be seen again, we somehow managed to attract and keep a full cohort of resident surgeons. "We managed" makes that achievement seem simple, but it became tough and then got tougher. The medical hierarchy steadily tightened the rules for the accreditation of hospital residences to such a degree that it became almost impossible to hold accreditation without university connections. Professional demands made our next move the formation of a joint residency program with the School of Medicine at the University of Maryland. This arrangement worked well and lasted well into the 1980s.

Competition for high-quality graduates of US medical schools constantly increased due to the declining number of graduates. These were the years when leaders of medical Associations and the administrators of Schools of Medicine looked the other way rather than focus on the problem of increasing numbers of foreign medical graduates. Year by year, foreign graduates continued to swell our medical ranks while medical schools cut their undergraduate admissions due to "a physician surplus."

The truth is, there is no surplus of American physicians, and never has been. Why the profession refuses an open discussion of one of its most pressing problems defies rational explanation. Why not bring the truth out into the open? Why not discuss what can be done about a situation which clearly needs addressing? Shall we shrink from the truth? Let's face this fact head on: *Nearly 100% of the presumed surplus of physicians in the United States is caused by the FMGs who came here to complete their training and then did not return to their homelands.*

From all indications, leading medical academics and medical association managements trust time to correct FMG problems, but current attempts at academic controls and wishful thinking can only make things worse. One modification of our program could be to eliminate citizenship for any foreign doctor based on marriage to an American citizen. That alone could help to prevent setting up a permanent practice in the US. Another possibility would be to remove all controls and let demand and supply settle who stays and who goes. Is this feasible? Maybe yes, maybe no. The point is the medical myopia that dominates the situation now needs the correction of free and open discussion. Politics obscured by medical myopia must go.

A lesser lesson in medical politics came in my hospital experience in Havre de Grace. It showed once again how some doctors can be more than mean-spirited; they can be vicious. In an earlier example of this fact of medical life, I described how my opportunity to reorganize the staff at Elkton General Hospital was foiled by a fine surgeon and deeply religious man at the University of Maryland. The origin of that opportunity was our success in reorganizing and upgrading Harford General Hospital in Havre de Grace.

To appreciate how my experience in medical meanness came about, it is necessary to understand life in the small town of Havre de Grace, MD. Anyone who likes small town life would find it easy to love life in Havre de Grace in years just after World War II. This town was pure Maryland, from its Catholic-inspired beginnings to its geography. Its homes and businesses sit overlooking the magnificent Susquehanna River just before the waters flow into one of the world's greatest estuaries, the Chesapeake Bay. The area is a favorite habitat of wildlife and game fish, including such favorites of the region as rockfish, blue crabs, Chesapeake Bay oysters, and clams. Canada geese, swans, and a huge variety of wild ducks migrate along the river and take up overnight residencies on the area known as the Chesapeake Bay Flats.

But people are people everywhere. Although most of the people in Havre de Grace practiced the Catholic religion faithfully, the community also had its seamier side. Its half-mile racetrack attracted typical followers of the ponies. Males were gamblers, touts, and assorted "high livers." Females included a temporary contingent of prostitutes. During the annual racing weeks, town business slowed to a semi-halt. Gossip circulated that some of the town's best known doctors let down what was left of their hair to join in the action. Rumors had doctors doing abortions in secret places at night, and one wildly circulated rumor had it that doctors were parties to making unwanted babies available for a price.

Truth or rumors and idle gossip, it was a messy situation that affected the focal point of medical practice in the region, Harford Memorial Hospital. Moreover, it was an open secret that Harford Memorial needed a clean-up. Doctors practicing at the hospital were accustomed to doing much as they pleased, when they pleased, and without paying any more attention than legally necessary to medical protocols: typical small-town stuff. The most notable of these free wheeling practitioners was Dr. Hugh O'Reilly who had been the town's sole surgeon doing general practice and surgery for some 30 years. A staunch Catholic in a community run largely by other Catholics, Dr. O'Reilly's influence in medicine and other areas was not to be trifled with. Membership in the American College of Surgeons gave him near control of the area's medical structure. At that time, elevation of new doctors to the College of Surgeons depended on the recommendation of local fellows like Dr. O'Reilly who had been an organizing member. With that kind of power, few non-members of the College dared to cross him. The fact that O'Reilly had been "grandfathered" into the College when it was too new to require examinations and surgical credentials meant nothing. Dr. O'Reilly was in; others were out.

Harford Memorial's trustees finally reached a firm decision to improve the hospital's methods and procedures. The goal was to clean out some undesirable practices, set up an improved staff organization, and generally upgrade the level of medicine conducted throughout the hospital. Promptly following the Board's decision, a number of the younger general physicians in Havre de Grace and surrounding communities like Aberdeen, Perryville, Port Deposit, Rising Sun, Bel Air, and Edgewood took part in discussions leading to a proposed staff reorganization.

Anyone not in medical practice will have problems understanding the sensitivity of reorganizing a hospital staff. Not only are massive egos and fragile temperaments involved, reputations and income can be affected up or down. Fearing resistance, those of us who participated in selecting hospital officers behaved timidly — there is no other word for it. Maybe such timidity is excusable when one's livelihood and reputation are subject to attack in a town where everyone knows everyone, and word gets around. Anyway, we selected only older, established physicians as the way to avoid unwanted friction getting the reorganization in place. Almost to a man, the doctors chosen were friends or otherwise closely allied with members of the Board.

The irony of our timidity was instantly visible. The men newly chosen to run Harford Memorial were just not suited temperamentally and professionally to their new responsibilities. Many of them were physicians the Board members believed to be sources of hospital deficiencies! In a word, the noble effort at reorganization was a flop. We put up with the situation for another year, and then seized the opportunity to elect qualified persons to offices where problems were most noticeable.

Surgery was one of those areas. I was elected Chief of Surgery. I promptly set up rules for the department and a monitoring system to make sure they were followed. Every surgical patient at the hospital began to receive a level of medical care higher than had been available in the past. I was neither surprised nor disappointed when I found that the least-qualified, most opinionated doctors with hospital privileges sought private meetings with members of the Board to express their discontent. Anticipating their response, I had taken steps to support my actions and policies, and when Board members faced me with a report of a disgruntled physician, I had chapter and verse to show who was right and who was wrong.

Every day was trying, and pushing through the hospital improvements against physician resistance damaged my personal relations with physicians with whom I had to work. Resistance to new requirements is understandable and quite human, but that doesn't make being the target of resistance any easier to take. If we had not seen clear evidence of improvements we could never have carried things through; however, we stuck together, persevered, and in months the hospital's greatly improved quality of medical care was clear to staff and public alike. One of the few pleasures of the experience came when nurses told me many times how glad they were to see order come out of the former chaos which they had been forced to contend with.

Not everyone was joyful by any means, especially those who were brought into line through less than pleasant corrections. The doctor most unhappy, and most willing to let everyone hear about his unhappiness, was the fervently religious Dr. Hugh O'Reilly. Until the reorganization, many doctors had hidden their distaste for O'Reilly out of self-protection. In the new staffing and revised atmosphere of the hospital, they made fewer efforts to hide their true feelings. Dr. O'Reilly got the message and didn't appreciate it. What we didn't know was that Dr. O'Reilly intended to avenge his lowered stature.

By the second year after reorganization, we had a staff and system in place strong enough to satisfy the credential criteria of the American College of Surgeons. The entire medical staff and the Board of Directors supported our application for acceptance by the College unanimously. It was a happy occasion to fill out the papers and send them in. At last we would be in a fully accredited hospital!

Two months went by while we heard nothing. During a staff meeting, someone asked if anyone knew why it was taking so long to be accredited. The secretary at the meeting brought out the papers and we began to review the process step by step to see if we had overlooked anything. Suddenly, Dr. O'Reilly audibly cleared his throat. Everyone looked at him. A self-satisfied smile creased his fleshy, well-lined face.

"Fellows, I think you are well aware that I am the only member of the American College of Surgeons in this hospital," he said. His smile increased as if in grandfatherly correction of small children. He was savoring a long-awaited moment. "I felt it was my duty to write to the College about some problems here. They have written me about a delay —"

He got no further. What he had done to us needed no explanation. "Who the hell do you think you are!" someone exploded. A doctor next to me, his face red with indignation, pointed a finger at Dr. O'Reilly and shouted, "I always knew you were a cheap excuse for a surgeon, but this is low even for you!" The outbursts were so violent, the silenced Dr. O'Reilly, no longer smiling, got up and left the room. We settled down after that and discussed what we could do to undo Dr. O'Reilly's mischief. I cannot pretend to understand Dr. O'Reilly's willingness to destroy the benefits of accreditation to the hospital and its practicing surgeons. If this were an isolated case, it could be ignored. Small-minded people and bigots rise to positions in medicine just as they do in other professions. In fact, it happens in medical politics so often that doctors learn fast to recognize their friends and enemies and act accordingly. One of the most dangerous acts in medicine is to challenge a physician exercising power over his peers. The damage such a person can do, *and does do*, is seldom seen outside the profession, but like the profession's curse, its medical myopia is only too real.

Dr. O'Reilly was a walking, talking example of Lord Acton's rule: power corrupts. The man was not a religious hypocrite. I am sure he was totally true to his faith. Yet he used his position as a senior surgeon to club other doctors into meeting his wishes. He was also a blatant user of his leadership in the town's Catholic church. If you were Catholic and needed a doctor, that meant you saw Dr. O'Reilly or one of the doctors he recommended. He also managed to discourage people from seeing non-Catholic doctors by smiling his weasel-smile and commenting "He's not of the faith, you know." Once this happened where other doctors and I were present, and someone growled, "What does being of the faith have to do with competence?" O'Reilly fixed his questioner with another grin and replied casually, "I just thought you ought to know. That's all."

We took no specific action with the American College of Surgeons at the time, but word about Dr. O'Reilly's letter to the College got around small-town Havre de Grace where everyone knows everyone. I remained uncharacteristically aloof from the situation and no one ever told me what soon resolved our accreditation problem. My guess is that the hospital was too important to the most prominent citizens of the community for its Directors to let Dr. O'Reilly hurt it with unjustified criticism. Within a matter of days, we learned that Dr. O'Reilly had changed his mind and wrote the College that he no longer found problems at the hospital. We were immediately approved and have held accreditation ever since.

Chapter Thirteen
Fraud And Punishment

My clinic in Havre de Grace was almost enough to occupy me full-time. There were enough broken bones just from accidents on the highways passing through the region to keep our orthopedists and an X-ray/cast man busy. The clinic provided a fully equipped Physical Therapy department and a support staff including receptionists, nurses, and office personnel. Altogether, the clinic employed 15-17 permanent personnel plus substitutes and relief persons. The clinic became known throughout the region for high quality medical and surgical services, and I was extremely proud of our reputation.

Heady days! Basking a little in my success and the recognition of my peers, I had no way of knowing my integrity would soon be tested as never before. Not only would my integrity be put on the line, I was riding for a fall.

Leading up to the test of my character were problems I have just described in improving Harford Memorial's surgical program. A special problem, typical of a small hospital in a rural community where everyone knew everyone else by reputation if not personally, was the hospital's policy in granting physician privileges. The policy was "fairness to all," and that meant I had to allow all doctors with privileges at the hospital to continue if I had any possible way to manage it. Unfortunately, many physicians had been given hospital privileges simply because they had been practicing in the region for years. Many of the older doctors were treating patients as they had been doing all their lives, with little regard for radical advances in medical techniques and medicines. Correcting hospital practices of well-regarded, but relatively inept older doctors was a never-ending headache because actions could not be taken that might damage these physicians' reputations. Days came, however, when incompetence became more than I could ignore. Trying to help and correct doctors as privately and sensitively as possible, those involved usually resented being told they were doing something wrong by a "young whippersnapper from the City."

When I agreed to reorganize and direct the surgical staff, I knew it was not the way to make friends. So what? I had never put friendship ahead of professional responsibility. This was no time to change. What could not be known was the amount of antagonism I was generating through my efforts to upgrade the staff and hospital practices. Sometimes being right can create more enemies than being in the wrong.

Not many months into the job of reorganizing the surgical staff, I sat down and faced facts. Progress was so slow it would make a turtle look like a sprinter. The time had come to make a choice. Either bring the hospital's surgical staff up to my professional standards, or resign. Was it time to quit a task generating unavoidable controversy — walk away and let someone else do it? Never having turned my back on a professional challenge, I just couldn't do that, but what were my options? No sooner had I asked myself that question than there was an answer. It was simple. Why had I never thought of it before? (Once again, it's always amazing that once a solution to a problem is found, it's a mystery why it was never found before.)

The way to upgrade the staff was to bring in doctors who would upgrade it. What doctors? How could they be brought to Harford Memorial? Under what conditions? The doctors I needed were under my nose! They were qualified senior and intermediate residents training under my supervision at Maryland General Hospital. If we developed a specialized training program for them under my direction, putting them on a temporary house staff of Harford Memorial should not be a big problem.

The more thought given to this idea, the more sense it made. If we brought in carefully chosen residents from Maryland General, it would improve the overall level of surgical care at Harford Memorial at a single stroke. Selected residents would gain valuable training as well. Most of all — yes, indeed, most of all! — the residents would be Ross Pierpont's eyes and ears in the surgical suite, the emergency suite, and the patients' rooms. I would know the quality of medical care in the entire hospital around the clock!

As the lead physician in surgical management at both Maryland General and Harford Memorial, I wrote a new residency program for Maryland General residents to train at Harford Memorial over periods of three to six months. Like the concept itself, getting the residency program approved was even easier than I thought. I pressed some personal buttons I had developed in both hospitals and won the approval of the program by both institutions without delay.

The program was an immediate success. Patient care improved noticeably, almost from the day the program started. It took pressure off the nurses' daily work; they liked the program and let others know it. The residents were pleased and training at Harford Memorial became highly desired because I did not hesitate to give the new doctors increased responsibilities in line with improved skills. In bowling terms, Pierpont was looking at a 10-strike.

One of my routine responsibilities at Harford Memorial was reviewing the applications of doctors for hospital privileges. I thought nothing of it when I received an application for minor surgical privileges from a young, ambitious general physician named Dr. John de Simona. He had opened an office in Havre de Grace and was doing well. Just as Dr. O'Reilly had built his very successful practice on his Irish-Catholic ties, Dr. de Simona cultivated first and second generation Italian-Americans in the county. There was no reason to deny him hospital privileges, and they were granted.

Observing Dr. de Simona's treatment of his patients at the hospital gave me some concern. There is something in me that rings an alarm when I see a doctor doing something I know from experience or instinct is questionable: "What explains that unusual diagnosis? Why did he deviate from procedures proven successful in treating a hundred thousand patients? Does the man have a character flaw we don't see?" My reservations melted away as Dr. de Simona accepted our criticisms and counseling in full cooperation. From a relatively inauspicious beginning, he became a trusted colleague. Dr. de Simona was a likeable person, and all in all a reasonably good doctor. His practice was solid and it grew. Observing development like that is one of the genuine satisfactions of medical practice.

Liking Dr. de Simona as I did, I had no way of knowing his coming to see me one morning was the first event in my downfall. Hailing into my office he said in his usual breezy, jaunty fashion, "See you a minute, Dr. Pierpont?"

I smiled. "Of course, John. What's on your formidable mind?"

"Ross, I've got a brother who's finishing his surgical training, and he wants me to help him get started. He likes what he sees us doing here in Havre de Grace — both of us have great respect for you — and he's asked me to ask you about a place on your Surgical Clinic staff."

I knew Dr. de Simona was "schmoozing" me with that "great respect for you" line, but Dr. de Simona was a natural schmoozer. I thought no more about it. "John," I said, "I've seen your brother only casually on a couple of occasions, and you know I don't make staff decisions on the spur of the moment. Your brother has several months to go before he finishes his training. Let me think if we have a place for him and I'll get back to you. Your brother's name is James, isn't it? "

"I'm John, he's James, two 'Js'," John de Simona said, grinning. "Thanks a lot, Ross. I appreciate your help."

With a full plate of immediate responsibilities to take care of, I put John de Simona's request on the back burner. John commented on his request for a slot for brother James to someone on my staff, who relayed the comment to me. When John reminded me, tactfully, of his request, I had no choice but to check it out.

Checking the character and ability of a doctor with other doctors is about as sensitive a job as you can get. Information has to come more through a discussion than from outright questions. Another physician, no matter how well he may know me, is not going to bad mouth someone he has worked with side by side. So I found ways to introduce the subject of James de Simona into conversations with his professors, and others who knew him. The few specifics I got suggested that brother James had some failings similar to those which had originally troubled me earlier with John. However, John had developed into a satisfactory generalist, and he had certainly ingratiated himself with the community.

Most troubling was not what James' professors and associates said. It was what they didn't say. Not one offered a word of praise for the man. Strange. I had no choice but to persist. Finally, I went to see one of his professors in medical school. The professor grinned at one of my roundabout questions of de Simona's ability and said, "Ross, you don't give up, do you! I'm not going to judge Jim de Simona for you. That's your job, and I think you've talked to enough people to know there's not much favorable going for him. OK?"

I said, "Herb, his brother has built a solid position in Havre de Grace and now has come on for James. I can't make room in my clinic for him at this point, and I don't have reason to reject an applicant who seems to be completing his training in a satisfactory manner."

Medical school professors have responsibilities not only for their students, but also their profession. I was playing that card. Herb Montgomery collected his thoughts in silence. At last he spoke very slowly. "I don't think he is a lot better or worse than others we are graduating — as an MD. For reasons I will not go into, the man does not inspire trust."

"If you had an opening in your practice, would you take him in?"

I had gone too far. Herb's normally genial look turned a bit grim. He said, "You do not expect me to answer that question."

His refusal to answer the question really provided the answer I needed. James de Simona didn't inspire trust, and Herb Chisholm would not put him on his staff. The only explanation was that James de Simona had some sort of character difficulty. Knowing this gave me a real problem. If I refused to give a part-time position to James de Simona, I would owe his brother an explanation. I had none, other than negatives I could not attribute to anyone. On the other hand, everything I had learned about brother James told me I should not take him on the clinic's staff. I put John aside several times hoping he would find another place for his brother, but John persisted. Finally I took up the situation with the staff seniors. I related everything I knew making sure they understood the difference between the facts of the situation and my interpretation of the facts. The staff reluctantly agreed that John's position on our staff earned the right to give his brother a trial. I closed the meeting by saying I would prepare a tightly written contract with an arms-length association between James de Simona and the surgical clinic.

I called John to tell him our decision. He immediately called his brother, who asked John to tell us our proposed arrangement suited him perfectly. He intended, he said, to build his full time practice in Baltimore City. John asked if I would have our proposed contract drawn up stating exactly what the terms would be. James would be only too glad, said brother John, to work with us.

James' contract specified he would work with his brother in Havre de Grace as the two of them decided, and our Surgical Clinic would back up their practice on an as-needed basis. James' base of medical activities would be in Baltimore.

We neither saw nor heard anything about brother James for a number of weeks. John came by one day to tell me that his brother had joined him in his practice and the arrangement suited them fine. The news was a relief; not having to worry about bringing brother James into the clinic suited me perfectly. About three months went by fairly peacefully. Then, out of the blue, James de Simona applied to the hospital for unrestricted surgical privileges entirely on his own.

This young Italian doctor had chutzpah!

Although I had no doubt that James de Simona did not have sufficient credentials for unrestricted privileges, I had no facts to back up my doubts. I have long argued that one of medicine's biggest troubles is the empowerment of doctors to grant or withhold privileges based on personalities, personal likes and dislikes, and subjective opinion. Now here I was, "knowing" James de Simona was not fully qualified and unable to stop him.

We labored over James' application for hospital privileges for a week and got nowhere. The net result was to give him temporary privileges. These did not involve him with the surgical clinic in any way.

James de Simona had not been on Emergency Room rotation more than two weeks before the resident staff brought irregularities in his diagnoses and treatments to my attention. Reports of irregularities almost invariably originated with his patients in the Emergency Room. High-speed automobile accidents on nearby highways constantly brought victims to the hospital's Emergency Room for immediate attention. When James de Simona was in charge of the ER, strange things happened. Patient after patient was diagnosed with a dislocated neck, hospitalized in a neck collar and traction, and treated for days. Most of his patients left the hospital fitted with immobilizing turnbuckle collars and followed for weeks or even months. A special eye-opener was the number of patients coming to see Dr. Jim from distant places. In one case, the patient came to little Havre de Grace from Connecticut. Irregularities that began as doubtful blossomed to a full-blown question of medical fraud.

I collected complete histories on six especially troublesome cases and called for the X-rays. The X-rays showed that the necks of de Simona's patients were normal. I called Jim de Simona in to explain. He glanced at the X-rays and answered without hesitation. "Every one of these was taken after I had reduced the dislocation."

I had to accept the explanation even though it left me more suspicious than satisfied. A few more days went by as I pondered what could be done to clear up an unacceptable situation. Then a resident reported Jim de Simona was doing unusual surgery on knees for torn cartilage. I asked a doctor I trusted completely to check the record of one of his operations for torn cartilage and get back to me. He reported James de Simona had not even entered the knee joint. What was supposed to be evidence of torn cartilage removed was nothing more than a piece of fat and fascia.

Calling for and reviewing the charts and pathology of the case verified what the resident surgeon and a second doctor had reported to me.

I remember sitting in my office looking at records of Jim de Simona's practice at Harford Memorial with a sinking feeling in my gut. The more I thought about this man and what he was doing, not only to his fellow physicians and the hospital, but to his patients, the more I had to squelch my anger. He was a disgrace to the profession, yet I lacked the power to remove him. The worst possible action I could take would be to charge Jim de Simona with wrongful action I could not prove beyond doubt. The man and his brother had made many friends in the community who would be certain to stand up for him. Unproved charges would accomplish nothing and could destroy me completely. The fraud for a doctor we had authorized to practice in the surgical department would continue.

What were the options? I could resign my position and say nothing, as I had thought about doing when facing the hospital's staff problems. Someone else could cope with James de Simona's fraudulent medical practice. The hospital could get someone else to conduct a further investigation. My final choice was to conduct my own investigation and steel myself for one of the most ugly experiences of my life: charging a fellow doctor with crimes against his oath and profession.

If I believed in myself, I really had no choice. I bit the bullet and pursued the investigation on my own. By now there was no way to keep a lid on the situation. Secrets in a hospital last about as long as the second shift. Investigation confirmed the worst.

We identified 115 specific cases handled by Jim or John de Simona in which surgical records were falsified, or cases wrongly diagnosed. We found specimens removed at operations misreported resulting in a false diagnosis of injuries and unjustified treatment, and more.

The income generated by the two de Simonas was enormous. They were referring cooperating Emergency Room patients to Elrod Hubbard, the slick lawyer who sat on the hospital's board and provided legal counsel to the hospital. Elrod Hubbard had filed more than a hundred personal injury claims with insurance companies. Medical fees and damages claimed from insurance companies totaled, as best we could tell, more than 15 million 1995 dollars!

I probably should have consulted legal counsel on my own, but I refused to turn this into a lawyers' circus. It was a medical problem. My strongest desire was to resolve it as a medical problem. Yet, looking at my problem from every angle, no answer came forth. If the de Simonas had not locked up the allegiance — possibly the complicity! — of the hospital's own lawyer, my way would have been easier. No question, the lawyer was the key, and there was no way to turn that key. Moreover, any action by me against the de Simonas was vulnerable to a charge of conflict of interest. The fellows on my staff and I were surgeons; the de Simonas were surgeons. Hence we could be charged with trying to knock them out of Havre de Grace and take on their patients for ourselves. Important in dealing with physicians is the matter of personal loyalties. To charge a physician you consider a friend with fraud, even with complete proof, is so distasteful to many doctors that, unfortunately perhaps, they prefer to pinch their noses against the stink. Unanimous support even from my own staff was not guaranteed.

Putting first things first, a first act was to protect the hospital's patients from potential harm. I instructed all residents to monitor the in-patient care of Jim de Simona's patients and report any departures from normal to me in person. Restrictions went into effect covering Jim de Simona's operating room activities for a case-by-case analysis. Material Jim de Simona removed by surgery would be compared with operative notes, and any discrepancies made a matter of record. The de Simona brothers knew full well what was being done to them. There was no doubt that John's original "respect for me" had been turned into hatred; however, they were smart enough to accept their restrictions and wait me out.

The de Simonas could be patient as long as I did nothing to restrict their access to the Emergency Room. This room was their practice expander, the source of patients who would cooperate in faked injuries and filing insurance claims. There was absolutely no way to stop the brothers as long as Jim de Simona was a doctor on call for the Emergency Room. Monitoring his ER activities was a practical impossibility.

I called a staff meeting to tackle the ER problem. Every doctor in the room recognized that we had no way to stop Jim de Simona as long as he could practice unsupervised surgery in the Emergency Room. At the same time, not one of us wanted to do what we had to do because it meant publicly admitting a member of our medical family was rotten. It would become very, very messy, and every one of us dreaded the explosion our action would trigger. Reluctantly, we agreed that the only way to stop what de Simona was doing was to take him out of ER coverage.

When the decision was reached, I looked at every doctor present and their faces reinforced my decision. I spoke slowly and deliberately: "Gentlemen, I am legally and professionally responsible for de Simona's actions. What has been said in this room today leaves me no choice. I take full responsibility for removing Dr. James de Simona from Emergency Room coverage."

Did anyone say anything in response? I don't remember hearing a single word as the doctors of my staff slowly got up and left the room. They were out of it. I would do what had to be done.

To my surprise, the hospital's gossip belt was strangely silent following the meeting. I went about my daily practice just as before, until the next month's ER rotation was posted. James de Simona's name did not appear on the list.

The brothers de Simona were frauds but not dumb. They knew that seeing me would get them nowhere so they didn't bother. Instead, they went straight to the Board of Directors where they had the attorney in their hip pocket. Naturally the Board of Directors gave them a prompt hearing. Although I was not present, I knew that the hour the de Simonas met with the Board was exactly the hour their cooperating attorney, sitting as counsel to the Board, would recommend that the Board reverse my action in removing Jim de Simona from ER coverage. Who stood to gain, who stood to lose, by such reversal? Gainers were the de Simonas and their attorney. The two doctors would be free to continue their plundering of the ER. Their attorney would continue to get fat legal fees from settlements by the insurance companies. The losers would be Harford Memorial, the insurance companies and the public. Harford Memorial would become a partner — unwittingly, perhaps, but nonetheless a partner — in the mis-diagnosis and fraudulent treatment of ER patients. The insurance companies would continue to pay fraudulent claims. The people would have to pay increased insurance premiums. And I was helpless to stop it.

News of James de Simona's request for a reversal of his removal from the ER spread throughout surgical services, and filtered back to me. Knowing the relationship between the brothers de Simonas and the Board's attorney, I also knew I had two and three-quarter strikes against me. The pitcher was winding up for strike three. There was no question of the outcome. Integrity had me in its grasp, and I had to lose. The only question was when and in what form the Board would set me down.

There is little doubt about which way the Board would have gone had it not been for J. P. Graham. J.P. had been the Chief Operating Officer of a multi-billion dollar industrial enterprise until he retired to live in Harford County. He was oriented toward corporate decision-making and strong corporate responsibilities, and known to be a strong backer of corporate policies once they were made. Not so incidentally, J.P. was the largest contributor to the Board of Directors and in turn Harford Memorial Hospital.

J.P. had a well-deserved reputation for fair play. My guess is that he doubted the Board was getting the full story about my decision, and he suggested a meeting between the Board of Directors, me as Chief of Surgical Services, and the President of the Medical Staff. In any event I was advised to appear before the Board with the President of the Medical staff, and to bring along a doctor from the visiting staff.

I invited Dr. Buzz Richards of the visiting staff to join me and Dick

Norment, President of the Medical Staff, for the hearing. Buzz was a true friend who knew the full story, and agreed to come although not overjoyed at the prospect. On a day as gloomy as the subject of the meeting, the three of us entered the Board Room together. We faced nine members of the Board with grim-faced Chairman Harry Taylor - a man I had known and liked for many years— sitting in the center. All had yellow pads and pencils before them. It was altogether a Boardroom scene right out of the movies.

Chairman Taylor's main interest was his Havre de Grace automobile dealership, with Harford Memorial Hospital as his prestigious hobby. He opened the meeting by putting into the record my action in taking Dr. James de Simona out of the Emergency Room rotation. It was a brief recitation that concluded by stating on behalf of the Board how members of the Board were concerned about an action which appeared arbitrary and unnecessary. He was invoking the hospital's standing "fairness to all" doctrine on behalf of doctors engaged in fraud. I have often wondered what was really on Harry Taylor's mind when he said to me, looking directly and confidently into my eyes: "Dr. Pierpont, I speak for this Board when I tell you we have great respect for you and your ability to manage the hospital's surgical services, but we also have the responsibility to protect the rights and privileges of all doctors here. Can you explain your action in removing Dr. James de Simona from the Emergency Room rotation?"

"Great respect for you..." What irony! That exact phrase had been mouthed months before by John de Simona when he asked my help in bringing his brother to Havre de Grace. Knowing I had to lose the hearing, I had time during the Chairman's prelude to study the Board's attorney. He studiously observed his yellow pad, making a few doodles to amuse himself. He knew, as I knew, what the de Simonas were doing. You lousy crook! How do you feel when you look at your children? You are worse than the de Simonas, defiling your position on the Hospital Board and every doctor here. Somehow, somewhere, I told myself, all of this will catch up with you.

Not only was the Board attorney my known enemy, I couldn't identify a single friend on the Board which was about to pass a verdict on my actions, but I had accepted this fight, and there was no backing away.

"Yes, sir, I'll be glad to explain my action. It became necessary because there was no other way to protect the hospital's patients, and in turn the hospital. Everything else was, and is, secondary to that responsibility. Please let me review for you my position as Chief of Surgery. My responsibilities include the surgical department's inpatient cases, the policies and procedures of the operating theater, and surgical activities of the Emergency Room. In addition, I am responsible for surgical staff appointments and monitoring all surgical activities that go on in this hospital. Up until now, the way I have met those responsibilities has never been questioned. My integrity in disposing of surgical problems of all kinds has never been questioned."

I looked from the Chairman to the Board's attorney. A slim, poised, well-tailored man about my own age, he looked me straight in the eye. The confidence of his body language was not hard to interpret. It said: "You've met your match, Pierpont. I hold all the cards, goodbye."

I continued to make sure everything went on the record. "Several months ago, Dr. James de Simona's handling of Emergency Room cases was brought to my attention by resident surgeons and others as being questionable if not improper. The questions about Dr. James de Simona's practices were so serious I initiated an investigation of his most recent cases to determine what was going on. I found, as a minimum, that James de Simona was regularly departing from general standards of patient care. I discussed the problem with my staff looking for a way to avoid continued improper patient care, while also avoiding removing Dr. de Simona from the surgical staff.

"We decided we could meet the problem by letting Dr. de Simona continue with scheduled patients provided our resident house staff closely monitored the conduct of this part of his practice. Fortunately, our resident house staff is fully capable of doing this. I grant you, our decision was not the best answer to the problem. It was the only way we could see to proceed at the time. This arrangement has not been completely satisfactory, but so far it has protected both the patients and the hospital."

The Board could have collectively yawned. They wanted nothing more than getting this hearing over with and forgetting it ever happened. I wouldn't let them off so easily.

"While letting Dr. de Simona continue, I also continued my investigation. Operative notes, X-rays, and the inspection of specimens from surgery conducted by Dr. de Simona have shown consistent deviations from accepted surgical procedures. The fact, gentlemen, is that Dr. de Simona has totally falsified records in more than 100 cases! Everything in his record showed medical misconduct, or worse."

At that, even the Board's attorney stirred a little. I should have repeated the statement of falsified records, but - well, who's perfect, and, anyway, it would have made no difference. Stubbornly, I went on: "My question continued to be what could be done to protect all concerned. Our monitoring of inpatient care and Dr. de Simona's willingness to cooperate in the management of his inpatient cases has made it possible to allow him to continue with scheduled cases. Unfortunately, the Emergency Room was an altogether different situation. It gave us problems without a solution. I am sure everyone on this Board understands there simply is no way to monitor what a doctor does in the ER when he is in control of that room with no other physician present to observe his actions."

I glanced around the Board to guess if they appreciated the dilemma. They endured my pause in total silence. If they understood, they hid it well. For the record, I continued: "As this Board well knows, I have never dodged the responsibilities I took on when asked to reorganize the hospital's surgical staff. I am charged with the standards of care in the surgical department. I am responsible for what goes on in the Emergency Room whether I am in the hospital or away. While my responsibilities go on around the clock, I have no way to stop a doctor from continued mis-diagnosing and unnecessary treatment in the ER, if he chooses to engage in such practices. Investigation has shown that James de Simona has regularly diagnosed his ER cases improperly and provided his patients with unnecessary treatment. What I have just told you, please remember, was found in more than 100 James de Simona surgical cases!"

I paused, looking at faces hiding whatever the men were thinking. "After consultation with the executive medical staff, we decided with greatest reluctance that we could not, in good conscience, permit James de Simona to continue operating unsupervised in the Emergency Room. That is why I removed him from ER rotation."

I stopped and waited. The Chairman made a note of some kind on the yellow pad before him, looked up at me, and spoke without conferring with any other member of the Board. My instinct was right. The Board had met and reached a decision about de Simona before I had spoken a single word. No wonder I had looked into blank eyes and grim faces. I might as well have spoken in Hindustani — maybe it would have been more effective in Hindustani.

"Dr. Pierpont, I am speaking for the Board when I tell you it is our desire for you to continue Dr. James de Simona in the Emergency Room rotation."

The memory of that moment has never dimmed with time. I sat there beside two fellow physicians who, I was sure, felt about our profession as I did, and still do. Nonetheless, I was alone. No one could make my decision for me. I had accepted responsibility for my action. I could share that with no one. Whatever I now did, my action and its consequences would be part of me for the rest of my life. Why not accept the Board's position about James de Simona? It was their hospital, not mine! It would make my life easier if I walked away from my earlier decision with the excuse I was simply accepting the Board's desire. The Board's "desire?" The word was a sugar-coated denial of everything I had, long ago, sworn to uphold.

I tensed as if a cold hand had grabbed my throat. I knew what I was about to say, and I had no choice in saying it. I spoke as if my voice came from a stranger. "Gentlemen, I can understand your request. I came here hoping you would understand mine. Surely you know that I am both morally and legally responsible for the medical actions of Dr. James de Simona in this hospital when I write his name in the rotation of the Emergency Room."

I stopped to make sure of what I had to say. "I have no desire whatsoever to compromise any action the Board cares to make. I will be glad to include Dr. James de Simona in the ER rotation if the Board of Directors makes that appointment and takes the responsibility for it. I just do not believe I can do the appointing."

Harry Taylor's taught face told how much strain he was under as he heard what I had just said. He knew, as of course I knew, the Board would never take the responsibility for including de Simona in the ER rotation. The Board had already discussed the case privately, had reached its decision, and the Chairman had called this meeting sure of a smooth, over-and-done acceptance of the Board's recommendation. After all, the Board was the Board. What crazy kind of doctor would defy the Board's decision? Now I had put the ball in their court, and what had been decided in private was suddenly in question. No one said a word as if the members of the Board were digesting an unforeseen development: Pierpont refuses to go along! The debonair attorney for the Board, who had listened to me as if watching a doctor out of his senses, scribbled a word or two hastily on Harry Taylor's yellow pad. The Chairman nodded and, visibly unhappy, looked at the three of us. "This Board will recess for 15 minutes. Excuse us, gentlemen."

Dick Norment, Buzz Richards and I left the room and stood in the corridor waiting. I felt played out, my guts tight as a drum, but I knew we had heard only the preliminaries to the sentencing which would come when I faced the Board in a few minutes. Dick Norment said, "Well, Ross, you laid it on the line. You're right, but you set those men back on their heels. There wasn't a happy man on that Board when you got through with them!"

I looked at Dick, grateful for his presence. Surprising myself by thinking how I would feel if I were on that Board, I said, "You know, Dick, I don't for a minute like what I did in there, but what else could I do?"

Buzz Richards said, "It's the only thing you could do and live with yourself, Ross. We're dealing with a man that doesn't belong in the operating room alone, and every mother's child on that Board now has to know it. You took the high road. They're on another road. The only question now is, what will they come up with?"

A member of the Board came out and asked us to return. As we entered the Boardroom, the expressionless faces of the men on the Board said plainer than words we were going to hear some ugly news. Chairman Harry Taylor spoke to me deliberately and politely:

"Dr. Pierpont, we have considered every part of this situation. I assure you, we understand your problem, and I hope you understand ours. On behalf of all members of this Board sitting today, this is our decision. We are asking you, at the direction of this Board, to include Dr.

James de Simona on your Emergency Room rotation in a routine fashion. If you fail to do this, you will cause a Board of Directors action to remove you from your elected position as Chief of Surgery and to cancel your privileges at Harford Memorial Hospital."

Everyone on the Board looking at me seemed frozen in time. I seemed to be looking at a tableau. The cold hand I had felt on my neck earlier now pressed harder as, for first time in my life, I tasted defeat. Its gall welled up inside me. Climbing my way up the pathway to medical success, I had overcome poverty; I had beaten back envy and sometimes hostility. I had spent the long hours necessary to close the gaps in my professional capabilities. I had reorganized and built Harford Memorial's staff into a group any doctor could be proud of. Always confident I was doing what I was meant to do, so far I had always won. Now I had lost. I was lost, for I knew what I was about to do and it would cost me more than I wanted to think about.

They had given me the choice between maintaining my place in the hospital and maintaining my integrity. It was the moment of truth and there could be no doubt. In a voice not quite as strong as I wished, I spoke with no further hesitation. "Gentlemen, I understand your dilemma. I hope you understand the position you have put me in. I am not an impulsive person, acting without thought. I did not arrive at an extraordinarily difficult decision without giving it every consideration. In the interest of your consideration, what has changed?"

It was a dumb question. Chairman Taylor tapped his pencil on his yellow pad and replied without hesitation. "That is our offer. Take it or leave it."

I took a moment to let the significance of what was happening to me, and Harford Memorial, sink in. A major part of my life was falling down around me in broken pieces due to a conniving, thieving, incompetent youth named James de Simona. The ethics of a hospital I had admired were being contaminated. I replied without more delay. "If we can do no better, I don't see how I can change my mind."

Members of the Board looked at us. We looked at them. There was nothing more to be said. In silence, we arose and left the room. As we reached the corridor and the door closed behind us, Buzz Richards reached to grab me by the arm. "Ross, that was a son-of-a-bitch! I have never been more proud of a man than I am of you right now!"

Dick Noment shook his head slowly and spoke just as slowly. "Ross, right now you must be going through hell, and I feel for you. I only hope that this will work its way out and you'll land on your feet." He paused. "You always do, you know!"

I managed a half-laugh. We reached the end of the corridor and went our separate ways. One price of integrity can be aloneness.

The Board immediately carried out its promised action. My surgical practice — and presence — in Harford Memorial was over. Fortunately, my thriving surgical clinic, and my practices in Baltimore City were unaffected. I also had my immediate family who understood and respected what I refused to compromise regardless of the cost. At this time my mother, now in her sixties, was in good health and resolutely on her own. "It's a hurting, but you'll come out ahead in the long run," she said in her best schoolteacher way. My brothers were also doing well in their fields and living in Baltimore.

Grace, of course, knew about the de Simona brothers up to the hearing. I had waited to tell her what had happened until I reached home, and when she heard the news she exploded. "Ross, this is crazy! You tell the Board the hospital has a doctor who's a fraud — who's in partnership with a lawyer filing phony claims for personal injuries with insurance companies! The Board protects the guilty person, turns around and punishes you — you, the doctor protecting the hospital and the patients!" I said nothing and she simmered down. "What are you going to do about it?"

I had asked myself that same question ever since I left the hearing and the hospital. I said, "Grace, I have the Surgical Clinic and my practices in Baltimore to take care of. The Board has assumed total responsibility for the de Simona brothers from now on. What am I going to do? I am going to do as I've always done. I am going to practice medicine the best damn way I know how and let this thing run its course. I don't know how it will end, but depend on it, Grace, it will end!"

I could have been prophetic. Out of nowhere, two days after the meeting, a man named Calvin Meyers called me. He introduced himself on the telephone as a member of the Casualty Underwriters Investigative Bureau of an association of insurance companies. "I have heard about your problems with Dr. James de Simona, and I'd like to meet with you as soon as possible. I may be able to help."

"Good," I said. "When do you want to meet?"

"Does this Saturday suit you?"

"Fine."

"Where can I meet you?"

I thought a moment. "How about the University Club at Charles and Madison Street, at one o'clock Saturday?"

Meyers said he would be there, and promptly at one PM that Saturday I greeted a six foot, two inch tall and obviously fit man in his mid-thirties at the University Club. Meyers was an impressive man with piercing blue eyes, sandy hair, and not carrying an extra ounce of fat. He was, in fact, a walking demonstration of type casting of the ideal FBI man, which he had been before he went to work for the insurance industry. I would never have enjoyed tackling with this guy physically. Now that I think of it, physical competition with Meyers would never have entered my mind.

Lunch on Saturday at the University Club was always quiet and casual. We got a quiet table in one corner where we could talk. Lunch included the usual get-acquainted chit-chat and pleasantries. Afterward, Meyers filled me in on the reason for our meeting. The association he represented was the insurance industry's equivalent of the FBI. His job was to help hold down insurance fraud and the enormous payoffs when fraud is successful.

Meyers said, "Dr. James de Simona has become very well known to us. He has generated a very large number of very questionable claims due to equally questionable injuries. My investigation of his cases has convinced me that fraud is involved in a majority of his cases we have analyzed; a lot of money is involved."

Meyers aroused my curiosity. "What value have you put on his cases?"

"Claims originating with de Simona and placed through the same attorney — I think you know who he is —"

I laughed, interrupting him. "He's only the counsel for Harford Memorial's Board of Directors."

"Right," Meyers said. "The claims I've looked into, all from the same attorney, are in the neighborhood of $15 million and still going up."

"How many cases are involved in that $15 million?"

"I'm not sure, sitting here, of the exact number, but they have gone over a 115 so far. Would you care to see some of the cases involved?"

"You betcha!"

As Meyers took batches of papers from his briefcase, he remarked, "By the way, we know all about you and the courage you showed when you wouldn't go along with the Board's recommendation on James de Simona."

Meyer's records added to what my staff and I had uncovered in our investigation at Harford Memorial. Case after case contained fraudulent reports describing severe injuries of dislocation not confirmed by X-rays, claims of non-functioning due to serious disabilities, and repeated general medical claims, all without a shred of medical substantiation. The pattern of De Simona's practices with cooperating patients consistently demonstrated fraudulent diagnosing and reporting. It added up to such a huge number of suspicious or outright fraudulent cases, the only question was how long the de Simonas expected to get away with it. I was sure he did not know the insurance association was on his tail. After getting me booted from the hospital, he probably had uncorked a bottle of champagne and toasted his connection with the lawyer who also served as counsel for the hospital's Board of Directors.

We spent that entire afternoon, five full hours, examining the records. We had reached a first-name basis by the time I put down the last one and said, "Calvin, this is all very impressive. You have worked your tail off to get the goods on de Simona. Now what are you going to do about it, and how can it help me?"

"Ross, what you told the Board defending your decision to take James de Simona off Emergency Room duty clued us to confirm what we had basically suspected to that point. Your courage and the investigation you conducted identified de Simona's fraud and the abuse of patient care beyond doubt in my mind. For my money, you went beyond the call of duty when you stood up for what is right knowing you would be tossed out on your ear for standing up for what is right."

"Thanks, Calvin. Very nice of you. I appreciate the compliment, but compliments aren't going to do a hell of a lot fixing this situation. What are you and the insurance industry going to do about it?"

Calvin Meyers made a face and pointed to the stack of his reports. "I'm going to use these to prepare a complete report that will recommend that the multi-billion dollar insurance industry come down with everything it's got to prosecute everyone involved in this fraud."

"That's it?" I said. "What happens when you turn in your report?"

Calvin Meyers' look said he wished I hadn't asked that. He turned away briefly, then I swear moisture might have glistened in those piercing blue eyes. "Ross, the insurance industry hates washing dirty linen in public. Especially when a hospital, doctors, and the Board's attorney are involved. It would be a long drawn-out case bringing dozens of individual claimants into court. The media would get involved — "

"Is that bad?"

"Well, when you deal with the public like that who knows what effect it will have on the insurance business? People who run insurance don't like negative publicity."

I know when my path has been greased for a soft landing. I felt myself beginning to bristle as Meyers confirmed what he had just prepared me to hear.

"Ross, someone high up in the Association will read my report and ask counsel for an opinion. Chances are almost certain, counsel will recommend no legal action and negotiated settlements as cheaper than going to court. The millions involved in these cases? A small increase in premiums will more than cover it."

I stared at Calvin Meyers for a moment and called for the check. I had to get out of there — to walk, to breathe fresh air! I was still subject to a flare-up of my old, latent ulcer. To sit in the Club's restaurant one minute longer and contemplate what I had just spent hours going over was to risk physical misery. Meyers recognized my frustration, and, being a gentleman, thanked me for the lunch, quietly took his papers and left.

I called Meyers about a week later to see if he had filed his report; he had. The insurance association had it "under advisement." Which is where it sits today, for all I know. Not long after I called him, I read where automobile insurance premiums had been raised 5% or so. As I read the announcement, I thought: Only a handful of people knows what goes on behind rate increases. I knew, and I deeply resented the irresponsibility of insurance companies which had put their image ahead of the truth. Claiming to serve the public while turning a blind side to actions which, unchecked, stand to injure people as well as their own business is hypocrisy of the worst sort. In the long run, it is not even good business.

In the immediate aftermath of my dismissal from Harford Memorial, my practice kept me busy. Even as I did my best to put the de Simona experience behind me, wheels began to turn at Harford Memorial. Unknown to me, some of the "stony faces" I had seen on the Board of Harford Memorial belonged to men now behaving in a very un-stony fashion. A couple of the Board's members, far from satisfied over the handling of the de Simona situation and my dismissal, made sure that information about the hearing reached J.P. Graham. News spread through the hospital staff that this extremely wealthy and powerful man felt the Board had treated me shabbily. Without a word to me of any kind, J.P. and at least two members of the Board let the rest of the Board know they were dissatisfied with my dismissal.

The Board now faced a new dilemma. They couldn't reverse their decision knowing I would never agree to let James de Simona back on the ER rotation. On the other hand, people too powerful to ignore insisted I should not have been dismissed.

I would have given a lot to have heard the arguments that swirled around me and my performance at the hospital. No, now that I think further about it, maybe it is just as well I never learned who was for me and against me, and why. One thing I especially would have liked to know, however, was how the Board's attorney felt about the controversy. In spite of his massive ego and confidence in his power with the Board, he had to have some very uncomfortable moments aware that Ross Pierpont and the de Simona problems were not about to go away.

One day not long after my hearing with the Board, Buzz Richards crossed the street from the hospital to my office in the Surgical Clinic. Entering with a half-grin, he said, "I guess you've heard some of the scuttlebutt about you making the rounds in the hospital."

I looked at him trying to figure out his small grin. "I heard J.P. Graham had held the Board's feet to the fire. Buzz, you know I try my best to pay no attention to hospital gossip — too many other things to think about. You didn't come in here to get a piece of candy. What's on your mind?"

"The Board has come to clearly recognize your unsurpassed surgical talents, Dr. Pierpont," Buzz said lightly. "They've made you an offer and asked me to give it to you. In a nutshell, you are welcome to come back with full privileges, except you are not offered the position of Chief of Surgery. I'm to give them your answer."

I leaned back in my chair. "Well!" It was the only thing I could say as an instant reply. Then the irony of it hit me and I had to laugh. I got up and took a quick turn from my desk to the window and back again. "Buzz, this is the most the bastards could do! They couldn't reverse themselves completely without becoming ridiculous. They couldn't make me Chief of Surgery again knowing I will never agree to let James de Simona back on the ER rotation." I studied him looking for a hint of his part in the proceedings. "How did this happen, do you know?"

Buzz said, "I didn't see any point in asking sensitive questions, Ross. I have a hunch, though."

"Yes?"

"I think J.P. Graham — for some reason that guy must think you're a good doctor — checked into your dismissal and didn't like the smell. If you want to know the truth, what is going on in the hospital with Jim de Simona right now still smells, but the Board looks the other way, and all the staff can do is monitor his inpatients as we've been doing. At least we're keeping him from gross malpractice."

Buzz made sense. I said, "I don't take kindly to having my ass kicked, especially when it's kicked for all the wrong reasons, but running the surgery service takes a lot of time and getting rid of its headaches suits me just fine. Let someone else cope with Jim de Simona and over-sensitive doctors who get their feelings hurt when things don't go their way. Tell them I accept the offer with pleasure: limited pleasure!" I hastily added. "Well," I said, "you don't have to tell them I have my limits."

Buzz grinned. "OK." His grin disappeared. "Something else I won't tell them is that they have lost the integrity of the staff, and themselves."

"Heavy stuff, Buzz," I said. "Don't let it get you down. If we concentrate on looking after ourselves now, it's going to be rewarding and fun."

After Buzz left, I tried to concentrate on my work, but I felt too good to stay cooped up. I kept my immediate appointments, canceled the last two of the day, and surprised Grace by going home early. She knew from my face that I brought good news. When I told her what had happened she cried out, "Oh, Ross! I'm so glad!" and threw her arms around my neck. Our daughter Christine wasn't sure what was being celebrated, but she laughed to keep us company.

It took time before I was finally vindicated in my restrictions on James de Simona, but his violations of medical procedures mounted until at last they were too much for the staff to ignore. This time not even the Board's attorney could save him, and he lost hospital privileges. I heard he left the state soon after that. In any event I never saw him again.

I did hear about him, however. Several years after his dismissal, I went to Scotland to play in a medical golf tournament. An orthopedist from Florida learned I was from Maryland and approached me as I was getting ready for dinner. "Do you know a Dr. James de Simona who practiced surgery in Maryland?"

"Good God, yes!" I said. My instant recognition of de Simona hit a sensitive spot with Dr. Johnson who asked if I would meet him on the hotel porch after dinner. "Of course. I'll be delighted," I said, truly anxious to know what this was all about. We met on the hotel porch just as an immense Scottish moon climbed like a golden ball in the cloudless eastern sky. Pulling two wicker lounge chairs together, we sank down and relaxed overlooking the greenery of the beautiful golf course. After the day of golfing, the setting was enough to encourage a nap, but my curiosity about James de Simona kept my juices flowing.

Dr. Johnson explained that he practiced in Palm Beach, FL, which I knew was an extremely affluent area. "About three years ago," Dr. Johnson said, "Dr. de Simona set up a practice which almost at once attracted my attention. As an orthopedist, I treat injuries and other problems that require braces and collars, but it seemed to me that Dr. de Simona had too many people wearing braces and collars, and performing unusual operations that made no sense to me. I began a quiet investigation

— I couldn't risk a charge of interfering with Dr. de Simona's practice. What I found so far indicates a systematic method of getting cooperative patients to agree to treatments which create the basis of insurance claims. But I can't prove it, and thought maybe you could help."

"Sit back, Dr. Johnson, while I tell you the story of Jim de Simona, his brother, John, and an attorney who got the lion's share of de Simona's accident cases."

Dr. Johnson and I compared experiences for more than two hours. It became clear that Jim de Simona was following the same course which had made him a wealthy young man in Maryland before he was exposed and left. When we said goodnight, Dr. Johnson was a very relieved physician who fully intended to address the de Simona problem on his return to Florida.

That appeared to end the de Simona saga for me, and I gave him no more thought. Months later, my secretary paged me to take a telephone call from someone in Florida. I instantly thought of Dr. Johnson, but the man on the phone identified himself as Ed Jacobs, an investigator for the National Association of Casualty Insurance Underwriters. Jacobs asked if I recalled a doctor named James de Simona.

"Yes. I know Dr. de Simona very well."

"Good, Dr. Pierpont," said the voice on the telephone. "We heard about you from Dr. Johnson, who has alerted us to fraudulent medical practices by Dr. James de Simona. You may be pleased to know we are going after Dr. de Simona on civil and criminal charges."

"That's very good news. I hope you succeed."

"I don't think you understand, Dr. Pierpont. My association needs your help. We want to know if you will testify for us in this action."

My internal reactions to this request was unfair to the poor soul on the other end of the telephone. How could he know what I had been put through while the insurance companies looked the other way? Now, after all this time, all this damage wrought by a conniving misfit as a physician, they come asking me for help! I put my simmering anger on the back burner and thought of how I would answer.

"Mr. Jacobs, I must ask you to give my message exactly as I tell you to your entire Board of Directors. Will you promise to do that?"

"Absolutely, Dr. Pierpont! What is it?"

"First, tell them what I have been through in fighting the fraud and other practices of Dr. de Simona. This happened at great personal and professional cost to me while your insurance association sat on the results of its own investigation. From where I look at the de Simona case, your people never considered what was the right thing to do, as I did, and paid for it. Your insurance companies copped out. They went for what cost least. After you tell them what I have gone through, tell them I said this: 'Go shit in your collective hats and pull them down over your ears!'"

"Wait a minute, Dr. Pierpont! That's a terrible thing for a doctor to say to me!"

My frustration somewhat vented, I said, "You are absolutely right, Mr. Jacobs. You have no way of knowing why I feel as I do. If you want to know that, sit still while I tell you what I have been through due to Dr. de Simona and the blind hypocrisy of your insurance association."

The insurance investigator listened in silence while I told him the de Simona story including the five hours I spent with Calvin Meyers resulting in nothing but increased premiums. When I finished, Ed Jacobs responded in a subdued voice. "My apologies, Dr. Pierpont. I will give them your message the way you gave it to me. If they want an explanation, I will give it to them. They deserve it."

Whether he did as promised, or got cold feet, I never asked or heard. Anyway, the last I heard of Dr. de Simona was that the insurance association had never acted to charge him with his medical misdeeds. Maybe the high-powered executives preferred to mess up their hats. However, hospital gossip some time later said he was supposed to be negotiating with the Internal Revenue Service to pay a $75,000 fine for non-payment of income taxes in an effort to stay out of prison.

Writing this with memories still vivid in my mind, I think of today's physicians practicing medicine in an atmosphere I never knew. Public officials pander to the public by proclaiming that the medical profession is a collection of men and women motivated by greed. Their unchallenged demagoguery erodes the patient-doctor confidence essential to successful medical care. Doctors who arrogantly keep patients waiting because they schedule appointments they have no chance of keeping on time aggravate the distrust.

Yet the physician's profession is a noble one. Not even the de Simonas can change that. Not even a hospital Board who tolerates unfit physicians can change that. Not even insurance companies who trade premiums for principle can change that. Every doctor true to his oath must recognize and accept the costs of living up to the profession he, or she, has chosen to embrace. Costs are high, sometimes terribly high, but if the choice is between integrity and compromise, the physician must be willing to pay the price of his integrity, as I once paid it in Havre de Grace. The public never knew the price I paid, and if it were spelled out, how many people would care? I'd rather not think about it.

Yes, I paid; indeed I paid. Not just in dollars but in my position in the medical community. Oh, how many laughs did I provide for envious competitors? Let them laugh, because neither Grace nor I ever regretted my decision. That decision made itself because it cannot be otherwise as long as I accept responsibility for human life. Every doctor who takes on-life-and-death responsibilities must be willing to make painful decisions sure he is right only by knowing his decisions are right. The key to making right decisions is not hard to find: it is the patient's welfare. No decision made because it is for the patient's welfare can ever be wrong, immediate consequences be damned.

Someone wrote that life begins at 40, and I reached that milestone in 1957. By the time I reached the point where my life should begin, I had carved my life into four different medical responsibilities. As Chief of General Surgery at Maryland General Hospital in Baltimore, I directed surgical residencies as well as conducting my own practice there. As former Chief of Surgical Services at Harford Memorial Hospital in northeastern Maryland, I had managed the surgical functioning of the hospital along with operating personally. As just Ross Pierpont, MD, I managed my Havre de Grace surgical clinic. My Baltimore office practice was my fourth responsibility.

I was busy. I was enjoying life to the fullest. What lay ahead for me? We would just have to wait and see.

Chapter Fourteen
"Gowns" Versus "Towns"
And "The Greek Church Massacre"

In the years just after World War II, doctors had no way to anticipate the changes in medical practice in store for us. We saw our patients, we treated them according to the principles we had been taught, we collected our fees - almost always adjusted according to ability to pay - or we forgot them. We had no Blue Cross, no Blue Shield, no HMO's, to tell us treatments we could prescribe or not prescribe. No one in the late 1940s could possibly foresee how profit-seeking hospitals, cost-based "managed care," and, above all, the towering bureaucracy of the Federal government, would steadily expand until they controlled us and our patients.

Those were days when medical care was an individual matter, conducted by highly independent doctors who answered primarily to their Hippocratic Oath. We were too busy working long hours to waste available time with a medical society and attending their meetings.

Those years were simultaneously when new specialties were being introduced so fast it was a struggle just to keep up with them. Surgery as a medical specialty that originally included all surgical services divided into such sub-specialties as orthopedic; colon and rectal surgery; thoracic and cardiovascular surgery, neurosurgery, transplant surgery; and plastic surgery. Internal medicine developed sub-specialties like cardiology, gastroenterology, endocrinology, and so forth.

The growth of specializations generated a demand for higher degrees of medical skills and more uniformity of physicians' training. Teaching hospitals felt the demand especially in the quality of residence training in internal medicine, surgery, obstetrics, and gynecology. In response, medical schools and all branches of the organized medical establishment set up new guidelines for physician training. These guidelines generally took the form of "Codes of Excellence." The codes were, of course, necessary and generally quite effective, but they also gave medical organizations final control of American medical practice. The main organizations were, and still are, the American Medical Association, the American College of Surgeons, and the American Association of Medical Colleges - more accurately, the faculties of the medical schools.

Before anyone fully realized what was going on, the codes of excellence set up by the national organizations were dictating what would be taught, and how, in the nation's schools of medicine. These organizations set up qualification panels to monitor trainees through rigorous examinations to determine the effectiveness of all aspects of their training, and, most especially, *to set up the qualifications to be applied in evaluating the credentials of each individual doctor.*

The ability to grant or deny accreditations handed power beyond belief to the faculties of the schools of medicine, and their allied organizations. Accreditation in one's specialty; for example, acceptance into the American College of Surgeons, or a similar organization, was absolutely necessary to a doctor's reputation and success. In Maryland, accreditation to practice in one or more of the state's hospitals was also a medical requirement, and "the gowns" of medicine (i.e., the professors of medicine in the state's two leading universities) were in full charge of accreditation processes.

The two institutions that went together in controlling medical care in Baltimore City, and in turn the rest of the state, were Johns Hopkins School of Medicine, and the University of Maryland School of Medicine. The power of these two schools to control medical care, and in turn the careers of individual doctors, rested in their ability to prescribe what is taught and how the schools' graduates would be accredited in their chosen fields. Day by day, these two teaching hospitals expanded their reach far, far beyond their conventional responsibilities of training new physicians.

The university professors concentrated their medical control primarily in The Medical and Chiurgical Faculty, The Baltimore City Medical Society, and to a lesser extent in some other medical organizations. Then came the "birth of the Blues" which expanded their power, because Blue Cross controlled payment coverage for all participating hospitals, and Blue Shield controlled payment for the services of physicians. These organizations, as always happens in the exercise of power, added ruling after ruling on top of previous ones to affect the life and practice of every physician in the state.

The system was ripe for abuses of power, but it affected me personally very little as my practice was going extremely well and growing. In those days of medical ferment, I had no personal reason to question what the medical "gowns" were doing to others in the state. I was one doctor among thousands, and who was Ross Pierpont to find fault with schools of medicine I admired. Little by little, however, I began to see that no one spoke for the ideas, needs, and interests of individual physicians. Since we had no voice, there was no way to be heard by those in power. I began to see we were losing control over our own destinies!

Now conscious of the arrogance of power exerted by the faculties of the state's two most-prominent hospitals, events taught me more and more that this situation had to be remedied before we were totally emasculated. But how? I had my hands more than full, working more than 80 hours a week. Daily events kept reminding me of the problem, and no one else I knew was doing anything about it. The weeks ground on, and little by little I grew to accept that I would have to fill the vacuum. Grace hated, absolutely hated, the idea, and I was anything but enthusiastic about it. Both of us knew, of course, that any action I took would be "taking on the establishment," with consequences I cared not to think about. When I finally made up my mind, Grace, loyal as ever, stood by my decision to see what I could do.

As a first step, I ran through the names of doctors who might be willing to join me in what was certain to become a nasty fight. The list narrowed to four: Dr. William Mosberg, neurosurgeon. Dr. William Ashworth, general surgeon. Dr. Willaim Lumpkin, general surgeon. Dr. Otto Phillips, anesthesiologist.

The five of us met one weekend in 1950, just four years after the end of World War II. "Gentlemen," I said, "I asked you to meet with me to see what we can do about our disenfranchisement by medical school professors and Blue Cross, Blue Shield. The fact we need to face, it seems to me, is that our doctoring is being controlled by the two medical schools, and we have no voice in their decisions."

Bill Mosberg grunted. "Ross, you know almost no one shows up at the Society's meetings. If we quietly pack the hall with doctors who agree with us, we can run right over them."

I quickly agreed. "Bill, you're dead right. I think I know where you're going, so go ahead."

Bill grinned thinking of his next idea. "Hell, their By-laws are so loosely written we can just nominate a slate of officers from the floor and have it seconded at once. By the time those 'gowns' realize what's happening to them, our people will fill all the offices."

Bill Ashworth laughed. "Bill," Ashworth said, "that would serve the arrogant so and so's right! And it'll probably work. But we'd better look at this a little more. We know we're honest and will do the right things. That's not to say the next bunch will do the same things we would do. They could be worse than we have now."

"Ashworth is right, Bill," I said. "This situation has been bothering me for quite a while, and I've been giving it a lot of thought. The question is, how can we do what must be done? How can we replace the Baltimore City Medical Society's control of our practices with doctors elected from our rank and file group - doctors who practice medicine every day and know the problems they have to face? How can we gain some form of control of medical policies when the way we practice medicine changes almost every day? Does everyone agree this is what we should be shooting for?"

As all four doctors spoke in agreement, Otto Phillips and Bill Lumpkin asked a question almost at the same time. "What's your plan, Ross?"

I grinned at them. "Come on, guys, what makes you think I already have a plan?" Everyone chuckled. "OK, I've already said I've been thinking about this problem for a long time. It seems to me that revolution is out - the wrong way to go. It would be ugly and cost us the support of moderate doctors. I think our first step should be to write up a change in the Society's By-laws, submit them for the usual slow process, and follow them until we get the changes we want ratified by the Society."

From Mosberg: "What changes do you have in mind?"

"The first thing is to get a two-month election period. The first month will be used to submit a slate of officers selected by the nominating committee, and at the same time nominations taken from the floor. At the end of the two month period, a meeting will be called to vote on the nominations, but no new nominations allowed. Just the vote. That rule is critical. It is one way to make sure everyone will have a chance to be heard.

"There will be plenty of time to review all candidates for office. The final vote will be by secret ballot. This will be evolution, not revolution. No one can possibly argue we're irresponsible or hasty. About your point, Bill," I said, addressing him directly, "if a new group takes over in the future and runs things into the ground, the Society has ample warning and the members would have no one to blame but themselves."

We broke up with everyone agreeing to proceed with my proposed action. The delay drew out for five long years as we drew up the changes we wanted in the Society's By-laws. At last we had them ratified by the Society's officials, who had no inkling about what we had in mind. After more procedural delays and a month's review by all concerned, our proposed changes were voted on and approved unanimously.

So far so good! The five years had been worth it.

During those years my small group had gotten together from time to time to complete our strategy. With the new By-laws in effect, the time had come to enlarge our five-man group to line up doctors for offices beginning with President of the Society, and on down the line to alternate delegates.

Time takes its toll, and the slowness of our progress had cut into our initial enthusiasm. This was dull work! And dirty work, at that.

Bill Mosberg spoke first. "Fellows, here we are! We've got everything in line. So what are we going to do to fill all of these damn offices - there's 43 of them!"

"There's five of us," Bill Lumpkin laughed. "If we fill five of the eight key offices, that will leave three more for someone else."

Otto Phillips missed the humor. "We're a great group of victors. We've won, and now nobody is monitoring the great reforms we set out to enact."

Bill Ashworth owned a sly, quiet grin and now he used it to nice effect. "Hey, Otto! We've got the opposition by the balls! Now let's squeeze 'em!"

"Stop being vulgar," I said, grinning.

The conversations skipped back and forth as we relished our satisfaction with a job well done - so far. No one had any illusions that our opposition would roll over and play dead. The "gowns" of medical schools relished their eminence, their power, and we knew they would fight bitterly to maintain their lofty authority. Their power could hurt, or help, physicians, and this power would be used to hold loyal and pandering subjects in line.

Fifteen or 20 minutes went by as I weighed various tactics. Finally, I said, "Fellows, this is going to be a tough, nasty fight. If we lose it we could hurt ourselves and everyone who is supporting us. Don't think for a minute the "gowns" don't know who's behind the changes in the By-laws, and the other things we've done. They know a threat to their power when they see one. Our goal hasn't changed. We want rank and file representation in the Society, and for it to be a cohesive force, not a negative. Why don't we show the present officers we want to cooperate, not fight them? We could split the offices. What about cooperation instead of opposition?"

Maybe our group was just tired and ready to concentrate on our careers; anyway, everyone went along with my idea of trying seeking cooperation with those on the academic thrones.

Like former New York Mayor LaGuardia, when I make a mistake "it's a beaut." Was I ever wrong trying for cooperation! It was one of the worst mistakes, maybe the very worst mistake, I ever made.

[There's a lesson here that should not be overlooked. If you are dealing with anyone actively exercising power of any kind, do not expect that person to willingly, voluntarily relinquish any part of that power, no matter how modest. The only exception I know is retirement due to age.]

Some of the younger university doctors saw merit in our ideas, and agreed to join our slate of nominees. It was a full slate made up, as mutually agreed, half of existing officeholders and half of our group's nominees. No position was to be filled by any of the five doctors who had engineered the changes now in effect.

We presented our slate of nominees from the floor at the meeting which preceded the Society's annual meeting and election of officers. The university "gowns" countered by presenting nominations containing only their well-known puppet personnel. Our offer of cooperation was up against a stone wall with blood oozing from every vein. The situation gave us a choice. We could attack the medical school "gowns," and thereby weaken the moral stance of our group, or we could ride things out to the end. After all, the voting at the annual meeting would be by secret ballot.

The vote took place. We didn't just lose. We were buried 10 feet deep.

It hurt, and it made me angry. I waited a few days, then called for a meeting, and our wounded group met once again. Fortunately, all of us have a strong sense of humor, and it came in handy.

Bill Mosberg even chuckled as he said, "Six years shalt thou labor, and cometh the seventh year thou shall get thy throat cut! How are we doing, lambs?"

"What's next?" someone asked, getting to the point.

Somehow, some way, life had taught me ways to draw on an inner strength when facing what appears as total defeat. Instead of being diminished by this bitter loss, it increased my resolve. I think the other doctors sensed this, although I have no way of knowing what they were really thinking. Fortunately, all five of us had such strong practices any enmity we had created with the university doctors would not seriously hurt our medical practices. Unfortunately, I could not say the same for other doctors who had originally joined our fight (but then copped out for the professors' nominees when the election came).

Instinct told me to speak up. "Fellows, we have not lost the war. We have lost the first battle. But only the first battle. I have talked with some of the younger doctors in the university group, and found that they voted for the professors' nominees either out of ignorance of what they stood for, or, in some cases, out of sheer fear of retaliation."

Bill Mosberg said, "Ross, I was wondering about that. "The professors can really hurt a young guy if they really get on his case."

"How well I know," I said. "I've been there."

"So I've heard," Bill Mosberg said.

"What killed us, according to the young doctor I've talked to, was the color of our ballot. The paper of our sample ballot was white. The 'official' ballot was green. Now if you're a young doctor trying to get established, and you have to choose between showing you're for the opposition's white ballot, or the official green ballot, in full view of professors, which do you choose?"

I let the question sink in, for the answer was obvious.

"I'll be dammed!" exploded Ashworth.

"Live and learn," uttered Phillips.

"All right," I said. "We can give up. Or we can go on and win this thing. So let's not get bent out of shape by what happened to squash a small bunch of amateurs playing in the big leagues." They looked at me. "The amateurs, that's us," I said. "Still, we got in seven people, which is exactly seven more than we had when we started."

I sensed that my friends, while discouraged, were still too proud to give up as long as they had a chance to turn things around, and it was no time to be weak-kneed. "It's going to take one more year to do what we set out to do. Fellows, we can't give this up, or we'll hurt others as well as ourselves in ways no one in this room is ready to acknowledge. And I mean hurt! In next year's election, we won't make the same mistakes, and this time we will win. I promise you, we will win!"

"Pierpont the optimist!" Ashworth drawled.

"What else?" I replied. "Damned if I will ever be a pessimist. And, gentlemen, I will never, never ever quit!"

During 1958 I dug in with all the energy I could muster; nights, days, weekends — whenever. Together, we left no option uncovered, no contact untouched, no promise we could keep omitted. The weeks rolled by and at last we had our slate of nominees ready. They included the seven doctor previously elected and 36 new nominees, a total of 43 carefully chosen, highly qualified physicians. Not one was from the university "gowns." This 43 was 100% our people.

As you can guess, the university group heading the Society had ways of keeping well informed about our group's activities, and the faces on most of the crowd in the meeting room on nomination night were visibly unfriendly. Conflict filled the air as the nominating committee rendered its list of nominees. No surprises there. The list was stacked with university "gowns."

The big moment came when the Society President said, "Are there any nominations from the floor?"

I watched the Society President visibly confident in his power to control events. As Bill Ashworth stood up, I thought: "Mr. Self-confident President, what will you be thinking a few minutes from now?" As if responding to my thoughts, the President was undisturbed, confident, going by the book. Speaking very slowly, deliberately, and coolly, Bill nominated a different President. The nomination was seconded the instant it was announced. (Now, what do you think, Mr. President?) Bill continued his nominations, one by one, until all 43 names were on the record. Not one of our names appeared on the Nominating Committee's slate, and vice versa.

My turn had come. Before another word could be uttered I moved for the nominations to be closed. The motion was seconded and carried. What, now, was our opposition thinking? A clue came as some professors challenged the closing of the nominations. Some were visibly upset when an objection about closing the nominations was voted down by a voice vote of approval.

The "gowns" realized they had been outdone by our parliamentary maneuver, but they were not equipped to cope with it. There was nothing they could do to change the closure, but they still wanted to fight against it. As I had anticipated, the debate, if you want to call it that, became less than dignified and professional, and the ugliness clearly hurt the professors' cause. Lines had been drawn between every doctor in the meeting, and speaker followed speaker trying to convince doctors to vote for the nominating committee's slate, accompanied by some veiled threats and name-calling.

It was one more example of seeing doctors I admired professionally reveal the ugliness of their feet of clay. They were willing to sell their humanity just to hold on to power.

Interest in the upcoming Society election buzzed from top to bottom of the medical profession in Baltimore. Soon, it became clear that the Med-Chi hall in downtown Baltimore would never hold the crowd that would attend the annual meeting. The Greek Orthodox Church of the Annunciation was around the corner from Med-Chi hall, and held more than 500 persons. It was selected as the site for the next annual meeting, and the big vote.

I had promised my fellow plotters we would not repeat our earlier mistakes, and I do not make promises I cannot keep. So I made discreet questions about the type of ballot the "gowns" would use in the election. Their ballot would be the same type as before, on green paper. Our printer obtained identical green paper and printed our candidates' names in matching places. There was no visible difference between our ballot and the professors' ballot except for the names of the candidates themselves.

The crowd of doctors exceeded the expected attendance, making it by far the largest attendance in the history of the Baltimore City Medical Society. The capacity of the church was not enough so late-comers found themselves standing in the corridors, but none of them left. No one left.

The tremendous interest and the crowd of doctors warned our opponents they were in deep trouble - even defeat. When the meeting was called to order, speaker after speaker arose to make impassioned speeches urging the return of the "gowns'" nominees to Society offices. They called upon the assembled doctors to remember all sorts of good things the present officers had done for physicians over many years. They said no greater good could ever come from this meeting than to re-elect the official slate of nominees.

The speeches were self-serving, out of order, and everyone recognized it. Our side saw our opponents only hurting themselves, and graciously remained silent to await the voting. We tasted victory, and how sweet it was upon the tongue after the anxieties and work of eight long years.

At last the voting could be delayed no longer, and the order came to deliver all marked ballots to the tally clerks. We had made sure that our green ballots were handed, in person, one by one, to every one of our supporters. No mistakes this time! As the ballots were handed in, a large number of green ballots accumulated on the floor. Some of the "gowns" picked up discarded ballots and looked them over in total disbelief. Exclamations complete with epithets soiled the churchly air. More ballots were picked up and I heard a surgery professor from Johns Hopkins exclaim: "Look at this! This isn't our ballot, it's theirs! It just looks like ours!"

The professors' discovery that they had been blocked from repeating their earlier maneuver came too late to change the results, of course. We five doctors had finally pulled it off, and we stood there together in the back of the church fully enjoying the consternation of our old teachers who were now seeing — for the first time, no doubt — democracy in action. It had taken us 8 long years of unending work and struggle to obtain a stake in the management procedures of our proud profession.

We had finally swept the "gowns" out of their arrogant control of our medical lives. The profession would be all to the good for it.

It was a night always to be remembered. It took me back to the struggle when other young physicians and I had "taken on City Hall" and won. In that victory, however, my role as one of the leaders of that cause came close to ending my medical career.

Here I was again, taking on, not one, but two faculties of the most prestigious medical schools in the region. Was I forever to be the racehorse answering the bell when confronted by situations in need of repair? Was I going to continue risking personal and professional status in causes not of my making? Then a different thought: Am I perhaps guilty of assuming more importance than necessary? I didn't know — and don't know — the answer to any of those questions. I gave little thought to them in the heady success of our triumph.

In the years that followed what came to be known as "The Greek Church Massacre," our "group of five" looked back upon the lessons we had learned the hard way. A different set of questions emerged in those get-togethers. Was it all truly worth the risks and the effort? Yes, we had replaced the autocratic rule over our profession with democratically elected doctors. We had created a good balance between teachers of medicine, accreditation procedures, and the expansion of professorial control over every physician's practice. The Society kept our process for nominating officers, allowing for reasonable differences of opinion and approaches to medical problems. Although practical, everyday results never turned out to be as great as we had envisioned, the fact remains that the University of Maryland and Johns Hopkins got the message.

Time will reveal if our changes in the Society will become important in regaining a system of medical care that cares for all. So far results have been far from encouraging. The time may come, sooner than we think, when individual physicians may need the Society's help in defending themselves against the tentacles of a managed care octopus.

* * *

The calming influence of time worked its usual magic after the "Greek Church Massacre," and members on both sides turned their attention to their daily responsibilities. I, for one, was extremely pleased that my leadership in opposing the medical faculties had no material effect on my own career. During the years leading to the climax of our eight-year struggle, I had become an increasingly active doctor on the surgical staff of the Maryland General Hospital. Soon after joining Maryland General as a member of the surgical staff, Dr. Warfield Firor was appointed Chief of Surgery as a step in strengthening the department. Dr. Firor's stature as a leading sugeon and former Chairman of the American Board of Surgery secured Maryland General's surgical credentials. It would be hard to exaggerate my pride in being named as his Assistant Chief of Surgery in charge of teaching and training the hospital's resident surgical staff.

When Dr. Firor retired, the hospital had no Chief of Surgery. As his assistant in the department, I became his logical replacement. The position would be an enormous, time-consuming responsibility, and Grace and I spent hours talking over what becoming Chief of Surgery would mean to our lives. Meanwhile, doctors on the hospital staff let it be known that as nature abhors a vacuum, they abhorred the absence of a Chief.

The day came for me to respond. I called the staff into a meeting and put the selection of a new Chief of Surgery on the table. Being careful to stay out of the ensuing discussion, I listened as doctor after doctor gave his ideas about what a Chief of Surgery should do. The talk ran its course until someone - I still do not remember which doctor it was - said in effect let's cut the talk short and Dr. Pierpont should move up and head the department.

It would be false to say the recommendation surprised me; I am neither bashful nor blind to immediate possibilities. Nevertheless, I had decided I would take the position only if the suggestion came freely and explicitly from the staff. I would not prompt any suggestion. There would be no hint of a power grab.

I responded by offering to act as Interim Head of Department. We should use the next month, I said, to consider potential candidates for the position, followed by an open election of Chief of Surgery for a three-year period. The position would be filled for each succeeding three-year periods as I suggested filling it now. If all concurred, I added, I would submit the staff recommendation to the hospital's Board of Directors for their consideration. The surgical staff unanimously approved my suggestions, and I wrote them up for the hospital's Board, which also approved them.

I called the next meeting as promised. A staff member promptly nominated me to become Maryland General's new Chief of Surgery for the following three years. An immediate vote followed, and I was unanimously elected for the office that would turn out to be my most demanding responsibility for the rest of my medical career.

I brought in a great doctor, Dr. Tom Flotte as Co-Chief of Surgery and head of teaching and training. I added "Head of the Visiting Staff" to my personal responsibilities. The arrangement was smooth and effective, allowing Dr. Flotte to concentrate on his teaching-training programs without distractions from other doctors. The Department flourished but we were not blind to some weaknesses in the training of our surgical residents. There were only two real possibilities for enhancing residency training: affiliate with Hopkins or the University of Maryland. Other Baltimore hospitals were looking for the same affiliation, so it became highly competitive.

Fortunately, Dr. Flotte had been at one time or another a close associate with the Chairman of the Department of Surgery at the University of Maryland. I was an alumnus of the University's Medical School. So it was natural to explore a working arrangement with the University's Medical School, where we prevailed. In medical "politics," as in government politics, personal relationships can make the difference in getting things done. Our affiliation with the University of Maryland lasted for years, and worked as I had hoped for the benefit of everyone concerned. It survives today.

Chapter 15

Medical Care Can't Survive Political Ignorance

The medical profession and its allied scientists have lived long in the belief that doctors and research scientists should work in a world "above politics." That attitude is understandable though foolish. Everyone realizes that those who engage in politics enter a soiling arena because politics is messy. From colonial days to the latest scandal, all too many politicians have used skillful lying, scheming, double-dealing, vote stealing, and other assorted nefarious schemes to gain offices and power. If that is what it takes to deal with politics, doctors say, it's not for me.

No one in his right mind would argue that life for doctors wouldn't be a lot nicer if they could simply practice medicine and ignore the politicians. However, the reality of American life is that politics is another word for power. The opposite side of that statement is that if you stay out of politics your power is zero. Both rank and file physicians and their avowed leaders have ignored politics, leading to an almost total takeover of medical powers by business, government bureaus, and the politicians who control the actions of state and national governments. We have presided over our own undoing. Today, far from keeping politics at arm's length, physicians are drowning in it. Doctors kowtow to politicians who know nothing about the proper practice of medicine, and care even less about it — if that is possible. The profession has been reduced to fighting for survival.

It has never been my fate to ignore the political system, although I am not sure just how and when I began to think about taking an active role. It probably was just an extension of my experiences in medical politics — which can be just as messy as party politics. Dr. Aycock's attempt to destroy me after leaving City Hospitals in Baltimore, including my initial rejection to membership in the American College of Surgeons, gave me an unforgettable lesson in the abuse of power.

I grew up in a family of Democrats and joined the Democrat party when I reached voting age, then 21. I began to take an active interest in the two national parties when I saw politics entering our medical system through the back door. That "back door" was the introduction of a non-medical system for paying medical bills; that is, Blue Cross and Blue Shield. These two systems are instruments of the political system, ultimately controlled not by doctors but by votes. These systems could only grow, and with it their power over private physicians.

The more I looked at the control of Blue Cross/Blue Shield by non-medical people, the more I looked at Maryland's political structure, and the more it fascinated me. From the Depression years of the 1930s and continuing to 1970, Maryland's political system was a "boss system." *The Baltimore Sun* even had a way of dividing the system up into "eighths." Boss so-and-so had 1/8th of Baltimore; Boss xyz had another 1/8th, and so on. Everyone knew who the bosses were, and the bosses did not, for the most part, invade each other's territories. Western Maryland was Judge Walsh country. Emerson Harrington ruled the Eastern Shore. Baltimore City, with about half of the state's people, called the shots of the Maryland system at that time, and was divided into largely ethnic bossdoms. Jack Pollack delivered the votes in the Jewish section of NW Baltimore (and did he ever!). The Coggins-O'Malley duo said who did what in the largely Irish NE part of the city. The Della-Wyatt organization ruled in the central-southeast zone. D'Alesandro delivered the Italian votes. Most of German, Polish, Lithuanian, and Greek votes fell into Bohemian groups loyal to Prucha and Macht. Alliances between these bosses literally made or broke candidates as late as the 1970s. They continued to exert measurable influence into the current decade according to the number of votes they could deliver.

The era of boss-rule was assisted by Maryland's political system based on the Electoral College idea. This gave unusual power to rural counties, which were relatively conservative, thinly populated, and the voters easier to control. To get elected statewide, a candidate was almost forced to win the rural counties. A major change occurred when the state adopted a one-man, one-vote rule. The rural counties lost their impact and the urban areas of Prince Georges County, Montgomery County, Baltimore County and Baltimore City filled the political vacuum.

Federal employees in Montgomery and Prince George's Counties, state and city employees in Baltimore City and Baltimore County, and mainly Democratic African-Americans in the urban areas gained increased voting power. The Democratic Party of Maryland, earlier a relatively conservative organization, shifted to a liberal — sometimes to a left ultraliberal — Party.

I watched these changes take place first-hand by contributing money and time to the campaigns of Preston Lane, George P. Mahoney, and Millard Tawes for Governor. I not only got to know the candidates and their advisors, I got to see the give-and-take (it was "give," and it was "take") first hand.

The more I saw of the political system at both state and national levels, the more convinced I became that medical practice was on a road to ultimate political/insurance company control. To no avail, I did my best to involve the medical profession in the electoral process. When prominent persons visited the state from the American Medical Association, the American College of Surgeons, or other organizations, I always brought up the importance of our organized medical leadership taking stands on political questions affecting the profession. I could almost punch a button to get the same lame excuse: "We can't get involved in government affairs without stirring up reprisals from people who don't like us. We don't need more enemies. We just have to stick to our scientific programs."

No one would listen to my Cassandra warnings. No one cared. If 1% of Maryland doctors saw where the state's Blue Cross/Blue Shield would ultimately take them, it would be a lot. Interest in the impact of medical insurance was as close to zero as you could get. The profession kept its head in the sand all through the late 1980s and well into the 1990s.

Lack of foresight and everyday wisdom dominated the medical leadership, the medical journals they edited, and on down through the rank and file. I found it incomprehensible then, and continue to find it incomprehensible now, that men and women who know medicine would not have foreseen the wreckage of Medicare/Medicaid. These systems were based on funds that existed only in a political dreamland. They promised care they could not deliver. Any experienced physician had to be blind not to see the systems were flawed from their beginning! Over-promised and under-funded, the system was born to fail.

Where was organized medicine when these blunders were whooped through Congress? Everywhere but where medical leaders should have been — facing Congressional committees, buttonholing Representatives and Senators, to at least go on record against these medical gorillas. Instead, not a whisper, not even a whimper, came from the organized medical community.

Do I exaggerate? To answer, look at what happened in Maryland when Title 19, Medicaid reached the state, and what I came to do about it.

The US Congress enacted Medicaid to provide medical care to those who couldn't pay for it. To establish inability to pay, each person had to meet very strict limits to income and assets. Patients who qualified were told the government would pay doctors their Usual and Customary Fees (UCF) for providing them with medical care. Usual and Customary Fees are just what they sound like: what physicians had been charging, no more, no less, than had been charged in prior years. If a doctor's UCF to set a broken leg had been $200, Medicaid was to pay the physician $200. If a doctor's UCF for an appendectomy had been $300, Medicaid was to pay that exact amount, and so on. If the full faith and treasury of the US Government had been behind this promise, Medicaid patients would have been among the best patients a doctor could treat. The opposite was true because Medicaid defrauded every Maryland physician who treated a Medicaid patient. If anyone other than the Federal Government had tried to do what Medicaid did to doctors, he or she would justifiably be sent to prison.

Most people, patients and non-patients alike, think the U.S. Treasury pays the expenses of Medicaid. The truth is that *Medicaid is financed jointly by the Federal Government and each of the various state governments*. This arrangement requires each state to establish its own Medicaid program, and for each state to share in paying for the program. Any state lacking the money to pay its share cannot take part in Medicaid, the costs of which vary state by state.

Five years went by while Maryland tried to get its Medicaid house in order. What took so long? The state did not have the money to pay its share of Medicaid costs established by the law's required payment of Usual and Customary Fees. When Maryland's Board of Health and Mental Hygiene looked at the estimated costs of treating the state's eligible persons, a horrible fact became obvious: *paying doctors their usual and customary fees would bankrupt the state!*

Some political realities soon became evident although doctors failed to recognize them before the enactment of Medicaid. First, Maryland is obligated to comply with the law establishing Medicaid. Two, Maryland lacked, and lacks, the money to pay the law's specified Usual and Customary Fees. Question: How can Maryland provide Medicaid? Answer: Don't pay the Usual and Customary Fees. Let the doctors take the shortfall. After all, how many votes do doctors have? No media "anchor" on the air would dare to defend doctors who refuse to participate.

I had studied the Medicaid law and knew it could not work as enacted. While the law was under study, I met with every one of the 12 members of the Board of Health and Mental Hygiene on a one-to-one basis. Fortunately, many members of the Board were political appointees of old friends I knew from associations gained in more than 20 years of participation in Maryland Democratic Party campaigns. I explained to each Board member that if the state failed to live up to its obligations to pay Usual and Customary Fees, as specified in the Medicaid law, I would be compelled to get a court injunction to stop the introduction of Medicaid in Maryland.

If I had to present my case to the Board at a public hearing, I felt confident I could win at least seven of the 12 votes. Of course, I could be wrong. As some politicians love to say, "Politics ain't beanbag!"

When word finally reached me that Medicaid would go into effect July 1, 1970, minus Usual and Customary Fees, I knew what I had to do. Anyone reading this will probably smile and say, "There he goes again!" So be it. Everyone involved in this situation knew there was no way Maryland could live up to the requirements of the law and meet its other obligations. Something had to give, and members of The Board of Health and Mental Hygiene, as well as I, knew what it would be. The Board's only option was: stick it to the doctors.

I prepared carefully for the hearing. One challenge I would need to face was a lack of solid legal backup for everything I planned to say. The situation called for more than just a good lawyer. I needed a law firm in back of me that knew its way around Maryland's political structure. I called Arthur Weinberg, of Weinberg and Green, not only one of the oldest and most prestigious law firms in Maryland, but also one with political sophistication.

Arthur agreed to support me at the hearing, although he was unfamiliar with the details of the Medicaid legislation. The day of the hearing, Grace, a colleague named Dr. Tom Crawford, and I picked up Arthur Weinberg and we headed for Annapolis. Arthur and I sat in the back seat going over the Medicaid law and what I intended to do at the hearing.

We hadn't gone a mile before I realized that Arthur wasn't just unfamiliar with Medicaid law; he knew next to nothing about it. No matter. By the time we reached the outskirts of Annapolis we had covered the fundamentals, and were agreed on how we would proceed before the Board. After a pause in our discussion, Arthur said, looking straight ahead and not at me: "Ross, you are planning to take on the entire medical community involved in Medicaid, not to mention some powerful people in the State Legislature. Are you ready to do that?"

It was a loaded question, and I looked at the back of Grace's head to see any sign she had heard it. I am sure she did, but she did not turn or say a word. My opposition to the medical community's plans for Medicaid could cost us in many unpleasant ways, personally and professionally, but Grace was always with me on an issue of right and wrong.

"I'm loaded for bear, Arthur," I said as a way to keep the conversation light. "These people are plain wrong, and that doesn't leave me any choice, does it?"

"Well, I don't suppose so — as long as you don't mind their opposition. What you say today is going to live with you a long time. It could get damn' ugly."

"Arthur, the question is whether I am right or they are right. I say I'm right — or do you have a different opinion?"

"No, from everything I see, you're right. The problem is, you are forcing their hand today. The Dean at the University of Maryland Medical School, who's for this action, called me about you. He said if the proposal to adopt Medicaid isn't accepted today, they will have to wait another three years just to have a go at it again." Now he looked directly at me. "You know it's been five years to get this far. You could add three more years to that."

"Arthur, I don't want sick people to wait another day, much less three more years! Are you asking me to walk away from doing what's not just wrong, but illegal? All I ask the Board of Health and Hygiene to do is to decide between obeying the law and breaking the law. If they don't like the law, let them change it, but I will not let them get away with making doctors deliberately violate the Medicaid law. Either they vote today to live up to the law, or I want you to get a Court order to block them."

"I can't argue with that," Arthur Weinberg said reluctantly. "You're correct, or I wouldn't be here. I'm still not sure just what you expect me to do."

"Just verify the facts, Arthur. When I testify, I will quote the letter of the law. I will then turn to you and ask you to verify that what I have said is correct."

He looked a question at me.

I said, "Just get up and wave that book of laws around so no one can miss it and tell them something like, 'Dr. Pierpont is entirely correct in his statement of the Medicaid law. Any other way of looking at it is contrary to that law and therefore illegal.' "

"Then what happens?"

"Then I am going to appeal to the Board to do the right thing and vote for implementation of the Medicaid law as written to include Usual and Customary Fees."

Arthur held back a chuckle. "You know they can't do that. They don't have the money. That's why it's taken five years to get to this hearing."

"We know that, Arthur. They know it, but here's my point. Not a handful of people at the hearing, and even fewer of the taxpayers of Maryland, know the truth about Medicaid law. People think Congress passed the Medicaid law, so everything is just fine. People unable to pay will get the care they need, the doctors will get paid, and everyone will be happy. Bullshit! If I have to get the facts out the hard way, then they come out the hard way. There is no way I can let this hearing end with the Board thinking they are doing what's right, when what they plan to do is stiff the doctors."

"Where do I come in on this?"

Having spent hours thinking of my action before the Board, the next step was clear in my mind. "I expect to stand there looking at the Board for a minute or two to let things sink in. Then I will say this to the Board: ' If this Board votes any other way than to act in clear obedience to the law of Title 19, Medicaid, Mr. Weinberg has prepared an injunction to be served immediately upon the Board of Health and Mental Hygiene. This injunction will stop this Board and the State of Maryland from acting to implement the Medicaid program by illegal means. We have no doubt our action will be sustained by the Courts which will prevent Medicaid from taking place for at least three more years.' Arthur, this is your time to get up and wave some papers in a great show of legal force and verify what I have just said."

"OK, Ross. I've got it," Arthur Weinberg said, noticing that Grace had stopped the car. "We're here."

The four of us walked into a hearing room packed to standing room only. As we went to front seats immediately before the Board members, I glanced around to see the cream of Maryland's medical profession: The Deans of the Medical Schools at Johns Hopkins and the University of Maryland, my alma mater; the President of Med-Chi; presidents of most of the counties' medical societies, an assortment of professors from Hopkins and Maryland medical schools, most of the counties' health officers, State Senators and legislative Delegates interested in health care, and of course many more people I did not recognize.

I couldn't help but wonder what these leaders were thinking about me as they saw us take our places. Whatever they thought, I knew it wouldn't be flattering. All of my prior contacts with medical organization leaders on political matters had put me at odds with most of my peers; on this day I was very, very much alone. To say I got any satisfaction in what I was doing would be a lie, far from it. The opprobrium of fellow physicians I held in great respect hurt me as much as it would hurt anyone, but they were planning to hurt the profession I love, and I could not remain speechless while they did it.

I looked neither to the right nor the left as the Chairman of the Board stood up and started the hearing. After summarizing the procedures, he said: "Here, today, we are considering ground-breaking changes of care for the poor and down-trodden of Maryland by instituting Medicaid tomorrow, under the provisions of Title 19 of the Medicaid legislation of

1965."

It's taken you guys from 1965 to 1970 to break ground because you know damn' well what you want to do is break the law, I thought, as the Chairman continued.

"Our problem is one of financial considerations in implementing Medicaid. We have examined all of our options and concluded that the state of Maryland cannot fund the Medicaid law as it is written. We are considering whether we can modify our payment procedures to change the wording of the law from a 'Usual and Customary Fee' schedule of payment to payment as 'fiscally available funding' which we recommend. We solicit your discussion." He paused, and I whispered to Arthur Weinberg: "Surprise!"

The Chairman said, "We will hear from those favorable to 'fiscally available funding' first."

The Dean of Johns Hopkins Medical School led off with an impassioned address about the poor, the halt, the blind, the downtrodden, and anyone in need to be cared for any time care is needed. He expanded on something he called the altruism of the fiscally probable and possible, and roundly declared the Board's recommendation to be the only humane and altruistic way for all doctors to do our sworn duty. As he talked, I thought how cleverly the Board was describing their proposed payment alternative: "fiscally available funding" indeed! It sounded so positive. Put available funding in a newscast, and not one person in ten thousand would know it was the opposite of what it sounds like. Average people would think it meant the state had funds to pay physicians' usual and customary fees when it did not. The term had been deliberately chosen to hide what everyone involved knew: adequate funds were not available and never would be. While I admired the Board's skill with the English language, the Dean closed his impressive, 20-minute speech. If this is typical, we will be here tomorrow, I thought.

The Dean of the University of Maryland Medical School spoke next and echoed his predecessor. Speaker after speaker followed until the Chairman took pity on our bladders and recessed at 3 PM for a few minutes. We resumed to hear more of the same, until those who favored the Board's position finished. To give the Board credit, they had marshalled an impressive array of medical talent to plead for the adoption of a process devised to avoid the clearly stated legal provisions of Title 19, Medicaid.

It was now about 5 PM. My time had arrived.

The Chairman said, "Now we will hear from those opposing Budgeting Ability to Pay, and favoring the Usual and Customary Fees." He looked at me, paused, and said, "Dr. Pierpont."

I stood up and said, "Mr. Chairman, where would you like me to go?" The words were no sooner out of my mouth when I realized how it sounded. "Mr. Chairman, let me change that. I know very well where you would like me to go. What I mean is, where would you like me to stand?"

The room broke up in the only laughter of the day. At least it was a break from the almost continuous tension and tedium of the preceding hours. I introduced Grace, my surgical colleague Tom Crawford, and Arthur Weinberg as my legal advisor from Weinberg and Green. As I said "legal advisor," it seemed as though the audience stiffened. I didn't see a friendly face in the crowd. There was no question where the members of the audience stood, they anticipated what I was about to say, and they didn't want to hear it. I was not a welcome presence in that room.

I looked at individuals in the audience, then said, "Let me say to all of you I understand how you feel about this situation, and I deeply sympathize with your concerns. All doctors here are sworn to treat the sick and the infirm. I, for one, fully intend to continue living up to my responsibilities without question, but there is another question here today. It is a problem not of your making, nor of mine. The Federal government enacted Title 18, Medicare, and Title 19, Medicaid without any real idea of the unintended consequences of those bills. They aren't physicians; they are politicians who just passed laws and then left it up to others to make them work. Those laws promise massive medical care for millions of the poor without the money to pay for it. They promise what they cannot deliver; and you here, today, know I speak the truth.

"I am not against medical care for the poor. I am for it. Everyone here today knows I am for it. But Medicaid, as passed five years ago — *five years ago!* — cannot work because it does not provide the resources to make it work. Unless real changes in it are made, every doctor will pay through the nose while it drags Maryland and every other state toward bankruptcy.

"I speak not only to those of you in this room, but to the citizens of Maryland. I speak not as a surgeon, which I am, but as a loyal citizen who has served Maryland without a penny in compensation on the Hospital Licensing Board, and Comprehensive Health Planning. I have a stake in this state, in our great profession, and I care about the people who cannot pay for necessary medical care. I have served them in my own practice without charge for more than 30 years. Not once in all of those years have I turned anyone away due to inability to pay.

"All that is beside the point of this hearing. We are discussing a federal law, and obeying that law. I feel a personal responsibility to that law, and am sure you do, too. Title 19, Medicaid, is perfectly clear. It says all patients are to be treated alike, and payment for their treatment will be on a 'Usual and Customary Fee' schedule. Neither you nor I wrote that law, but it is the law of the land. Am I correct, Mr. Weinberg?"

Arthur rose and thrust the open book containing the Medicare law first toward the sky, then toward the Chairman and members of the Board presiding over the hearing, and finally a full 360 degrees to the crowd. "Dr. Pierpont, you are absolutely correct! He states the letter of the law, and there is nothing in it allowing this Board to change it. I see no way around the mandates of this law."

Arthur looked around the crowd as if to underline his statements and sat down.

I resumed: "We have no choice here. As law-abiding citizens, even though we may feel we know a better way to implement Medicaid than the law allows, we cannot avoid obeying it. That means endorsing its provision for 'Usual and Customary Fees,' not rewriting the law to suit ourselves. I now must tell you where I stand on this issue. If any other decision is made, Mr. Weinberg is prepared to file an immediate injunction to stop the order from proceeding. The unfortunate effect of that step would stall Medicaid in Maryland for another three years." I turned to Arthur Weinberg. "Am I correct about this, Mr. Weinberg?"

Arthur stood up to answer. "Yes, Dr. Pierpont, I have the injunction here to proffer against any illegal proceeding by the body of the State of Maryland." He was so emphatic he nearly shouted over a room crowded by very tired, worn-down people.

    I turned and, one by one, shook the hands of every man sitting on the Board. Speaking to all of them, I said, "Gentlemen, I thank you for your time and patience in letting me speak."

    That night I got a call about the hearing. Seven members of The Board of Health and Mental Hygiene had voted for implementing Medicaid on July 1, 1970 with the legal Usual and Customary Fee schedule. Five were opposed.

    I had carried the day single-handed, but it became a flawed victory. As Medicaid went into effect, the State of Maryland got around the law by keeping two sets of books. Merely agreeing to the Usual and Customary Fee schedule did not provide the money to pay the fees. The State never had the money to begin with. So they never paid the fees, the state just said we owed you. One set of books shows the amounts of money charged; the other set shows the payments doctors actually received.

    Some years later, I decided to take a look at the numbers. I found that fees left unpaid to Maryland doctors for treating Medicaid patients exceeded several billion dollars. At least my efforts, in stopping a proposed illegal action, had created a record of how much we "heartless and greedy doctors" had donated to serving the poor. To my own contributions, I also add the $1,500 I paid to Arthur Weinberg as his legal fee. When I wrote his check, I almost felt like calling him to say he owed me the money for the lesson in medical politics I had taught him. I didn't of course, but the lesson of the experience is still important, for it shows what one person can do in the political arena. Persistence, determination, and integrity can pay off.

    Earlier I wrote that I saw Medicare/Medicaid as promising services impossible to deliver with the money available, and flawed from the beginning. How accurate was my 20-year-ago appraisal? Headlines from news stories in The Wall Street Journal of April 7, 1998 begin to answer that question: "For Medicaid Patients, Doors Slam Closed," reads one headline. A leading nursing-home company says it plans to "...go out of Medicaid in all [of its] 300 buildings if we don't see a little change in the Medicaid program." Adds the Journal, losing money on Medicaid patients is "a standard complaint by nursing-home owners."

A second report in the same issue of the Journal informs that some "major health -maintenance organizations are pulling out of the largest Medicaid programs. The list includes Medicaid in New York, Connecticut, Ohio, Missouri, New Jersey, and Florida. If the trend continues, according to patient advocates quoted in the news stories, the most likely outcome will be for many millions of the 32 million Medicaid participants to be "thrown into Medicaid mills" letting care suffer and costs soar again.

Maybe there is hope. In a turnaround for the American Medical Association, the nation's largest physician organization, the President-Elect for 1995, Stormy Johnson, actually appeared before the Health Committee of the Heritage Foundation and made a speech.

Events of those earlier times convinced me more and more that the United States would move inevitably toward politically dominated health care. As I saw it then, and continue to see it now, every encroachment by politicians into medical care meant more and more paperwork, more enrichment for lawyers and high-priced CEOs of health care organizations, and — worst of all! — the transfer of treatment decision-making from physicians to politically appointed, or for-profit administrators.

What else have we learned about Medicaid and political controls imposed upon medicine? Politicians — and some doctors — keep putting "Bandaids" on the current system's flaws, but it is on life support. It is only a question of when and how, not if, this ill-conceived law must die.

To beat the drum once again: in the absence of medical leaders' involvement in the political/for-profit takeover of the finances of health care in the United States, a hybrid system emerged as ugly as a weed and continues to grow like one. The system grows ever more wasteful, makes accounting clerks out of physicians, is uneven in the care patients receive, and ultimately must collapse when its life-support mechanisms wear out.

As I had no choice but to stop the organized attempt to subvert Medicaid law in 1970, I felt I had no choice but to continue personal involvement in the political affairs of Maryland and the Congress. This gradually would drive me to do everything I could to keep then-Senators Daniel Brewster and Joseph Tydings from returning to the US Senate. Those efforts were destined to teach me more about the inner workings of political parties than I ever wanted to know.

Chapter 16

The Rewards of Parenthood

Sometime between the "Greek Church Massacre" of 1950 and the Medicaid Showdown in 1969, Grace and I developed a new and demanding core of values. At the time of our marriage, every day meant doing what it takes to survive, accompanied by building success in my chosen field of general surgery. Grace had experienced the long hours and poverty of training to be a registered nurse, and working with young and inexperienced doctors, so she knew well what lay ahead when we married. She adapted without undue strain to life as the wife of $135 a month resident surgeon at the University of Iowa Hospital followed by the equally cash-short start of my new practice in Baltimore.

Actually, life was good for us in Iowa, partly because we didn't expect too much. Our savings from after-hours work in Baltimore gave us some extra money and, heck! the hospital paid me in cash every month. Grace had some free time during my duty hours, and enjoyed the luxury of spending a year as a student at the University of Iowa.

When we returned to Baltimore and I opened my first office, she and I became a workaholic team. Two things made our working hours possible. One was that both of us had grown up in a culture where fatigue was ignored as long as it provided time for necessary sleep. The other was that we loved each other very much, respected each other's needs, and trusted each other totally.

Now that I read that sentence, I realize how much I have always taken for granted about Grace!

I don't think she took much about me for granted. To her, I believe, I was, and still am, simply a man that is. That's all: *just is*. What I am now is what I was, and will be tomorrow.

When we, and I do mean *we*, opened my practice as a fledgling surgeon in Baltimore, we became a perfect team. For seven years Grace was my nurse, my bookkeeper, the team's shopper and housekeeper, and, when we found time, lover. After my practice grew in Baltimore and Havre de Grace to the point we hired secretaries and acquired our own office building, Grace happily spent more time at home, but her hand was always steady on the tiller monitoring all of our business activities, finances, and social activities.

The idea of starting a family was naturally a part of our lives, but in the early years of our marriage it was out of the question. Children wouldn't have been fair either to us, or children. Then somewhere in our sixth year of marriage, we knew the time had come to do something about it. Like all young couples, we had no doubt that as soon as we wanted children — bingo! They would come. Well, we now wanted children, but nature didn't want us. Months passed, nothing. We began to doubt ourselves, and anxiety didn't make things any better. Finally, albeit reluctantly, we had to face up to the question of sterility. Did we need to consult with a fertility clinic? Which of us would go first? With our medical training, obviously we knew all there is to know about human reproduction. We were also realists, so we were just one more discussion from making a fertility appointment when Grace came to me one day, beaming. "Ross, I think I'm pregnant!"

A few more days went by, and doubts were replaced by the sure thing. We were on our way to becoming proud parents!

Grace being Grace, there was no way mere pregnancy was going to stop her from doing things important to her, as long as there was no physical danger to our child now growing day by day in her uterus. We had planned a trip to Canada that summer, had bought a spanking new Ford convertible for the trip, and Grace insisted on keeping our long-sought vacation. One leg of our travel was around the Gaspe Peninsula. This became a rough ride over newly laid gravel lasting one and a half days, mostly at 60 miles per hour.

I was more than a little concerned about the roughness of the ride, but Grace had no problems. I found that I could "flatten out" the wash-board gravel if I drove fast enough to sort of "glide" from high ridges to high ridges, "soaring" over the low grooves in the gravel. Another bit of ingenuity involved getting rid of the billowing clouds of dust raised by the front wheels and filling the convertible if we drove at customary speeds. Driving fast with the top down not only "leveled out" the gravel road, the dust cloud followed the car instead of filling it and laying a white coat on our noses, eyes and ears. Anyway, we persevered and saw the Perce Rock, the penguins, boats on their sides in the mud when the tide was out, and the cod fishing we had always wanted to see.

The only bad moment of Grace's pregnancy happened when she became tangled in the leash of our cocker spaniel and bounced down four steps! Eight months pregnant — you can bet her tumble brought us up short, but not even her fall bothered her or the baby.

Things held to our normal schedules until Feb. 4, 1952. At 3 AM —"emergencies" in the middle of the night were old hat to me as a doctor — Grace prodded me awake and said, "Ross, I am starting early labor pains." We waited long enough to be sure, and at five that morning she said her pains were slowly increasing. It was time to go.

I helped her dress and we drove to Maryland General Hospital, where I was on the surgical staff. I registered her into maternity as her obstetrician had directed and made sure her anesthesiologist, an old friend, was advised to be on hand as soon as needed. When both of us were confident that everything was in order, and Grace was now in the best of hands, I took off for Havre de Grace where I had a patient waiting for surgery. It was a typically busy morning for me, but I took advantages of breaks in my work to telephone friends at Maryland General and make sure Grace's condition was normal for delivery. By 1:30 PM, I had enough. I canceled everything for the rest of the day and drove to the hospital, arriving about an hour later. Later that afternoon, our first born child, a daughter, entered the world.

Christine was to be our only child.

Grace's pride and joy with her new daughter could be seen just by looking at her face. She was one mother who was going to see that her daughter had everything she needed, including an ocean of tender love and care. As soon as Christine was old enough to go places, Grace wanted to take her with us wherever we went and it was possible to do so. I fully agreed. By the time Christine reached age two, she never missed dinner with us. That was fine, but honesty compels me to add that during Christine's childhood I wasn't much of a father in terms of being present for her. I never added up my working hours, but they probably exceeded

80 per week. My flow of patients grew constantly, my management responsibilities increased, I operated six days a week in two or more places, made hospital rounds, kept office hours, taught anatomy to new medical students, supervised the surgical staff and visiting surgeons at Maryland General Hospital, and took care of personal business. Attending childhood parties, going to school meetings, and the sporting events Christine participated in school was rare — which is to be kind about it. It is too late for recriminations now, but nothing has, or will, compensate either Christine or me for my lack of involvement in her formative years.

Fortunately, Grace never failed Christine. She went to everything where parents were invited. She worked with Christine on her homework, and all of her other childhood activities, without regard to time. In a word, she was tremendous.

A unique condition of Christine's childhood made her into a little lady well before her normal time. My professional attainments in surgery, along with the money produced by my successful practice, brought us into frequent contact with older persons, usually highly educated, professional, political, and executive-level people. Many became family friends leading to a flow of invitations to dinners and meetings. Learning table behavior through dining daily with us, and reflecting the poise she had gained at the hands of Grace, Christine was welcome at many of these affairs. Most often, she was the only one of her age present. Fortunately, she was able to keep all of her normal childhood playfulness, and playmates, while acquiring a quiet confidence that did much for her throughout her high school and college years. I have always felt that Grace's training of Christine as a child served her well, and that includes bringing up our four grandchildren in Germany.

But children are, well, children. An inevitable crisis happened when Christine was 15 and developed a serious "crush" on a very nice boy. Naturally, we knew zero about the "crush" until Christine came home wearing the boy's high school pin. No one said a word about the pin, but dinner was a bit strained though otherwise uneventful. I noticed Grace was well into dinner before her face regained her normal complexion instead of being unusually pale.

After dinner, Christine excused herself to go upstairs and study.

Grace busied herself a moment with the dishes, then turned to me. "Did you see the pin she's wearing?"

"Of course - how could I miss it?"

"What are we going to do about that? The girl is only 15!"

I waited to respond. "Grace, the first thing we are going to do is be careful. Let's not lose the game giving in to our own dismay about this. She knows we had to see the pin. She's probably waiting to see what we say about it."

"Well, that pin has got to go! I'm not going to see Christine burdened by that kind of commitment. Ross, Christine is a conscientious person. She doesn't commit herself to something like this without thinking what she's doing. That pin has got to go!"

"I'm not arguing with you - I agree - but we could make the situation worse and trigger a serious reaction against us old fogies who don't understand. Remember, she's as strong-willed as we are. Let's approach this as respect for her having a mind of her own. Let's take it easy."

As noted, we Pierponts have strong wills and Grace showed hers. "I'll go easy, but I'm her mother and I am going to get at this tonight!"

Not long after that, we called Christine into a family talk. Christine showed no surprise that we wanted to bring up the matter of the high school pin. Grace made an effort but could not really disguise her feelings, so I tried to keep the discussion easy-going. I couldn't be sure where our talk was going to lead, until Christine finally said, "He seems so sincere about me, and I do like him a lot." She paused. "I really think he needs someone."

"Oh, God!" I thought. Not a maternal instinct at 15! Where the hell is this going?

Grace was now calm and smooth. "Christine, I was your age, too, you know, and I think I know how you feel. We all need someone, but that pin says something more than just friendship. It sets you and the boy apart from your other friends. Are you ready to trade all the rest of your friends, boys and girls, to 'belong' to just one person?"

There was a long silence. Christine spoke slowly, in a low voice. "Mamma, I think it's because I feel sorry for him, for some reason. I just don't want to hurt his feelings, but I don't want to be tied up completely, either."

"Christine, you could hurt him more by going on wearing his pin. You will find you are not ready for just one person; you have too many other people you want to be with, and if you wait to find out you really don't want to commit yourself to this boy, you will really hurt him. Why don't you explain this to him, and give him back his pin?"

This was mother-daughter talk, and discretion held my tongue.

Christine turned to me. "You haven't said anything, Daddy. What do you think?'

Christine was my child, too, so she knew without asking what I thought. She just wanted to hear me say it. "Christine, I think you know your mother is right. I think she's right. Don't hurt that boy's feelings - he probably is vulnerable right now, so tell him you really like him a lot and how much you appreciate his gift, but it isn't right for either of you right now."

Christine looked as if tears might appear any moment, but she collected herself and said quietly: "I'll give him back his pin tomorrow."

She did as promised but the house endured mostly silence the next couple of days. More temporary crushes flared up from time to time but nothing serious and she graduated at the top of her class at one of the toughest schools in the state, Roland Park Country School.

Then came her freshman year at Wellesley.

College students of every stripe and sensibility were caught up that year in protest of everyone in authority. The Vietnam war became the flash point of opposition to "the establishment," from the Federal government on down to college faculties, even individual professors. They seized buildings, rioted, refused to take examinations, and on it went. Christine was not exempt from the pressure of her college peers, but we had no idea how bad it was until the day she called to tell us what was going on at Wellesley.

Grace was listening on another phone, but I answered. "Christine, I understand what you are saying. I see the anti-war sentiment here, too. Many things going on are awful, but right now you need to live a life -"

She interrupted, sobbing hard. "Daddy, you don't know! You're not here! You don't understand!"

"Christine, I am doing my best to understand. I understand you are in a beautiful college, you have the company of fine friends, and you are doing a great job in your education, but it is a little hard for me to truly understand your position when I think about my campus - eight feet of city sidewalk, shared with a million other Baltimoreans. Your mother is listening, and we both love you and share as much as we can in what you are going through, but your job is to take what's handed you as we in our time took what was handed to us. Your job is to do what you are there to do."

I had barely finished when Christine blurted again, "You don't understand!" Still sobbing, she hung up the telephone.

I did not wait to call back. The phone rang several times before Christine picked it up and answered. I said, "Christine, I was with you all the way, but you hung up on me. If you ever do that again, don't bother to call back."

I do not say things I do not mean and both Grace and Christine knew the importance of what I had just said. Grace's face was drawn and pale as she reached to take the telephone from me. She listened quietly as Christine, between sobs, apologized. Grace replied, "Christine, we are both with you in everything you do, but you must stand with us and support us, too. You mean everything to us, and we respect you."

After that disturbing episode, our parent-daughter relationship became downright peaceful until Christine became a "Born Again Christian." She became active in the Wellesley Christian Fellowship and attended an Evangelical Free Church. Grace and I met a number of these very intelligent and likeable students, even attending an immersion baptism of her and equally devout others. One of her student friends, a young man named Bill, was close to a genius she admired very much. One day when we were talking about her friends at Wellesley she mentioned that Bill was very religious.

"Religious is fine with me," I said.

"He has very strong opinions about things," Christine said.

I laughed. "So do I."

"Well, Bill thinks everyone should give their money to help the poor."

I didn't laugh. "Christine," I said very slowly, "you may not think much about it, but your father grew up poor, went to school poor, studied medicine poor, interned poor, and started my practice poor. Your mother trained in nursing poor and married me poor. No one can tell Grace and me what it's like to be poor. So I feel for the poor and I help them all I can. I truly understand being poor, and you should know your mother and father have no intention of ever being poor again!"

That ended our introduction to this particular philosophy of Christine's Wellesley friends, including dissemintation of wealth to the poor.

The focus of Pierpont family life after Christine graduated from college was getting her ready for a one-year teacher-training course in Germany. Maybe it sharpens the senses when you watch someone you love get ready to leave you: really leave you. One day I sat in Christine's room watching her pack, and the thought suddenly came to me, how wonderful life had been to me. Looking at Christine busy with her task, I could also have been watching Grace, for they had so many characteristics in common - a blond, five-foot eight inch, slim and well-proportioned woman. Oh yes, woman! She had inherited Grace's bright and easy smile, infectious laugh, a way of carrying herself with confidence, and a way of speaking that radiated honesty. What you saw in Christine was what you got. The old saying, a beautiful mother will raise a more beautiful daughter came to mind, and how right it was. (I reminded myself not to say that to Grace.) Who's to blame if I felt an overwhelming sense of pride in Christine and the lady she had become - even if all the credit belonged to Grace, not me?

It also helped immensely that she had never given us a real behavior problem, no cigarettes, no drugs, or dubious activities with the opposite sex. Parental pride aside, she was every inch a lady.

Without warning, or even looking up at me, Christine said, "Do you think I should write a note to the boy I met once in Boston?"

I blinked. "Who in the world are you talking about?"

Now she looked at me and smiled that radiant smile. "He was a Rhodes Scholar I met with a Harvard friend of mine. He came over here from Germany on a Rotary Exchange last winter and Bill thought since I was majoring in German, and he was German, it would be fun for the three of us to have dinner together."

"I don't remember him," I said.

"I'm not sure how to take him. Bill introduced him as 'Baron Lippold von Klencke,' and the two of them during dinner talked a lot about his 'castle.' I think they were having some fun pulling my leg."

There are times to be silent. This was one of them. After a pause, Christine spoke thoughtfully. "He was nice. A real gentleman - you could tell. Bill said, 'Lippold, if Christine's assigned somewhere in northern Germany, you have to look after her.' I don't remember just what Bill's friend said about that, but it was something like, 'Of course, Bill.'"

Grace came by just then and I greeted her with one of those parental "something's-going-on-here" looks. Grace sat down and I said, "Grace, Christine just told me about a Rhodes Scholar from Germany she met in Boston, and the idea she could meet him again when she's in Germany."

Grace said, "Christine, that's nice to hear, but aren't there others you'd want to get in touch with? After all, you were at Degendorf for the Goethe Institute for three months, and at the University of Munich for a year. I thought you made some good friends at those places."

Christine thought a moment. "Mother, none of them live in northern Germany."

The three of us were silent until Grace wrapped things up. "If he seems like you described him, why not just write him a note saying you're coming, and let it go at that?"

Christine took Grace's suggestion, and we thought no more about it until Lippold von Klencke's reply arrived a few days before she left for Germany. He invited Christine to visit him at Haemelschenburg and would help her find an apartment in Holtzminden. That sounded much more attractive to Christine than arriving with no place ready for her. Offer accepted.

After arriving in Germany, Christine spent her first week with fellow Fullbright grantees in Bad Gotesberg, then left for Bad Pyurmont. There, Lippold picked her up and helped her settle in an apartment in Holtzminden. As we found out later, it was to be love at second sight.

As days passed, Christine was clearly adjusting well to her upcoming teaching assignment, and Grace and I liked what we heard. Christine's assignment turned out to be teaching English at the gymnasium (roughly Germany's equivalent of an advanced American high school) in Holtzminden, a small city on the Weser River. The school was 40 minutes from Lippold's castle in Haemelschenburg.

Not long after Christine had settled into her teaching assignment,

Lippold called to invite her to visit the castle over the next weekend. Christine accepted, telling us all about it later. Still excited and enthusiastic, she described how the two of them drove along the Weser River, through a countryside of beautiful small mountains and rolling hills in middle-north Germany - a region not usually visited by American tourists. The approach to Lippold's castle was through the Emmer Valley leading to the family estate of some 1,200 acres.

Her excitement came right through the wire to us as she told of her first sight of Lippold's castle (Schloss Haemelschenburg). "My jaw must have hit my chest!" she said.

She had always been captivated by European castles and chateaux, and this castle, or palace, was a superb specimen. Its construction was virtually continuous through 30 years from 1588 to 1618 as the center of one of the most important baronies of what was then the Hannoverian Kingdom. As guardian of law and order for the area, the castle contained a court, a justice, a below-ground dungeon, arms room, horse stables, large floor-to-ceiling porcelain fireplaces (in original times the sole source of heat), a chapel, and 50 rooms, all accessed over a drawbridge moat.

If ancient words could be recovered, what tales, what fates, would those rooms tell!

This huge structure is divided into two wings separated by what originally had been the stables and lofts. One wing is "the Baron's wing," and the other the "Knights' Hall." Today, the most beautiful of the rooms are in the original stables section. A dining room seats up to 50 persons. The ballroom is 40 feet long, 30 feet wide, with a decorative ceiling 18 feet high. A large reception room and adjacent library are next to the dining room and ballrooms. Antique furnishings and furniture, and hand-worked filigree complete a magnificent setting.

That was the beginning. I think both Grace and I sensed Christine was more than just pleased with her "fox hunt weekend." Sure enough, the letters and telephone conversations contained increased references to Lippold, along with dissatisfaction with her lodgings in Holtzminden. My internal warning flags waved. Then came a letter that led me to tell Grace I thought it was time to go to Germany and find out what was going on there. Grace brushed my concerns aside as a doting father's imagination. I let it drop, then brought it up with the next letter.

Grace said, "If I am going, you have to come with me."

"Now, wait a minute," I replied. "We're not conducting an invasion. This is only a scouting trip, so we'll send out a scout, not an army. You go over there and straighten out her lodgings, and just incidentally check up on this great Lippold von Klencke guy."

Grace not-too-happily agreed, and arranged with Christine for a visit to straighten out her lodgings. Once in Germany, they took only minutes in Christine's lodgings to decide a change was in order. They had no trouble finding a small studio apartment owned by a couple with an adopted daughter. The entire family welcomed Christine and Grace like one of their own, and Grace called me to report everything was now fine.

Next came settling "the Lippold question." Christine arranged dinner with the three of them, and Christine's affection for Lippold became obvious before the main course was served. Grace was so appalled she could not finish her dinner. Calling me to report what she had found, she said, "Ross, there's no way I am going to lose my daughter to live in Germany the rest of her life." Of course, she had been too wise to say that at the dinner.

Lippold invited Grace to a fox hunt the next weekend, and Grace was delighted to accept as another step in finding more about the relationship between the man and her daughter. During the days before the hunt, she found ways to comment on the chill and unhealthy dampness that went with living in a stone castle. Christine did not take the bait.

On arrival at the castle for the foxhunt, Lippold and his mother, Baroness Viktoria von Ruperti Klencke, greeted them with champagne and tea. Grace retired early in anticipation of a long day for the hunt. Later, she told me, her room was not just warm, she became so warm she tried to open a window. No luck. After a warm night, she was met at breakfast with a question from Baroness von Klencke: "I hope you slept well. Was your room warm enough for your comfort?"

"Oh, yes indeed. Quite warm enough, thank you."

Christine couldn't restrain herself. "Not too cold in a drafty old castle, right?"

All laughed and Grace joined in although a little embarrassed to realize her room had been given extra heat from the castle's oil-fired, hot water system. After breakfast, the hunters gathered in jovial spirits. Bon vivant Count Rotekirsh (Red Cherry) gallantly paid close attention to Grace. The hunt day ended with dinner and dancing that continued until about 3 a.m. in the castle ballroom. During the conversation of the evening, Grace learned that Lippold was an only child, his father having been killed during World War II. His death came, they said, when he stood up in his lead tank to issue an order. His instant death made Lippold, born 2 weeks later, the sole heir to the castle and estates.

The evening was a charming, unforgettable experience and Grace could not help liking Lippold and his family; however, she was still determined she would not live to see her only daughter spending the rest of her life in Germany. Christine, of course, had different ideas of her own and they began to come out when she brought up the subject of inviting Lippold to the United States for the Christmas holidays. Grace studiously ignored what began as a possibility and gradually enlarged to a certainty. Things came to a head when the three of them, Christine, Lippold and Grace, were together preparing for Grace to return to the states. Christine alerted Grace with a soft nudge of foot to shin. "Mother, aren't you going to ask Lippold to our home for Christmas?"

"No, I don't think -"

Grace stopped in mid-sentence.

Lippold was sitting across the room, saying nothing, while Christine and Grace talked. Now, Grace got up and approached Lippold. "Lippold, Christine and I have been talking about our plans for Christmas at home. We would like you to come over and visit us and meet Christine's father. Could you arrange to do that?"

Lippold's immediate acceptance of the invitation was almost as unanticipated as Christine's threat to stay in Germany for Christmas. To say we were ready for him when he actually arrived, bag and portfolio in hand, would be an exaggeration. We had asked him, he was here, and the question now was, where to go from here?

Later, as all four of us sat in the living room, Lippold brought up his desire to marry Christine, who listened in silence. But Christine was Pierpont-raised and she had known from the beginning what she wanted. "Mother, Father, I have listened to Lippold and to you. I love Lippold, but I still want to think about it. Besides," she finished emphatically, " I promised Lippold on the trip over that we would not get engaged under the Christmas tree."

We looked at each other and the question was settled with no need for more words.

In March of the next year, Lippold proposed again, and this time Christine accepted.

In a ceremony too magnificent to ever forget, Christine and Lippold were married before 500 guests that included Lippold's mother and Grandmother von Ruperti on Sept. 21, 1974. When Grandmother von Ruperti, tall and perfectly erect, strode gracefully down the aisle dressed in a black satin suit with a flowing white ascot and collar framing patrician features capped by perfectly groomed, snow-white hair, her effect on all of us was electric. Our new Grandmother became second only to Christine as the star of the occasion.

No one could have prepared me for what happened at the reception. As soon as we arrived for the reception, we formed the customary reception line that included Christine, Lippold, parents, and Lippold's Grandmother. While we stood awaiting our first guests, Lippold's mother, Viktoria, turned to Christine and spoke directly to her: "Christine, I wish to congratulate you, and welcome you as the new mistress of Haemelshenburg."

Totally unprepared for Viktoria's statement, we stood looking at her until Christine broke the silence. "Thank you, I appreciate it."

Only later did I realize that with Viktoria's congratulations Christine had become responsible for the management of the estate and its 1,200 acres.

Chapter 17

A Pierpont In Germany Carries On Centuries of Responsibility

Different traditions; a foreign language; new and different friends; unprecedented responsibilities and parenthood. It was up to Christine to digest them all.

We had never made the mistake of trying to live our lives through Christine, and now that she was married and living abroad we knew we could only follow her life from a distance. Her life, of course, would be totally new. The three of us were somewhat familiar with the small town of 500 people dominated by the Schloss Haemelschenberg, but we knew nothing about the social conventions and structure of the local society.

Not for nothing had I learned bitter lessons about the costs of violating protocols. Could I give Christine the benefit of that experience? In a brief get-together before she left for Germany, I tried: "Christine, I hope you are aware of the position you hold in the castle. When Baronin Viktoria, a lady twice your age and Lippold's mother, congratulated you on becoming the mistress of Haemelschenburg, she meant what she said. All of those duties you have admired her for handling so skillfully are now your responsibility."

Christine was still in a glow from her marriage and wasn't ready to think about anything as dull as responsibilities. "Oh, Daddy, you misunderstand all of that. Everything's changed now. We are all equal now. Germany's modernized."

Grace saw what Christine wasn't ready to see. "Christine, I'm not so sure you are right about everything being changed. Remember how Viktoria was called on to settle disputes among the villagers in that anti-room to Lippold's office? Those people in the village, when they need help, still look to the castle for it. I think your father's right."

Christine didn't want to hear it. "I'm going to act like all of the others," she said firmly. "That's the way it has been for me, and I'm not going to pretend anything. We'll all be friends together, you'll see."

Grace and I left it at that until I looked at her one more time at the airport. I smiled at her; she smiled her bright smile back. I said, "Oh, by the way, Christine, if you find the people aren't as egalitarian as you think, remember, 'Daddy told you so.'"

That was all until a letter came saying they were greeted when they arrived at the castle by a huge welcoming sign over a large table loaded with food and beverages. The whole village had turned out as if a holiday, and a brass band played Lohengrin's wedding march. "The depth of affection and the loyalty of the people," she wrote, were overwhelming.

"All at once," she continued, "I realized that although I had never thought about my station as Lippold's wife, the greetings of the villagers told me very clearly that they understood."

It was also clear to her, now, that some of the people would be watching for mis-steps, and failures to live up to the demands of formal German protocol. No one ever knew it affected her. Some said, later, it was as though she had been trained for it. Also, it helped enormously that Lippold supported her in every way.

After all, Lippold was a classic product of German tradition and education, who had become a civil servant of the German government. That term describes a totally different position in work and in life than found in our civil servants. To be a German civil servant, one must be a university graduate followed by a degree in German law, or postgraduate education. Lippold had extended his university education by 2 years as a Rhodes Scholar at Oxford in England.

If qualified by the required education, one may apply for the civil service. Acceptance means 2 years devoted full-time to mastering every phase of German public policy and management; transportation public and private; banking at Federal, state and local levels; medical care at all levels; insurance; labor; industry, and more. At the end of 2 years, applicants are examined for six months. Any failure of any part of the examinations brings immediate release - no second chance. Winners in this rigorous process carry their successful grades on their diplomas for the rest of their lives; however, winners are also on probation for the next 3 years, followed by lifetime tenure except for the most flagrant violations.

This system evolved over hundreds of years and, to me, comes about as close to Plato's "Republic" as you get. It is a system of government designed to bring the nation's best and brightest into the management of the nation's affairs.

As Christine and Lippold settled into life as husband and wife, we learned to enjoy the union of two brilliant, talented, and active young adults. One of Christine's pleasures was strengthening the religious activities in the village. These took place for the most part in the beautiful chapel, which is the oldest Lutheran church building in the world. It was built in 1563, during the time of Martin Luther's Reformation. Christine used her teaching skills to strengthen the Sunday School training of children, organize women's groups, and work more closely with the German religious hierarchy. Religion is second only to Government in importance in Germany. Within a few years of her marriage, Christine was honored by election to the regional Church Council.

In a notable and amusing exception to Christine's religious success, her egalitarian approach to worship at the Chapel ran headlong into the realities of local tradition. As noted, the Chapel was built in the early days of the Lutheran Reformation, when people were identified by their class. The Chapel's main entrance admitted about 90 worshippers for seating on the first floor, with space for about 40 more in a rear balcony. A second entrance at the front of the Chapel opens to the nave on the same level as the raised pulpit. Visiting aristocracy, who sit in an enclosed pew built at floor level, use the front entrance. The front entrance is also designated for use by the von Klencke family, who sit in a different, enclosed pew built above the floor-level pew. This pew is reached by going up a few small steps.

Christine's two great beliefs were in her religion and egalitarianism. If equality were ever to be realized in Christine's world, it surely would take place in her church. Before marrying Lippold, she had gone to services there many times. Always she had been seated wherever she wished. Now, she told Lippold, she would sit where everyone else sat and be just like everyone else in the eyes of God. She was so fervent, Lippold was convinced and agreed to the change. Tradition gave way to the power of her persuasion.

As the mother and father of the von Klenckes of Haemelschenburg, we were often invited to important social events. One of these was the "Celle Ball," a Ball held by the Hannoverians on the 29th of December every year to mark the "coming out" of the younger groups with their elders. It is a strictly formal affair with white tie and tails for the men. The ladies dress in the finest gowns with family jewels in full display. The Prince of Hannover, who would be the King of Hannover if such an office still existed, is the honorary Grand Master of each Celle Ball. Seating is as formal as the guests' attire. "The Committee" meets in advance and assigns everyone invited to sit with different partners. As men come into the Ball, they pick up place cards on a table in the champagne reception room, and seek out the lady with whom they will sit at dinner.

The Balls maintain a strict tradition that dinner must be over, and each man must dance with each lady at his table before joining the partner he came with. I have been placed with a Countess, a Baroness, a Hertzoggin, and others. Every one of my assigned partners for the evening has spoken English, a genuine help for everyone in view of my poor German. Grace was assigned partners of high prestige for her first two Balls. For the third, she was seated at the left hand of the Prince of Hannover, making her the honored foreign guest. In this society, her seating was a high honor, not lost on other ladies attending the Ball.

Dancing was a new experience - for my partners as well as me. I "managed" the quadrille if not trampling one's partner qualifies as "managing." Waltzes were popular, and I chose them for dancing with a new partner whenever I could. The setting, the formal evening attire, the jewelry, and the music remind me, now, of watching one of those opulent old movies depicting European royalty.

For young Hannoverians, the Balls are a different evening altogether. They congregate in an adjacent ballroom with a rock band pounding out the rhythms. Will that be life in the castle when Christine's eldest takes over, I would like to be around to see. All things being equal, however, I doubt the possibility.

While the Celle Ball is a social highlight of life on the estate, a German Hunt Ball is far more important socially. A typical Hunt Ball given by Christine and Lippold takes place the evening before The Hunt in the ballroom of the castle. As invited counts, countesses, barons, baronesses, government officials, and prominent citizens arrive - perhaps 125 in all - the Brass Band of Haemelschenburg serenades them. Dinner features wild boar accompanied by red wine, fish accompanied by white wine, and dessert accompanied by champagne. A hunting horn band keeps the pace of the dinner lively, and a dance band takes over following dinner and toasts in the main ballroom. Although the Hunt will begin the next morning at about seven, the dancing and socializing normally continue until about 2 a.m.

A Hunt Ball hosted by Christine and Lippold is typical of Balls held the evening before many other similar Hunts throughout Germany. Hunts are private and take place on private estates, such as Haemelschenburg, or on forested land leased from a city or state. Invitations to a Hunt Ball, and the following Hunt, are signs of social status and prized accordingly. Christine and Lippold receive several thousand dollars in return for leasing their estate for the Hunt.

Centuries of tradition establish well defined rules of the Hunt which are strictly enforced. The purchaser of a hunting lease must hire a hunter who keeps the observation towers in repair, establishes the stands for each hunter, and sees that the game on the land does not starve. The hunter also keeps a count of wild boar, fallow deer, red deer, roebuck, and estimates the number of foxes, hare, rabbits, and other types of game on the land to be hunted.

To minimize any possibility of injury to the hunters, each hunter has a "stand" that limits his field of fire. Each hunter must wait for deer, fox, rabbit, or other game to appear within his individual field of fire before taking a shot. If the shot misses, there is no second chance. He must wait for another animal to appear in the field of fire allotted to him.

This type of Hunt usually begins about 7 AM, with a hearty German breakfast accompanied by schnapps and brandy. After breakfast, the hunters assemble in full hunting regalia along with the Beaters. Beaters wear bright yellow raincoats for warmth and visibility. The job of the Beaters is to form a broad semi-circle away from the hunters, then walk toward the hunters at an angle which keeps them out of the line of fire. As they walk, they drive game ahead of them into the hunters' fields of fire.

The sound of a hunting horn at about 8 a.m. is the signal for the morning hunt to begin. About 11 a. m. the hunting horn signals that the morning hunt is over. Everyone returns to a hunting lodge, or a tent, where a huge fire awaits, along with a full dinner. A typical Hunt menu could include goulash or split pea soup, roast beef, potatoes, a salad, plus dessert with fruit and cheese. Successful hunters display their trophies, and stories of the morning activities vie with each other for excitement, often over glasses of beer, wine, champagne, or brandy and cigars.

The afternoon of the Hunt is basically a repetition of the morning's activities, ended by the hunting horn about four o'clock in the afternoon. The lease-holder of the Hunt owns all game killed during the day. One typical hunt included five wild boar, three roebuck, one fox, one fallow deer, eight hare and ten rabbits. Local merchants are eager to buy all available game, and sometimes the lease-holder will keep some for himself, or give it away as trophies.

The Hunt, which began with a festive Ball, now concludes with a grand supper either at the home of the Hunt's lease-holder, or, sometimes, at a restaurant.

In addition to annual, all-day Hunts, the estate at Schloss Haemelschenburg is a favorite for fox hunts like the one Christine saw the first time she visited the castle. On the day of a foxhunt, 40-50 participants in brilliant hunting garb gather in the castle courtyard astride their chosen horses. Simultaneously, the Master of Hounds, the horse breeder and farmer on the estate, arrives with about 15 excited, yelping, jumping dogs. When all are ready, the pastor blesses the hunt and the hunters guide their horses out to their starting places.

This is not a Hunt for a live fox. If one shows up in the hunt it is by accident. The "prey" of the hunt is fox scent.

The hunting horn sounds the start of the hunt, the dogs charge off looking for a fox that exists only by its scent, and forty to fifty horses with their riders surge toward the first jump. Some horses refuse jumps, others unseat their riders, while the hounds continue their endless yelping. More riders lose their mounts at the river jumps, but no one is hurt seriously and the ambulance remains idle. About a half-hour from the first sounding of the hunting horn, successful riders are at the halfway point where they refresh with bubbling champagne. In another half-hour, the finishers have crossed the finish line.

To end the hunt formally, the Mistress of the Hunt (Christine) arrives in an open surrey pulled by two well-groomed horses. The horses stop, she leaves the surrey and presents a trophy to the winning hunter. She then goes to the mount of the winner and inserts an oak sprig into the bridle at its head. It is always the same, always things as expected and as they should be.

Although Christine fully accepted her responsibilities in Haemelschenburg, and the traditions that went with it, she remained at heart a believer in social equality. Nonetheless, her egalitarianism did not prevent her from being dazzled at the wedding of the young Prince of Hannover.

From her description of the wedding, it was like the Celle Ball, or a Hunt Ball, on a far grander scale, or like the royal weddings in England we have seen in movies or on television. The reception after the wedding took place at Marienberg Castle, one of several castles still owned by the Prince. Following convention, seating arrangements were by place cards, and Lippold and Christine found themselves seated in an ornate, flower-decorated parlor with the Queen of Spain, Sophia; Isabella, the daughter of the Queen of Greece, and the niece of the elder Prince of Hannover. "I have never seen such opulence!" said Christine. "Diamonds, rubies, sapphires in crowns and tiaras, necklaces, and bracelets. If I ever needed to be impressed with 'royalty,' I got it then. It wasn't just impressive, Daddy. It was overwhelming. So," she concluded, and I could imagine her smiling, "you win."

Although she grudgingly recognized the class distinctions so evident at the wedding, at the same time she was pleased at the way everyone she met behaved with total courtesy and acceptance. She was never conscious of being seen as somehow different, as an American. In fact, she said later when we talked about it, "I had no problem talking with royalty, and they seemed to enjoy talking with me as an American."

Although Christine and Lippold's life still includes exciting balls and fox hunts, their daily life is built upon hard work and long hours. Four children were born to them in the first twelve years of their marriage, and they still come first in Christine's life. Lippold leaves for work in Hannover each morning by seven, and he does not return until 6-7 PM, Monday through Friday. As top aide to Ernst Albrecht, Minister President of Lower Saxony, his responsibilities often call for travel to the capital, or weekend meetings of government officials.

In addition to mothering four very active, though well behaved, children, Christine oversees all castle and estate activities. From her "headquarters" of a 19-room apartment on the second floor, she manages a restaurant, a hydro-electric plant, several rental properties, and castle tourism. Between 20,000 to 25,000 tourists visit the first floor and former dungeon of the castle every year.

The 1,200 acres of the estate support a farm and forestry operation. About 700 arable acres are farmed by Herr Langels, who lives on the estate in a classically German farmhouse. Herr Langels raises large-boned, rangy Trackener horses used for fox hunting and dressage. When trained, they can really put on an impressive show. Zuckerrueberg (sugar beets) is a major cash crop. The farm also produces wheat, rye, and a variety of garden vegetables.

The forestry operation, under the sub-management of Herr Seidensticher, grows Norway spruce, Douglas Fir, Beech, and Oak trees on the slopes of nearby hills and low mountains. Both the planting and harvesting of trees in Germany are strictly controlled.

Although the responsibilities of Christine and Lippold are demanding, they are never too busy to welcome Grace and me for frequent visits. It helps, of course, that we stay out of the way and take care of our own four-room suite on the second floor of the castle. Our visits have stimulated me into a close study of the German political system, and especially the German medical care system. Being a physician, medical care is my first concern and will be explored later in this narrative.

Chapter 18

Anarchy, War and Peace

One day while Grace and I were visiting Christine and Lippold, I found myself looking closely at the castle's 3-foot thick walls. These were made of enormous gray boulders mortised into place one by one, 5 stories high. Each boulder had to be hauled for miles over land and water to reach the carefully selected site. The effort that went into building the castle encouraged me to take a closer look at the origins and purpose of the place. Although my great grandparents had emigrated from Germany to America, I knew only the basics about them, and even less about my ancestry. I wanted to know more.

It seemed to me then, and still does, that the well-kept castles of Germany are symbols of German personality. They represent the respect — no, the affection — Germans have for tradition and order, for wanting things "where they belong." Tradition, I believe, was the glue that bonded the German peoples together through centuries of anarchy, through the upheaval of replacing Catholicism with Lutherism, through regional and national wars, and through the hardships of the most ruinous inflation ever inflicted upon a modern nation.

Two Barons von Klencke directed the work of hundreds of artisans for 38 years before completing the castle, all 50 rooms of it not counting the dungeon. But what moved Georg von Klencke to start such a long-term, enormous project when poverty was a way of life, and animals plus a man's hands and back provided the sole source of construction power?

Schloss Haemelschenburg (in English, Haemelschenburg Castle), like dozens of similar castles studded throughout Germany, was built as part of a regional Government system. The Knights' Wing in Schloss Haemelschenburg was no decorative add-on. It was a necessity, the place where the Baron's armed knights lived, trained, kept their weaponry, and their horses. These armed men were on call around-the-clock every day of the year to sally forth against marauders, or to defend the castle against attack, if that became necessary. Their presence was, for the most part, sufficient to deter all but the most desperate of raiders, or, of course, organized armies. The presence of the dungeon, and the fate of those sent into it, was a constant reminder that attacking the rule of the Kings of Hannover, implemented in the Barony of Haemelschenburg by the Baron, was not a healthy enterprise.

In the years Baron Jurgen von Klencke ruled his important Barony, in what is now north-central Germany, the entire continent of Europe was in political and religious turmoil. What we call Germany today was a conglomerate of some 350 warring "states" under a system of Emperors, kings, dukes, counts, and barons. The Duke of Hannover, the capital city of Lower Saxony and including Schloss Haemelschenburg, literally owned all he surveyed, including the Barony of Haemelschenburg. The law was what he said it was. Conditions worsened in 1517 when Martin Luther's Reformation divided Germany into a Catholic south and a Lutheran north. Jurgen broke with the Roman Church and, joining forces with Martin Luther, built one of the oldest Protestant churches in the world.

Land was the source of wealth and stability in those turbulent times. The only way to "own" it was through Letters of Occupancy issued by the Dukes. The power to issue or withhold such letters is not hard to imagine. The sole proof that the von Klenckes "owned" the Barony of Haemelschenburg consisted of Letters of Occupancy issued for each generation by the Duke of Hannover, through more than four centuries of occupancy. Finally the estate became the von Klencke's private property.

For Baron Jurgen von Klencke to maintain his position and ownership of the Barony, he had to maintain an effective fighting force. From all indications, he was a good commander, and his fighting force was effective. While his Barony remained at peace during many years of his rule, the Dutch were fighting the Spanish and both sides wanted fighting men wherever they could get them. Baron Jurgen von Klencke played no favorites; he rented his knights to whomever wanted them and paid the most: sometimes the Dutch and sometimes the Spanish. Gold received from the services of Jurgen's knights, plus income from good crops and local taxes, gave Jurgen the money he needed to build Schloss Haemelschenburg. He also had a big plus - the dowry of his wife, Anna von Holle.

In addition to the protection of its thick walls, the Schloss has a forbidding moat with access only through the same type of drawbridge seen in dozens of movies. Using the moat for sewage disposal increases its deterrence power. Moats are also effective ponding systems that purify raw sewage. In the castle's moat, water flowing into it from five springs on the nearby mountain keep it oxygenated to assist in breaking down the waste deposits. Carp help in the cleansing and provide a fresh fish supply. These are thoroughly purged before they can be eaten at Christmas feast and banquets. Caught fish are put into clean, pure water in the castle's fountain where they naturally cleanse themselves over five or more days - not a lot different from getting clams to cleanse themselves of grit.

The baronial system functioned reasonably well from the time Jurgen built the castle until centuries later. Gold collected from renting out the knights, collecting taxes for the king and retaining a slice of that income, and general self-sufficiency was enough. Fox hunts, wild boar hunts, and fishing were necessities for survival, not a sport, especially in winter when foods ranged from scarce to bare survival. When collection of taxes for the king stopped, Jurgen's successors supported themselves by raising horses, farming, and forestry.

Not even the two World Wars radically changed the system. The populated centers of Germany suffered enormous destruction and massive dislocations, but farmers who were not invaded did surprisingly well. Farmers also survived the hyper-inflation following World War I because they had the necessities of life for their own survival, and could sell or barter their surplus foods and wood to meet other needs. People willingly traded all sorts of possessions in return for something to eat and a place to sleep. In World War II, bombed-out people fled by the millions into the safer countryside, where they turned to the nation's farmers to survive. During World War II, Lippold's mother turned Schloss Haemelschenburg into a haven for 96 refugees still living there when the war ended.

In talking with Viktoria, Lippold's mother, I found that the events of World War II were very much alive in her memory. The violence of the war, she said, seemed almost to have passed by the castle until the conflict's last few months. No bombs fell, no pitched battles occurred as went on almost daily not many miles to the south. Then came the day when her mother-in-law, Anna, answered a knock at her door and found an American Colonel standing before her, a pistol holstered on his hip. A large number of armed American soldiers stood behind him. Anna said the Colonel saluted her and said, "Madam, war is a crime I cannot do anything about. I have to inform you that we are commandeering this castle for occupancy by my troops."

Anna had gone through too much in her life, including the loss of her son and close relatives, to let the Colonel's announcement destroy her poise. "Herr Colonel," Anna said, "I have made my castle into a home for 96 people. Some are very old, and some are children. I am a widow. My son, Leopold von Klencke, was killed at Metz 2 weeks before my grandson, Lippold von Klencke, was born."

The Colonel responded politely. "Madam, I fully appreciate your feelings, and your position here. I do not want to cause you more problems than I have to, but I hope you understand that my first responsibility is my men. This is the only available shelter, and I must use it until we are ordered to move on."

"Thank you, Herr Colonel. I understand and will do all I can to obey your orders as quickly as we can."

"I appreciate your cooperation," the Colonel replied. "This is what I must ask you to do. First, every door and cabinet must be unlocked and left unlocked. Locked places must be checked for safety, and my men will break locked doors open if they have to. All of my troops will be warned against stealing or destroying anything in the castle, and we will do as little damage as possible. I give you my word on that."

"You are most kind, Colonel. I will call the people together and tell them they must leave their rooms for your troops to use."

After the Colonel returned to his troops, Anna and her daughter-in-law, Viktoria, moved all of the inhabitants into the Chapel. The only things they took with them were bare necessities. Although the American had assured her there would be no thievery, Anna took the precaution of moving some best wines from the wine cellar into the crypt beneath the floor of the church.

Viktoria said that after a few days went by uneventfully, the Colonel came to see them. "Frau Anna, I am constructing quarters for my men in the meadow. As soon as the equipment arrives, we will move there and return your castle to you."

The inhabitants of the crowded Chapel got the news with sighs and some tears of relief. Good to his word, the Colonel returned the keys of the castle to Viktoria. She remembered being surprised when he saluted her and said, "Frau Viktoria, I want to thank you on behalf of the United States Army for your cooperation. I have checked the rooms and believe the castle has not been unduly harmed. If you find anything wrong, do not hesitate to let me know."

Although we talked many years later, Viktoria still remembered the unexpected courtesy and thoughtfulness of the Colonel, and how much she appreciated the carefulness of his American soldiers. She said she put aside the bitterness she felt over her husband's death at Metz, and did her best to respond graciously, "All of us thank you. We are grateful for your courtesy and the fine behavior of your men. Not everyone would have been so thoughtful."

The joy of little things when not much is expected! The 96 refugees driven to the castle by the war were delighted by the simple privilege of returning to their rooms.

In addition to the disastrous loss of life, some officials in the British government were talking about German land reform. If this happened, it could lead to breaking up lands such as the estate at Schloss Haemelschenburg. If anything went wrong for Viktoria and her baby son, Lippold, ownership of the estate would be wiped out. To prevent this, the father of Viktoria's dead husband, Lippold's Grandfather von Klencke, adopted Lippold, the first born son of his first-born son. Under the rules of the time, the ownership of the estate at Haemelschenburg passed to Lippold in his infancy, with Viktoria as his guardian. After the adoption, Wolf von Klencke, Lippold's uncle, had no claim on the estate.

I had made an effort to get to know Wolf, and fortunately for me he spoke English fluently. His childhood was a clue to the grown man. Many families have a child that "kicks over" the traces, and Wolf was the "kicker" of the von Klenckes. While a schoolboy, he found a way to sneak out of the house at dawn and go fishing with a farmer friend instead of going to school. He chuckled easily as he told me how he'd tie one end of a string to his big toe and the other end to a ball before going to bed. Then he dropped the ball out the bedroom window where his farmer friend would find it in the dawn and yank on it to awaken Wolf. Wolf would yank back to let his friend know the signal was received, and without a sound to awaken any grown-ups, the two boys would go fishing.

Wolf was full of stories about his youth, about his loves, about his war experiences. A solidly built man about five foot ten, with sky-blue eyes and blond hair, he seemed always ready to laugh or say something interesting: truly a man who has lived and loves to live. I liked the man.

I knew that Wolf had served throughout World War II as an officer in the German Army, and the question of mostly aristocratic officers carrying out the orders of Hitler, a fanatic most of them despised, had always intrigued me. Wolf von Klencke offered me my first real opportunity to get some answers. "How could you take orders and risk your life for that brown-shirted maniac?" I asked Wolf.

"We were officers," Wolf said as if that should explain things. "We had sworn to obey our Fuhrer. It will sound strange to anyone not trained in the German Army, but I personally did not think much about Hitler, any more than your American soldiers thought about your Franklin Roosevelt, or your Harry Truman, or English soldiers thought they were fighting for Winston Churchill. My loyalty was to my men, and to my commander - and trying to stay alive myself." He smiled. "It's kind of important, staying alive if you can."

"The German General Staff had to know the kind of man Hitler was," I said.

Wolf's face again creased in that charming, easy smile that made him well-liked by many women. "If they did, they didn't tell me." Serious now, he added, "I never met anyone on the General Staff in five years of taking their orders, many of them I didn't understand, but it's impossible for an army to do its job if everyone in it waits for explanations before following orders. I was trained to lead men in battle, and it was expected of me."

It was expected of me! There it was again - that respect for tradition and what is expected of each person according to status. He expected to lead men in battle. His men expected to follow his leadership: no questions - just do it.

As we talked on I learned that Wolf as a very young infantry officer had been in the lead command in the occupation of Austria. He led troops across the Polish border and entered Warsaw, then crossed the Czechoslovakian border, and led his troops into Prague. Most of our conversation surprised me at how easily Wolf usually talked about his years in fighting. I detected no anger, no resentment until his face went grim in remembering the death of his brother, Leopold. He was as tight-faced when he spoke of his two brothers-in-law, Viktoria's brothers, dying in the Russian fighting. Another brother-in-law, Franz von Bitter, had been captured and imprisoned by the Russians until 1949, years after the German surrender: five men, four dead.

As I thought of Vikitoria's two brothers and her husband sacrificed in a despicable cause, I remembered how she had handled her encounter with an American Colonel who had commandeered her home. My admiration for the woman could not be higher.

"Uncle Wolf," I addressed him though I was as old as he was, "what did you do as the commander of infantry troops when you went into Austria, Poland and Czechoslovakia?"

"I was only 22, and young enough to be a proud commander of my battalion. Like a damn fool, I stood up in the lead car like it was on parade and in we went." He stopped, thinking. "Ross, I really was a damn fool! I wonder why I wasn't shot by those people. I'd never do that again!"

It was up to me to say something, but what? "I guess some people are born to be lucky, Wolf. Maybe you were one of them."

He let down, relaxed a bit. "Yes. I was lucky. It was awful, and I am lucky to be alive."

Wolf, I learned, was in the bypassing of the Maginot Line in France and had arrived at the heights overlooking the beaches, crowded with fleeing British, Belgian, and French troops, at Dunkirk. I had read considerably about the British evacuation, and asked Wolf what he had seen of the Allied disaster.

"We were ordered to attack. We attacked. The Brits just gave way. It was so easy I couldn't believe what happened. The Brits are good, but they gave way and there we were looking down on them crowding the beaches along with the French and Belgians."

This was my chance to get some questions answered. "Why did the German Army stop on the heights at Dunkirk when you had the British,

French and Belgian armies trapped against the sea? Why in the world didn't you go on and end part of the war then and there?"

"No one knows why we waited and let the British escape. The order came down from Hitler to halt. So we stopped. Why? I don't know."

(William L. Shirer, in his book, The Rise and Fall of the Third Reich, argues that the orders not to attack came from Hitler.)

"Are you saying you never found out why Hitler gave orders to stop the advance?"

"No one would ever say why we stopped. Our generals said, later, there was nothing to stop our advance. No reason at all, but the order from headquarters, maybe from Hitler himself, was, halt. We halted!"

Wolf searched his memory for a moment. "Of course we talked about it. Some of the superior officers said Hitler refused to believe we had driven the British to the beaches at Dunkirk, and were in position on the heights. You may not know it, but Hitler had always admired the British and knew their military history very well. I'd heard some officers say he felt we and the British were really kindred spirits. After all, German kings from Hannover, who couldn't speak English, had been crowned kings of England. Hitler hated the Russians, and was said to believe the British would come to their senses and join Germany in fighting the Communists and Russians - the 'infidels' he called them. He had no respect for the French or Dutch or Belgians, but he held the English in high regard."

Wolf sipped his wine. I remained silent to avoid interrupting his train of thought. "Headquarters kept sending us messages about our ammunition and other supplies, and morale. Someone in charge must have thought we had advanced so fast we'd outrun our lines of supply and they had to be restored before another battle. Hitler was supposed to wonder if the British had led us into some sort of trap. He just refused to believe in our enormous success. So we sat there and watched 'zem' go."

Wolf relaxed into jargon English. He had no way of knowing at the time his force had advanced so easily, a British counterattack had bit 10 miles into the flank of the German 7th Panzer Division, near Gerd von Rundstedt's headquarters, that 35,000 French troops continued to defend a key city inland from Dunkirk, and that German strategists were concerned about the obstacles presented to German armor by numerous water barriers around Dunkirk.)

"They had little boats," Wolf continued "Bigger Boats. Rafts out to ships at sea. For three days we did nothing but watch 'zem' go day and night. By the fourth day, we had petrol, diesel fuel for tanks, and food, and we were ordered to attack."

He smiled, remembering the events of the day. "At the first shots, white flags went all over the beaches. We stopped shooting and signaled for their commanders to show themselves. They did as directed. I was ordered to go down the hill to the beach and bring their commanders to our headquarters to arrange the final surrender. It was a funny feeling to get into my command car and tell my driver to take me to headquarters of men who, moments ago, would have shot me to death without a second thought. I stood erect in my car and saluted three generals, British, French, and Belgian. "Gentlemen,' I said, 'Please to get into ze car to go to our headquarters.'

"The French general was first to get in, then the Belgian, but the English general stood erect looking straight ahead and not obeying my instructions. 'General,' I said, 'Please get in ze car.'

"Nein,' he said.

"Why you not get into zee car?" I said.

"I won't ride in a car with them, the British general declared.

"Why you not ride with 'zem'? You finished fighting beside 'zem,' "I said. I respected the general's rank, though he was an enemy, but this was going on in front of watching troops, and I was getting a bit angry.

"My orders made me fight beside 'zem', but I don't have to ride with 'zem'!" the British general declared again.

Wolf's normally cheery face lost its glow. "I looked down at the general and said, 'Then, sir, you will walk in front of my car to our lines.'

"I motioned my driver to move on, and the British general, like an arrogant ramrod, walked in front. I respected his pride, but he was defying my orders to ride with his former allies. I motioned to my driver to speed up until he was nudging the general. The startled general glanced back then walked faster in front of the car. I sped up the car more. The general broke into a trot. More speed and the general had to run to keep from being nudged."

Wolf chuckled as he remembered what must have been an incredible scene. I remained silent. "He finally tripped and fell down. I stopped the car, and went to see if he was hurt. His face was red as a beet, his mustache dripping wet. Panting, out of breath, he looked up to me and his eyes told me that he knew he was beaten again. 'I'll ride,' he said. I did not help him as he crawled to the car and climbed into it. I respect the Brits, but not one who does not respect his fellow officers.

"No one talked during the trip to our headquarters where the generals signed their surrender. What would have happened if we had followed up our advance and captured 30 or 40 divisions of the British army instead of letting them run away to fight us another day?" Wolfe thought over his question. "Maybe you Americans wouldn't have come in against us. We wouldn't have fought on two fronts at the same time. And Hitler - "Wolf stopped. "It's something - knowing what we know now - I don't want to talk about any more."

Some wise person once observed that the army that wins in war is one that makes the least mistakes. Had the German Army not halted its advance and driven the British, French, and Belgian troops into the English Channel, or into a German prison, had the German Army gone on to defeat Russia, the world would look a lot different today.

The following afternoon, Wolf and I sat on the ramparts outside the library in the warm sun. Wolf lamented his tennis elbow and said he was thinking about selling his properties in Hamburg and moving to Munich for the rest of his life, but I wanted to know what he had done after the battle at Dunkirk, and I asked him about it.

"The rest of the war?" he said. "They gave me 75 men and told me to maintain part of the ring we held in the siege of St. Petersburg. My line was more than a thousand meters - a little less than your mile - just across the river from the heart of the city. We were too strung out to do much good, but once in a while we captured a Russian soldier near the river. It always happened in the mornings. I could never get them to tell me how they got where we captured them.

"Those Russkies are tough. Really tough. One day I looked out the window of my command post, and I saw one of my Russian prisoners chopping wood. He had a blood-stained hole in the back of his tunic, probably taken, I thought, from a soldier who had been killed. Then he turned to pile the wood, and I noticed a hole, chest high, in front of his tunic. To satisfy my curiosity, I went out for a closer look. It was as cold as hell, the Russian cold, with snow falling - how well, I remember that Russian cold!" He seemed to shiver a little at the memories, though we were in warm sun.

"Ross," he said, "You're a doctor. You'll never believe that as I walked around that man standing there in his army tunic, I was looking at a man with a bullet hole in his chest. 'Russkies,' I said, 'Take off that tunic.' I gestured to show what I was saying. 'Now your undershirt.' When he stood there bare-chested, I saw a hole from the front of his chest to his back. There he was, chopping wood in below-zero weather in the snow with a hole in his chest! When I tell you those Russkies are tough, believe it they are tough!"

"How did it end in Russia?" I asked.

"In a hell of a hurry!" Wolf exclaimed, and laughed. "I can laugh now, but I didn't then. One morning at dawn the sentry heard unusual noises and woke me. I looked out toward the river and couldn't believe it! Where they had been only water the night before, I now saw a bridge. What looked like a full Russian army was lined up on the river bank and starting across the bridge.

"Ross," he said, with his voice rising impressively, "those damned Russkies had built their bridge under water, under our noses, during nights. How they did it in icy water, I will never know, but it did tell me where our prisoners had come from. They had gotten mixed up in the water and came out on the wrong shore where we captured them."

I shook my head impressed by such a feat, too. "Amazing! What did you do?"

"Blew retreat and got out of there as fast as we could. Otherwise we'd spent the rest of the war in one of the Russkie's hell-hole prison camps, or died from disease or starvation, or been shot."

Wolf showed signs of wanting to end the talk, but I had one more question. "What were you doing when the war finally ended?"

"I was in Holstein when we heard Hitler was dead and we had surrendered. I immediately found myself some civilian clothes and buried my uniform, burned my papers and identification. The Russians and Americans were taking anyone in the Army prisoner, and that wasn't for me: not after the years I spent dodging bullets. Everyone I saw was doing the same thing, every man for himself.

"I was 300 kilometers from home, and the only way to get there was to walk, so I started walking like all the other refugees. I finally got to the Weser River, where the bridge was down but the superstructure was still above water. I started to climb through the girders when a shot rang out and a bullet ricocheted above my head, and someone yelled 'Halt!' I pulled out a handkerchief and began to wave it - what else?" He grinned, chuckling at the memory.

"My luck was still good. He was an American soldier pointing his rifle at me when all hell seemed to break loose up-river from us. It meant more to him than grabbing another German refugee, so he turned and scooted away. I finished working my way through the bombed-out bridge and made it the rest of the way home without trouble. My war at last was over! I was alive! That was all that mattered at the moment."

I said nothing as I noticed a small tear drifting down his cheek. From an attitude almost of triumph at living through years of combat, his mood became somber. He looked down at his feet and said softly, almost to himself: "My brother and Viktoria's two brothers, they were not lucky like me. I miss them very much."

As I looked at him, I thought: You! Your brother, Lippold's father! Viktoria's brothers! You were our enemies, fighting us to the death, dying yourselves, because you were expected to obey your superiors' orders - in turn the orders of a vicious, genocidal monster - and you obeyed. What do we make of a world like this, a country like the Germany we faced in World War II? Could I look into the face of Wolf von Klencke now and see there the face of an enemy?

Had we met on the field of the battle, he would have tried to kill me, and I to kill him. As I looked at "Uncle" Wolf now, I felt no anger, no bitterness, no enmity. I knew only regrets: so much lost, so many lives spent on nothing!

My desire to learn more about my, and Grace's, German ancestries had drawn me to a road well beyond gathering some history about von Klenckes, Pierponts, Zimmermans, and Schmidts. I gained a better understanding of what it was like to grow up a German between the World Wars, though it was superficial, of course. Yet I had vicariously experienced traditions, expectations, and approaches to life ingrained in Germans over many centuries. Grace and I were now and forever part of life at Schloss Haemelschenburg through Lippold, Christine, and our four grandchildren.

Chapter 19
A Lesson In Bigotry — From Liberals

When Grace and I opened the door of our home upon our return from carefree days as guests of Christine and Lippold, it closed the door of my brief immersion into five centuries of German culture. The next day I climbed into my work clothes — my surgical gown and gloves. We picked up where we had left off.

The discipline of a lifetime took over. From the time when I was a skinny eight year-old huckstering fruits and vegetables and smelling of our cows, to my sleep-when-you-can years in college and medical school, to the 24-hour days of my residency in surgery, to the opening of my first office in Baltimore near the end of World War II, and every year thereafter, work was the music we danced to.

Fortunately, the work continued to pay off. In the early 1950s, I found myself in need of more offices. Grace and I talked it over and we responded by buying a four-story town house in the Mount Vernon section of Baltimore. This is a neighborhood of century-old mansions complemented by a Gothic style Methodist Church and the renowned Peabody Institute (of music). Grace and I loved this elegant old home and we retained as much of it as possible. The first floor and wide staircase leading to the second floor were paneled in burnished mahogany. Hand-carved, floor-to-ceiling fireplaces were focal points of the main rooms. Marble-pedestaled floor to ceiling mirrors, and sliding doors also reaching to the 15-foot ceilings, added their own unique charm. Our wonderful downtown office building was also charming in a different way. It paid for itself in renting space to others. One office was taken by an old City Hospitals associate and fellow surgeon, Dr. Donald Hebb, who joined me as a partner.

My offices in Havre de Grace, a town half-way between Baltimore and Delaware, were not as impressive, just busier. As I mentioned earlier, we had our own building in Havre de Grace where I had taken in seven partners. When I wasn't actually operating five or more days a week, I continued to direct teaching resident-surgeons at Maryland General Hospital, and taught anatomy on Mondays and Wednesdays at the University of Maryland School of Medicine.

I was busy as a mother hen with one leg, and I loved it.

Loving what you do is great, but there's a limit. Grace and I had taken two steps to ease our mutual responsibilities. One was to hire Charles Shipley to drive me between offices, a serious need of mine described earlier. The second step was to hire Elaine as a full-time maid and all-around housekeeper. Both Charles Shipley and Elaine worked with pleasure for all - including Christine — for more than 33 years.

The freedom given to us thanks to Charles and Elaine made it possible to devote time to an absolute necessity — managing the business part of my practice. The medical profession is notorious for ignoring the economics of medicine, and medical schools have virtually ignored it. I expected no help from other physician-associates and partners, nor did I receive any. Over 45 years when I had many physicians as partners or associates, not a single one of them gave a dime's worth of time to the business side of the practice. In my domain, it was strictly "Pierpont, you do it."

The demands of running the business side of my practice took huge chunks out of the day. I have already listed some of the business responsibilities, but the addition of Medicare/Medicaid and a variety of insurance plans added a new layer of work. I could never have managed it without two things. One was Grace, who monitored everything we did. The other is what I had learned managing money as an eight-year old and pre-teen huckster, selling subscriptions, managing two cows, and working behind the counter in the stores of a drug chain.

Hoarding money and paying my own way while growing up made business management almost second nature to me. I knew where every nickel went, and if I made a mistake handling my money in my formative years it was as unforgettable as what happens when you touch fire. I also learned something at least as important: don't do things yourself if other people can do them better. The most effective part in managing the business side of my practice was to find the right person to do jobs with special requirements, then watch to see that those jobs were done on time and well.

One job I handled personally was negotiation of insurance coverage. Although we had a very high amount of surgical practice involving insurance, we kept things simple. Whatever our patients could reasonably afford, that is what we accepted. If the payment was just by insurance, fine. If it was nothing at all, we accepted that, too.

It's hard to believe, today, that we operated on such a simple policy. But we did, and it worked to nearly everyone's satisfaction, doctors and patients alike.

Then the politicians decided to manage medicine for us. Please read carefully the next sentence: *We were forbidden by law to treat anyone at no charge.* If a patient could not pay, our only choice was to collect the charges from Big Brother, the Federal government.

Grace and I had adapted many times before; we did it again. In fact, income from all parts of my practice, combined with the profitable results of a few investments, started to soar. We reached a bracket in taxable income so high it made little sense, monetarily, to put in the hours I did. Fortunately, more and more friends who were very successful financially introduced us to the power of tax write-offs. Investing in oil and gas provided opportunities to hold on to some of our hard-earned income, so we "tested the waters" with a few investments and had profitable results. Eventually we limited such investments to Russell Johnson and his son. Between us, we grew to arrange multi-million dollar oil deals in West Virginia. We drilled dry holes as well as profitable ones, relying on 90% tax write-offs and honest operators in the fields to keep us on the plus side.

It was exciting, reaching its peak in the 1970s. In those years, looking for something else as an interesting and profitable sideline, I satisfied my lifelong interest in sports by joining a group forming a franchise in ice sports. Baltimore had built a new Civic Center, and it looked like a natural home for ice sports including hockey. The two leaders of the group were "Jake" Embry, a former operator of a top radio station, and a part-owner of a Baltimore brewery, Zanvyl Krieger. We tried for a National Hockey League franchise, but had to settle for a farm team named The Baltimore Clippers. I was the team physician as well as a major investor.

Our franchise started out great. In addition to hockey, we had Holiday on Ice, Ice Capades, and occasional attractions like the Royal Marine Tattoo. Then came two blows we could not anticipate. A judge ruled that no one could own athletes in hockey or any other sport, which destroyed the value of the hockey team. With a stroke of a judge's pen, $750,000 went down the tube. At the same time, political insiders persuaded City Hall to void our rights to the ice shows. We had nothing. Jake Embry and Zanvyl Krieger wisely walked away. I stubbornly refused to give up and organized a new group that went back in the American Hockey League as the Baltimore Clippers. The effort cost me more than I want to think about, even now. It still hurts! But in one of the strangest quirks of fate ever seen, the losses of my ice-sports venture turned into one of my best investments. Hold on for this one.

On a typical routine day in my practice, I took a phone call and heard: "Doc, this is Larry Ziedel. I don't think you'll remember me, but I used to be a hockey player."

"Larry... yes, sure I know who you are. Good to hear from you. You played right defense for the Quebec Aces, and were always getting into a fight."

Larry laughed. I said jovially, "With that big nose of yours, you kept me busy straightening it out and sewing it up."

Larry said, "You've got a memory, Doc! Anyway, the reason I called is I'm a stock broker now. I know you don't want to buy stocks from a dumb hockey player, but I owe you a favor. You always were great to us hockey players, and whenever we had a problem in Baltimore you were always there to help us."

What's this guy up to? I thought. What I said was: "Thanks, Larry. I appreciate it."

"Doc, I called because an investment advisor left our company here in Philadelphia, and has gone on his own in Baltimore. His name is Dan Dent, and this guy built a record here beating the managers of the accounts of Mellon, DuPont, Wannamaker and others, better than anyone. I have nothing in this if you call him, but you should do yourself a favor and get in touch with Dent as your investment advisor. I'm telling you, you can't go wrong."

This is wild, I thought. Of all the hockey players I treated, this one calls me with advice about an investment advisor. OK, stranger things have happened. We exchanged pleasantries and both of us went about our affairs while I thought no more about it.

Weeks went by. Larry Ziedel called again. He sounded neither surprised nor disappointed when I admitted I hadn't called Dan Dent. He said, "Doc, you really are missing out not seeing Dan — oh, by the way one of his clients is Robert Goodman. Do you know him?"

I laughed. Bobby Goodman had handled the 1966 campaign of Ted Agnew for Governor of Maryland, plus the campaigns of a dozen other political candidates, and was one of the best-known political advisors in the business.

"I know him well, Larry. He invested $10,000 last year in the hockey team. He lost it, too."

That same day I called Bob Goodman who promptly announced he was not interested in investing more money in hockey.

I chuckled. "I'm calling about something else, Bobby. I've been told you have a good financial adviser in a guy named Dan Dent."

"Good? Good? The man is sensational. He's made me enough money to pay all of my back alimony to my wives, even left some over for myself."

Bobby had more success picking political winners than in picking brides.

Abhorring indecision as usual, I immediately followed the telephone call by calling Dan Dent. I couldn't have done anything better. Following his advice has assured my financial comfort for longer than I expect to live. My point, I guess, is that where the turns of fate will lead no one can foresee. I hadn't done any more for Larry Ziedel than I've done for — quite literally — thousands of others during my years of residency, practice, and sports activity. Somewhere, somehow, what I did for Larry registered and he "returned the favor." I've always heard if you cast enough bread on the waters, you'll catch some fish. Maybe.

Alas, what I caught in my investment in Baltimore's Southern Hotel was not fish, but a disaster along with an expensive lesson in hypocrisy, bigotry and deception delivered by "pillars of the community." The Southern Hotel was, and remains, a Baltimore landmark. It has 400 rooms, a roof garden, a large ballroom, and had a reputation for fine dining. It had always been one of the city's favorite watering holes for the financial district's executives and the state's political elite. Following World War II, business and social activities fell off in the hotel area. The waterfront two blocks away was a total mess with polluted water, rundown warehouses and boats.

During my period of exciting, "tax write-off" investing, one of my very successful friends asked me to be the tenth man in a group of well known and financially successful men taking over the Southern Hotel for $600,000 in cash plus the assumption of a $750,000 mortgage. This savvy group was a power house that seemed to assure the success of the venture. It included I. H. Bud Hammerman (a real estate operator who was later to destroy Baltimore County Executive Ted Agnew when he was Vice President), Philip Tawes, son of Governor Tawes, George Hocker, the "bag man" and mentor of Governor Tawes, Merrill Bank, top executive of Maryland Cup and Sweetheart Straws Corporation, and Paul Hampshire, owner of a leading firm in construction.

On paper, it couldn't have looked better. My only question was to make sure the company would be taxed as Subchapter S so that profits or losses would flow directly to each investor. Before joining the group, my attorney, Schale Stiller, and I met with Bud Hammerman to clear up some details. Schale repeatedly emphasized to Hammerman that the new corporation had to be a Subchapter S corporation, which meant it could not have more than 10 investors, or I would not invest with others in the group.

"That's not a problem," Hammerman said. "We met the requirement of no more than 10 investors in the corporation. This is a Subchapter S corporation."

Schale wasn't satisfied with the answer. "Are you sure of that, Mr. Hammerman?"

"Absolutely," Hammerman replied firmly.

At the first meeting of the group, I again raised the Subchapter S matter. "Gentlemen, are we a Subchapter S corporation? If so, we had better make sure we meet all of the requirements before we issue any stock. It's easy as hell to go wrong and forfeit the designation."

Bud Hammerman said, "Ross has a good point. Let's review the regulations."

He had no more than started to review the regulations when Merrill Bank stopped him. "Just a minute, Bud. You know I told you I was splitting my shares with my boys." He didn't need to say more. It was now clear that with more than ten shareholders we would not qualify.

I don't know what I looked like, but Hammerman turned brick red when he looked at me and quickly turned toward Merrill Bank. "What do you mean, Merrill?" He almost choked.

Merrill Bank said firmly, "Bud, I told you that when I joined the group."

I should have walked out then and there. All of $600,000 invested would be treated as ordinary capital contributions and taxed as such. Any profits would be subject to ordinary corporate taxes. Any dividends would then become individually taxable — income taxes would be paid twice. There would be no opportunity to take advantage of IRS Rule No. 807-907, allowing a tax write off. My old friend, Paul Hampshire, knew what I was thinking and took the lead at convincing me to stay. Others chimed in. Against experience and better judgment, I went along.

From the first day after we took over the hotel, it was down hill. All investors ponied up more money from time to time, but that was the end of the others' involvement. As I demanded action to forestall the inevitable, they listened and did nothing. I finally, in desperation, became Chairman of the Board. My first act was to hire a new hotel manager. His first acts were to investigate the garbage cans outside the kitchen, replace the night clerk renting rooms by the hour and skimming the cash he collected, and inventory the linens and liquors. He immediately stopped vendors from putting expensive foods into clean hotel garbage cans for pickup by the Chef's accomplices. We had a good Chef; he was better as a thief. New night clerks ended the "hot sheet" business. Daily accounting for linens and liquors stopped that "shrinkage."

It wasn't nearly enough. Occupancy never reached 60%, then the minimum for a profitable hotel operation. It was time to close. I knew, and know, nothing about how to operate a hotel, but I learned how to close one. I placed monitors at all four corners of the hotel, at all exit doors, and in the elevators early the Saturday morning of the closing. At 9 AM, the manager began advising all guests the hotel was closed and they would have to leave. Employees were notified similarly. All were warned that stealing would be prosecuted. Some pilferage happened, but not much.

All investors saw the closing coming, and we had meetings trying to think of a way out of a badly losing proposition. Needless to say, all now realized the cost of losing a Subchapter S designation for the corporation, but it was too late for that. Our money was gone, and we still had a $750,000 mortgage to pay. Bud Hammerman was the only one of the 10 who made any money on the deal. He received the real estate commission on the purchase. He profited on the expensive refurbishing and probably on legal fees and organization expense.

It took about three telephone calls to find out no one in the hotel business had any interest in the Southern at any price. I explored making the hotel into a retirement home by selling rooms or suites with a monthly upkeep charge. Rooms on the first floor and mezzanine were ideal for outpatient treatment without leaving the building. Facilities for religious services were available. The ballroom was an attractive meeting place, or exercise room. The kitchen and dining areas could be put into operation with almost zero expense. The roof garden also had appeal.

I worked up a proposition in which a church or charitable organization could take over the hotel virtually as a gift. The organization would take title to a million-dollar property, while we, the investors/owners would be entitled to a charitable gift deduction. After hosting a number of dinners with Board members of interested organizations, I found them frightened by the scope of the proposed program even though they always admitted there was almost no way they could lose. The Boards always had at least one or two members with zero business experience, and less understanding of tax and mortgage management, if that is possible. The idea that a church organized for the glory of God could take over and operate a religiously-oriented 400 room home for men and women in the twilight of their lives, by assuming a $750,000 mortgage, seemed to them to profane the purity of their church. They were too close to a "holier-than-thou" attitude for my broad view of religion, and I ended these discussions close to frustration.

One day Bud Hammerman called to tell me that the federal government was pressuring the Raytheon Company to participate in the Kennedys' pet poverty programs. Raytheon, he said, was making multi-millions on defense contracts, and needed to get off the hook. Maybe Raytheon could use the hotel in a Federally-financed poverty program.

I told him he had a great idea. He promptly said he was so impressed by my other ideas and approaches that I was the ideal man to negotiate a deal with Raytheon. Hammerman's flattery meant nothing to me — quite the opposite, but the others and I were swallowing huge losses and no one was doing anything about it. I checked out the Raytheon company and confirmed their enormous contracts with the Pentagon. The situation looked promising. I called Raytheon, and after a few more telephone conversations, made an appointment with the Chief Executive Officer of the company, Tom Smith, and a vice president, Brainard Holmes.

I drove to their headquarters near Boston where Smith and Holmes were cordial but very dubious about their ability to take on a poverty project. My ace was that the Kennedy Administration, through the Defense Department, had made it known they expected Raytheon to participate in their pet program. The only question, really, was where and how. Both men knew why I was there, so Tom Smith got to the point. These were my kind of people.

"Dr. Pierpont, your ideas are interesting. But we have looked into several of the programs in place, and, quite frankly, we're not impressed."

I said, "What programs have you checked into?"

"We looked at Poland Springs, and one other like it."

"No wonder you're not impressed. Programs like Poland Springs are wrong from the start because they're in the wrong places. The training they offer is idealistic nonsense. You can't train city people in an isolated place with programs that have no meaning for them. They're taken out of their familiar environment and given training with no bearing on what they will be up against when they try to get and hold jobs in the real world. We suggest a poverty program that is entirely different."

Smith and Holmes hadn't climbed up the Raytheon ladder as fools. They said nothing and left it up to me to go on. I said, "The Southern Hotel is located in a place poverty people know and understand. It is in the business district of Baltimore with jobs that these people can be trained to fill. In addition to regular types of job opportunities open in a city the size of Baltimore, we have 14 hospitals training resident physicians. We have nursing homes and other types of care facilities in the city and surrounding areas. All of these places need nurses aides, maids, female attendants, and jobs like that. I am positive we can establish a program that will be successful training young women in poverty to become productive, tax-paying, decent citizens of the community. The place is ideal. The need for trained young women is there. What else can you ask?"

"Tom," Holmes said to his boss, "This makes sense." He repeated, "Yes, this makes sense to me."

Smith looked at him, said nothing, and Holmes took the cue. He turned to me, hesitated and said: "Dr. Pierpont, do you know 70% percent of the people in poverty programs are black?" I looked at him. He said, "Does that make a difference? A problem?"

Of course I knew the racial makeup of the poverty programs. As far as I was concerned, it didn't make one hoot of difference. I replied, "Not at all. The fact is that a high percentage of the people in jobs like those we would train women to fill are black now. I am a physician, a surgeon at a Baltimore hospital, and other hospitals, as you know. As I see this program, I expect the program to do practical training in cooperation with the hospitals and nursing homes where we expect most of the graduates of the program to find jobs when they graduate."

Bullseye! The idea of cooperative training hit the mark, and CEO Smith was finally ready to talk business. We talked on and on for hours, until the day was growing dark outside the windows. Smith wrapped it all up by saying Brainard and others would work with me on a preliminary basis with the full intention of coming to a final and positive decision. The presumption, of course, was that all was as presented. At that, we all shook hands and I left the room glowing with satisfaction. The Southern Hotel was going to be transformed from an albatross into a lovely, profitable swan!

Smith was good to his word, and things moved rapidly. He assigned a Raytheon executive named Andy Johnson as our liaison, who promptly met me to inspect the property. I had already talked with the human resource people at hospitals, and they confirmed their need for trained help like the program would provide. Johnson was impressed with that information and asked if I had anyone in mind to run the program.

"In my opinion, the program should be run by a woman since the program is for women," I said and handed him a slip of paper with a name on it. "This woman is intelligent, level-headed, with years of experience in female education. Why don't you interview her?"

Johnson followed through and called to say my recommendation had worked out. He then added that things looked very good, and Smith wanted to set up a meeting to bring Raytheon's "critique group" to Baltimore and go over every detail. A week later, a group of eight Raytheon men joined me and toured the hotel, the area including the city's shady "Block," and ended at City Hall to meet with Mayor Theodore R. McKeldin, a Republican in a Democrat stronghold.

By this time we had also acquired representatives of the poverty program from Washington, the only negative element in the meeting. Mayor McKeldin met everyone with his famous "exuberance," and asked his development secretary for his opinion about the Southern Hotel program.

The development secretary pursed his lips thoughtfully and said, "Mayor, I'm just not sure. We're spending millions in area redevelopment, and from what I can see these people may not be just the ones for the area."

I had checked out the development secretary and spoke before McKeldin could either confirm or deny the man's comment. "Mayor, that's an interesting comment Bill has just made. I would say, very interesting in view of the fact he has moved out of the city and into Hampstead."

McKeldin, well known for his loyalty to Baltimore City, was not amused. "Bill, you moved to Hampstead — out of Baltimore? You're my development secretary for the city!"

Bill did the best he could in the situation. "Mayor, it's my children, you know. Not me."

McKeldin did not hide his embarrassment. No one filled the silence until the Mayor finally said, "Well, I think we can arrange for what you need, gentlemen."

He excused himself and I thought watching his back as he left the room: "You old four-flusher! It's the question of blacks in the heart of Baltimore again. You were hoping your development hot-shot would give you a way out of this, but it didn't work. You couldn't back away from the poverty program for the city, and especially for the black votes you need to beat a Democrat in the city."

I was to find this was a question that would never go away. It came up indirectly at our luncheon meeting after we left City Hall. A top

Raytheon executive asked, point-blank, how we would handle the attraction of the strip joints in "the Block." I pointed out that since the bars in "the Block" did not admit blacks the "problem" was minimal. It was a weasel-word answer followed by a related question from the same man.

"Ross, this program will attract hundreds of active young women with strong sex drives. What are your ideas about handling this problem?"

The question took guts. Think of the liberal media quoting a Rayatheon executive asking that. Embarrassing would be the kindest way to describe the hullabaloo. I felt sure the man was reluctant to ask it, but had to bring it up.

"Fritz," I answered (we were on a first name basis now), "I know that is a question that has to be answered, and I'm glad you brought it up. I've thought about the question, myself, because it goes to the heart of the program. The one thing we cannot do is conduct a program contaminated by promiscuous sex. This program is going to bring in young women with all kinds of backgrounds and personal standards. By definition, they're coming out of poverty. Our job is to take those women as they come and make them responsible, self-supporting adults ready to take their places in the community. But let's face some reality. Fritz, did you, or any of the rest of us when we reached the dangerous age— " I glanced over the men listening to me — "have parents who made you put your pants on backwards?"

Laughter filled the room. I said, "No offense, Fritz, I just had to make the point. We're dedicated to making this the best damn poverty program in the USA, a model the Kennedy people will point to with pride. It will be something Raytheon will be proud of. We intend to turn out mature women, not irresponsible children in an adult body.

"Yes, intercourse will occur. With that many women in training, no one can stop it 100%. If a woman becomes promiscuous, if pregnancy develops, we will follow the law in each case. If carrying the baby to term is wanted, with or without adoption, we will work with the Volunteers of America to handle that. Whatever the decision, if the woman is responsible and otherwise complying with the program, we will complete the training needed for her to take a productive place in the community. This is what we promise this program to do, and I say, here and now, that this is what you will get to the best of our ability."

I spoke with total sincerity, and as I stopped the room burst with applause. I'm not sure I remember just how I took that, because most things I say are not ended in spontaneous applause. I reported the meeting to the other investors, and as may be imagined, they were graciously appreciative though it didn't trigger any applause that I know of. Ten days later Raytheon confirmed acceptance of the plan with a lease of the hotel for $275,000 per year triple net, subject to final approval of my program by the US Government.

About three weeks went by while everyone marked time. Finally, I took the long-awaited call from Brainard Holmes in Raytheon's headquarters. "Ross, there's a problem with the contract."

"What?"

"The contract is complete and waiting on Sargent Shriver's desk for his signature. He is stalling and we don't know why."

Sargent Shriver was a brother in law of President John F. Kennedy and Attorney General Robert Kennedy. He had total access. Blanket authority.

I asked, "Do you have any idea why Shriver is stalling?"

"Not yet. But let's say I have a good idea."

The next day, Holmes called and said, "Ross, it's your Maryland Senator Joe Tydings blocking the deal. No one is sure why, and I can't tell you all I know — I'm sure you'll understand why — but I am almost positive Senator Tydings has intervened personally with Shriver to block the project."

Why on earth would Joe Tydings block the poverty project? My brain raced but came up blank. My personal relationship with Senator Tydings had been relatively close and always cordial. I supported him in his Senatorial campaign with effort and money. I attended his deficit dinner at the Mayflower Hotel in Washington where I contributed $800. I had been the Tydings family surgeon at their home in Havre de Grace. I was the doctor who put a cast on the arm of Joe's wife, after her horse hit a chicken coop and threw her. Joe had to know my involvement in the poverty project. Now, according to Holmes, this man, this supposed friend, was blocking something that meant an awful lot to me. Why? Why? Why?

I had to get to the bottom of it.

I called Tydings' office a number of times and never reached him. I left messages to call me back, something he would normally do within hours, but now he was avoiding me. One day, two days, three days passed with Tydings ignoring my calls. His inexplicable refusal to acknowledge my calls was unusual to the point of confirming the accuracy of Holmes' information. Joe was blocking the project.

On the surface, Joe Tyding's pressure on Sargent Shriver — a Kennedy in-law who presumably was in favor of the Kennedy poverty program — had no purpose behind it. There had to be a reason, something powerful enough to make Joe go to Shriver on a personal level. I couldn't think of a single reason to explain the Senator's personal interference in Raytheon's poverty project. Then I remembered McKeldin's development secretary and his opposition to the project "— *these may not be just the people we want to put in that area.*"

Bingo! Someone doesn't want several hundred young, black women coming out of poverty to live in a hotel once a Baltimore landmark in the heart of the business district! But opposition on that basis was not a Kennedy-liberal position. It wasn't a Kennedy-appointed Sargent Shriver liberal position. Someone had to have enough prejudice against blacks to force Tydings to go against his supporters, and in particular, me. It would take a lot to make Tydings spend political capital to block the Raytheon proposal and make enemies of ten well-known, former friends.

OK, who was the "someone?" I could only guess. The more I thought about Joe Tydings' inherited "old money" background, and the various possibilities, the more I crossed off other ideas and the more I focused on the Mercantile Safe Deposit and Trust Company. The "Merc" was an "old line" Baltimore bank with headquarters just around the corner from the Southern Hotel. This bank had little known, but enormous control over major Baltimore businesses as the trustee and administrator of some of Maryland's largest inheritances. One of these was the Black/Abell holdings which included the powerful Baltimore Evening Sun, the morning Sun, and WMAR TV station. It was hard, if not impossible in those days of "boss" politics, to get elected to anything bigger than dogcatcher without the Merc's support.

What's more, the "Merc" held the mortgage on the Southern Hotel. That gave the "Merc" a big financial interest in what happened to the property. The idea that the "Merc" did not want a predominately female-black training program almost next door to its headquarters had a certain logic. That logic pointed to the "old money," socially prominent owners of the "Merc" as the source of pressure on Joe Tydings. Was it true? In a way it really didn't matter. What mattered was that someone had pressured Senator Tydings into an uncharacteristic action deliberately planned to destroy our group's Raytheon project. And to cost me, personally, buckets of hard-earned and after-tax dollars.

If Holmes and I were right in diagnosing the situation, the only way to get the contract signed was to get Tydings to reverse his opposition. Until that happened, Sargent Shriver would sit in silence on the contract until I was dead and buried.

My car radio announced news of a student sit-in, and I said out loud, "A sit-in!" A Ross Pierpont sit-in at Tydings' office would be so different the media would cover it out of sheer novelty. With a sit-in I would expose Tydings' bigotry in opposing Raytheon's poverty program. That bigotry would turn black voters in the state against him forever. It would shame him with his liberal friends in the press. The Kennedys would be appalled and so would the rest of the leadership of the Democrat party, which had more to worry about than one misguided Maryland senator. A sit-in had a real chance of forcing Joe to go against whoever had aroused his opposition in the first place and stop him from opposing the Raytheon poverty program.

A call to an old friend from a TV station lined up a news release blitz. Grace agreed to go with me, bag and baggage, to sit in Senator Tydings' Washington office until he saw us publicly. We planned to leave Baltimore for Washington at 12 noon on the chosen Monday and take up camp at Joe Tydings' door until the press got the complete picture.

What picture? The picture of a "champion of the underdog" — and especially the black constituency of liberals and the Democrat party — blocking a model poverty program favored by the Kennedy Administration. Before I was through, I would make even President Kennedy take notice!

The news release called for embargo until 12:00 noon but an eager beaver at a local TV station put it on the air that morning at 11:30. By the time I returned to my home from Havre de Grace about 11:40 that morning, prepared to head for Tydings' DC office, the street was full of reporters, TV cameras, and rubberneckers. I made my way through and as I opened the door Grace was standing before me highly excited and holding the telephone.

"Ross! Come here! Quickly! Joe Tydings has been calling and calling. Here, take the phone."

"Tell him we'll see him in hell, but before he gets there, we'll be waiting for him outside his office in Washington." I spoke loudly to make sure Tydings heard me.

Grace put down the phone and we started toward the door baggage in hand as the phone rang again. Elaine answered it and called to say Tydings was again on the phone and wanted to talk to me. I called back, "Tell him I've left for Washington."

I paused at the door. Elaine said, "He says he knows you're there and wants to talk to you."

I ignored her and as I reached the front steps the TV people called, "Hold it, Doctor." They came up with microphones, but Grace interceded. The contention had gotten to her and she said, "Ross, please talk to him. What can it hurt?"

I gave in. "Sorry, folks," I called to the reporters. "His excellency, Senator Tydings, has decided it is time to talk to me."

I took the telephone, and Tydings said, "Ross, I don't see why you're so upset. Come on down to my Baltimore office. I'm not in Washington."

"Where have you been the last two weeks when I called you two and three times a day?"

"I didn't get the message," Tydings said. "It must have been a mixup in my office."

Do what you can to me, but never, never lie. Tydings was lying and we both knew it. "You're lying, Joe. I didn't know you've sunk that far. You know you have ducked me. We both know the reason. The Raytheon contract."

"Ross, I'll see you in Baltimore now. I won't see you in Washington."

"Fine! But you will see us in Washington, Joe. We have food, time, and whatever it takes. We can wait."

"Now, just a minute! You'll be arrested for trespassing —"

"Good! I hope so," I hung up.

The tension had upset Grace, who at heart is an extraordinarily gentle person who despises confrontations. I could see she wanted this ugliness ended. I thought things over briefly and yielded. I said to Grace, "OK, let's go see him." Together, we went out and told the press we were going immediately to Senator Tydings' office in the Baltimore U.S. Courthouse. The press loved it and away we went downtown. At Tydings' Courthouse office, we waited until the press had again assembled, and I said, "Ladies and Gentlemen, what is between Senator Tydings and me is public business. No secret deals. I am willing to meet with him here in front of everyone to hear what we say. If he won't come out, I invite you to accompany me into the Senator's office."

A young aide to Tydings spoke up. "The Senator has said he will see only you and Mrs. Pierpont, Doctor."

I looked at the reporters and said, "The problem between Senator Tydings and the group I represent affects Baltimore and in fact the whole country. The business between us is public business, your business. I want you in our meeting. You have just heard that the Senator, elected to represent you, and whose salary and staff expenses you pay in taxes, doesn't want you in our meeting. I want that to be understood. Have I made myself clear?"

Someone called out, "Why doesn't the Senator want us in the meeting?"

"Ask him!" I said, and turned to go into Tydings' office with Grace.

Tydings and his chief aide, Hardin Marion, both in their shirtsleeves, stood up as we entered. The greetings were perfunctory, the atmosphere unfriendly. We sat down in two chairs facing Tydings' desk. I waited to see how he would open the meeting.

He said, "Ross, what did you want to see me about?"

I had to restrain myself when this intelligent man had the gall to ask why we sat in front of him. I reminded myself I had a job to do in meeting Tydings, not vent my anger. I said conversationally, "Joe, you know why we're here. That is why you would not answer any of my telephone calls."

He said nothing, to avoid admitting he knew the problem, and waited for me to continue: political negotiating strategy! By now, my anger had begun cooking as I said, "If you are going to play coy with me, I want to know why you have taken it upon yourself — you, Joe Tydings — to block the Raytheon poverty contract. I want to know why you are blocking the best poverty education project ever developed for the Kennedy Administration's poverty program."

Silence. Tydings could not keep from getting red in the face. He would not look at me as he uttered a response obviously discussed in advance. "I will not line the pockets of real estate speculators."

That did it! Only one of 10 men in our group, Bud Hammerman, had any significant real estate interests. The rest of us, well known and respected in unrelated fields, included a son of Governor Tawes, a key executive of one of the state's largest businesses, the owner of a prominent sub-contracting firm, the closest confidant and advisor of Governor Tawes, other well known and respected men and me, Doctor Ross Pierpont. Now this weasel sitting before me as a United States Senator was trying to hide his bigotry by charging decent men as speculators using the poverty program to "line our pockets!" He knew the charge was false, but he knew no other way to hide his opposition to the Raytheon project based on race.

His refusal to answer my telephone calls, his demeanor now, and lowering himself to a lie meant one thing: Tydings was locked into something too big for him to resist. He had no way to relent in his opposition because he was doing the bidding of someone too powerful to deny. Where did this leave me? The only thing I could do was to make his bigotry and falsehoods clear and on the record. Past experience had taught me to prepare for this eventuality.

"Senator, I thought you might come up with something like that, which you know is a bald-faced lie. There are no 'speculators' trying to line their pockets on the backs of the poor, and you know it. You also know, I know, and everyone in on this knows, that real estate profits have nothing to do with your opposition." I paused to look at Tydings' senior aide, to make sure there was no way for anyone to misunderstand I was calling Tydings a liar to his face. I played my trump. "I thought you might use an excuse like that. I have a surprise for you." I pulled a sheaf of papers from my briefcase and held them for all to see. "These papers show that all partners to the Southern Hotel project have agreed to donate the entire Southern Hotel property, Raytheon contract included, to any non-profit institution named by the NAACP of Maryland. We will be out of it without a dollar, without a dime! How's that for 'real estate speculators trying to line their pockets,' Senator?"

I heard a sound from Tydings' aide, something like a gasp. Tydings was so shell-shocked he looked right, left, and to the ceiling to find an answer. He found none. Grace and I waited. Finally, he managed to repeat the excuse I had just blown to bits: "I will not line the pockets of real estate speculators."

I rose and held the documents close to his face. Telling myself to remember the old political rule, "Don't get mad, get even," I spoke very deliberately but could not hide my disgust and fury.

"Joe Tydings, I supported you. I thought you were an honest, decent man. Now I tell you, you are a no-good, lying son-of-a bitch — now I promise you one thing. If I live, I will see your ass out of the Senate and into the street."

Those are my exact words, uttered years ago, but burned indelibly into my memory. Tydings tried to defend himself again: "I will not line the pockets of real estate speculators."

No way could I let him get away with that. I leaned over his desk until we were face-to-face about a foot apart. He tried to look past me, but could not avoid me as I said, "I've thrown your lie about 'real estate speculators' into your teeth, Joe. Bite your lie hard. Force it down so its taste won't make you vomit. Maybe you didn't hear me, or maybe you didn't understand, so let me tell you again you are a no-good, lying son-of-a bitch. If I live, I will see your ass in the street."

I turned to Grace and said, "Let's get out of here, Grace." Responding to my words and anger, she was trembling in sympathy.

We left and the rest is memory. We gave up the Southern Hotel and its mortgage to the Mercantile Safe Deposit and Trust Company, then chaired by a Baltimore "blueblood," Tom Butler. The Raytheon poverty project died a slow, painful and very expensive death for those who had invested our energies and money in it.

As for my experience with Joe Tydings and the liberal wing of the

Democrat party, it was an eye-opener. Before, my contacts had been with candidates who cut a few corners, who compromised, and who made deals — Joe Tydings had been one — but I had always believed you could trust a decent man not to go back on his word. Not to stab you in the back. I had been exposed to Kennedy liberalism where it counted, and the experience taught me much. Tuition for the lesson appeared prohibitive, but in the long run would prove worth it.

I learned what can happen to the goals of men who lack, collectively, the power of just one man in the "right" place. I saw one man, Senator Tydings, misuse his power to destroy a plan offered by one of the nation's largest corporations to reduce some of the ugly effects of urban poverty. What I also was beginning to see was that the politicians running the United States were just beginning to find medical care to be the greatest possible opportunity to extend their power. This new awareness in the aftermath of the Southern Hotel disaster convinced me I should take a more active role in real politics.

Meanwhile, I had made a pledge to Senator Joseph Tydings. It would take time. It would cost me. But I do not indulge in pledges I do not keep.

Chapter 20
How Maryland Politics Kept "Ted" Agnew From Becoming President Agnew

One evening a group of us were chatting after dinner, and someone asked what made me the way I am. It was not only a very personal question, I had nothing in reply. I had been entirely too busy with patients, Christine, and Grace, to meditate about "the making of Ross Pierpont." Still, the question lodged in the back of my mind: who, what am I?

The question came back to me after an extremely hectic day of operating at my clinic in Havre de Grace. Charles was driving me back to Baltimore, and it was sheer pleasure to stretch out in the back seat and let my mind wander. The man I am, I thought, comes out of the driving need of my life, and the training by my mother.

From the earliest days I can remember, by word and example, every hour of every day, Mother drilled into my very soul to hate a lie, never hesitate to stand up for what is right, and never, ever accept defeat.

The driving need of my life was and remains survival. From my mother, down to all four of us boys, the rule of our lives was to do what it took to survive. Don't waste time thinking about yourself, and things you want and don't have. What needs to be done, do it and move on. The need to survive was the force that took me through pharmacy school, through medical school, through the grueling hours of residency, and working six and seven day weeks with Grace to build my practice.

Refusal to accept defeat was what led me to promise to Senator Joe Tydings if I lived I would one day see his ass upon the street.

That promise became a magnet that drew me irresistibly into Maryland's political arena. Before Tydings, I had learned many of the unique aspects of a unique political system, Maryland politics. In a word, Maryland's politics were crazy. How else can you describe a system that expected its governors to be honest administrators while paying them $4,500 a year through the 1940s, and $15,000 a year in the 1960s? The strange thing was that this crazy system produced some good governors who adapted to the system rather than try to change it.

I have already described the Maryland government's system of exercising power through the Governor's "bag man." Some years there were two bag men. One of these was a totally trusted "lieutenant" who "arranged" gifts and other sources of funds to enable the governor to feed and clothe his family. I always found it amusing to observe the ability of various governors to pretend no such thing as bag man appointments existed while they were operating the process from beginning to end. One especially sanctimonious Governor I shall leave nameless was able to espouse all things right and holy while using a bag man known for creating a schedule of compensation for licenses, appointments, and contracts. His going rate, if I remember correctly, was about $25,000 for a judgeship, $15,000 for a magistrate, $5,000 for a contested liquor license, and so on. A typical case I remember involved the transfer of a liquor license from a prestigious Charles Street location in Baltimore to a nearby residential area closed for liquor licenses. The applicants got exactly nowhere until $10,000 was ponied up for the sanctimonious Governor's bag man, upon which the transfer was approved with miraculous speed.

Although the Maryland spoils system was accepted by the voting public, it was, of course, corrupt and perilous to practice. A decent man and competent Governor, Marvin Mandel, got a bit careless in one of his negotiations involving a race track, was tried, convicted, sent to prison, and disbarred. His conviction was ultimately overturned, but his life as a disgraced ex-Governor, ex-convict is hardly inspiring. Another Governor neglected to leave his Maryland money system when he went to Washington as the nation's Vice President. He was riding high until one of his bagmen blew the whistle on him. Ted Agnew, Vice President of the United States under Richard Nixon, was forced to resign in disgrace. My experience with the rise of Spiro "Ted" Agnew is one of the more fascinating "could have beens" in modern politics, as you will soon read.

Talk to politicians today about such shenanigans, and they will tell you those things happened yesterday. They are obeying the first rule of defense in politics: deny everything, remember nothing. (Where have you seen this rule in use before?) Don't tape record (President Nixon learned this.) Don't keep a diary (Oregon's Senator Packwood, and others, confirmed this one.) If you are caught after stealing money from the

Congressional Post Office, resign while charging entrapment. If you are Speaker of the House, or a high-ranking legislator caught in lies and trading favors for money, it's ok if you just resign and leave to await the Capitol crowd's acceptance of your reformation.

The crown of crowns for applying the first rule of politics goes uncontested to the present inhabitants of the White House. In practicing selective amnesia and erecting stonewalls impenetrable to investigators, the landlords of the Lincoln Room give would-be competitors a record to shoot at.

If someone established a *Josef Goebbels Award for the Most Effective Use of Big Lies,* who is today's most likely winner?

My first real exposure to politics was in connection with medical legislation. In 1962, the Congress let it be known it intended to start legislating medical care. I found out all I could about the proposed new laws and saw, 36 years ago, that Federal intervention into medical care was a prescription for waste, distrust, and ultimately the downgrading of our medical system. As I described in my Governor Tawes-arranged meeting with Dan Brewster, and later when Maryland acted to implement it, I did my best to point out the flaws in the system and enact nothing until the flaws were corrected..

What I foresaw when I went to Dan Brewster about the unintended consequences of Federal intervention into health care is sadly proving only too true. Today, most physicians cannot survive without taking orders from administrators of HMOs and insurance plans. They have no choice when patients come to them eligible for Medicare and Medicaid, both riddled with totally despised paperwork, fraud, and waste. How much waste? My estimate is up to 500 billion dollars a year. I charge that Medicare and Medicaid are ill-conceived, under-funded, and over-promised, and will debate anyone anytime who wishes to challenge that assertion. An example illustrates the insatiable appetite of the monster generated by today's patchwork of government-funded, employer-funded, and not-funded- at-all healthcare. Health insurance and HMOs are not as bad, merely sadly lacking and oriented toward the wrong "p," profits, not patients. In June, 1998, United HealthCare Corp. announced it was paying 5.38 billion dollars for another health care company. Aetna has bought another health care company for other billions of dollars.

Where do you suppose those billions of dollars come from? They come from profits reaped from the medical skills of physicians and billings to Medicare-Medicaid. We taxpayers are footing the bills.

This nation is so wealthy we probably can stand even the present, horrible waste of resources. Two far worse problems are the unequal quality of medical care and more than 44 million people with no health care provisions whatsoever. Any thinking person who does not shudder to contemplate what will happen to unprotected people when the economy inevitably has a sinking spell is hardhearted indeed. This subject is so personal, and so critical to the future of the United States, I will take it up in detail in a later chapter.

My mid-Sixties experiences with Dan Brewster, and the Democrat Party of Maryland led me to take stock of myself. My practice was thriving. I had no need to get involved in the corruption of Maryland or national politics, but I faced a question: did I believe in what I said, or was I a bystander getting my kicks by baying at the moon? If I entered the political arena, it had to be done the only way I know: Go to win or stay out. Second, do not put a price on anything I do. That meant if I ever tried for public office, I would have to put up Pierpont money, plus any contributions from personal friends and associates who agreed with my positions. It meant my support would never be a quid-pro-quo in return for party'-delivered votes.

Money is no guarantee of success in winning elections. Steve Forbes and many other very wealthy individuals have spent what most of us consider fortunes and came away also-rans. Ross Perot spent millions; he has less power than when he started. Over a span of 28 years, *not one of 19 candidates who financed their campaigns for statewide office with their own money, won election!* The opposite side of that coin is that it is virtually impossible to win an election without money — usually weighed by the ton. If there is any doubt about that, look at the depths to which the Democratic National Committee sank in raising its millions for the 1996 Presidential campaign. The Republicans didn't stoop so low, but theirs are far from clean hands, too. Political campaigns need too much money to be effective — which means to win.

My approach to public office was in line with maintaining my integrity. Fortunately, or unfortunately, that position never put me in obligation to those who, at the time, managed the party's resources. The trade-off to organization bosses and big-money contributors is: You want me to help you; I want you to help me. You want my support, I expect your vote on anything that matters to me and to those I control. Otherwise, let's talk another time.

Beginning in 1966, a series of events led me to enter politics as a Democrat. It was the last of two terms for Millard Tawes as Governor. He and I had become friends, and I looked on him as a good man and Governor. At the same time, I had also become close to Ted Agnew, the County Executive of Baltimore County. I had played a lot of golf with Agnew, got to know him on both personal and professional/business levels, and quite frankly I liked the man. Obviously, many others in the Republican Party liked Ted, too, for he was on his way to the Republican nomination for Governor for the next (1966) election.

Leadership in the Democrat Party without Tawes as Governor and final authority was becoming a mess. Governor Tawes had bestowed his blessing on his friend, Attorney General Tom Finan from western Maryland, but Finan ran in a party at odds with itself. George P. Mahoney, an affable, glad-handing, wealthy contractor in Baltimore County was running an ultra-conservative approach, seen by liberals as playing a thinly-veiled race card in "block-busting" Baltimore City. His slogan: "Your home is your castle. Protect it" hit the mark with middle-class whites. Clarence Miles, the third leader, had built up a lot of credits with other Democrat Party leaders, and had attracted liberal financing. But the candidate who looked to me like a solid shot to win the primary nomination was Carlton Sickles, a liberal Congressman in wealthy, government-oriented Montgomery County. Sickles had two powerful groups behind him: the Kennedys and their followers, including Senator Joe Tydings, and organized labor. In all, six candidates had filed for the Democrat nomination.

One Sunday morning our foursome regrouped at the 19th hole after a round of golf. My companions included a friend, Steel Phillips, Jack Dunn, and Ted Agnew. With Agnew, the expected Republican candidate for Governor, in the group, the conversation naturally turned to the election.

"How's it going, Ted?" asked Jack Dunn. "Does it look like you can beat — well, who will you have to beat?"

Agnew didn't hesitate. "No one knows which of those guys is going to win the primary. It could be anyone. What I do know is that their fighting in the primary is going to divide the Democrat party beyond belief. With me, Republicans will be united while all of the Democrats who lose their man in the primary will be looking for someone else to vote for. Unless I beat myself, I'll beat whichever one the Democrats nominate."

He made sense and always did, at least politically. But his statements were also mandatory. How could he possibly admit any doubts to probable supporters? His self-confidence also did not quite agree with the way the election looked to me. I said, "Ted, I'm not so sure you're right. I have a pretty good idea of the strengths of the four top runners, and if the Democrat losers lick their wounds and get behind their nominee, you'll have big problems."

Agnew wasn't swayed. "C'mon, Ross — you're always seeing something behind the trees —"

"My golf ball!" I broke in.

Everyone laughed. "No seriously, Ross. My people have analyzed the votes behind all four top men, and they're shallow, limited loyalty. Whoever, they nominate, I'm going to win."

The others waited for me to answer. I reflected a moment and said, "Ted, if I am right you are underestimating the Kennedys, the government-employee vote for Democrats no matter whom, and the clout of organized labor behind Sickles. With Tydings and labor behind Sickles, you're a cinch to lose nearly every black vote in Baltimore City, plus union votes. Add to that at least 90% of the Jewish vote for Sickles. It has to be close, no matter how you look at it."

My comment was a "downer," and the usually ebullient Agnew became thoughtful. I stepped into the silence. "Ted, I am going to help you win," I said brightly.

"You're going to do what!" Steel Phillips almost shouted.

"What the hell are you talking about?" asked Ted Agnew.

As my comment about Sickles suggests, I had been studying the political field of Maryland at the statewide level almost as a hobby. The

Democrats had the black vote locked up. For a Republican to win statewide, black votes had to be siphoned from the Democrat. I spoke deliberately. "I am going to become the best known liberal in the Democrat party. Not only that, I am going to run for Governor against all of the others on a liberal platform."

The group exploded in laughter. All heads in the grill turned in our direction to see what the fun was about. Little could they have guessed. Finally, someone said, "Ross, you might walk like a liberal, talk like a liberal, even act like a liberal. But you 'ain't' no liberal!"

"Amen," said Jack Dunn. "For the heck of it, what are you talking about?"

I became dead serious. "I am going to do something I've wanted to do for a long time. Everyone associates black with liberal. We all know that in everything else but voting, black people aren't liberal; their values are conservative. Doesn't matter. The media and the white public link black and liberal as the same thing. Some people have joked about maybe I should become a candidate myself, and that got me thinking. Why not? I'm not going to get into the ring with those other four guys, so I am going to run for Governor as never done before."

Jack Dunn, Steel Phillips, and Ted Agnew could do nothing but look at me.

"I am going to file as a Democrat for Governor with a black candidate for my Comptroller."

"Damn!" was the best Ted Agnew could muster. No one else said anything.

"Don't any of you see that the black vote will swing this election?" I said. "Maryland is 20% black. One of every five people you see is black. It's time to show those Democrat-owned black voters they've been blindly supporting a party that's done nothing for them since the Civil War. This state, 20% black, has never had a black statewide candidate. Ted, as Governor, you can do more for black people in Maryland than any one of the Democrat candidates will ever do. That's why I am going to help you win."

Agnew, the politician, raised the obvious question. "Who will finance and run your campaign?"

"I will."

Agnew persisted: "You're talking a lot of time and money, Ross. Are you sure you want to do this? "

"I'm sure." I replied.

Sometimes that's how decisions are made with effects beyond anything foreseen. After answering more obvious questions about my intentions, with Ted Agnew leading the questioning, the four of us parted company that Sunday more thoughtfully than any of us could have been imagined when we started out for the golf course.

The next months would test everything I believe in, and demand every ounce of energy I possessed. My first step was to meet with Juanita Jackson Mitchell, a prominent member of Baltimore's black community, and Dr. Carl Murphy, head of the Afro-American newspaper. The office of the newspaper was arranged to let Dr. Murphy wheel his office chair from one place to another. He was a white-haired, dignified and still-handsome black man I judged to be in his seventies. Ms. Mitchell sat beside me along with three other black men and women facing Dr. Murphy's huge and paper-filled desk.

Dr. Murphy wasted no time. "I have asked you to come here to meet with Dr. Pierpont, who has approached me with a very thought-provoking idea. There has never been a black candidate for statewide office in Maryland. He is considering running for Governor with a black person of our choosing for Comptroller. If we agree to do this with him, we will name the person to run with him."

He paused. We waited in silence. I could not help but wonder what the others beside me were thinking. It had to be: what the hell is this all about!

Dr. Murphy said, "Dr. Pierpont has obligated himself for the necessary filing fees and all expenses of the campaign. We are not being asked for any money."

Juanita Mitchell turned to look at me. "Dr. Pierpont, why 'Comptroller'? Why not Attorney General, second on the ticket?"

I smiled. "I knew you'd ask that." She smiled in return, as did the associates beside her. "The reason is that candidates for Attorney General attract the attention of every lawyer in the state. Every one of those guys is anxious about that office, and they think their experience entitles them to judge the qualifications — usually negatively — of the candidates.

We don't need that kind of potential opposition. But the real reason for Comptroller is the office itself. The Comptroller is second in line of succession to the office of Governor. If the Governor dies or is removed from office for some reason, the Comptroller moves up to the top spot in the state. Agreed?"

"I never realized it that way," Ms. Mitchell said, "but you're right."

The following discussion was brief as all agreed to my offer. Then, totally surprising me, Ms. Mitchell turned to look at me squarely. "Dr. Pierpont, you have always been a solid backer of our community from the time you joined the NAACP. But coming here today I kept asking myself if you had any hidden agenda in doing this. I have always known you for a deep and intelligent man of your word. Though I am not real sure about why you are doing this — I think you can understand that —"

I nodded. "Of course."

"I also know this about you. Whatever you are doing, and why, and even if something else we don't see is involved, I know you will never do anything to hurt us."

"Thank you, Ms. Mitchell. I appreciate that very much."

Dr. Murphy wound up the discussion by telling me he would call me when they had arranged for a Comptroller candidate. A few days later, he called to say they had selected a man named Archie Williams for the slot. I thanked him and added I welcomed any help and advice his group could give. Typically, he replied, "You do what you can and I'll do what I can. Good luck and goodbye."

That was that. The labor of a statewide campaign began with no letup. It was seven days a week. Every week for three months. Grace and I saw each other mainly on the campaign trail. My main effort was to communicate to the black community, and indirectly to the white-owned media, that for the first time in Maryland one-fifth of the state's population had a candidate on a statewide ticket. To communicate that message, I bought a Volkswagen bus, mounted an amplifier and microphone on it, plastered it with signs and photos of myself and Archie Williams and hit all black-dominated areas of the state.

The stakes were huge. Voter registration in the areas we covered were more than 90% Democrat. I tried to pump up my fellow candidate, but of course he knew we had no chance to win, and had no stomach for a night and day effort. By primary election day, he had almost dropped from sight.

When the votes were counted, a dazed Democrat party found itself with an unwelcome nominee for Governor, George P. Mahoney. Only 1,800 votes separated Mahoney from a popular Democrat Agnew could not have beaten, Carlton Sickles backed by the Kennedys, Tydings, unions, and liberals. That 1,800 vote included 4,500 votes for Ross Pierpont, plus another 1,000 votes in a mishandled ballot box. Sickles challenged me for those votes and party loyalists urged me to concede them to him. I refused, insisting they were mine. It was a no-decision contest because no one could guarantee whose votes were for whom. The entire ballot box containing votes for (Sickles? Pierpont?) was discarded.

Now the important thing about so few votes. If Sickles got those 1,000 votes he would have been so close to Mahoney that a recount would have become necessary. The outcome of a recount, considering the absolute control of the voting system by Maryland's Democrat machinery, and the loathing of Mahoney by the party regulars, is for innocents to guess.

The Democrat agony continued after Mahoney was finally acknowledged as the party's candidate. Jewish voters refused to accept him. Blacks were, in my estimate, 99.9% against him. The Baltimore Sun and other newspapers derided him as a blatant racist, bordering on senility, and otherwise unacceptable as Governor of Maryland. To any real liberal, Mahoney was anathema.

The primary forced Maryland's Democrats to choose between their candidate running on a racially-tainted platform and a Baltimore County Republican!

This two-to-one Democrat state elevated Ted Agnew to the Statehouse in Annapolis, and a future for Ted absolutely no one could possibly have foreseen. While Agnew was Governor, Richard Nixon tapped him to be his candidate for Vice President. This son of Greek immigrants, only months earlier a minor figure in national politics, became second in line for the highest office in the nation, the most powerful position on the globe. Had Agnew held on to his office when Nixon resigned, Ted would have succeeded Nixon automatically. He did not reach the Oval Office, of course. He had taken with him to Washington the money-grubbing dealing that went with Maryland's offices of County Executive and Governor, and one of his associated bag men blew the whistle on him to save his own skin. Ted Agnew had no choice but to resign as Vice President in disgrace. Gerald Ford then moved into the Oval Office in place of Richard Nixon.

Another election after the one in 1966 has special interest. This was the election of the next U.S. Senator in 1968. My part in the 1966 election of Ted Agnew was based on my opposition to a Tydings-Kennedy-union-big government man in that high office. The Senatorial campaign mattered in another way. Failing to persuade Senator Brewster to oppose the enactment of Medicare/Medicaid as President Johnson proposed, he had helped put it through. Doctors were already finding these programs as I had warned: over-promised, under-funded, and, most important, an unsound way to provide health care. If I could be elected Senator, maybe I could influence the enactment of sound medical care legislation.

At the time, Senator Brewster was a drunk. The party's position on him was basically that he was better than any newcomer, such as Ross Pierpont. He was above all a party loyalist while I was seen - correctly — as an independent.

Discussions invariably led to the Democrat organization's unhappiness with Senator Joe Tydings. In essence, the party leaders were saying while they would not support me against the alcoholic Brewster, they would back me against Joe Tydings — sometimes referred to as "that arrogant son-of-a-bitch." That was equivalent to the national anthem to my ears, but I lacked the name recognition necessary to beat Tydings head to head. My relationship with the media was also a problem; to reporters and news editors I was just a wealthy, conservative doctor dabbling in politics in some sort of ego trip.

I had no real hope of beating the incumbent Senator — challengers never win; they can only replace an incumbent who loses. Without the active support of the Democrat Party, and Brewster's wise decision to stay on the sidelines and keep quiet, I wasn't a dark horse. I was close to invisible. The real prize was Senator Tydings. To beat him, I had no choice but to campaign ahead of the next election, and I did so.

I hired an experienced advertising agency, who developed a hard-hitting campaign complete with volunteers, radio, TV and print advertising. I still get some pleasure from my expenditure of $600,000 when I re-play my "pledge of sober thought in my conduct of your affairs in the U.S. Senate. Vote Pierpont in the Democrat Primary in September."

Oh, the howls of pain that went up in Brewster's tent when they heard that announcement. What really hurt them was their candidate was having one of his worst episodes with the bottle at the time it aired. I campaigned the state as hard as I could, and met each area's Democrat leaders wherever I went. All were cordial and reiterated their support if I would just take on Tydings two years later.

One episode in the campaign especially stands out. I had approached Jack Pollack, the undisputed boss of the largest Democrat organization in Baltimore City, the largest Democrat stronghold in the state. Jack had a reputation for delivering what he promised. Earlier, I described how Pollack taped a hotel-room meeting with Millard Tawes and used it to get even with Governor Tawes when, according to Pollack, Tawes double-crossed him. However, Pollack's recording was so poor it was successfully challenged and Jack's case fell apart.

I offered $40,000 for the Trenton Democratic Club's endorsement and support. Jack called and asked me to meet him at his office. His office was plastered with framed newspaper cartoons typically labeling him as "1/8 Boss." Other assorted lampoons portrayed him as a symbol of corrupt Maryland and Baltimore City politics. He enjoyed himself immensely as he pointed out some of the cartoons he liked most.

Jack did not waste anyone's time. "Ross," he said, "I know you as a straight-shooting man and maybe my friend. I've never known you to do anything wrong, and I am not going to do anything wrong to you. You have offered $40,000 for our support and to do what we could do for your campaign. I could take your money, and do what I could. But I won't take your money.

"First, I don't think you can beat Brewster in the primary. OK, you're right about the bum, but the party won't give up on him. You can't beat an incumbent Senator and the state's Democrat organization against you like that. So I won't take a friend's money and not produce."

I said, "Thank you, Jack. I'm sorry to hear that, but I respect your honesty with me."

Jack said, "Come and see me in 1970 when Tydings runs. Then I'll tell you a different story." He stood up, so did I. We shook hands and he said, "Keep your money, or spend it wisely, and good luck."

Legends of Jack Pollack of many hues abound. But I found him a man of his word, strong enough to walk away from $40,000 in cash when he did not believe he would be honest in taking it.

A different episode in the Brewster campaign is worth mentioning to illustrate the absolute necessity of telling supporters what they want to hear. As the meeting with Jack Pollack shows, I had to go after every ounce of political support to counter Dan Brewster's power of incumbency. This took me to Ocean City where all candidates would appear before a meeting of cities and counties officials. On the way there, along with a supporter, John Hubble, I stopped to see Sam Setta at the Wishing Well Motel in Easton.

I didn't relish this meeting because Sam Setta was a curmudgeon and close to a mossback Democrat. His firmest belief was that property rights, especially his property, was a sacred right. As was typical of Sam, when a local newspaper published a photo of Sam and his motel, it was with Sam holding a shotgun. According to the newspaper, Sam meant to keep his motel for white guests only.

This was a sociable call, though obviously one with political intent. I bought a bottle of Jack Daniels, and the three of us chatted about my campaign to beat Brewster. Sam knew Brewster, and as expected did not like him. When we got up to leave, Sam threw his arm around my shoulder and said, "Ross, you've always been a straight shooter. That's good enough for me, and I am for you."

In the car, John Hubble burst out laughing loudly. He was a big man with a laugh as big as his body. "Doc," he said, "I have just seen a master at work. How you managed to give satisfying answers to all of Sam's far-out questions I'll never know. But you did. You did it!"

"John, it's no trick. You know I don't play tricks. The point is, people hear what they want to hear. It depends on how you say it. You know by now I am not going to say something I don't believe. But I am going to say what I believe, in ways I think people want to hear."

"Damn if you said anything new," John said and thought a moment.

"It just sounded different."

"Right," I said.

The next morning,in Ocean City, John Hubble picked me up to go to the political meeting. He greeted me with a copy of the *Baltimore Morning Sun* containing an anti-Pierpont editorial. It was a classic example of the way liberal bias in the news media has eroded its credibility. The editorial showed my face atop a huge black cat (could the symbolism be more obvious?) with a caption reading: "The Fat Cats Have Done It Again."

The accompanying article stated I had the largest sit-down dinner of a non-incumbent. Then came statements that my dinner had "skirted and used campaign financial laws." To suggest the dinner was even more evil-doing, the article wrote of "non-reporting of this huge dinner," and that "The Fat Cats Have Done It Again!"

The *Sun* article specifically admitted everything I had done was legal. Unable to condemn me with facts, the writer and artist deliberately resorted to a derogatory — and highly memorable — label coupled with that well known image of bad fortune, the black cat. The paper's objective: hurt me as much as they could. Who the hell is going to vote for a "fat bad luck cat?"

Some may find my interpretation paranoid. Why would the *Sunpapers* be out to "get" Ross Pierpont? Well, think about it. I was a known conservative. A prominent and wealthy doctor, I was a spokesman for medical opposition to federal government management of medical care, describing it publicly as under-funded and over-promised. Brewster voted consistently for more government management of medical care. He was "old money blue blood" of the Baltimore County aristocracy. *And a liberal.* For all practical purposes, Danny Brewster and the owners of the *Baltimore Sunpapers* belonged to the same "club." Oh yes, the reporter and the cartoonist knew how to curry favor with their bosses. They would never get in trouble by helping Danny Brewster and hurting Ross Pierpont.

That long day continued with stops in Annapolis, Prince Georges County, and ended in an apartment in Montgomery County. It was a meeting where I had nothing to lose because these were votes I normally had zero chance to get. I was shooting for the support of two left-wing

Democrat ladies and one of their friends who had arrived somewhat noisily on a motorcycle. This man also sported a braided, Chinese-style pigtail that went well with political views somewhat to the left of Mao Tse Tung. Since I had no chance for these votes uttering left-wing sophistries, I answered their questions by economic and political facts as I saw them. The ladies' male friend soon tired of it all and excused himself. We continued to talk over our political positions for at least another hour. When we got up to go, both women threw their arms around me, one even kissed me, and said, "We like you, Dr. Pierpont. Count on us 100%."

Hubble waited until we were driving away then said, "I've seen it all! I've seen you be a conservative that drew Sam Setta's arm around your shoulders. Just now I saw the conservative independent 'fat cat' Dr. Pierpont kissed by left-wing liberals who promise their enthusiastic support! The greatest part of this whole operation was that you didn't waver from the things you've always said. It was just that your explanations had a different ring to them —"

"So that everyone heard what they wanted to hear," I interrupted him. John laughed that huge laugh of his. "About that friend of theirs on a motorcycle," he said, "he said he was for you, too." Another laugh. "You probably could get the gay vote, too."

I said, "John, look around you. Every one of these apartment buildings holds 1,500 votes. If I can't get help inside those buildings, meaning my literature slipped under the doors, I'm dead."

John's joviality disappeared and he became serious. "Doc, I've worked in politics a long time. You're so different I'm not sure you could ever make it in politics. Most politicians I know would be on their heels if they don't keep winning. The difference is, you're better off out of office than in. Socially, and sure as hell financially." He paused and I remained silent. Then he said, "I hate to tell you this, but a lot of people think you're completely nuts even to run for office. Look how we spent today. Look what newspapers say about you. It's a wonder to me you would expose yourself to attacks like that. Who needs it!"

John Hubble had repeated what I had heard more times than I remember. Even Grace said something the same though she totally respected what I was trying to do. After a long silence, I finally said,

"John, you are absolutely correct. What you have to realize about me is this: I have a damn failing. Any time I see something that needs to be done, I have to try to do it. I've been like that as long as I can remember. Too late to change now."

That line of thought took me back to my first big attack on the misuse of power, the mismanagement of my fellow doctors at City Hospitals. "What drives me to run is what the people in power are doing to this country. I'm talking about the Brewsters, the Tydings, and the media's terrible misuse of its power - look at the biggest powerhouses, The Washington Post, and The Baltimore Sunpapers. The people running things think they know what's best for everyone - right now they're doing their damnedest to turn doctors into robots, hired hands answering not to the needs of patients, but to the profits of bean counters. What they're doing to medicine, they're also doing to education - schools are a mess and getting worse. Do these people believe in freedom that made this country great? Hell, no, John! They believe in security blankets.

"John, I just can't help it; I have to do my best to stop what they're doing to us. Why me? Who else? Is anyone else doing what I'm trying to do? I don't want to sound noble, but am I any different, any less, than the handful of men who pledged their lives and fortunes to get the King of England off their backs? Sure my efforts cost me, cost me one hell of a lot, and not just money. But some of the men who pledged themselves to found this nation did lose their fortunes, and some lost life itself when they and their families became marked men and women for the British to hunt down.

"Why do I run, John? Because I look at a drunk in the Senate. I look at Joe Tydings, an autocrat and self-serving liar. I look at a Democrat organization in Maryland that takes black votes as its property, bought and paid for. With my knife, I help to cure sick people. With my brain- and money - maybe I can help to cure this nation of misfits and incompetents who are running things."

It was a long speech, but it did me good to say out loud some of the thoughts that had been just meandering through my mind. My attempt to knock Brewster out of the Senate got me 40,000 votes. I had known from day one I could not overcome the incumbent backed by the party's organization, but the actual defeat hurt badly. It helped then, as at other times, that my life had been built around a determination to survive - never, never, ever give up. It also helped that while I despise the gloss-over and double-speak (now refined by linguistic hired hands into "spin") my love of my country has never gone down. I think history will show that the making of these United States has been humanity's finest hour to this moment in time.

Stay with me while I ramble some more. Politics in our democracy is organized chaos. No other word can describe such interplay of every individual's needs and opinions, every organized group's goals and opinions, every ethnic individual and group with still more opinions, every nationality, every creed, and every religion, every pauper and homeless, every entrepreneur and captain of industry, every doctor, lawyer, pharmacist, dentist, podiatrist, chiropractor and "Indian chief" - yes, in this nation every one of these groups and individuals "knows best!" Every one says my ideas of what we need are just as good as your ideas.

Wonder of wonder, for some reason it works!

Chapter 21

I learn why they say, "Politics 'ain't beanbag!'"

An election is a lot like any other contest. There's a winner. And a loser. But there are differences. Losing an election lasts a long time. You make friends, some of them reliable. You make some enemies which are always reliable — they'll do everything they can to keep you down and out. I have never seen any act of mercy for a loser in a political contest. He's down. Hit him again!

My loss to Danny Brewster was a killer. I had spent more money than I had ever intended, after-tax dollars, at that. Campaigning day and night, I had virtually estranged myself from Grace and close friends. All I had for the time, effort, and money was a tad more than 40,000 votes. I took my place with all the others who had run self-financed statewide campaigns without winning a single election.

On the bright side, I had 40,000 Democrats who believed in what I had to say. I had made personal contacts with professional politicians from the Atlantic coast to the rattlesnake-occupied mountains of Garrett County. Voters and politicians alike, every one of them, including those who did not agree with me, now knew where Ross Pierpont stood. I had established a reputation as a hard campaigner and major personality in future elections. I firmly believed that my determination to campaign with truthfulness and integrity had registered across the state.

I had learned to roll with the punches, and to recover and punch back. The ups and downs of my surgical experience, where life, not votes, is at stake, served me well. It is a harsh learning experience to think you are winning a battle to save a patient's life only to have a sudden, unexpected pulmonary embolism snuff out the life willingly entrusted to your skill. It is humbling beyond description to tell the patient's hopeful family what has happened with honesty, candor, and sympathy. Winning or losing in politics is a weak image of a medical defeat.

Yes, there was a lot on the plus side. But it didn't endear me with the professional Democrats when Brewster went down to defeat at the hands of a Republican, Charles Mathias. Losing a senatorial seat is a serious blow to any political organization, and I had strongly opposed

Brewster. I did my best to mend my fences with personal calls to the Democrat leaders I had met, and thank them for considering my candidacy. While they were unhappy with the loss of Brewster, a large majority of them were unhappier still with one of their own: Senator Joe Tydings. They let me know without question that they would work with any respectable candidate who would oppose Joe.

I used these meetings to let it be known I, too, wanted Tydings out of the Senate. Democrats I talked to about him always wanted to know what I had against the man, especially since some of them had seen me support him. I avoided personal explanations by referring to Tydings' liberal record. It was enough for them to hear I didn't like Tydings' dancing to Kennedyite music, and his later devotion to legislation that implemented Lyndon Johnson's "Great Society."

What none of them knew, of course, was the promise I had flung into Tydings' face when he killed the Southern Hotel program. Anything I could do to see Tydings' carcass out of the Senate and on the street, I was ready to do.

Fortunately, I had gained enough information in my Brewster campaign to convince me that Tydings re-election in 1970 was anything but a sure thing. What I couldn't foresee was the virtual disintegration of the Democrat Party on the national level. Maryland was still a political province of "old line," conservative politicians. Nationally, Johnson had ridden roughshod over Congress to hammer through all kinds of liberal programs. Welfare boomed. Medical practice came more and more under federal control as Medicare and Medicaid expanded the covered and their coverage. Affirmative action, well intended but ultimately one of the worst of the programs, gave bureaucrats new powers, new fields of endeavor and billions in expenditures.

When Johnson at last saw that the overblown intentions of his Great Society had led to unintended and unfortunate consequences for his Presidency, he bowed out of office. Teddy Kennedy, Jesse Jackson, and George McGovern rushed into the vacuum. They belonged to each other, but they didn't belong to me. Even this many years later, I can only wonder how the Democrat Party ever fell for the charms of such a trio.

Unable to associate myself with the McGovern troops, I checked my options. There was no question in my mind that Tydings had made so many enemies in the Party I had a better than even chance to beat him in the primary. (You don't beat incumbents; you have to be there when they beat themselves.) However, I also knew that left-leaning power brokers aligned with the Ted Kennedy-McGovernites would back Tydings against me. How much they would help Tydings was an unknown. Friends suggested that I run against Tydings, win the Senate seat as a Democrat, then become a Republican.

To present myself to the public as a Democrat while knowing I felt strongly against the Party's fiscal, social, and political policies was out of the question. At heart, I was no longer a Democrat. The situation left me with no choice but to see where I might stand with the Maryland Republican Party. Although Republicans were a pitiful minority in Maryland, the Party controlled the Presidency and was doing fairly well nationally. The Chairman of the Republican National Committee was a Maryland Congressman, Rogers Morton. I knew Morton casually from running into him a number of times during the Brewster campaign.

I made an appointment to see Morton, and what I learned from him was startling. He and others leading the Maryland Republican Party considered Tydings unbeatable! Our conversation is etched in my memory.

As I entered Morton's office in Washington, he greeted me effusively. He was a hearty, gregarious bear of a man, about six foot six, whose geniality came naturally and made him well-liked on both sides of the political aisle. His charm was a key to making him the Party Chairman.

Greetings done, I got to the point. "Congressman, I am here as a friend in need of information."

"Shoot."

"How are you planning to take over Joe Tydings' seat in the Senate next year?"

Morton shook his head. "You know Maryland too well to think that can be done. Oh, there's some rumblings against him — happens all the time. But you can't beat someone with no one. The sad fact is we're up against a Party four times our size. Tydings is a lock to repeat. Anyway, why do you ask? You're a Democrat."

"I don't like what's happened to the Democrat Party and I don't like Joe Tydings."

Morton smiled. He knew I had supported Tydings in previous elections. "Ross," he said, handing me a sheaf of papers. "Look at these and weep. These polls show Tydings getting about 80% of the vote against anyone we put against him."

I glanced at the numbers. Morton was right — as far as the polls went. The pollsters had asked the wrong questions with the wrong opponents.

"Pretty gloomy," I said. "But you can't give Tydings a free pass. Are you going to run Glenn Beall against him?"

"Hell, no!" Morton exploded. "We're not going to waste a House seat for the satisfaction of opposing a sure winner! We probably will field someone who needs the exposure and understands what he's up against."

"If I understand you, you really don't have a candidate against Tydings."

"You understand correctly."

"What would you say, Rogers, if I changed to Republican and ran against Tydings?"

Rogers Morton shook his head. "Ross, you found out what you're up against when you ran against Brewster — "

"Brewster lost," I interjected.

Morton smiled."That was sweet. Sweet. But I can't encourage you to change parties and take on Tydings. Don't get me wrong, it would really save me some problems if you did. But it's too risky. I wouldn't have any money for you."

"I don't want the Party's money. All I am asking for is your guarantee of recommendation, and full Republican support. I don't want to run against you and Tydings both."

I had handed Rogers Morton more than a little to think about. His decision, whatever it was, was going to affect both political parties for years — the term of the next Maryland Senator would last through 1976. Morton gave his burly body a half-turn in his chair while he considered what I was offering to do. I broke into his thoughts: "One more thing, Rogers. I need your promise you won't run Beall under any circumstances."

"That, you've got," Morton said. "I'm positive he won't run against Tydings, and so is he."

That was satisfactory as far as it went. But I had learned the hard way, in politics don't take anybody's word about what another person will or won't do. "Do you mind if I go down to the "Hill" and talk to him in person?"

"Hell, no, Ross. He's seen the polls. He'll tell you the same thing I told you."

We parted in agreement that, insofar as the Chairman of the Republican National Committee was concerned, Glenn Beall could not beat Joe Tydings and would not give up his seat in Congress to make the attempt. Beall personally confirmed Rogers Morton's statement. He had no intention of campaigning against the incumbent Democrat Senator.

"Glenn," I said to the Congressman from western Maryland, "This is August. I want to see what happens between now and January. If everything stays as it is now, and based on your decision not to run against Tydings, I will come back to see you and Rogers in January. At that time I'll let you know if I will change to Republican to run against Joe Tydings."

"I hope you do," said Beall. "I surely don't intend to."

January, 1970, came and I met with both men in Washington. If they had not changed their positions, I said, I was going to file against Tydings. They were delighted to resolve the question of who would take on the Democrat. They were full of promises to help, give me full support at the Republican Party level, except for campaign money. They said I was alone in taking on a losing effort, so no Party money would be donated to my campaign. I said, "Gentlemen, I am going to take on Tydings with your assurance you are not going to file Glenn Beall against me."

"You've got it," Rogers Morton said. Beall agreed.

I left them smiling, as I relished the thought of carrying out the campaign I had planned for months. What neither Morton nor Beall knew, as I did, was that Tydings was in deep trouble with both the rank and file and most local leaders of the Democrat Party. The incumbent would beat himself, provided I presented an acceptable alternative.

Within weeks, I visited every Democrat boss in the state who was on my list of "disaffected locals." These were old line Marylanders who respected fiscal responsibility and integrity. In each visit, I explained my disgust with the deterioration of the Maryland Democrat Party led by the alcoholic heir to the Kennedy mantle, coupled with Jesse Jackson and ultra-liberal George McGovern. Every one agreed with me vocally, and my meetings became very pleasant. Again and again, each one confirmed their anti-Tydings feelings. Local Democrats wanted him out. They were bothered by losing a Democrat Senator in the person of Tydings, but they also understood the need to clear the Party of what he stood for. Virtually to a man, they promised to help me run against him.

Even when I told them I would change to Republican to run against the man, they understood. One honest Democrat was typical: "Ross, at least we'll have a man we can trust and someone we're not ashamed of introducing as our U.S. Senator. Count me in."

These meetings were extremely reassuring, but I had no illusions about winning in a walk. It would be a hard battle against experienced pros who had liberal money and union support. My first job was to get rid of the "Tydings can't lose" illusion. I set out to focus attention on the arrogance and hypocrisy of the man, things I knew first hand. I worked hard with a statewide group of anti-Tydings activists who called themselves the CAT. Citizens Against Tydings."

Volunteers helped me put a large, heavy-weight paper bag on the counters of nearly every pub and convenience store in Maryland to ask for contributions to my anti-Tydings campaign. It was simple. It was devastating. Contributions flowed in, small but they added up. They also focused the glare of publicity on Tydings' shortcomings.

When I changed from Democrat to Republican at the end of January, a newspaper strike cut into the campaign, but we overcame the lack of coverage in other ways. New polls were taken in mid-April and stunned the state's political pros. From a "can't lose" position going into my campaign, Tydings had fallen to "can't win." The liberal press took one look at the polls and hoisted hurricane warnings: the conservative "do good doctor" from Baltimore was in line to unseat their fair haired Senator. The only real surprise to me, and a stunning one at that, was to find "old money," nominal Republicans suddenly finding hitherto unknown virtues in my Democrat opponent!

A few days after the polls were known, Rogers Morton called to ask me to meet with him and some Republican National Committee members. I had no illusions they were calling to offer me campaign money or other support. I had kept Morton and Beall informed throughout my campaign, and there were no surprises that I knew of.

I went alone to the Capitol Hill Club a few blocks south of he House Office Building in Washington. Only a member of Morton's staff was there to greet me, and I waited for him in the Club's ultra-posh reception room. Brightly lit large photos of Eisenhower, Lincoln, and the incumbent President Nixon looked back at me from the walls.

A commotion at the doorway signaled Morton had arrived. Well-wishers and favor-seekers clustered around the man's huge frame somewhat like baby chicks hanging near Big Mamma chicken. Morton saw me and covered the distance between us with about a half-dozen long strides. Smiling broadly, he grasped my hand and said, "Ross! Good to see you. Thanks for waiting. Let's go upstairs for some lunch."

He led the way to an elevator and we went up to the third floor and a private dining room where a table was set for four: Rogers, myself, and two senior aides.

Rogers dominated the luncheon conversation and I waited patiently for him to get to the point of the meeting. "Things look pretty good for you, Ross. How do you feel?"

"Fine," I said. "You've seen the polls. We're riding high if we don't get knocked down by the bumps. I expect to win this election. Nothing taken for granted, but I still expect to win."

Again that affable, engaging smile lit up Rogers' face. "You have done one hell of a job in a short while! You know I told you Tydings was an 80% winner. You proved me wrong about that. Any more rabbits up your sleeve or in your hat?"

"Nothing magical, Rogers. I'm counting on my name recognition, my position as an alternative to a hypocritical liberal, and a record Tydings isn't able to challenge."

Rogers Morton toyed with his dessert a bit. I sensed that for some reason he was a little ill at ease. "How do you find your former Democrat friends taking this? Are they nervous?"

"I've talked with every one of them — kept them fully informed and asked for their help and advice. They have been upfront with me, too. As a matter of fact, they seem quite satisfied backing me against

Tydings. Better than I expected, really."

My answer described my worst concern in taking on Tydings. It is one thing for political party leaders to glibly assure me of their help, neutrality, whatever, when the event is off in the future. It is something entirely different when plans become reality, and public reactions take place. Fortunately, undercurrents of animosity toward Tydings were, if anything, strengthened when the local leaders had a place to express their feelings. Tydings, himself, helped me as he reacted to negative attitudes he hadn't felt before. The Senator was not used to rejection.

Morton arose from the lunch table and we moved to easy chairs. His huge body filled a chair as he sprawled comfortably, showing his girth from advancing years. He liked to extend his legs full length, feet crossed at the ankles. Morton, I thought in silence, when are you going to get to the point? I didn't have to wait much longer.

"Ross," he said, "as you know I didn't give you a chance of the proverbial snowball in hell. But you showed us stuff we didn't know. We really appreciate everything you've done. And done damn' well. Until you came to see me, we were ready to concede the Senate seat."

"That's what you told me when I came to see you and Glenn Beall in August — and again in January when I told you I had decided to run. I look at what's happened since those talks and don't mind saying I don't believe anyone else, not even Glenn Beall, could have done it."

Morton stared at the toe of his right shoe. "Ross, being Chairman of the Republican Party is sometimes a terrible job. But someone has to do it. And that's me. Now I have to be honest with you. The Party has met and decided Glenn Beall should run for Tydings' seat."

I was prepared for a lot, but not this! Morton's words swept through me like a hot flame. This man before me, this honorable Chairman of the nation's alternative political party, the party setting national standards at the White House, had given me his solemn word that they would not run Glenn Beall for Tydings' seat! Beall himself had confirmed it. Twice! I had gone to the mat and shown them wrong in saying Tydings could not be beaten. Now, he and his party had coldly, cruelly decided to double-cross me. Their repeated promises were as worthless as smoke.

As my successful campaign against Tydings crumbled into ashes at the feet of big Rogers Morton, I clenched my teeth hard to control my anger. Only then did I let go. "Rogers, what the hell are you saying to me? Are you saying you and Glenn Beall are two-timing liars? Are you saying you sold your good word, your soul, dammit! to reap the harvest of my work? Or are you just saying you and Glenn Beall are two lying sons-a-bitches!"

"Now, hold on, Ross," Rogers broke into my outburst full of pain.

"No, Rogers, you hold on! You just admitted you were ready to concede the Senate seat to Joe Tydings. Like a fool, I trusted you. I burned my bridges taking on Tydings when your experts told you I couldn't win. And I gave my word to Democrat leaders in Maryland when I asked for their help as a Republican. Too late, I find that the people who told me not to trust you and Glenn Beall were right. Your solemn word means no more to you than a fart in a hailstorm."

Rogers Morton tried to look pained. The effort did not become him. "Ross, politics, as they say, 'ain't bean bag.' It's a battle for survival every election. Sometimes, to survive, you have to change your mind, no matter what it costs. What you have no way of knowing is, I'm obeying orders from the boss. President Nixon looked into this and told me he wanted Beall to run."

Liars! I have never been able to tolerate anyone who lies, a gift from my mother. She often warned us while very young: "Ross, a man who will lie is a man who will steal."

I spat out words like bullets. "That's how you excuse breaking your word with me! And making me break my word with my supporters. The Republican Party of Nixon and Morton deserves its reputation for weaseling and lying. When people say you and Republicans in Maryland have no principles, no integrity, Lord how right they are! My mother always warned me, a man who will lie is a man who will steal."

Morton let my anger flow right past him. Almost unperturbed, he even chuckled as he said, "Have I stolen anything?"

"You're damned right you have. You have stolen my faith in you and the people you represent. You have tried to steal my integrity. You have done your best to steal my good name. Rogers, I promise you: I will never forget it. You are a louse."

Even as I said that, I remembered saying almost exactly the same thing to Joe Tydings, and I thought what the hell am I doing here?

For any real impact on Rogers Morton, I could have just said, "Thank you for the lunch." He was the soul of patience as he said, "Ross, calm down. Whether you believe me or not, the boss in the White House calls the shots. I can't blame you for feeling the way you do, but we'll try to make it up to you."

I just looked at him, silenced by his ability to destroy everything I had done so calmly.

"I am sorry, but I'm stuck with this job. I only hope you will reconsider and not run against Glenn Beall. If you do decide to run, I hope you will run a gentlemanly campaign against him."

"You call yourself a gentleman?" I retorted. "Rogers, I am going to be honest with you which is something you have not been with me. Tell Glenn Beall for me that the first time I meet him I'll tear off his right side. The second time I'll tear off his left side. Then his rear end and his front. What's left, I'll stomp on all the way to the election. He has it coming. You have it coming. Is there anything else you would like to know?"

"Ross, again I apologize. I hope you will reconsider what you plan to do." The huge man sprawling before me dismissed me politely. "Thank you for coming. "

I stood up, and Morton got up to extend his hand. I said, "Thanks for the meal and the treachery. I won't forget either. Goodbye."

I don't remember leaving that room anymore. Fury does that to me. As I waited impatiently for the elevator — I needed to get out of there! — years of survival training took over. "Hold on," I said to myself. "Don't get mad. Get even."

Chapter 22
I Keep My Promise to Senator Tydings

The Maryland Republican Party rubbed salt into my wounds. By June, prominent Republicans were pressing me to withdraw in favor of Glenn Beall. This favored soul marked time in the wings, preferring to appear above the fray, and letting it be known he did not want to give up his Congressional seat to run for the Senate if I ran against him. Grace took things — I started to write, "gracefully," but to avoid an unintended pun, make that patiently — as long as she could. "Ross," she finally said, "you promised me you would not run if the party did not back you. Now they're not backing you and are fighting with you. You can't do this to yourself! I think it's time to forget it."

"Grace," I replied, "I know how you feel, believe me. Will you look at it another way? The Democrat party has not changed. They just want to get rid of Tydings. A weak candidate like Glenn Beall will be a one-term Senator. If I am elected, I will bring not just a Senate seat to the Republican side, I will bring with me a close association with the state's *Democratic* leaders. It is even possible I could help to change the entire political structure of the state — who knows?"

"But is it worth it?"

"What is the nation worth to us, Grace?"

I have no doubt that, to some, my ideas will read pretentious — maybe they are. But it was how I felt, and I am not about to pretend otherwise. As the primary neared, two top Republicans, Alexander Lankler and my double-crosser, Rogers Morton, asked for a formal conference.

I faced a dilemma: Available information indicated that Democrats against Tydings were lukewarm about Beall as his replacement. I had strong doubts that Beall could win. On the other hand, I had zero chance to win the Republican primary with the party's money and organization against me. Some die-hard, "old money" Republicans would rather go down to another of their string of defeats than support an outsider — and former Democrat— who challenged their "leadership." To this day, I do not believe Rogers Morton told the truth when he said President Nixon had ordered me dumped in favor of J. Glenn Beall, Jr. I believe Morton "owned" Beall. He controlled him in the House of Representatives, and would control his votes in the Senate. *He also knew he would not control me.* His prestige and leverage in the Republican Party nationally would soar if he took an obscure western Maryland Congressman from "can't-win-against Tydings" to a win over the "can't-lose" Senator. The man he now wanted to elect was a lightweight. He was a very handsome, very pleasant and relatively young man whose best luck was being born a - ding-a-ling! — Beall. In western Maryland, and indeed throughout the state, the Beall name carried great weight. Glenn's father was a self-made man who had won election to the Senate years earlier. He had been a hard-working Senator, and was highly respected by politicians and the public alike, Democrats included. Carrying four-to-one Democrat Maryland while running as a Republican is an indication of Beall Senior's popularity.

I think the opportunity to elect Glenn Beall Jr. to the Senate was simply too great for Rogers Morton to pass up. I had exposed Tydings' vulnerability in my early, relentless campaign and that the Senator had paved the way to his own defeat. Rogers Morton's questions were how he would tell me I was a reject, and how much damage could I do to Beall's campaign.

Other than the duplicity involved, Morton's position was a fact I either had to accept or fight. The controversy led to some bitter confrontations in June, 1977. Grace attended most of the meetings of my supporters, and became increasingly unhappy with the situation. Fortunately for me, she understood my reasons for running, and believed in what I was doing.

Most of my group knew enough about Glenn Beall's weakness to believe he lacked the stomach for a hard fight against me. John Conway, a major supporter, summed it up like this: "Beall just doesn't have the guts to face you in a bruising primary. Let's not give up."

Rogers Morton had made one thing crystal clear to me. He was not about to keep his word to support me if I filed against Tydings. His man was Glenn Beall. We arrived at the deadline for filing in June, 1970 still at loggerheads. A last minute meeting led to a compromise offer. Morton said if I would not run against Beall, the Party would donate $100,000 to a campaign of me against the popular Democrat Congressman from

Baltimore County, Clarence Long. For me to take on Long as a Republican would be a long shot if ever there was one. Long was the epitome of constituent service. I think he spent more time in his various Baltimore County offices than he did in Congress. It was a saying in Baltimore County that if you needed something done in Washington, Long was the man to get it done for you. Loyalty from his supporters was legendary. Even Republicans liked him.

I had never doubted my belief that Joe Tydings had sown the seeds of his own defeat provided there was a united front against him. If I opposed Beall as vigorously as my supporters urged, and the state Republican Party officially pitted itself against me, the resulting split could have the very effect I could never accept: Tydings' re-election to the Senate. I had promised Tydings I would see his behind on the street, and I would keep that promise whatever I had to do.

Maybe Morton knew more about my desire to see Tydings defeated than I guessed. He was a shrewd man with almost unlimited contacts.

My loyal supporters, opposed to my withdrawal, agonized with me to the last minute. It came and I went to meet Beall and his supporters in a private room at the grand old Belvedere Hotel in downtown Baltimore. I went into the room by myself, where I delivered my answer to the waiting assemblage of Republican Party officialdom: "The first order of business in my opinion is to get Joe Tydings out of the Senate. That is the reason I approached the Republican Party in the beginning. Everyone here knows what has happened since then." I paused to study their faces. Glenn Beall toyed with a pen. Morton, the liar and double-crosser, could have been wondering what he would order for dinner. Lankler licked his lips, a bit anxiously. A handful of other "old line" types looked at me in silence. These people were totally bored! If I generate a primary fight, it will be bitter. The odds are my votes will not win against the old school tie Republicans in the Party.

"Worse, the fight would cripple Glenn, and a weak Beall would not draw enough Democrat votes in the general election to beat Joe." Beall's face tightened and took on a tinge of pink. He deserved what he had just heard. I continued: "I am not really interested in taking on Clarence Long in the 2nd District, though, no doubt, doing so might make some friends of the grateful opposition here. *My overriding consideration is Joe Tydings,* a fact most likely known to you. My best judgment,unfortunately, is that if I continue to run against Glenn and split the Party, Tydings will win re-election by default.

"For this reason, I am willing to withdraw from the Senate race and will do everything I can to elect Beall..." I could not resist adding the kind of thought that does not make friends: "...even though from my view of the Republican Party in Maryland, Beall's election could turn into a long-term disaster for a resurgent Maryland Republican Party."

I turned and left the room. I had no stomach for congratulations for doing what I felt had to be done, but which I believed would be harmful to Republicans in the long run. Hating lies and liars, despising double-crossers, I had been handed a situation in which I had no choice but to deal with them as best I could, or totally withdraw.

That day was one of the saddest days of my life.

Unfortunately, that day has also been representative of so much in both political parties.

Most of us have been taught that honesty is the best policy, but that message has surely become sidetracked on its way to high-level politicians. The current occupants of the White House do not do anything so crude as lie. Heavens, no! They have brilliant "spin doctors" who are expert at manipulating the media to "alter the facts through a deliberate and reckless disregard for the truth," as a professional public relations man defined their techniques of evasion and deception. As happened to me in the campaigns of 1969-70, they are not only getting away with the deceptions, they are basking in incredibly high "approval ratings."

Is Maryland any different? Not if you believe Jack Pollack's tape recording of the promises made by Millard Tawes when he was running for Governor and broken once elected. Not if you believe the Mayor of Baltimore and Baltimore Sun reporters. The Democrat Mayor says Democrat Governor Glendenning made promises he then failed to keep, leading the Mayor to turn on the Governor and support a female challenger. A prominent Democrat state legislator has been quoted as saying it is time for the state to put an honest man in the Governor's Mansion, "which leaves Governor Glendenning out." Widespread doubts about the Governor's honesty obviously make no difference to any number of public men. An example is former Governor Donald Schaefer, who has decided he now likes the Governor and urges his re-election.

An amusing sidelight is that the fight between the present Mayor of Baltimore and the Governor is about "state-authorized gambling." Governor Glendenning strongly resists any new gambling in Maryland, while his most prominent supporter is the former Governor who rammed a Keno-enabling law through the state legislature making public gambling statewide.

The men I had to deal with in the campaigns of 1969-70 were less sophisticated than our current political "leaders." Their method was simple: Say what you need to say, promise what you need to promise, to get elected. Once you are safely in office, who is going to throw you out? No one. What can people hurt by broken promises do to you? Nothing. The cost and effort necessary to evict an elected officeholder makes the effort impossible.

Politicians are fond of saying, "A day is a lifetime in politics." They believe that. They practice it.

I really had no business trying to oust the popular Congressman Long, but by now I was too deep into Democrat-Republican differences to do nothing. I accepted the Party's offer of $100,000 and promise of support against Long. Now Morton and his cohorts showed their true colors once again. Repeated requests for the promised campaign funds met only delays and explanations; Morton was negotiating for time. I finally managed to get $6,500 as a "down payment."

I ran for nomination in the Republican primary the only way I know: all-out. I had to, because seven months earlier I had been a Democrat. The effort paid off with 53% of the vote against two other well known — and competent — Republicans. With nomination in hand, we closed ranks against the popular Long. The principal fund-raiser in my campaign pulled in the largest turnout ever in Maryland for an unelected person as 800 people joined me at the Eastwind catering place, including some prominent Democrats like Jack Pollack.

As I was winning the Baltimore County primary, Beall won the Republican primary for the U.S. Senate. In the weeks that followed, polls began to show that Beall was slipping against Tydings. The labor vote, black vote, and the 4x1 Democrat advantage in voter registration were holding behind Tydings. A predicted June margin for a Republican against Tydings of 150,000 votes was melting and Beall was in trouble.

If Beall lost, no matter how my own campaign went, the chance of my lifetime against Tydings would vanish forever. I set aside my feelings about Beall and Morton and joined the Beall campaign as often as I could.

I have never thanked God for a rainstorm, but in the election of 1970 I probably should have although it killed me against Clarence Long. The rain was so continuous and so heavy on election day, only truly committed people turned out to vote. The final result was a victory for Glenn Beall of 45,000 votes. Clarence Long continued his reign as the constituent king of the House of Representatives, although I did manage the largest vote against him at that time.

I waited until the votes were beyond question and dialed Joe Tydings. When he came on the line I said, "Joe, I promised if I lived I would see your ass upon the street. I keep my promises. How does your new situation feel to you?"

The only sound I heard was the bang of a telephone hung up. "Well," I said out loud, "Joe Tydings you just have no *savior faire!*"

As for Beall, in his next election he lost ignominiously to a virtually unknown, scholarly Baltimore lawyer, Paul Sarbanes, and never won another election after that.

After the 1970 election, some friends and I got together socially and were reminiscing about what happened, and what might have been. Someone said, "Ross, you've spent a bundle on running for office with nothing to show for it —"

"Wait a minute!" I interrupted. "No one knows better than I do that I belong with that group of candidates who financed their elections personally and not one has been elected. I'm not happy about that; I'm a lousy loser. But how did it happen that a little-known Republican from Baltimore County become Governor against a Democrat with a four-to-one registration advantage? How did Carlton Sickles lose the Democrat nomination when solidly backed by teachers, government employees, and most blacks? If my handful of votes had been in Sickle's column, giving him the Democrat nomination, he would have beaten Ted Agnew. Think of public and private unions, blacks, and the Maryland Democrat Party all behind a Governor Sickles with their hands out! We would have become the most unwanted state in the U.S. as far as attracting companies to locate here is concerned.

"I think I bruised Dan Brewster so badly when I ran against him that he never recovered, and Mac Mathias replaced another Democrat Senator. Not least of all, for many reasons, was the victory of Glenn Beall, a lightweight if ever there was one, over the darling of McGovernites, Kennedyites, and laborites — Joe Tydings. On the whole, I won some things that matter to me even if I didn't win actual office."

Those were some positives, but a galling negative from Morton's and Beall's double cross that radiated through the Republican Party was the unnecessary loss of a Congressional seat to a Democrat Byron, and a Senate seat to Democrat Paul Sarbanes. If there ever was a case of incumbents beating themselves, Beall vs. Sarbanes was a classic.
Joe Tydings, like Glenn Beall, never won another race after his first loss. But Joe proved that the only thing to expect in politics is the unexpected.

About five years after losing his Senate seat, Joe called me and said he would like to talk over some things of mutual interest. I was intrigued in spite of what I thought about him. We settled on his coming to my house in northern Baltimore on the next Saturday afternoon. It was a gloomy, rainy day and I was relaxing while watching a football game on TV. The doorbell rang. I opened it to see a dripping wet Joe Tydings, wearing a larger-than-life smile, hand extended in a friendly hello.

He could see Grace standing behind me and included her in his greeting. "Ross!" he said, fairly booming for Joe Tydings. "It is really great to see you again. Grace, it's good to see you looking well."

"Come inside, Joe," I said. I took his dripping coat to the kitchen to dry out a little, then rejoined him and Grace in the living room. I shut the TV off and said, "What can we do for you, Joe?"

"Ross, I came here to ask if we could bury the hatchet and get on with some things."

I stroked my chin, listening and waiting for him to go on.

He said, "We were good friends before and I feel badly about what's happened. I want to get back into things in Washington, although I'm doing well in my law practice. I've been thinking about running in '76 and before I can do that I need to clear up any personal problems — especially burying the hatchet."

"Well, Joe, let me tell you about that hatchet. You happen to be talking about a mighty expensive hatchet — a couple hundred thousand on top of three million. There's always been more than the money, though. I'm talking personal decency, betraying friends for no reason I can see, and — well, that's enough for now."

My gut still turned over to think of one of the saddest — not to mention expensive — episodes in my life.

Joe was tough and I am sure he anticipated almost exactly what he had just heard. "You know, Joe," I added, almost quietly, "What you and your friends at the bank did to keep down the black community in Baltimore was wrong. Money is no excuse for that. It's things like that that convinced me I couldn't go on being a Democrat. I'm sure you know I'm a Republican now."

I glanced at Grace. She sat quietly observing Joe with not-very-friendly eyes.

Joe said, "Ross, there are more things than what you have just said I am very sorry for. But please believe me when I say the reasons for what I did were not what you have just said —"

I did not let him finish. "You'll never prove that to me, Joe. Let me put it to you like this. I respect your courage in coming to see us today. I understand what you are thinking about, because I've been there— oh, have we ever been there!" Again I glanced at Grace, as she managed a small smile. " I understand why you don't want anyone raising such issues in a primary campaign against Paul Sarbanes. The black vote is crucial in Maryland primaries — n'cest pas? The shoes you're wearing are a little tight, Joe. Trust me, I understand."

Joe showed again he was tough as he managed a laugh. "Ross, one thing you haven't changed in for sure — you're still blunt and you know the angles that make a difference in an election."

I started to answer, but he held up a hand asking me to wait. "Ross, we understand one another. I'm very successful in law and major representation with Congressional committees. I am just closing a case with a million dollar fee to me. As I said, it's not the money. It really isn't. Just like you, I want to see things happen that matter to me. I want to be back in the U.S. Senate. I am asking for your support if I run, and if we can bury the hatchet at least stay neutral if you can't support me. It's up to you and Grace to make that decision."

I saw no point in continuing the conversation and said, "Thank you for coming, Joe. We'll talk things over and try to be fair."

As I said the words, I couldn't help thinking, "That's more than you were with me!"

Joe put on his raincoat then looked me in the eye. "One more thing, Ross. If you ever need anything from me, and I can help, give me a call." He had nerve, this guy, for he added with a trace of a smile: "This time I promise to answer."

The meeting ended and we went about our daily affairs. Then one of the strangest events in my political endeavors took place. It was less than two weeks after meeting with Joe Tydings that I took a telephone call from a man I hadn't seen in months.

"Ross, this is Herb Brown. I wonder if you could do me a favor."

"Herb, it's been a long time. Sure I'll help if I can. What's it all about?"

Dr. B. Herbert Brown was a local businessman-educator. He owned a small business college in downtown Baltimore. By guts, persistence, and ability he had developed, single-handedly, a practical institution for night school and part-time business education. His school filled a real need in the community.

He said, "The seat of Chairman of the Board of Regents at the University of Maryland is open. I would like to be the new Chairman."

"Nothing like setting your sights high, Herb. But I need to know more than you want to be the Chair. Where do you stand with others? When is the election?"

"Ross, the election is Monday."

"Which Monday?"

"Next Monday."

I laughed. "Herb, this is Friday. You're calling to become Chairman of the University's Regents on Monday. Why didn't you wait a couple more days until it's over?"

Herb laughed. "I didn't think of you till today. I remembered your run-in with Joe Tydings, and that Joe has the position in his pocket. Can you do anything about that?"

Now, that was a question! "Herb, two weeks ago I would have said,

352

'Sorry, I can't do a thing.' Some things have changed, and maybe I can. I'll let you know."

After Herb hung up, the irony of the situation became totally amusing. I had short-changed my practice, neglected family and friends, and spent huge sums of money establishing myself politically with the goal of booting Joe Tydings from his seat in the Senate. Goal accomplished, promise fulfilled, Joe Tydings visited me for the first time in five years. Today, an old friend asks me for help in becoming the Board of Regents Chair instead of Tydings' own choice. In spite of the feelings I still had about Joe Tydings, the challenge of finding out how good his word was became irresistible. I dialed his number and he immediately took the call. Just like old days!

"Ross, good to hear from you. What's on your mind?"

"Well, Joe, a good friend of mine called me a short time ago to ask me to help him in a tough situation. I know you are very close to the people at the University of Maryland — I taught anatomy there, you know..."

"I know. They tell me your reputation as a professor is tops."

"Thanks, Joe, I try my best. My friend tells me that if anyone can help him at the University you're the man to talk to."

After a slight pause, Joe said, "Yes, I am very close to the University administration, Ross. What's the problem?"

"Joe, Herb Brown, my good friend, really wants to be Chairman of the Board of Regents. I told him I would do my best to help him get the job. He's a good man and would be a real asset to the University."

The telephone was silent. I had put Joe Tydings between the well known rock and a hard place. Finally, Joe said, "The meeting of the Board is Monday, just three days from now."

"Oh? So soon?"

"Three days." Another long pause. "How important is this to you, Ross?"

I couldn't help it; I had to treat him with a dose of his own double-speak. Instead of a direct answer, I said, "Joe, would I have called you if it wasn't important?"

Joe must have swallowed hard before he finally answered. "No, I guess you wouldn't. Tell Brown he'll get a unanimous vote of approval

Monday."

"Joe, that's really great of you. I know Herb will appreciate it. I'll let him know as soon as I hang up."

I put down the telephone and burst into laughter. After I got over that I called Herb Brown and told him he would be the next Chair of the Board of Regents. His effusive thank-yous filled the telephone.

As promised, Brown was elected unanimously as the Chair the following Monday and served the University with distinction. (Sometimes I wonder about the guy who was in line for the Chair, but, alas, you can't have two winners.)

As a footnote, Joe Tydings never made it through the next Democrat primary, losing to Paul Sarbanes. One of the saddest campaigns ever mounted by a Republican ended when Sarbanes wiped up the mat against Glenn Beall in the general election. Maryland's Republican position was left to be represented in the Senate by a full-blown liberal, Mac Mathias. The eggs laid by the likes of Rogers Morton, Chairman of the Republican National Committee, had hatched into impotent barnyard roosters. Pride, ambition and greed were caponizing the Republican Party of Maryland.

Chapter 23

The Decline and Fall of Political Machines

My first involvement with political power was the fight we carried to City Hall to obtain relief for residents at City Hospitals. That effort was about as unsophisticated as you can get. I learned a little more about the power of political officeholders when I became friendly with the leaders, bosses really, of the Democrat Party in 9 to 1 Democrat Baltimore City, and at least 2 to 1 Democrat Maryland.

I do not exaggerate when I write that in those days political bosses were the real powers in Baltimore City, the various counties, and, in turn, the state.

I had truly enjoyed going behind the scenes of Maryland's city, county and statewide government as a Democrat. In postwar Maryland up until the riotous sixties, I could be proud of Democrat policies, although some of the state's policies were so unreal as to be ridiculous. The party functioned statewide through a constitution granting tremendous powers to the Governor.

I remember one episode in the Savings and Loan debacle when a group proposed taking a new, stronger regulation to the Governor. Someone asked, "What happens if he doesn't go for it?" An old hand in Maryland politics looked at the questioner as if looking at a child. "If he doesn't like it, we'll just put it away and go home." Chances of passing anything through the Maryland Legislature against a Governor's wishes were classified as "slim and none."

The Maryland political saga from the 40's to the 80's deserves repeating. In 1940, they got a Governor's Mansion to live in and $4,500 a year. Can you appreciate the Governor's elation when he was handed his monthly pay check of $375? Twenty years later, Maryland raised its Governors' pay to $15,000. This windfall was for more than a full time job, as Governors were expected to make special appearances at candidates' gatherings, state and national party conventions, appearances in Washington, weekend bull roasts, and other fund-raisers. Without defending the payoffs accepted by Governor Ted Agnew, where was he supposed to get money for daily life, much less put two sons through college? The system was a scandal waiting to happen. Which it did when Governor Marvin Mandel was tried and convicted of accepting illegal "gratuities." The system also brought Agnew down, although it did not catch up to him until he was Vice President.

These and other scandals did not truly upset me as much as the changes occurring in the Democrat party at all levels. From Democrats that took this nation through the Japanese and German threats of World War II, through the rebuilding of Europe with the help of the Marshall Plan, and the restoration of a peacetime economy, the party became a playground under the thumbs of playboy Senator Ted Kennedy, charlatan Jesse Jackson, and hopelessly impractical George McGovern. The Party refused to recognize the threat of Communism and Russian expansionism. People who challenged Communists and Communism were labeled McCarthyites and shunned. Behind such men and the true source of Democrat policies and positions, including a despicable pandering to African-Americans for their votes, were Big Labor bosses, Big Education bosses of the National Education Association, militant black organizations like CORE, and, perhaps worst of all, the Tort lawyers.

Increasingly disturbed, I remained a Democrat through most of the era of the political bosses. Baltimore City in that era was the key to the political control of Maryland, and it was divided into recognized fiefdoms. Northeast was predominantly Irish territory dominated by Coggins-O'Malley until Riccuti-Curran knocked them off. Jewish Northwest was a Trenton Club fief bossed by Jack Pollack. South Baltimore was Della-Wyatt controlled. The Poles, Lithuanians, Ukranians and comparable ethnic groups in east Baltimore responded to the Macht-Prucha organization..

Counties also had their bosses. Judge Walsh presided over Allegany County. Emerson Harrington was the lord of the Eastern Sho.' The Lee clan dominated Montgomery County.

Two ethnic groups are conspicuous by their absence in this lineup: African Americans and Germans. This was an era when Democrats "owned" black votes, and otherwise paid no great attention to them. German-Americans were a different matter. German immigrants were the largest contingent nationally and in Maryland. But they split their influence between Catholicism and Lutherism, which left them comparatively weak in Catholic-dominated Baltimore. A typical if cynical comment of the times was that Baltimore was "owned by the Jews, run by the Catholics, for the benefit of blacks."

The political bosses gained and exercised their power through patronage and money. Bosses controlled liquor boards, judgeships, zoning boards, road building, slot machine gambling, horse racing, and each party's Central Committee. What they also controlled was "walk-around money." This money, spent by organization volunteers at polling place level, was the key to many an election. The organizations saw that their candidates dominated their neighborhoods with lawn signs, neighborhood advocates who promoted the candidates anointed by the boss, mailings, and above all the official organization ticket. If you were on the official ballot, supported by walk-around money, you were a leg up on winning the election. A candidate left off the official ticket could usually wait for the next election. In short, the bosses provided the winning margins of votes, bought or otherwise, that elevated eager candidates to office. Once in office, most candidates voted for laws, appointments, or regulations as directed by the boss who put them there.

The Sunpapers, and to a minor extent, the Baltimore News American newspaper, wielded tremendous power. At the height of its influence, not to be reached again, the Sunpapers devoted front page editorials extolling Harry Hughes, a candidate otherwise "a lost ball in tall grass." Repeated, powerful and free front page "endorsements" elevated the modest Hughes to Governor.

I had no professional instruction in the uses of power, political or otherwise, but I knew it when I saw it. Or felt it. Mainly I saw it in the power - sometimes brutal power in my case - exercised by the leaders of medical organizations. I experienced it totally when banished as Chief of Surgery and even as a practicing physician at Harford Memorial Hospital. I bent to it when I bowed out of the campaign against Senator Tydings rather than try to defeat Tydings, the Republican Party organization, and its money.

What I saw happening to the practice of medicine in the United States convinced me that medicine in the future would come under political control. Once the Federal government wrapped itself around health care via Medicare/Medicaid, government money - or withholding it -

would control all but a handful of physicians and hospitals if not stopped.

If not stopped! Could I be the person, one doctor, to stop a juggernaught?

Who knew, and who knows? But I did know this: if someone doesn't try, the outcome will be as inevitable as taxes and death. My life from its earliest beginnings, the lessons I learned in overcoming obstacles through the years, gave me one option: do what I can.

Looking back, I can see that this is how I arrived at my political actions, including resigning from the Democrat party and becoming a Republican. None of this was a result of sitting down and thinking about some sort of detailed program. When a political situation called for change, and no one seemed more suitable than I to charge into it, I just did it. My goals were to get recognition and an official position where my insights could prevail.

That, in a way, is how I happened to spend a lot of money, and Lord knows how many hours, trying to replace Clarence Long, Democrat Congressman in Baltimore County.

In order to replace Long, I first had to win the Republican nomination. Why there would even be a primary contest was a question because Democrat Long was generally seen as unbeatable in his predominantly Democrat district. Long was also one of the hardest working Congressmen ever in terms of service to voters. He spent more time dealing with the problems of individual voter than he did as a legislator. Give the man credit, he knew the power of responding directly to voters, and he developed an extremely effective way of reaching out to them. He had equipped a van emblazoned with "Clarence Long, your Congressman at work!" which he parked in front of post offices in his district where he met with constituents. An aide greeted voters outside the van and found out why they wanted to see Long, after which Long, assisted by another aide, met with them inside the van.

The tactic gave Long an image of a Congressman never too busy to listen to citizens' problems, and it was enormously effective even with voters who had no need for a favor.

My opponents in the Republican primary were two "old-line" Republicans, John Seney and Phil Knox. Both were fine gentlemen who had zero chance to beat Clarence Long. I felt no need to tear the Republican organization apart and virtually ignored them, but the "old-line" Sunpapers did not. I was stunned when the Sun declared John Seney their Republican choice, stating editorially that Seney was also the choice of a large majority of the District's Republican organizations.

The Sun's statement was wrong and obviously damaging to my campaign. I found that the author of Seney's endorsement was Bradford Jacobs, a son-in-law of someone in the family of the Sunpapers' owners. To correct the error, I went to the editorial department of the Sunpapers to confront Jacobs and demand a retraction.

With a subordinate supporter beside him, he sat behind a desk where I laid his editorial before him, and beside it the written endorsements of a majority of Republican organizations in the Congressional District. He looked from the endorsements to me, unable to hide his embarrassment. I finally broke the silence: "I have shown you that your statement in this editorial is wrong. The question is, what are you going to do about it?"

Jacobs had the power of the newspaper empire behind him. He also had no intention of embarrassing himself with a retraction. "I'm not going to do anything. What do you expect me to do?"

"Do what any honest and responsible reporter would do! Retract your damn statement as wrong and write the truth. I have majority support of Republican organizations in my District, and now you know it."

Jacobs' fellow writer shifted and Jacobs saw the movement. He reached to pick up the endorsements, then thought better of it and pulled back his hand. Anger covered any embarrassment he might have felt over his error. Growing pink in the face, he growled, almost choking: "You've got one helluva nerve coming in here like this! I've got a right to my opinion."

"Of course you do. But not to print a damn lie. Now you know what you wrote was wrong, a lie. The man sitting beside you now knows you lied. From your refusing to retract it, we know you have no problems with printing a lie to influence voters."

As I spoke, Jacobs stood up. "This interview is over! I have nothing more to say to you!"

I shouted something to Jacobs' retreating back. Whatever it was meant nothing of course, except that this episode colored my relations with Brad Jacobs and the *Sunpapers* from then on. Anyway, I went on to win the primary with more votes than my two old-line opponents put together.

To win against the entrenched Congressman Long, I knew I had to do something beyond conventional campaigning. I had to find a way to get Long to beat himself, if that were possible. I found that the man had just two weak spots. An economist by profession, he totally lacked a sense of humor. He also had blocked a second bridge across Chesapeake Bay.

Long had stopped the proposed and preferred crossing of the Bay because he promoted a bridge built in the vicinity of Edgewood, a small town about 20 miles northeast of Baltimore. Long's supporters in Baltimore County generally favored his site, which got him their votes. Meanwhile, the fight over location was costing millions in lost tolls, caused horrendous waiting in line on both entrances to the existing bridge, and who knows how much development of Ocean City.

Long's site selection was not purely political. We found that the Congressman had the foresight to buy a large piece of land in line with the site he promoted.

Knowing Long's inability to laugh at himself, we built a campaign to take advantage of it while bringing his record to voters' attention. My loyal supporters built a portable carriage that held a large American flag, a Maryland flag, and huge, colorful posters. The posters displayed Long's voting record showing his public statements and how his votes in Congress were different - Long was two different men.

To get our message to voters, what could be better than going where Long had his visitations? When he went to District post offices, we followed just behind. Meanwhile, I had an advance crew stake out our position on the sidewalk where anyone seeing Long's van would see ours. As we pulled into place, with music filling the air, I would get out and introduce myself to the people arriving for a session with the Congressman. I answered questions outside; Long answered questions inside.

The campaign began to take hold, as we urged people to recognize the difference between Long the private person and Long the Congressman. The man's dignity froze him as people began to ask him one or more of the questions posed by our posters. He tightened up, argued with aides, and fought our presence every inch of the way. He even took a couple of weeks off. But when he resumed his post office visits, we resumed our side-by-side comparisons.

One day in August it was 101 degrees with no breeze, and Long gave up using his van for a place in the air conditioned Edgemere post office. I advised the Postmaster that Long's actions were illegal, and, when he ignored me, my crew went inside, too. We were ordered out, which I refused to do unless the Postmaster made Long leave, too. A very upset by now Postmaster directed Long to leave and was indignantly informed he was dealing with Congressman Long, who would not leave until he was finished his interviews.

I interjected that if Long remained, I would have no choice but to call the legal section of the U.S. Postal Service in Washington. By now, the Postmaster had enough. "Everyone, all of you, get out of here!" he ordered. I left with my crew and we had a laugh over the episode as a still-declaiming and irate Congressman Long came out of the post office followed by that day's collection of constituents.

A week later, parked at a post office near York Road north of Towson, a man called out to me, "I wouldn't vote for either of you jerks! Look at that no-parking any time sign."

As he marched on, I called my trusted aide, Reid Braswell, pointed out the sign and said, "Let's get out of here and leave this place to Clarence."

After we drove across the street, Reid called the County police and told the desk sergeant: "Sergeant, I am calling about Congressman Long parking in a no parking zone in front of the Post Office on York Road across from Yorktowne Plaza. I got a $25 ticket last week for parking in that zone. Does he get to park in a no-parking zone because he's a Congressman?"

Assured that something would be done, Reid hung up the telephone and we watched. A couple of minutes went by and we heard sirens. Motorcycle police pulled up at Long's van and stopped. Two policemen approached Long, and a crowd gathered to listen as talk and arm-waving went on. After the police left with nothing happening, Reid called County police again. He poured it on. "Sergeant, two policemen came, talked to Congressman Long, and left. He's still there making his own rules, defying the law in a no-parking zone. You have County Executive Dale Anderson's telephone number, please give it to me so I can protest to someone high enough to see that no one is above the law in Baltimore County!"

The sergeant asked Reid to let him correct the situation, and again we waited a couple of minutes. This time, motorcycle police were accompanied by a squad car. Long tried to talk his way through the situation while his loyal audience watched. But the police would have none of it, and finally a Congressman beside himself with indignity packed up and left.

As the campaign came to a close, Long encountered a man apparently bent on attacking a woman near a telephone booth in our District. His chivalry aroused, Long intervened on behalf of the woman. The man promptly sued Long for assault and interference. Naturally, I heard about the case and Reid Braswell and I went to the Harford County court house to hear it. I was still practicing medicine in Harford County and many people in the courtroom knew me. Judge Stewart Day, presiding, also recognized me and said, "Dr. Pierpont, if you are a witness in this case I must request that you be sequestered."

I responded, "Your Honor, I have just come in from campaigning against Mr. Long and I'm here to see how my old friend is making out."

People laughed except for Long, who looked like he was eating a porcupine.

Judge Day restrained a smile and declared a fifteen minute recess. As he left the room, he beckoned for me to follow him. I noticed he was limping badly, not like him at all. When we were alone in chambers, the man was obviously in pain. "What is the problem, Judge?"

"My right foot," Judge Day almost whispered with pain. "It's killing me!"

I told him to take off his shoe and sock, and as he did I saw a badly swollen foot and a glistening redness over the meatcarpo phalangeal joint of his big toe.

"Judge, you've got the gout."

"What? You sure, Ross? I've never had the gout before."

"You've got it now." I picked up his telephone and called the local medical lab. Recognizing the man's voice when he answered, I said, "George, anyone there who can bring a prescription over to the courthouse?"

"Sure. What's the problem?"

"I'm sure Judge Day has acute gout and you can prove it with a uric acid determination. I'll leave him a prescription for colchicine. You give him the verdict for me, George. And thanks very much."

The prescription I left for the judge was an old but reliable drug for the immediate relief of acute gout. His uric acid, I found later, was high at 14. The prescription worked and I received a very nice thank you both in person and in the mail. Shades of what I could do in such a situation under Medicare rules today.

Clarence Long was found not guilty.

Research had found chinks in Long's supposedly impregnable position, which I penetrated with billboard, radio and other advertising. But the overwhelming Democrat registration, a strong and well-financed Democrat party, and Long's undeniable popularity did me in. I got more votes than had ever been run up against the Democrat, and smoothed the way for Helen Delich Bentley, Republican, to defeat him in 1984. Bentley proceeded to hold the seat for five terms.

At this point, I was not noticeably closer to my goals than when I started. A medical Cassandra, my concerns and recommendations fell on deaf ears, and I lacked an official platform from which to speak. It was time to get going.

I had recovered from my losing battle against Clarence Long when an election of a new Mayor of Baltimore City came up. The Democrat boss control of Baltimore City had always made it impossible for a Republican to be elected to any major office in the City, beginning with the Mayor. The City Council was Democrat, the Mayors were Democrats, and the bosses behind them were all Democrats. An aberration occurred when Theodore McKeldin, who called himself a Republican, was elected mayor. The reality was that McKeldin's policies and friends were all Democrat, not Republican. He held the office of Mayor with the help and affection of the Sunpapers, the City's Democrat bosses, and the skill of one of the great "bag men" of all time, Bill Adelson. "Republican" McKeldin's chief advisor was a Democrat. Surprise!

I faced the fact that there was no effective Republican Party in the City which still dominated Maryland. As far as I could find out, no one, including the nominal Republican Mayor McKeldin, had ever made an effort to increase Republican registration. Republicans in the City had absolutely no one capable of opposing the leading Democrat contender. This was William Donald Schaefer, then President of the Baltimore City Council, known to be favored by the powerful Jewish boss, Jack Pollack, and a prominent fundraiser, Irv Kovens.

I attended a number of meetings with other real Republicans, including black Republicans - yes, there were, and are, black Republicans in Baltimore City. Good ones, too. As discussions went on, it became clear that if I didn't take on the contest against William Donald, there would be no contest. I had the electorate polled, and found that Schaefer was unusually popular, with very high name recognition. To be blunt about it, he had no known weaknesses to expose. He had also adopted the most popular positions on the few issues of that time. For me to run against him was Don Quixote at his worst, for I had to lose, had to waste my time, money, and probably add some more enemies to my list.

The question became, would we Republicans allow Schaefer to become mayor by default. We could not, would not, if I had anything to say about it.

Since the few Republicans in Baltimore had no visible "standard bearer" to oppose Schaefer, it was me or nobody. Hell, to some I was nobody. Archie Jones, a black Republican from the McKeldin days, was against me because he saw my candidacy weakening his own position as a black leader. However, common sense - or what passed for it - prevailed, and the Central Committee voted for me to be the Republican nominee. We nominated Margaret Dyer to join me as candidate for City Comptroller.

A bright spot occurred when George L. Russell, a successful black lawyer, filed against Schaefer, and the two of us joined in a strange relationship by appearing almost side by side, Democrat with Republican, at many political meetings. We became friends, and remain friends to this day.

I tried everything including a meeting with a Irv Kovens, a political powerhouse in Baltimore City, and his wealthy friend, a contractor named Victor Frenkil. Though they were my long-time friends, they knew my chances and would not give away their support of Don Schaefer.

One of a few amusing episodes lightened the campaign when I attended a City Council meeting with supporters carrying signs about Schaefer's refusing to debate me on city issues. The Councilmen were waiting for Schaefer to appear and open the meeting as Council President. A Councilman, Willy Myers, recognized me and beckoned me to come where he sat. When I reached him, he said, "Ross, Johnny Hines has a terrible hernia hurting him."

I said, "Where is he?"

"Over there." Myers pointed to Hines and called to him, "Johnny, come over here."

When Hines reached us, I could see his hernia inside his pants it was so protruding.

I said, "John, we have time. Let's go take a look at that."

The two of us went into a men's room near Don Schafer's office as President of the City Council. I had John Hines lower his trousers in a relatively private area of the men's room, and suddenly there was a burst of activity. I looked around, and there was Don Schaefer relieving himself at one of the urinals while members of the press had followed Hines and me into the men's room. What we hadn't known, of course, was that the reporters finally saw a chance to get the two candidates for mayor in one photograph, and were taking advantage of it.

I calmly turned back to John Hines, but the always-excitable Schaefer panicked as flash bulbs popped. Well, put yourself in his position. Not literally, of course. But having your picture taken under such conditions is enough to upset even a poised candidate for mayor. Schaefer is not known for his poise. His first reaction was flight, and he forgot what he was doing. Looking down at himself, he saw his trousers were now soaking wet. Without a word, he rushed past the reporters and into his private office. By the time he changed and came into the Council room, everyone there was chuckling about it. To give Schaefer his due, he carried off the meeting without a sign of embarrassment, and with professional efficiency.

The pictures were never published, although I saw some which had been marked to make sure no one could be identified. Much later, John Hines died and I visited the family at the funeral parlor. While standing with John's son at the coffin, another person approached. I turned, and there was Don Schaefer looking me in the eye. We stared at each other, speechless, until the humor of the occasion hit us, and both suppressed smiles while we turned to view John Hines lying in his casket.

I lost to Don Schaefer, of course. But I managed to get some things into the record through meetings and position papers. This is quote without one word changed from one of my position papers on the impact of drugs on Baltimore in the year 1972.

> *The future of this City is at stake.*
> *Not only has drug abuse reached epidemic proportions, killing more of us this year than will be killed in Viet Nam, crippling more of us than were wounded in any war, the problem has only begun to show its magnitude. Should my opponent take over as Mayor, his views deserve comment. He*
> *says: "Baltimore ranks first in the rate of growth of drug addiction, in proportion to its population. We must educate children about drugs in school. There are no 'magical answers' to drug problems, but (a) a program of turn in the pusher will help; (b) Law enforcement must be improved, as by a task force; (c) Methadone is a problem as much as it is an answer.*
>
> *It is hard to be kind about such nonsense. My opponent's "program" would be laughable were the future of Baltimore not at stake.*

That position paper laid out a proposal to neutralize the drug impact 28 years ago, when Baltimore had a future. Its addicts then were estimated at 9,000 to 10,000, a manageable addict population. Once again, I played Cassandra, the media and voters put their blinders on, and today Baltimore suffers from a virtually incurable illness due to drugs. Addicts have grown at least five-fold to number more than 10% of the adult population. The cost of illegal drugs in crime, money, and living in fear is out of control. The city's health commissioner states that, today, 85% of all crimes committed in the city are drug-related.

Failure to cope with drug and crime problems when these were manageable has brought Baltimore City to the brink of bankruptcy. More than 56% of Baltimore's population is now on welfare; the numbers grow. Twenty-eight years ago, no one listened when I pointed out that Baltimore's vacant houses were cancers destroying the health of neighborhood after neighborhood. No one cared when I pointed out that the City's housing program for impoverished people would be a disaster. Crowding hundreds of people, I said, many if not most of them single-parent families, into multiple-floor apartment buildings would prove unmanageable. Without individual responsibility of occupants, such housing was doomed. Ownership monitoring of the buildings, I argued, is the only system that will work. I urged that housing supervisors be used exclusively for final control and backup of tenant-owners, including policies to evict tenants guilty of drug use, possession, or criminal activity. Now we see that well-meaning but fundamentally ignorant policies have led to easily-foreseen financial and social disasters. Former tenants enjoy the spectacle of million-dollar buildings crashing in rubble to the ground.

Twenty-eight years ago, I charged, and repeat now, that Baltimore's public school education was not only defective, it bordered on disastrous. Soft-headed egalitarianism and social promotion were turning out illiterate diploma-holders. To correct an educational system clearly ineffective that many years ago, I called for a tracking system to monitor children according to ability, motivation, and achievement. Direct responsibility for the failures of today's public schools lies at the hands of those who have established and run them: rubber-stamp school boards, teacher education schools, education administrators, and teachers' unions that swap educational achievement for more money and protection from discharge. Ultimate responsibility for all of the above: elected officials who ultimately control public school goals and policies, if not methods.

Let there be no mistake: In Maryland, that responsibility lies primarily at the door of Democrat officialdom and the Democrat party.

How did Democrat management of the City, and the liberal media, respond to my analysis of the City's needs? The media went lock, stock and barrel for "boosterism," which made great stories labeled "news," and gave me the deadliest treatment of all: the silent treatment. Pierpont? It's a laugh. No one pays any attention to him. He's a needler, a Republican needler at that. Why do anything about black problems like housing, drugs, and education, when black votes for Democrats are a lock at more than 90%? Baby, we're in power! Don't mess with a winning situation!

Bossism and one-party Democrat rule has taken Baltimore down hill until its survival, not its future, becomes the question. Three years have gone by since David Rusk, urban scholar, said Baltimore was moving past the point at which poverty and failing institutions would make the city's recovery impossible. Welcome to the Pierpont camp, David Rusk!

One positive of the losing campaign against Schaefer was my increased acceptance by rank-and-file Republicans. This became important the year following the mayoralty campaign. This was the year of the Republican National Convention where the re-nomination of Nixon and Agnew was a foregone conclusion. But these Conventions are exciting events, and this one gave me an opportunity to build a better-run and more democratic Republican party in Maryland. Until I got into the act, delegates to National Conventions were always hand-picked by a tight little group of elected officials in Washington, plus some patrician types and people who commanded influence. This group also controlled the organized activities of the Maryland Republican Party.

Not long after the dust of the mayoralty race had settled, the "old guard" called a meeting to organize Maryland's slate of 25 delegates to the National Convention. The "old guard" had failed to notice that the introduction of open voting for delegates had opened the door to organized opposition to fundamentally despotic practices within the Party. The "old guard" consisted of long time party regulars led by Rogers Morton, Senator Beall, and Senator Mathias. John Conway, Jack Brandau and I were now elected delegates and leading new opposition to the past practices of party regulars.

We had talked with other elected members of the delegation to find out where they stood with regard to following the lead of Morton/Beall/Mathias, or determining future policies of the Maryland Republican Party with Pierpont, Conway and Brandau. We lined up eleven, two short of the thirteen needed to win control. I could not envision myself remaining active in the Party with the "old guard" continuing its self-serving, often defeatist practices. As every possibility went through my mind, one and only one solution to the dilemma seemed possible. I called upon my two associates to discuss things.

I pointed out that the Senators and Morton had managed to frighten any more delegates from joining us, and unless we did something unheard of, defeat was inevitable. I do not take kindly to defeat, so I said, "We are two votes short of the thirteen we need, and there are only two delegates we can hope to join us."

I let that sink in. Jack Brandau said, "Who are you talking about?"

I was now enjoying myself, for I had learned a lot about the allure of power in negotiating with others, and I knew what I had in mind would work. It would not only work beautifully, it would also give Morton, Beall and Mathias fits.

"We have to get Madie Mitchell and Dr. Aris Allen to join with us."

After an appropriate silence, John Conway exclaimed, "Ross, you can't do it! We've talked our butts off with them and they won't budge. We don't know which way they'll vote."

I said, "Suppose, John, we put Dr. Allen up for Chairman of the delegation."

Both men looked at me. Dr. Allen and Madie Mitchell were African-Americans. If we achieved what I suggested, Dr. Allen would be in line to become Chairman of the Maryland Republican Party.

I said, "With our eleven votes and their two votes, Aris Allen chairs the delegation, and Madie Mitchell has to go along with that no matter what Morton tries to tell her."

John Conway slapped has palm against his forehead. "Damn, Ross, you're right. You're right!"

Jack Brandau was laughing as he said, "What a hell of an idea! Sometimes you have to rise above your principles in politics, but this is worth it."

"Hold it, Jack! This is not only for us, it is doing the right thing. Dr. Allen is one of the finest men I have ever met. He's a state office holder, and he will be the first black person to chair a delegation in either party since the Civil War. We'll make history with this move!"

Dr. Aris Allen was not a man who took positions lightly. We had a long talk about everything each of us stood for, and fortunately he knew my record in Republican campaigns. I was not a wheeler-dealer trying to use him for personal gain. After he agreed to the proposal, we told Madie Mitchell who positively glowed with the news. No one had to tell her Dr. Allen would be in line for Chairman of the Maryland Republican Party.

At the next meeting we elected Dr. Allen Chairman, thirteen to twelve. The reaction of the "old guard" was predicable. You can't do this was one of the kindest responses. In a weak-kneed attempt to derail Dr. Allen, they pled to make Senator Beall Chairman "so he can have the deserved prestige of handling the telephone for the delegation." They carried their hope to replace Dr. Allen with Glenn Beall right to the floor of the Convention in Miami Beach, Florida. At stake were not only Chairman of the delegation, but also the positions of National Committeewoman, and National Committeeman. These prestigious positions in the national party would be elected by the Convention delegation, which we controlled thirteen to twelve.

Our group put up Louise Gore, a prominent Republican from Montgomery County, for National Committeewoman, and Dick Allen, a farmer from Maryland's Eastern Shore, for National Committeeman. The Morton/Beall/Mathias group's big gun was none other than Tilton Dobbin, Vice President of the Maryland National Bank. Dobbin, we found, had been assured of his election before coming to the Convention. That kind of thing was typical of Morton's technique. After knocking a Vice President of Maryland National Bank out of becoming a National Committeeman, I reminded myself never to go to that bank for a loan.

We elected Louise Gore and Dick Allen, and Rogers Morton went ballistic. Openly declaring war on us, he exerted pressure that most kindly would be labeled nasty. I was personally vilified within my Party, and had some uneasy moments. Would our lines hold? They did, without giving an inch. (It helps when you know you don't want to be with your opponents.) Rogers Morton sent a messenger to tell me that he intended to bring our Maryland fight to the floor of the convention to reverse our elections. "Tell Rogers," I said to the messenger, "I look forward to meeting him in open debate on the merits of democratic principle as it applies to differences between properly elected members of a delegation. We will debate before the eyes and ears of the public. Let me know when we start."

That ended the threat. Dr. Allen, as expected, did a masterful and even-handed job of leading the delegation. President Nixon selected Dr. Allen to be his escort to the podium for his acceptance speech. It was a grand feeling to watch this happen for we knew we were making history, and all thirteen supporters of Dr. Allen and what he represented savored the moment.

I had my own moment of personal glory when one of the Convention's managers came to tell me I had been awarded time to present a new and fairer method of electing delegates to the National Convention. I had worked on this proposal very hard and had sent copies of the proposal to every delegate is his/her hotel room. To grant me time to present my proposal from the podium was more than I dared hope for.

But it happened. I had never been on such an elaborate dais before, and the experience answered a rather silly question that had always bothered me: how did they get all of the different speakers of widely varying heights to appear at the same height when they spoke? They simply had a hydraulic lift, and a technician raised or lowered it to put each speaker at the same eye height. I used my full ten minutes, of course, and someone moved that the proposal be studied by the Republican National Committee and reported back at the next meeting. The motion carried by a voice vote.

Dr. Aris Allen served with honor as Chairman of the Maryland Republican Party, went on to high positions in the Federal Government almost to the time of his death from prostate cancer. We thirteen delegates who voted for him had everything to be proud of.

We could not be proud of the fund-raising activities and expenditures of the Maryland State Central Committee in the months following the National Convention. In one case, a state chairperson was using scarce funds to maintain the offices of elected officials in Washington. Investigation also found that the Party's money was being used to enhance the positions of the Central Committee for politician gain. A threat of indictment appeared, but it all settled down and nothing happened. These episodes showed one reason Democrats controlled Maryland and Republicans took their leavings. The boss system in Maryland made sure that elected officials supported Democrat Central Committee activities by attending fund raisers, selling tickets, and more. Not only were Republican elected officials conspicuous by their absence from the Party's fund raising events, and other activities, they got complimentary tickets and in some cases paid travel.

The change in Party organization following the National Convention led to some high level resignations, all for the best. Wonder of wonders, actual efforts to increase Party registrations began to appear. These have borne fruit. Today, Democrat registration continues about 10 to 1 in Baltimore City and far outnumbers Republicans in Prince George and Montgomery Counties. The reason is purely race. African-Americans by and large refuse to vote Republican. Letting Democrats take their vote for granted does black citizens no favors, and little signs are emerging that well educated blacks are finding this out. The uninterrupted slide of Baltimore City in almost every category of livability is a case in point. What more can be said of a City where two of every three births are to an unmarried girl, and most of these mothers are still in their teens?

Hopeful signs? A real two-party system in Maryland where seniors and African-Americans do not unthinkingly vote for the candidates promising the largest hand-outs could work wonders.

It always amazes me to hear people say there is little difference between Republican and Democrat policies and principles, not that Republican policies and principles are the be-all and end-all. The easiest way to describe the difference is in two words: collectivism and individualism.

Collectivism, the Democrats' way: Democrats believe that the way to resolve a problem is to handle it at government level: pass another law. A typical result of this approach is social engineering and pandering to low-to-no income people through income tax laws. This once-simple law now fills thousands of page volumes two feet thick. Not even tax experts know for sure what the laws say. Another example is our healthcare problem. It was perfect Democrat policy for them to appoint a secret panel without one member of the medical profession on it, and authorize this illegal panel to draft new laws that would take over 15% of the nation's gross national product, totally revamp doctor-patient relationships, and put the control of trillions of healthcare dollars into the hands of - guess who - desk-riding bureaucrats of guess-which political party. It says a lot when there is no need to name that political party.

The examples can be expanded endlessly. The environment needs protection, pass a law. Wages for unskilled persons are too low, pass a law. Disabled persons need better facilities, pass a law. Homosexuals need official, public recognition, pass another law. Senior citizens need better health care, pass some healthcare laws. High government officials need corrective oversight, pass an independent counsel law. People drive too fast, pass a 55 mph law. When the law libraries are finally filled with enough volumes of laws, Utopia will at last be, guess what, the law of the land!

Problem resolution by big government has big, ugly children: problem resolution by collective organizations like Big Labor, and Big Education. The excesses and failures of both types of organizations are the ultimate result of their problem-solving approach. Who is surprised that teacher unions put the interests of teachers and administrators ahead of children's interests? How could it be otherwise? Coercive acts of the California teachers association are only the most obvious example of the consequences of attacking education problems through collective organizations whose rationale for their existence is their existence.

Collective organizations in lockstep with collective government, supported by the trial lawyers, is the ultimate definition of today's Democrat party.

A complicating problem with the collectivist approach is that the intentions are always good, always sound reasonable and affordable. Some of the collectivist actions are necessary. Only when one looks at the ultimate collectivist method of problem solving can we see the bottomless pit waiting at the end of the collectivist road - methods of control adopted by failed communist and socialist governments.

Individualism: True Republicans believe that each individual is the best place for solving problems. Is this fanciful? Those who say so should ask how this country managed to become the greatest nation on earth. It is the result of individuals. Thomas Edison who freed mankind from depending on sunlight/candlelight to conduct our daily activities. Henry Ford who freed mankind from horse-transportation and made it possible to live and work anywhere. The Wright Brothers. The inventors of computers. Alexander Graham Bell. These are the individuals, not contingency lawyers and not legislators, who changed not only America, but the world. Today, enjoying their inheritance, are the hundreds of millions of Americans who recognize and resolve their problems in terms of individual and family needs - freedom, not government edict, makes it possible.

Our history shows clearly that a necessary government can exist without destroying Republican-style individualism. The Declaration of Independence, the origin of our government, is a document stating individual resistance to the King's collectivist edicts. It is no accident that the Declaration was signed, not by a dignitary, but by one individual after another who took pen in hand to pledge his individual life and property. Our Constitution succeeds because it defines the need for collective decision and action, while restraining government coercion of individual rights and freedom.

The danger today is willing substitution of Democrat collectivism and government control for Republican individualism and freedom — individual responsibility for one's acts and their consequences.

In Maryland, the population has submitted to a one-party (Democrat) system for decades, and it costs us dearly. We have had two governors found guilty of corrupt paybacks, one of them a heartbeat from the Presidency. We have had County Executives go to jail for illegal acts. Two state legislators were forced from the last session of the State Legislature. In my opinion, our current Democrat governor sits in the Governor's State House office aided by (1) stolen votes in a 1994 election, (2) 90% black votes in Baltimore City and Prince Georges County, (3) the payback of government employee unions, and (4) the payback of the teachers unions. Is it any wonder that this Governor's Secretary for Economic Development left him in disgust, and that Maryland is pitiful in attracting top national companies with top-paying jobs?

The way the present Governor won his original election to the Governors' Mansion is charming. It is a real insight into the conduct of one-party politics.

The polls had closed at 8:00 p.m. on election day. Republican Ellen Saurbrey appeared to have won the 1994 election to Governor with a majority of 10,000 votes. When this became known, the Democrat machine came alive. At approximately 11:00 p.m. from Baltimore City's polling places, which had closed 3 hours before (at 8:00 p.m.) 15,000 votes for Glendenning suddenly turned up. Where had 15,000 votes been for three hours? Why had someone sat on so many Glendenning votes long after the polls closed? The situation smelled and encouraged Sauerbrey to contest the election. The media promptly charged in to label Sauerbrey "crybaby," "bad loser," and plead "let's get on with the State's business." Control of the election machinery in a one-party City and State made sure nothing happened, except that the "crybaby" image pegged on Sauerbrey hurt her badly in the next election. Since Glendenning had already bought the allegiance of blacks, teachers, and thousands of public employees, in a Democrat state, she probably had no real chance anyhow.

The problem of challenging Democrat power with Republican power came home to me when I was running against Don Schaefer. Senators Beall and Mathias asked me to visit them in Washington, and needing all of the Republican help I could get I promptly complied. After typical chit-chat, I said my campaign strategy was to tell voters Baltimore had real and future problems that I ascribed to the City's political machinery and behind-the-scenes seats of money power.

Senator Mathias, friendly but serious, said: "Ross, there's such a thing as going at things too strong. You are doing a good job, and great for you. But you can't step on too many toes without hurting yourself and the Republican Party."

Beall took the cue: "Ross, some friends in Baltimore have called us to say they think you are being too aggressive. They'd like you to back off from some of your charges."

I stared at them. Was nothing beyond them?

Mathias said, "Ross, the only way Republicans can get anything done in Maryland is to go along. We have no choice but to go along with the many people who help us and help them with their problems. Stirring up the black population isn't going to help anyone."

What in hell was going on here? What were they talking about? "I came here thinking that at last you two might want to help me fight Don Schaefer for the good of Baltimore. Is this 'back off' of yours my thanks for helping you beat Dan Brewster, Mac."

In the silence for a moment, I began to realize why I had been asked to see them. I had analyzed the pension system of Baltimore and found the system's management committee was placing enormous sums of money in Baltimore banks of the committee's choice. That was safe investing, but bonds and low-yielding savings accounts were falling behind inflation. The system was not generating enough to pay its obligations. It was wrong policy, so I publicly said so, ignoring the fact that influential Republicans were part of the system's advisory group.

No wonder they had squealed to Beall and Mathias. I was hitting them in their wallets!

Since I had no proof of that, I simply said, "You guys have taken me away from my campaign to tell me to back off. You are telling me not to stir up the black community, how to handle a Baltimore which is my home and nothing to either of you. Both of you are from Western Maryland with about 1% black voters. You want to lecture me about blacks? I have been a member of NAACP for 10 years. I took a black lawyer as Comptroller in one of my campaigns, and a black woman now. I count George Russell, black candidate for Mayor against Schaefer, as one of my friends.

"Glenn, you know damn well you lied in your teeth when you promised time and again you would not run for the Senate. Don't tell me Rogers Morton pressured you; a man would have had the guts to refuse. Don't either of you give me this crap about blacks, something you don't know one damn thing about."

They exercised the wisdom to keep quiet. Good, I had more to say.

"You talk about stepping on toes, and my guess is that some of your friends don't like my criticism of their managing the City's pension system." Without a word coming from them, I continued. "I am right about criticizing them, and I can prove it. Is it more important that a few of your banking supporters run that system for the benefit of the banks, or for the benefit of the people in the system? Oh, now that I think of it, there are other things for criticism. Failure to monitor the public housing, which may interest your friends, too. I don't need to justify my campaign to you. I am trying my best to bring out issues for the City of Baltimore in what both of you know is, from the beginning, an almost impossible fight."

Mathias tried to be friendly and light-hearted about the situation. "Ross, I'm sorry you feel that way. I thought we were beginning to see things the same way when we had lunch a couple of months ago."

"OK, so now you two are trying to tell me to cool it and run a nice, gentlemanly losing campaign. Is that right?"

"Well, not exactly."

"If not exactly, where is some help for me? How much money will you raise - you could do it, you know. Where is some money from the RNC, from the Maryland Republican Committee?"

Beall finally woke up. "Ross, we didn't call you about money. We wanted to give you some friendly advice."

Advice from Glenn Beall? That was enough for me. I gently told them never again call to advise me about matters they knew little or nothing about, and left.

As it happened, Hyman Pressman, who won the City Comptroller's job in the election took the time to call me about pension fund management. "Ross, you were right about the pension fund. We are doing the things you recommended and removing the banks from advising us about the fund, or controlling it."

Some reward for my efforts. I said, "Thanks for calling, Hyman. I appreciate it."

As must be obvious, my Baltimore City campaign went with my leadership of the delegates to the Republican National Convention in arousing internal Party opposition. So far, I had ticked off Rogers Morton, former Chairman of the Republican National Committee, Senator Beall, and Senator Mathias - not much left of the old guard leadership in Maryland's Republican organization.

Some leaders! Senator Mathias was a darling of the Maryland press, and in truth a likable fellow. Someone even dreamed up the title for him, "Conscience of the Senate." Behind the facade, however, was a "one-worlder," with socialist leanings, wherever they might take us. He regularly attended Bilderberger's secret meetings in Europe where he hobnobbed with some of the world's most powerful (richest) men.

As may be expected, Democrats counted Republican Senator Mathias to be one of their most dependable votes.

Of course, I had no way of knowing Mathias' international doings when he came up for re-election in 1974. What I did know was that Mathias followed the typical Republican route in Maryland of posing as a Republican, to get Republican votes, but vote Democrat to get crossover votes. It's a nice, workable formula if your conscience permits it.

As mentioned, I had gained with rank and file Republicans when I broke the strangle-hold of Morton/Beall/Mathias and elected Dr. Aris Allen Chairman of the Republican delegation to the '74 National Convention. We made some small gains in Baltimore City and the State Central Committee. Miscreants of the Central Committee were dismissed, not to return. Progress has occurred, but our need is to get the influential, wealthy supporters to contribute money and effort to the degree needed. We aren't going to achieve that until the Republican Party has a completely open, democratic organization at all levels.

In spite of the shortcomings, we have actually become competitive with Maryland Democrats, largely due to the left-ultraliberal shift of the Democrats not only in Maryland but in the nation. When people look at Jesse Jackson, Kennedy, Rangels, tort lawyers, a homosexual ambassador and Barney Frank, custodian of a homosexual whorehouse, and bosses of huge labor unions, including the hardboiled, backward stance of the teachers' unions, they begin to see that Republicans offer a better choice. Only the image of a plutocratic, minority-biased Republican Party stands in the way.

We still had far to go when I saw the Republican dilemma as Senator Mathias announced for re-election to the Senate. Mathias was a shoo-in once he had the Republican nomination; Democrats and the liberal press loved him. Not so with Republicans, who saw Mathias as a Democrat in Republican clothing. Organizations that monitor voting records showed Mac to close to the ultra-liberal left.

What would it take to beat him in the Republican primary? The answer, as I saw it, was a bona fide Marylander, bona fide Republican, with bona fide conservative credentials. I met those requirements easily. I considered my personal stock in trade to be unswerving loyalty, living up to my word, and "saying it as it is."

I decided to do everything I could to knock Mac Mathias out of the U.S. Senate.

About the same time, Helen Delitch Bently, a loyal Republican and friend, had also found Mathias vulnerable, capable of beating himself as is necessary in fighting an incumbent. If both of us contested Mathias, we would divide the vote and he would win easily. I filed before Helen made up her mind, with the result she withdrew from consideration.

Neither of us could have foreseen what came next. I was indicted for drug dealing. Was Mathias behind this? Not personally. He would not be so dumb. What we do know is that the charge was so stupid the judge who finally, a hundred thousand dollars in legal fees later, heard the case and commented that the charge would never have been filed it had not involved Dr. Pierpont, a Republican candidate for the U.S. Senate.

Some day, I hope to get the full truth behind the indictment. That it was personally motivated is beyond serious question; the charge involved only my written, fully recorded help for an obvious addict. He turned out to be a Baltimore City Police Department plant who managed to find me in Havre de Grace and plead for help. The charge was so ridiculous it can be explained only as an attempt to destroy me personally and politically. I wrote the complete story in my book "Indicted," where all individuals' names, places, and events are fully and accurately described. Nothing is made up, nothing left out. (Even this brought warnings I might be sued for defamation of character! No one ever followed through to sue as threatened.)

Stupid indictment or not, it derailed my effort to beat Senator Mathias. He won the primary and went on to win the general election easily. The "Conscience of the Senate" served his six-year term then retired to take on management of the B.C.C.I. bank. He was in charge of this notorious bank when it was cited for laundering dirty money and other breaches of U.S. banking laws.

Helen Bentley at first did not like my pre-empting of the right to take on Mathias. Events proved it was the best thing to happen to her. I remain convinced that the anti-conservative elements in Maryland who had brought me down would have done the same thing to her, had she run. She had developed a record as Chairman of the Maritime Commission and was subject to charges of contributions from those who had to work under her rules. It would have been a fatal charge for Mathias to exploit.

The combination of strain on both Grace and me caused by the indictment and my efforts to unseat Mathias was enough for Grace to question doing anything more. One thing bothering her was the obvious disinterest of people when I discussed solutions to complicated problems. She said, in effect, my opponents give simple answers people can understand. My answers were too complicated for people to understand.

Alas, she was right! I said, "Grace, there's no way to make the drug problem simple. Or recidivism simple. Or medical care for all simple. Let the mountebanks mouth their platitudes. I cannot say things I know are misleading - in some cases a bald-faced lie. Just can't do it!"

Like so many things, the era of sound-bites in the news and 30-second announcements, enabling candidates to put themselves before the public, is a mixed blessing. It ended the era of bossism. But it has elevated perception over fact. Image over substance. Media power and costs have also changed running for office into a gigantic money game. The image of Al Gore, Vice President, soliciting funds from impecunious nuns and lying about it, is sickening. The selling of the Lincoln bedroom in the White House takes sickening to nauseating. The sell-out to trial lawyers is beyond contempt. Republican fund-raising is not as notorious, but never let it be said it is above criticism.

The problem I see with all of this is that the need for money-grubbing, and buying the votes of unfortunates through handouts, threatens to destroy the qualities which have made America great, a truly unique nation in the history of man. As I write this, I do not know what my future holds. But I know this: If I believe in integrity, in stability, and fairness to all regardless of race, creed, sex or station, I cannot look away when I see things to be wrong. Principle and conscience, to me, override wealth and prominence. Involvement is not a one-day affair, it is never ending effort.

This personal assurance is my strength when I hear, or read, derogatory remarks. How many have I heard! Of course they hurt! If I am cut, do I not bleed? But I look at the Democrat Party I left, and the condition of the Republican Party under Rogers Morton when I joined it, and I regret nothing.

I look at my great old city of Baltimore where I spent almost all of my adult life, and I see its schools foundering, its crime and drug problems ruining the lives of innocent families, its incredible number of vacant houses, its tax rate, all accompanied by white flight, and I cry for it.

I also look at a Republican Party which has captured four of eight Congressional seats, and growing strength in the counties. There is much to do, not least of which is the coming struggle to determine the fate of medical practice in Maryland and the nation. I will never, ever give up doing whatever I can toward solving the crime, education, and medical problems of my state and my country.

Chapter 24

Money. It Matters

If you haven't grown up when earning enough money to take care of necessities occupies your waking hours, it is difficult to understand how someone who grew up that way respects money. As a well known friend likes to say, "Money to me is like sex. It doesn't bother me a bit. It's the absence of it that gives me trouble."

What's money worth in times when you could buy a barrel of oil — 52 gallons — for 10 cents? Oil sold for $2 a barrel, not a whole lot more than today's price for one gallon of premium gasoline. These were the years of modest economic recovery from the Great Depression.

Many people have asked Grace, and me, how we managed to find the time and money for my campaigns for public office. The answer is not complicated. By the time I began running for office, my practice produced more than enough money for daily life, and my investments on average earned additional money. As for time, I didn't schedule operations on patients nights or Sundays. So I needed only minor time off from my daytime surgery to campaign.

I have already described my clinic in Havre de Grace, and my methods of forming surgical partnerships. A little reiteration seems justified: Our core principle was that we would never turn anyone away, and all would be treated to the very best of our ability without concern for the size of the fee, or no fee at all. I allowed no one to press for collection of charges which would compromise the ability of the patient to pay. Our charges were what the patient could afford, no more, no less. One result of this policy, which came to hurt us terribly after the enactment of Medicare/Medicaid, was what was called our payment profiles. Our surgical and monetary profiles were among the lowest in Maryland.

We were good at what we did, kept very busy, and made out well financially.

While in my thirties, Grace and I had set aside enough money for me to invest in some common stocks. Whether it was research, good advice from brokers, or good luck, my stocks did well and enabled us to reinvest our profits. But income taxes were becoming "impossible." They were taking more than 50% of my earned income, and going higher. It was time to find a better way to hold on to my earnings.

I was about 40 when I learned about oil and gas exploration. Tax laws encouraged exploration, with savings as high as 70% write-offs on the intangible costs of well drilling. When the result was a dry hole, the write-off was 100%. What was called "tangible write-offs" could be charged against taxes at 20% per year for five years.

This added up to a situation where the entire well could be written off directly against taxable income, plus a tax-free depletion allowance of 28% of the income from a producing well.

I understand it all very well now, but I took my lumps in learning. Fortunately, Weeb Eubank, then Coach of the Baltimore Colts football team, helped when he introduced me to an honest man in the oil business — yes, they aren't as rare as some would have you believe. This was Russell Johnson of Oklahoma City.

Our largest oil ventures with the Johnsons were in 1979-80 when oil prices hit $40 a barrel due to the Middle East oil embargo, a value illustrated by the 10 cents for a barrel of oil at the bottom of the Great Depression, and $2 a barrel as late as 1957. With oil and natural gas prices at the wells reaching record levels, the West Virginia Big Injun Sand and other producing areas were as hot as the prices. Those were heady days as Johnsons/Pierponts collaborated on million-dollar explorations in West Virginia, Oklahoma, and Texas. Our projects were moderately profitable even when prices fell to sustainable levels.

Raised where tradition and family were primary matters in one's life, I found the lives of people in the oil and gas fields of mountainous West Virginia totally different. These people were as ruggedly independent as their mountains. One never-forgotten sight was large plastic pipes suspended treetop to treetop across public roads. These pipes were carrying natural gas from the wells to a major pipeline! It was cheap, and it worked, but from a safety and environmental standpoint I can't imagine it happening anywhere else but West Virginia.

West Virginians owning land with gas under it liked us. Under our drilling contracts, they received a royalty of the customary one-eighth to one-quarter of a well's production. An additional, popular "perk" was all the gas they needed for a lifetime if the well came in productive.

The search for profitable investments which also reduced taxes produced any number of scam artists who took the gullible and greedy to the cleaners. To make matters worse, the IRS took a dim view of some presentations and declared tax-deductibility incorrect or invalid. As usual, only the lawyers made out in these cases as the lawsuits, counter-lawsuits and other types of disagreements abounded.

No one wins all the time, and my share of losing propositions included owning our home, investing in calmness, real estate, an iron foundry, and hockey teams. I wasn't satisfied when a judicial decision wiped out one investment in a hockey team. I had to turn right around and do it all over again! But you never know. The fact is, my second try at sponsoring a Baltimore hockey team turned one of my worst investments into absolutely my best investment. Since I have already described my good luck in hooking up with Dan Dent as my financial advisor, I will add only that he relieved me of the responsibilities of making day-to-day decisions about investing money. Dan beat every investment index I know of for 20 years. Some record!

Probably the most rewarding investment I ever made grew out of my close relationship with Tom McNulty. A basic reason for that is the human side, for I genuinely liked Tom. He was a gregarious Irish Catholic, a "Renaissance man" with views broad enough to add membership in the Masons and the highest Catholic Order of the Knights of Malta. With an Irish tenor voice of thrilling range, Tom frequently lent his voice to weddings, and he sang for years in his church choir. Our different religions were a non-factor in our friendship, and we also saw things alike personally and politically. One of his typical contributions to my political goals was to pilot me around Maryland in his private plane and appear with me in campaign stops. Grace and I deeply sympathized with Tom's devotion to his only son, born with Downs Syndrome. Tom and Mary, his wife, knew nothing about Downs Syndrome when Tommy was born. They not only adjusted, they devoted their lives to giving Tommy all the love and attention he needed. The result was a very well behaved, healthy youngster except for the obvious problems of the Syndrome.

Tom had started a charge-card business which he eventually sold, leaving him with the ownership of an AM radio station, WWIN. One day Tom seemed, for him, preoccupied and I wondered what was on his mind. It turned out to be his radio station. WWIN had been doing very well in reaching Baltimore's African-American market in spite of a poor number on the dial, but the radio market was changing drastically with the tremendous growth of FM stations. WWIN had declined in sales with more declines in sight. Its continued profitability without a sister FM station was in doubt. Tom asked me to join his Board and give him any assistance I could. I immediately accepted and bought some WWIN-radio stock. The Board now consisted of Tom, Paul O'Malley, George Whattam and me.

We met several times to explore the best alternatives. Tom felt sure the station, with emphasis on cost controls, would stay profitable with its niche in the black Baltimore market. I was not so sure, but said nothing. Not long afterward, we had a meeting and Tom got to the crux of things. "I've really gone through our position in Baltimore every way I can see it. I've reached the conclusion that if we are to stay competitive, we need to buy an FM station. What do you guys think?"

What Paul O'Malley, George Whattam and I knew about buying an FM station was that it took a lot of money. Paul said, "How do we go about that, Tom? It sounds like a lot of money."

Tom laughed. "You think radio stations come cheap, Paul? It's changed fantastically the last couple of years. I remember when you could hardly give an FM station away. Nobody wanted the debt, never mind the purchase price. Now..." he paused dramatically while we sat waiting. "Now, an FM station could cost two million or more. That's if we can find one in Baltimore!"

"How much money have we built up in the kitty, Tom?" Paul said.

"Six hundred fifty thousand, give or take a thousand."

"That's earning something, isn't it?" Paul asked.

Tom said, "Not enough. Our trustees aren't aggressive enough. It helps but it's not the answer we ought to be looking for."

I thought of my experience with Dan Dent. "Tom," I said, "I might have an answer for us." I told them about Dan Dent and Tom instantly asked me to find out if he would take the account. With no one objecting, that part of the meeting was settled. We agreed to meet again when we had more information about an FM station and our $650,000 investment money.

Dan Dent was agreeable to take on the account, especially when I told him the group's direction was to invest aggressively. Dan needed to know our specific financial goals, and I didn't hold back. "Dan, we need you to raise the fund to a million-six by the end of next year." His eyebrows shot up. "Time is of the essence, Dan. None of us are young people, you know!"

He grinned, saying, "Take a year, Dan. Don't just double our money. Do better!"

I said, "You've got it, Dan."

As years do, one went by and darn if we weren't in position financially to start shopping for an FM station. Questioning around, we found that WFBR, another AM station in Baltimore, owned the rights for an approved FM station which it had never exercised. Tom and I both knew the general manager of WFBR, and after discussing our strategy we authorized Tom to negotiate with the station to buy its FM rights. He brought back a deal of $1,500,000 with no sales fees or commissions.

Within minutes, WWIN-AM became WWIN-AM,FM— the WIN TWINS. What a beautiful deal! Two stations in operation with very little added expenses and double the rates for advertisers buying the combination. Money left over from the investment managed by Dan Dent, and other savings provided another $200,000 to upgrade the tower and signal strength of the TWINS. Advertising income responded perfectly.

Naturally nothing stays perfect, so our pleasure was dimmed by bad news about the health of the station's General Manager. He was diagnosed with cancer. Tom had grown close to Sheldon Earp, the GM, and he also felt as though the WIN Twins was one of his progeny. He had built the station and it seemed almost as much one of his "children," as young Tommy. The situation had changed from delightful to sad.

When we met to discuss the situation, Tom was forthright. "Fellows, we're all getting older and Sheldon is in real trouble. I don't know how much longer he'll be with us. We have to consider selling the station. I can't operate it alone, and the rest of you aren't radio people. Tell me what you think."

We three "non-radio people" knew Tom was right and said so one way or another.

Tom said, "OK, everyone agrees. The next step, it seems to me, is for all of us to explore any contacts we have to see who can make the best deal."

Sometimes things happen beyond the expected. The next day I bumped into Jack Dunn Jr. at the golf course and for no good reason mentioned my interest in selling the WWIN-TWINS.

Jack worked for Legg Mason, a Baltimore brokerage company. He looked at me as if I had fallen out of the sky. "Ross, I don't believe it! This is right down my alley. My job with Legg Mason is buying and selling radio properties!"

"Well, you may have one to sell," I said. I referred him to Tom McNulty to see if they could reach a mutual agreement. That went smoothly, and in a surprisingly short time Jack came to us with an offer of nearly $5,000,000 for the real estate and the two licenses.

This was terrific, but more good news occurred when we closed the sale. The buyer was a minority operator, who had financial preference in radio station ownership. Because we were selling to a minority person, the proceeds were tax-exempt if invested in another minority enterprise of like interest.

The law of unforeseen consequences had come into play. Legislation enacted to further the interests of U.S. minorities would now help four ex-radio station owners. We simply turned the money over to Dan Dent to invest 100 cents on the sales dollar, with no tax.

Dan did his typical research before investing. The opportunities were limited, but he found one that met the prescribed formulas and invested our millions within the required time.

I think, looking back, that Tom had an inkling he had little time left, for both he and Mary died in 1996, leaving son Tommy who lives on in his fifth decade. Tommy is well cared for from Tom's multimillion-dollar estate. The rest of Tom's money was dedicated for the retarded.

While investing in public real estate deals was one of my worst experiences, I had much better results investing in private real estate. The difference is, primarily, the investor has control of his money in private deals. Even so, investing in real estate often requires more than enough capital — money — to last through enough delays to make Job look like a sprinter. Large loans with interest to pay keep coming due. Without reserves, the deal will melt into nothing or be lost otherwise.

The never-broken rule is: it always takes much longer than planned.

John Hubble, a very streetwise and knowledgeable real estate broker, and former Clerk of the Court, brought me into the purchase of 32 acres of land at I-95 and Caton Avenue, just inside Baltimore City's western limits. This is a strategic intersection to be sure because this piece of property sat squarely on a future interchange of eight-lane I-95 and a main roadway into the City.

A third partner was a wily, secretive man named Elvin Brazeal.

It was a good thing that Elvin knew real estate because acquiring this property defied explanation. The deal ran something like this: Undeveloped land lay on both sides of planned streets yet to be paved by the City. We would acquire land on both sides of the undeveloped "paper" streets. A parcel on one side gave us ownership of the land to be used for streets, up to the middle of its side of the street. A parcel on the opposite side gave us ownership of the land to be used for streets up to the middle of the other side of the street.

Sounds complicated? It was. Each parcel of land had to be acquired one by one, and there were 11 acres of "paper" streets.

Sounds expensive? It was. But the end result, if successful, would be very profitable. It was a tough call, but Brazeal and Hubble were the height of confidence. Grace and I talked it over until she finally threw up her hands over the complications. It was a bet, a gamble, but the risk was in my judgment worth it. I decided to bet on them. Time went by and my two associates finally came to me one day to announce we finally owned all parcels needed.

For the next act we went to the City to close the streets and acquire them according to law. Hyman Pressman searched through City laws and finally uncovered one which he said gave the City the right to price the 11 acres of street lands at $333,000.

"Thirty-*three* thousand, Hyman?" I said, accenting the final three. "Where did you get the *three* thousand to tack onto 330?" Hyman either did not see, or appreciate, my dry humor and he said nothing to explain the odd amount. We haggled with him, which was tough because Hyman exercised haggling as an art. Finally we caved in to get on with the deal and settled for one third — $111,000. My money.

That was a piece of cake compared to haggling with City engineers, accountants and politicians until I began to wonder if they wanted to bring in the dog catcher. It was serious business, for we were talking about locating and building water mains, sewers, flood control, and other construction of financial substance.

The City people had us by the well-known sensitives and there were plenty of days I wished I had never met John Hubble. Then bingo! Elvin Brazeal had gone through the recordings of site acquisitions, including acquisitions for the I-95 interchange with Caton Avenue. In those musty records he found that the Baltimore City had failed to take a portion of the paper streets property legally. *We owned a piece of land making up a section of the I-95 interchange!* We had been dragged through so much, entirely at my expense, I could not resist writing to Mayor Schaefer.

"Dear Mr. Mayor," I wrote, "as you know we own land used as a section of the I-95 interchange. Since we have been unable to arrive at a settlement of other matters involving our other lands, my idea is to recoup our expenses by erecting a tollgate on our section of the ramp. Our toll will be reasonable, of course. We will name it after you. 'Schaefer's Tollgate.'"

Schaefer's well known low boiling point was evident in his rejection of a tollgate.

The possibilities were not lost on City officialdom which to this point was interested only in squeezing us as much a possible. Debates maintained decorum, but bureaucrats simply are handicapped by lacking a sense of humor.

Our offer to the City was to relinquish title to our piece of the interchange if, in return, the City would correct the water and sewage problem and set up proper flood control at City expense. This was not the kind of arrangement Schaefer and Pressman were accustomed to making. They were always on top making others give in to their demands. Knowing, finally, they had no choice they agreed, and the papers were drawn up and signed.

By this time my lien on the property had climbed to $500,000. That much money should be put into proper focus. At the time, college graduates were glad to get jobs paying $10,000 a year. You could buy a new car for much less. Gasoline was 30 cents a gallon.

I was ready to sell and move on instead of paying interest on the loan every quarter. When we got an offer of one million, five hundred thousand, I said take it. Brazeal said no, we can get more. Hubble agreed with Brazeal, but would go along with my decision. I said, "I'll stay as long as you wish, provided someone else assumes the half-million dollar debt and pays the interest."

Silence.

We sold the property and divided the capital gain of $800,000.

If that sounds great, remember the years, cash paid for purchases and interest, risk of failure, emotional strain over the haggling, and not least of all having to prove our improvements were in the best interests of the public. Without that, no permits, no development, no sale.

Fortunately, it really did work out to the benefit of all.

Elsewhere I wrote that the first law of man is to survive, and I am a survivor.

Don't ever forget something else. The same law of surviving applies to the person on the other side of your deal.

Chapter 25

How Does Healthcare Work In Other Nations?

Attending medical conventions through the years gave me some exposure to medical practices outside the U.S. Many foreign doctors I met were outstanding, and their presence in U.S. conferences suggested they were at the top of their profession in their countries. My other, direct experience with the products of medical schools in other nations was frequently negative.

For many years, our entire medical care was in transition. Beginning in the mid-forties, the individual payment system was deemed unfair to those with little money.

This idea brought on the problem solving proposed by Blue Cross to serve hospitals and Blue Shield to serve physicians. To finance Blue Shield when it first started, doctors remitted to it 25% of their fees.

These first changes expanded rapidly until the Federal government saw a way to milk it for votes. President Lyndon Johnson took the lead with his "Great Society" and the result was Medicare and Medicaid, enacted in 1965. I studied these programs closely and found them flawed from the start. What had been wasn't working; Medicare/Medicaid could only lead to frustration and lower-quality medical care. What could work? I decided to explore what other countries were doing. Maybe nothing worked.

I got in touch with Vice President Agnew and asked him for a letter to accompany me in looking for a system proven elsewhere that might work in the United States. Shortly after that Grace and I were taking a break in Europe, and I found the opportunity to look at European systems up close. One lucky break was in meeting Margaret Herbison, a "front bencher" in the British Parliament, and Minister of Health for Great Britain. Mrs. Herbison invited us to visit her at home in Schotts Lanarkshire, Scotland.

Grace answered for both of us. "Mrs. Herbison, that sounds marvelous!"

We settled on a mutually convenient date, and I hired a car with a knowledgeable chauffeur to drive us to Lanarkshire. It was a lovely drive without a care through the beautiful, serene Scottish countryside. We arrived about 4:00 in the afternoon at a modest home on a smallish lot, planted in the formal style of British gardens - perfectly kept, colorful and altogether charming. It was the kind of orderliness - and tradition - I thoroughly admire.

Mrs. Herbison welcomed us in person and immediately asked us to drop her title of Health Minister. Pleasantries completed, we entered the living room where a comforting fire glowed in the fireplace. An older man and woman rose to greet us as we entered.

Mrs. Herbison said, "Grace and Dr. Pierpont, may I introduce you to Sir Arthur Woodbourne and Mrs. Woodbourne? Sir Arthur wrote the National Health Act in 1946, just after the war. I though it would be nice to ask Sir Arthur to join us. I hope you do not mind."

Mind? How much could I ask for - the Minister of Health and the author of Great Britain's health care legislation! I couldn't dream of asking for such thoughtfulness. I said, "We are positively delighted, Mrs. Herbison! You couldn't be more kind and thoughtful to an American who, right now, begins to feel we are imposing on your good will."

"Not at all! Not at all! Now, will you have a sherry with us?"

We chatted over the sherry, then our hostess led us into her dining room. We looked upon a table absolutely loaded with all kinds of beautifully filled dishes containing some of the most exquisite food I have enjoyed anywhere. Grace again and again commented how delicious everything was. It was so irresistible we ate more than we intended.

This was our introduction to Scottish high tea. Resisting the urge to take a high-tea nap, we returned to the living room where we discussed the British and American healthcare systems for nearly four hours. The British system, in my opinion, has serious flaws in it especially in terms of American expectations in health care. A main problem is the central government's policy of limiting the options of physicians by matching all types of care to the money available. An example is kidney dialysis. Anyone over age 55 with kidney failure must either pay the cost of dialysis personally or do without. This kind of exclusion extended to all other medical care. A person in need of care could be put on a waiting list provided the type of care was on the approved list. When the waiting person's name reached the top, the care was government-paid in full. Persons who could pay for private treatment could have it virtually at once if they paid by private insurance.

My comment about this situation reminded Mrs. Herbison about the time she became ill in Cleveland, Ohio. She called the hotel desk clerk who said the hotel doctor would see her, and the fee would be charged to her hotel bill.

"I think my mouth flew open." She laughed ladylike at the thought. "It was appalling! Such a thing is unthinkable in Britain. A doctor would come at once on an emergency basis and no demand for money would be made. Of course, if a patient in Britain offers payment any arrangement between doctor and patient would be perfectly acceptable. But never would cost be interposed ahead of service in an emergency situation. I feel sure your American system would never be acceptable here."

I responded in like fashion. "I have the same problem imagining your system in America – I don't think Americans would accept it. Americans don't have –" I paused to think of an accurate word – "I guess it's the 'stoicism' of you British. We're impatient and impetuous, and my experience with all kinds of patients tells me our people will never put up with the waiting and restrictions you have here - most of all, the waiting."

She thought that over. "I suppose you're right. We are a bit different in what we put up with here, due to our limitations." She seemed to be thinking, and then added: "Dr. Pierpont, you might look into some of the things the Germans are doing in healthcare. I hear what they're doing is very interesting."

"What sort of things are you talking about?"

"I really shouldn't say too much because I've never had reason to get deeply into their system. What I have heard in conferences is that their system is different and quite good."

Both Grace and I are of German descent, so it struck me as odd that after all my years in medicine I knew nothing about the German healthcare system. General conversation then led to the controversy over abortion. Sir Arthur Woodbourne held the floor for a review of the medical case for abortion. It was an insoluble problem in the Great Britain of 1968, according to Sir Arthur, and the government was following what he called a middle ground.

Mrs. Herbison started to add something but was uncharacteristically interrupted by Mrs. Woodbourne who had sat quietly in a rocking chair before the fireplace while the conversation swirled around her. She was a striking woman. Nearly as tall as her six-foot husband, she had a black patch over a blind eye, and a shock of carefully coifed white hair made her appearance even more striking against her jet black velvet suit.

Her strong voice when she broke into the conversation left no doubt she had strong opinions about abortion. "Dr. Pierpont, they are not going to tell you the truth about abortion! It has nothing at all to do with health! It has nothing to do with necessity. It has to do with religion! It's the Catholics and their votes that keep them from any sensible decision for the people of Britain. That, sir, is the problem and the truth!"

We laughed as Sir Arthur declared, "Well, that's that!"

And so it was. We expressed our heartfelt thanks for a delightful and informative visit and returned to our waiting car. The ride back was relaxing, and we reached our hotel just after midnight. It had been a long, wonderful day.

The hospitality of our new friend, Mrs. Herbison, included a guided tour of the House of Commons, the House of Lords, and lunch in the Parliament dining room. When we left her and Great Britain to continue our trip, I felt positive that the British system of healthcare had absolutely no chance of working in the U.S. It is what is called a single-payor system which breaks down financially from time to time. When that happens, all suffer as a result.

We looked into the French system while in Paris, and found it to be reasonably good. As to be expected, the big problem was finding enough money to pay for necessary care, and stopping - or at least minimizing - patient overuse, especially by the elderly.

In meeting with French officials, we found they were more interested in the Ayatollah Khomeni and the Viet Nam peace talks than in medical problems. The daily buzz about the peace talks centered on endless discussions about the shape of the conference table - round, oblong, or square. Oblong won, and later we took a side trip for the fun of it just to see the great table for ourselves. What can be said about sensible men squabbling about the shape of a table while men were dying horribly?

While finding little of healthcare value in Great Britain and France, another incident occurred which still amazes me. This time Grace and I were traveling through Scandinavia with another couple, Dr. Phil Heuman and his wife. Marge was a large, good-looking and unusually outgoing woman we liked very much. We had looked into the healthcare systems of Norway, Sweden, and Denmark and found them very complete and doing a good job for the citizens. Physicians, hospitals, and other sources of medical care, along with the patients, were tightly controlled. It was their only way of keeping costs in line with available funds, with a resulting loss of physician discretion and personal liberty. All were basically socialized and quite expensive systems, none of which people would accept in the United States.

The whole exercise left me a bit down and disappointed, a feeling not helped by knowing our vacation was ending. We were having breakfast one morning when a thought nibbling at the edges of my mind broke through to full consciousness. I said, "Phil, one comment keeps coming up when we talk to medical people about their systems."

Phil sipped his coffee. "So that's what you've been so quiet about."

"Over and over, we hear that the Germans are onto something about healthcare that none of these countries seem to have. What the devil is it?"

Phil said, "Ross, the funny thing is these people still hate the Germans so much they don't want any part of anything German. I'm surprised anyone has mentioned a German system. Maybe that's why no one has ever given us a clue as to what the German system is, or why it's different. There's not a French or Danish politician alive who would dare say let's handle medical care like they do in Germany." He added quickly: "Maybe he wouldn't stay alive much longer if he did."

It was 20 years after the war. But that attitude about anything German still ruled the day.

With my German ancestry, and pride of it in my childhood, the total detestation of things German was, down deep, unsettling. What could I do about it? Nothing. I had no intention of letting the feeling prey on me.

"Phil, that's the way it is, but look beyond the hatred. Every comment, however limited, has been favorable to something called 'the German system.' Well, what the hell is the system?"

Phil shrugged.

"Remember what the Belgians told us. The Dutch, who detested everything Germans stand for, kept the German medical care system after the Nazi occupation ended. It was the only thing the Dutch kept."

The conversation languished on dry ground for a while. The question between what I knew about healthcare, and how what I knew might differ from the German system occupied my thoughts. In two more days, any opportunity to learn more would be gone. I said, "Phil, do you know anybody, anybody at all, in Germany?"

"No."

"Neither do I. The only name I know is Willy Brandt. He's their Foreign Minister, or their Chancellor, or something. Why don't we call him about the system and see what he says?"

Phil looked at me in astonishment. "We call him? Sure, just give us five minutes or so."

I laughed. "OK, I'll call him. What's there to lose?"

"Your sanity, perhaps. Just how do you expect to reach the foreign minister, or Chancellor or whatever he is in Germany? We're sitting here in Denmark!"

"I'll call him up."

"You'll what?"

I was getting excited and intrigued by the possibility. You get a number, you ask for Willy Brandt, and he answers or he doesn't. No big deal about that. Our wives joined us, and Phil had five minutes of fun regaling them about my temporary insanity. I smiled like the Cheshire cat. We had some time, this was going to be fun, and I knew it! Both wives wasted no time telling me I had gone bonkers, and to forget embarrassing myself and them.

What they were telling me was that I was on the right track.

I called for a telephone and placed a person-to-person call from Dr. Ross Z. Pierpont, American surgeon, to Willy Brandt, Bonn, Germany. The operator asked where she could find Herr Brandt. Good question, and I thought quickly, "Please try the headquarters of the Government. He is Chancellor, or Prime Minister, I'm not sure which."

"Stand by, please."

The conversation between the telephone operator and someone in

Germany was beyond me. At last I heard her dial a number and on getting an answer in German she switched to English so I would understand. "I have," she said, "an American surgeon on the line from Copenhagen Denmark. He wants to speak person-to-person to Chancellor Brandt. He has an introductory letter from the American Vice President Agnew..."

From Bonn: "Jus' a moment."

The next voice I heard was in perfect English. "Good morning, sir. This is Willy Brandt. To whom am I now speaking?"

"I am Dr. Ross Pierpont from Baltimore, U.S.A, Chancellor. I am representing Vice President Agnew about medical care systems. I have heard you have perhaps a model system that could be accommodated to the United States."

"Doctor, it is very kind of you to call. I believe we do have one of the finest medical care systems, though of course we have some problems. But in most ways it does a fine job for us. Can you come to see me and discuss our system? It will be nice to have you."

Could I come! I controlled my excitement. "Thank you very much, Chancellor. Unfortunately, very unfortunately, I have come by this opportunity late and I am scheduled to return to the United States day after tomorrow."

"Oh. Wait just a moment."

I held the phone for what seemed forever, but really just a couple of minutes.

"Dr. Pierpont, there is a midnight train out of Copenhagen which arrives here in Bonn at 7:30 a.m. If you will come on that train I will meet you for breakfast and arrange for someone to show you through all phases. You can catch the train back to Copenhagen at 1:02 p.m. and be back by 8:30 p.m."

Was I floored? Put yourself in my shoes. I asked Brandt to hold for a moment while I spoke with my wife and friends. When they realized I was not joking, there was no question: we would go. I said, "Chancellor, we will be there on the 7:30 train."

"Good. I will see you then. Goodbye, Dr. Pierpont."

I took a deep breath and turned to Grace and my friends. We looked at each other, absorbing what had just happened. The head of the German Government had taken a phone call from a total stranger and offered his personal time to meet us for breakfast and explain German medical care!

"I don't believe it!" Phil said. "This is not happening."

It was happening. It was for real.

We toured Copenhagen for the rest of that afternoon, and the concierge was waiting for me when we returned to the hotel. "You are the American Dr. Pierpont?"

"Yes."

"Please come with me. We have had several calls from Chancellor Brandt from Germany. He wishes you to call him right away.

I didn't like the sound of it, but immediately went to the nearest telephone. When the connection was made, I said, "This is Dr. Pierpont for Chancellor Brandt."

He came on the line at once and said, "Dr. Pierpont, thank you for returning my call so promptly. I am most sorry to trouble you, but I do not want you to make an unnecessary trip. I am leaving in 10 minutes due to an emergency at the East Border which demands my personal attention. I did not want you to find no one here since it is not possible for me to return and join you for breakfast. Please accept my apology. Also please feel free to call me as soon as you are here again. I will place as much time as necessary to cover all of your medical questions. Again my apologies but I must go. They are waiting for me to leave at once."

I swallowed my disappointment, assured him I understood and thanked him for his interest.

Later we learned that the "border incident" was the Prague, Czechoslovakian Spring Uprising of 1968. I know that Willy Brandt, at one point the leader of World Socialism, and individualist Ross Pierpont, would have encountered major differences in our viewpoints, had we ever met. I also know that Brandt was a brilliant humanitarian of great sensitivity and thoughtfulness at a time of great stress in every incident of European life. The Prague uprising was only one example.

I made other efforts to meet Chancellor Brandt personally but nothing ever came of it. In effect, I was asking the German equivalent of the President of the United States to meet with a non-official surgeon. Not meeting him was disappointing, but nothing was really lost. He was not the medical system, and the system wasn't Brandt. My loss was purely personal. I would have to explore other ways to gain the knowledge about the German system. No great problem – I just had to do it.

Chapter 26

No Ending

Stories and books, I am told, should have a beginning, a middle and an end. This has no end because what I have started will end only when the United States has a medical/dental program for all regardless of age, sex, or income, cradle to grave. Or I die — whichever comes first.

This nation *must* replace Medicare/Medicaid. Earlier I described these programs as over-promised and under-funded, frustrating patients and physicians alike. They are surviving only by officially-sponsored hypocrisy and the power exerted through a misled Federal government by insurance companies and managed care officials who are raking in obscene incomes. Insurance companies are essential in providing medical/dental care, but their role needs a new approach.

It takes time for the people to catch up with really big lies like Medicare/Medicaid, but it's happening. Hardly a month goes by without another HMO announcing it is withdrawing from Medicare because reimbursements do not cover costs. Elderly people most in need of medical attention are stripped of health protection. The second-largest nursing home company in the nation teeters on the edge of bankruptcy, blaming Medicare reimbursement rates for its losses. The company's stock, down to 25 cents a share, is suspended from trading. According to a front page story in *The Wall Street Journal*, June 30, 1999, "independent drugstores have failed or sold out in the past two years, and many that remain simply refuse to fill some or all Medicaid prescriptions." Why do they turn away business? They lose money with Medicaid reimbursement rates. Far from least of all, the problems of trying to cope with mounds of paperwork and bureaucratic hassles push doctors toward total frustration.

The richest nation in the history of mankind presently ignores more than 44 million people with no healthcare/dental insurance. The situation is a time bomb hidden by current high employment and accompanying overall prosperity. When the inevitable cycle of the national economy turns down, ending the incomes of millions of uninsured people, the shock to the nation will be felt to its foundation. These people will become sick; they must be treated by someone, but by whom? For nothing? The pressure on doctors and hospitals to take care of indigents by the millions could become unbearable.

Is there any excuse for this, when we know better?

No.

As I wrote earlier, I have studied other nations' healthcare systems in the hope of learning what works, what doesn't, and why. One of my first lessons was that our national bill for medical care — inadequate care at that — is too high. According to the nonpartisan Congressional Budget Office, more than 15 cents of every dollar the United States produces in goods and services goes to pay for medical care. This ratio of expense is far higher than that of any other industrialized nation while leaving more than 43 million people uninsured! The biggest factors in our excessive medical costs are reams of useless paperwork, non-medical overhead, and actual or threatened malpractice suits. Malpractice insurance for a general surgeon today is from $15,000 to $50,000 per year. A neurosurgeon is socked with insurance charges from $40,000 to $75,000 per year. Tort lawyers' contingency fees provide handsome living these days. Their handsome living shows that about $150 billion a year can be saved in legal charges and malpractice insurance alone.

In my investigations of other nations' health coverage, I found the system in modern Germany to be as well designed as a Mercedes. The system goes back as far as 1883 when the Emperor Bismarck first set it up, and naturally it has been refined over the past 100 years. Today, it covers every living person in Germany. With virtually no exceptions, the people are more than satisfied with it even though *it costs about 30% less than our Topsy-grown system in the U.S. — a system that leaves patients and doctors alike unhappy while leaving those 43 million Americans with no pre-paid healthcare whatsoever.*

What works in any other nation is not guaranteed to work in the U.S. As I told the British Minister of Health, Americans are too impatient, too demanding, to put up with some of the rules and practices accepted by Europeans.

Where do we go from here? The first thing is to admit we can learn something from Canadian and European experience. Canadians have a single-payor system much like the one in Great Britain. Both are in worse shape than our own Medicare/Medicaid. Why not use the experience of other nations, plus our American experience, to establish principles that will guide a new American medical/dental system for as long as can be foreseen. As to principles, I propose the following:

Pierpont Medical/Dental Healthcare System In Principle

1. All inhabitants of the United States shall receive medical and dental care without regard to age, gender, and ability to pay.

2. All persons with income shall contribute to the costs of medical and dental care through deductions from their income. Amounts needed, and deductions required, are subject to negotiation with the citizens of the state selected, and their representatives. For planning purposes, a suggested amount could be a 12.5% contribution from gross income, tax deductible, up to an income ceiling of $40,000. On a monthly basis, the maximum contribution would be $416 per month per family. Medicare deductions from Social Security payments, and health care insurance payments would stop, taken over by the system's universal and total partnerships.

3. All persons shall be free to choose any participating healthcare professional, or establishment for needed services. Healthcare professionals also should have a corresponding freedom of choice.

4. The system shall be organized in groups. These will be one of two types.

> Rule one: Groups will consist of residents within geographical boundaries. Boundaries shall be identical with one or more boundaries of the political subdivisions within each state. Residents of each subdivision shall belong to the area conforming to its political boundaries for purposes of funding, paying for, and receiving their medical/dental care.

Rule two: Groups will consist of employees, and their families, of companies that wish to set up a medical/dental program for such employees. These programs may be set up as long a they comply completely with all requirements of this Medical/Dental Healthcare System.

NOTE: Other, acceptable modalities can be allowed.

5. Members of each insured group shall elect a non-paid Board of Directors to serve for five (5) years. This Board will supervise what is in essence a mutual, medical insurance company. Each Board will select, through open competition, an administrator to conduct its group's business, and shall oversee the activities of this administrator.

6. The administrator, in cooperation with local medical/dental societies, shall assure maximum medical/dental care at prescribed costs, and shall prevent abuse by patients, establishments, and health care professionals.

7. Since governments at different levels will participate in the resolution of any and all legal claims, persons and establishments providing medical and dental care shall be granted sovereign immunity from legal action alleging personal liability for professional services. Charges of inadequate or wrongful care shall be settled by the least-costly method: internal negotiation or arbitration where the patient receives all of any settlement money. Should these methods fail to provide a satisfactory resolution, the involved person(s) may penetrate the shield of sovereign immunity by appeal to a proper court. This step preserves all participants' rights.

8. Persons and establishments providing medical and dental care shall be paid through fees for personal services and the use of medical/dental equipment, plus reimbursement for the total costs of patient-required equipment, medicines and other consumables.

9. A schedule of medical/dental services and materials will be established between all participating parties as a point system according to the time and skills required, or the purchase price of medicine, healthcare equipment, or other consumables.

10. To guarantee all participants service and solvency, the system will clear payments through their mutual insurance companies to its participating healthcare professionals and establishments once each month.

The first step in introducing a medical/dental health plan covering all Americans, conception to casket, is to make sure it will do what it is designed to do. There is no way — surely, Hillary Clinton proved this — that anyone is going to turn one sixth of the U.S. economy over to an unproven system, no matter how attractive it reads on paper. The way to do this is to put my proposed system to the test. My suggested criteria for a pilot test:

Waivers by the Federal government to allow the test.

A state small enough to minimize risk,

Close supervision to assure universal availability of medical and dental care,

A state large enough to be representative,

Data collection to assure scientifically acceptable findings.

Maryland, Missouri, Delaware, Coloraldo, and Indiana appear logical choices to meet the desired criteria, but there are others.

A primary objective is to draft enabling legislation leading to a complete debate of every aspect of the plan. Participants must include medical professionals, officials of governments which will administer the test, and the people who will be covered.

Two outcomes are possible. The debate will show my proposed program is not acceptable by all parties affected, and the test is dropped. The other outcome is that questions and possible problems will be uncovered, the questions answered, and the test proceed.

A question to be answered: Does my proposed system turn medical and dental care over to the government as attempted by the Clinton administration? No. In my proposed system, the Federal government's only function is to provide a less, but adequate, amount of money to the states as is now provided through Medicare/Medicaid. State, city, and county governments are to provide oversight of any insurance company doing business with groups obtaining medical/dental care through such company. These governments will assure that the medical/dental groups are managed according to law and regulations, including the point system established to allocate a dollar-value to each type of medical/dental service provided. State, city or county governments will set up special Boards to adjudicate disputes not settled on the group level. In this activity local and Federal governments will participate only as partners in the total healthcare system.

Background to these suggestions: American as ever, ignoring my political leanings, and wanting to be helpful, I sent my findings to Hillary Clinton's Task Force, registered mail, return receipt requested. Since they had already decided to function without benefit of any physician's experience, no doubt this explains why they ignored my information. It took personal intervention with the post office to get the return receipts two months after delivery.

Clintonesque, they used my materials in their own way. Not long after I had sent my approach to health care to Mrs. Clinton, my son-in-law, a civil servant in the German Republic, called me from Germany. His colleagues in the German health system were somewhat amused, he said, to have a Clinton delegation ask questions about what I was writing about health care. His report did not come as a surprise.

Clinton-care came up at a large meeting of a Pharmacy and Pharmaceutical group in the person of Congressman Benjamin Cardin. I had known Cardin from my Democrat days, and now we were on opposite sides of the political fence. Cardin began speaking about the need for healthcare reform, and within minutes Bill Wilson, sitting beside me, nudged my ribs. "Ross," he whispered, "Cardin is describing Germany's health system."

I do not exaggerate in saying that both Bill and I recognized parts of Cardin's address as paraphrasing points I had made again and again about healthcare. When he finished, I promptly stood up and congratulated him on his understanding of what healthcare was all about. To my surprise, he responded: "Ross, I've been talking about the German system."

As the meeting broke up, Cardin's wife approached me and, laughing, said: "I almost fell out of my chair to hear you congratulate Ben."

I smiled in return. "It's the first time he's been right in my eyes. Any time Ben is right, you can bet I'll congratulate him."

What happened next is an example of knowing the right things to do, then doing something else. The Clinton team looked at the opportunities provided by micromanaging 250 billion dollars a year, and all of the votes, appointments, perks, and deals that money controlled. The mere thought of giving that up was enough to reverse the Clintons' entire approach to health care. The result was predictable. They issued a proposal crafted to give complete control of healthcare to Federal bureaucrats. None of this included inputs from experienced professionals who had devoted their lives to healthcare. It was a classic example of relying on the once-prestigious, now disgraced, principle of meeting human needs through centralized management, a management concept famously proposed by a man named Karl Marx.

If anyone is offended by my aligning of Hillaryist medical care with Marxist-style medical care, please look at how Hillary Clinton put her plan together. Look at how it would have been put into force, and how anyone deviating from its rigorous rules would be punished. It is beyond argument that her task force was established in secret and met in secret, outside U.S. law. Her method of effecting this plan would be pure coercion. Neither the patients nor the medical professional would have any say whatsoever as to the services provided, the sources of those services, nor methods of payment. Everything would be handled by government edict. Yes, punishment of physician "offenders" would be right out of Stalin's Russia: jail.

To me, there is no question that our present system of medical and dental care must give way to something better. The questions are when, how, and what the replacement will look like. I devote my waking hours these days and nights to arguing for replacing our present horribly inefficient system with the one outlined here. It is fair to all. It provides total coverage from pre-birth to burial. It gives freedom of choice to patient and practitioner alike. And it saves an almost incredible $500 billion a year.

Medical organizations should be leading the way in this inevitable change, reaching everyday Americans with the truth devoid of political scheming.

Wake up, doctors! Wake up, dentists! Wake up all Americans! This nation has shown time and time again, that once aroused to a need it responds generously and promptly. I, for one, cannot believe the people I have grown to love and trust will allow a program to continue that wastes its hard-earned money and tolerates million families to risk their future without the protection of healthcare insurance.

This need makes an ending impossible. There can be no end to my story until we have corrected the waste and failures of our present healthcare system.

Appendix
A U.S. Healthcare Sytem For All

This book would be incomplete without describing the kind of healthcare system needed to replace the present, failed one. However, it is impossible to describe in detail, within the limits of a book, a system designed to replace one that fills thousands of pages of regulations and consumes more than 15% of the total U.S. gross national product — with costs constantly escalating. What I present in this Appendix are the goals of my system, and the broad provisions of the way it would be initiated and operated, to include a transition that does not take away any of the protections of existing programs.

When Greg Wilson lost his job, the loss of income was just the beginning of the family's troubles. Unpaid medical bills mounted because the family's health insurance, formerly paid by Greg's employer, had vanished along with his job. Expensive medical care for son Lawrence, age 9 and asthmatic, had to be dropped. Treatment of daughter Linda's birth defect had to be postponed indefinitely. The worst blow fell when Greg's wife, Donna, miscarried and had to be hospitalized. The Wilsons found themselves struggling alongside the other 43 million Americans naked of health care coverage.

Sylvia Gilson's mother, 90% immobilized by a stroke, was improving almost daily thanks to care provided by a major hospital and paid by mother Gilson's Health Maintenance Organization. One day the mail brought Sylvia a one-page notice: "Effective immediately, the (Name omitted) Hospital will no longer provide medical services for persons enrolled in any Health Maintenance Organization." That was the beginning of a nightmare for Sylvia that has yet to find an ending.

Experiences like that alarm all Americans — and are not even "the tip of the iceberg." Consciously or instinctively, Americans know that our present way of providing medical care is a not just disappointing. It is a disaster waiting to happen. The only question: who suffers the disaster as hospitals and Health Maintenance Organizations lose money, cancel coverages, and walk away from any further responsibilities? The system has declined into a morass of unkept promises, angry physicians, healthcare executives whose first responsibility is profit, a mountain of confusing and very expensive paperwork, and unpaid debts.

A recent study found 91% of Americans discouraged by their health care. In one state typical of others, 87% of its people (nearly nine of every ten!) looked on health care as in crisis or in trouble. Few are the doctors who would dispute those attitudes.

What goes on here? No one seriously questions that this nation possesses the most highly developed health care in the world, delivered from the hands and brains of the best-trained medical force ever assembled on this planet.

Compare what is available with what people receive. The United States lags behind at least 7 other developed nations in critical health categories like life span, immunizations, completeness, "portability" of coverage, and freedom to choose physician, hospital, or other health care services.

Stories abound of people failing to get specialized attention, or sometimes any attention at all on a timely basis. Prescription drug prices steadily escalate. Medicare/Medicaid drift steadily toward insolvency while Seniors press for more coverage at still greater costs. The number of American families without health care protection mounts in times of unprecedented prosperity.

If the economy turns down and unemployment mounts, the number of people with no health protection, and no way to pay privately for their care, will jump far beyond the 17% in that position today. Indeed, the number of such persons is growing year by year without the stimulation of unemployment. Surging demands from these legions of unprotected people seeking free medical care and medicines could shake the structure of this nation to its very foundation!

Today's horror stories could look mild by comparison.

The time has come to replace the costliest, most wrong-headed, most cumbersome, non-functional system in the world with one that delivers complete medical care to every person, birth to burial. To repeat, the system must cover every person, birth to burial. Change that to pre-birth to burial. Care to assure healthy mothers delivering healthy babies is the greatest medical bargain possible.

The replacement system must be patient and doctor friendly. Our tradition of freedom to control one's destiny requires a system with freedom to choose one's doctor, hospital, or other source of care. Freedom to choose must also allow health care professionals, and institutions, a comparable freedom of services, or products, they agree to provide.

A basic concept of the new health care system is that of universal partnership. Every person, and every organization, involved in health care across the nation will be partners who share the system's responsibilities, activities, assure its solvency, and its services.

The function of medical boards, societies and associations

Control of the system's charges and payment functions resides with its partnerships, which creates a key role for the partners' medical boards and societies, dental associations, hospital associations, nurses associations, podiatry associations, physical therapy associations, and similar organizations.

All health care providers agree, upon coming into the system, to render all services for which they are licensed and approved. In turn, the interests of all individual providers, and their patients, will be monitored through their associations. Problems, charges and payments for services rendered, and peer review of fees and quality of service will be managed by local chapters, or divisions, of the various professional groups. This means that every health care provider in the new system must be a member in good standing of his/her professional society or association.

Each local partnership, in cooperation with the provider's national society or association, will establish the value of products and services provided at each level of service, for each category of health care. Values will be expressed as points (dollars).

To make sure each local partnership stays financially sound, the insurer will average the costs of services and products provided each month within each medical category. This determines the amounts to be paid to providers within those categories. If the budget for a particular treatment provides funds for 100 treatments, but only 50 are actually billed, payment to providers would be doubled that particular month. On the other hand, if 200 treatments were billed, payment to the providers would be reduced by half.

Experience demonstrates that in normal circumstances averaging is fair and should work out over a full year as predicted, assuming records are correctly maintained. If, however, things get out of balance in a particular medical category, the program is readily adjusted through internal investigation and meetings of the organization's Board. This simple procedure eliminates the enormous waste of time and money currently used to settle problems through legislative processes at city, county, state or federal level.

It is essential for everyone to understand that the new health care system will replace the present system by expanding existing coverages, not reducing them. Nor will the new system be installed instantly nationwide. The first step is to prove its merits, and savings, within a single prototype — or demonstration — state. This requires action by the U.S. Congress and the selected state to enable my new, universal care to replace health care programs within the demonstration state.

After the system has proven its ability to replace our failed system with a system that covers every person birth to burial within one state, it can be rolled out state-by-state until all states are covered.

Cases of dissatisfaction are inevitable, and when disputes happen they shall be settled through the local organization's internal grievance procedures. When internal procedures fail to resolve a dispute, it will be referred to the appropriate supervisory body at the desired level of government (city, county, state, or federal) for adjudication. ***This brings city, county and state governments, plus the federal government, into the new system as working partners.*** In this capacity, governments at each level will make sure that local organizations operate within all laws, especially insurance laws. They will supervise, when necessary, the resolution of any dispute that arises about the provision of health care. When governments cooperate in resolving disputes, sovereign immunity is created for all partners in the system. Sovereign immunity will drastically reduce legal expenses by eliminating trivial lawsuits while assuring fairness in settling patient grievances. If, however, government intervention fails to resolve the dispute to the satisfaction of the aggrieved party within the system, such party retains the right to appeal the problem to the courts.

The outlined method of resolving disputes accomplishes these desirable ends:
1. Resolution is accelerated.
2. Hearings may be with or without legal counsel as an aggrieved party desires.
3. Financial settlement with the aggrieved party, when appropriate, is accelerated.
4. Retention of all rights of action by all parties to a dispute when the procedure fails to provide a satisfactory solution.
5. Saves time and money.

This is an all-payor system, not a single-payor system.

Single-payor systems in Great Britain and Canada have shown their financial structure is deficient, making them unable to deliver proper health care to all covered persons *in a timely manner*. For all practical purposes, these systems periodically go bankrupt.

My all-payor system positively assures timely care for everyone, and everyone pays a fair share. Therefore the partners who make up each local organization obtain funds to budget health care on a yearly basis. Annual budgeting allows them to allocate funds for each category of care provided. Although planning is on a yearly basis, budgets are reviewed in each organization's regularly scheduled meetings. If unexpected developments call for adjustments, the system is flexible in permitting a resolution by agreement of all parties involved.

Since everyone pays into the all-payor system, participants gain a feeling of pride and responsibility — "big brother" is not giving them handouts.

1. Persons on welfare pay from their welfare money, by check or other method, while supported by welfare agencies that keep them above poverty levels.
2. Unemployed persons participate in a similar way.
3. Persons with income to $40,000 per year pay a percentage of their income, subject to some variations involving major industries. The estimated average payment should approximate 12.5%, plus or minus 2%. Other health care payments cease, or may be

voluntarily added based on personal preferences. For example, persons earning more than $40,000 per year may decline to participate. However, experience in other nations indicates that most people with higher incomes use the system as "basic" health care and add to it through the purchase of additional, private insurance, as described in the next section.

4. A small percentage (less than 0.5%) may "fall through the cracks" and must be coped with on an individual basis.

Collecting insurance premiums; administrative services

Each local organization of policy holders (e.g., a mutual insurance company) elects by secret ballot a Board of Directors which establishes a procedure for managing its financial matters including premiums collected. These Boards handle only this part of the system's function, not its daily operations. Such Boards normally serve for a 5 year period at no charge except for reimbursement of expenses.

To manage the system's daily operations, each local organization acquires an Administration Company by the use of competitive bidding. Normally, the costs of administrative overhead in an all-payor system average about 10% instead of the 20% to 40% expended by present-day HMO's and health care insurance companies.

As just noted, persons covered in this system pay insurance premiums into an insurance company which they own, making them mutual insurance companies. Insurance companies, in competing for local contracts, will normally design services and rates for individuals who desire levels of care beyond what is offered by the system itself; e.g., private rooms, private nursing, etc. This benefits both the insurers and policy holders.

Charges and payments: no more mountains of paperwork!

When a product or service is delivered, the provider prepares a 3-part bill fully identifying what has been provided including its predetermined points. The provider and patient sign the bill. The provider keeps one copy, the patient keeps one copy, and one copy goes to the provider's society, or association, for peer review. Upon acceptance and approval by a society, or association, the bill is sent to the patient's in-

surer. The insurer pays approved bills once a month to all providers in the covered area. All bills and payments are averaged to assure the solvency of the system.
This is the total paper work needed to establish fair charges and pay for them.

Savings

Removing the expenses of the federal government's micro-management of our present system produces instant savings of as much as 225 billion dollars per year.

Another estimated 150 billion dollars can be saved per year through reduced legal costs.Reducing unnecessary paperwork and insurance overhead will save another 150 billion.

As the waste is cut away from our failed health care system, and every living person is covered birth to burial, our all-payor system also offers each individual freedom to choose one's provider, *with no loss of coverage at any time, for any reason.*

One more benefit: The savings generated by replacing the failed system with my proposed system will provide sufficient savings to make each person's contributions for medical care 100% tax-deductible.

Conclusion

There is no question: the American people are saddled by a system of health care that cannot endure. The only questions are when it will change, and what will replace it.

The all-payor system I have prepared for the people's consideration is based on a system functioning well in Germany for 11 years. This system has been successfully adopted to meet the individual health case needs of at least 12 other nations. These include nations as varied as Japan, Korea, the Netherlands, Sweden, and more recently Isral.

Are we too proud, too arrogant, to learn from others? Can anyone honestly argue that my system does not deserve a fair test in a demonstration state? It may not be the only system to replace our present failed system. But I have looked world-wide for a more promising system.

There is none. I have looked to professional associations for ideas about replacing failing Medicare/Medicaid/HMOs. So far as I can find, there are none.

I have no pride of authorship in proposing a new health care system for the people of the United States. So I close by offering this challenge: if someone claims to have a system better than the one I have just outlined, by all means let us move to test it promptly. If no one can propose such a system, put my system to the test in a demonstration state and let the results speak for themselves.

THE PIERPONT HEALTH CARE SYSTEM

A Solid Answer to America's Health Care Nightmare

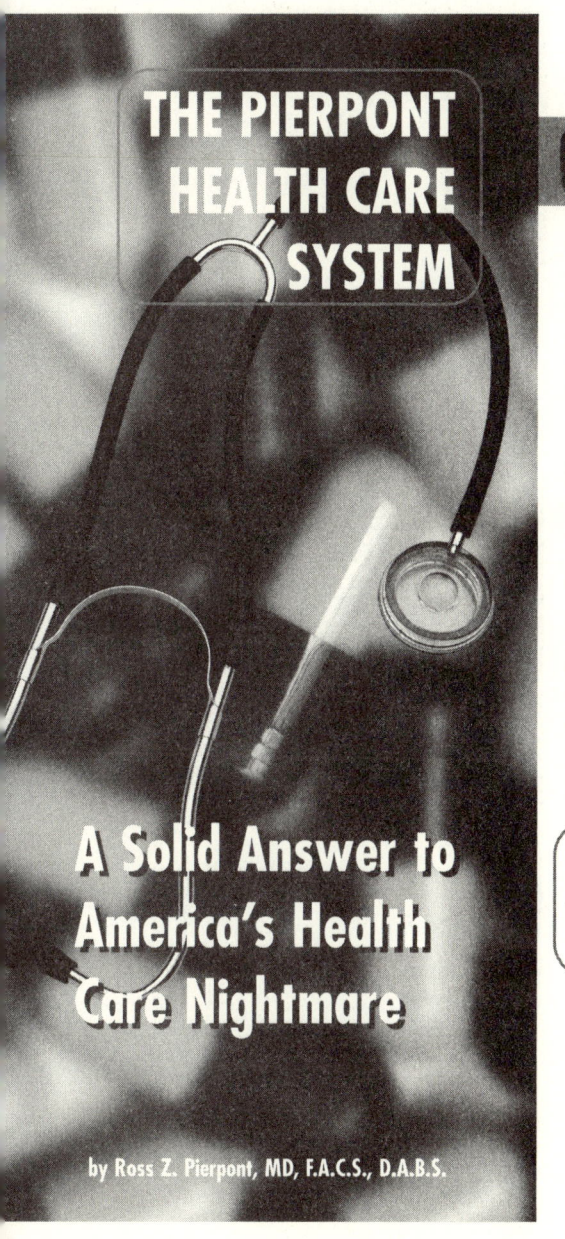

by Ross Z. Pierpont, MD, F.A.C.S., D.A.B.S.

Getting America's Health Care System Moving: Now is the Time for a Better Plan

In 1993, President and Mrs. Clinton made a futile effort to reinvent our health care system and fight the unholy duo of government micro-management and trial lawyers. The effort was futile because the President and First Lady simply wanted to institute bigger government, and their staggering lack of success is clear for all to see. They were rebuffed soundly.

And the fact is, they knew better. They knew that a system for total cradle-to-grave health care and freedom for every person in the United States has been identified, and is available NOW: The Pierpont Health Care System.

The Pierpont Health Care System can save Americans as much as half a trillion dollars a year. Most importantly, each and every American can have less expensive health care, with universal access, freedom of choice and total portability. That was the goal when Medicaid and Medicare were introduced more than 30 years ago and, sadly, it's still just a goal now.

The present system is a failure.
The Clinton plan was a failure.

The Pierpont Health Care System is a solid answer that works.

The Twin Towers of Failure

Since the introduction of Medicaid and Medicare in 1965, the American people have been promised a great deal and delivered very little. The system was supposed to provide comprehensive coverage at a fair price for all Americans. Instead, it has become a patchwork nightmare, with the government and the trial lawyers killing the system, inflating its costs and confusing the insurance companies.

The result: 43 million Americans are without sufficient health coverage in the present health care system, which also denies universal access, freedom of choice and total portability.

Some alarming facts that highlight the fallacies of America's current health care environment:

- State, local and Federal governments micro-manage our health care system to the tune of $250 billion a year;
- Health care claims one (1) of every seven (7) dollars spent in the United States;
- Health care costs account for approximately 15.5% of our gross national spending, and that figure is expected to be closer to 20% within the next decade;
- The U.S. is the only industrialized nation in the world without universal access to health care;
- Americans pay more on average for their health care, but do not receive more care than citizens in most other "G-7" nations like Japan, Germany and at least seven others;
- Among industrialized nations, the U.S. ranks anywhere from 16th to 21st in life expectancy.

The Problem: Medicaid/Medicare

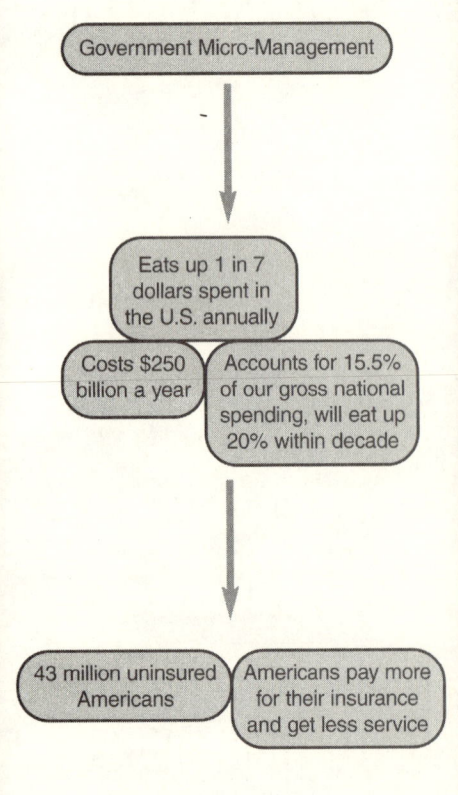

Government Micro-Management

↓

Eats up 1 in 7 dollars spent in the U.S. annually

Costs $250 billion a year

Accounts for 15.5% of our gross national spending, will eat up 20% within decade

↓

43 million uninsured Americans

Americans pay more for their insurance and get less service

The Solution:
The Pierpont Health Care System

- Partnership of all providers throughout the entire health care system, along with Federal, state and local government

↓

- Government only oversees and adjudicates
  - Cuts management cost from $250 bil to $25 bil
  - Tames the "900 lb gorillas"; government micro-management and frivolous litigation by trial lawyers

↓

- Lowers costs

↓

- Universal, comprehensive, compassionate coverage from cradle-to-grave

A Health Care System That Works

The best way to cure the American health care nightmare is to roll our current system into the Pierpont Health Care System. Designed by Dr. Ross Z. Pierpont, a veteran of more than 50 years in medical practice, education and administration, the Pierpont Health Care System is an adaptation of the successful, century-old German model. The basics:

- ALL are insured, and each person has ownership in their mutual insurance company;

- A Board of Directors is elected every five years to operate the company;

- Everyone pays into the citizen-owned and operated insurance company (organized by place of residence or employment);

- The system assures quality care for all, and is fully portable from cradle-to-grave;

- Government's role is reduced to overseer and adjudicator, reducing annual management costs by 90%;

- Allows for sovereign immunity with the government as a partner;

- Disputes are solved internally, cutting down on the frivolous litigation so prevalent in our current system;

- If the patient is dissatisfied with the internal settlement, they can penetrate sovereign immunity and go into civil court;

- Cuts down on paperwork - Every patient gets a bill for a visit or treatment, similar to a restaurant check;

- Copies of this bill go to the patient and to the provider's society for immediate peer review;

- This bill is processed for peer review by the provider's society and sent to the mutual insurance company for payment;

- Tames the "900lb gorillas" that are crushing America's health care system with overhead: governmental micro-management and frivolous litigation;

- The overall cost savings of as much as $500 billion per year is sufficient funding to pay the debt and deficit, strengthen social security and still contribute to an across-the-board tax cut;

- Also, the cost of health care premiums would become tax deductible.

American health care is excellent, but our present health care **system** is an abject failure, weighed down by the bureaucracy of government micro-management. Based on a proven model, the Pierpont Health Care System puts power and choice of care back in the hands of the American people.

We can:

- Restructure the role of government as only a supervisor and adjudicator, not a micro-manager;
- Keep trial lawyers out of the process except for the rare necessity to penetrate sovereign immunity; and
- Bring regulation and control of our health care system to the local level.

We must all work together to make sure that our health care is what it should be, and let our leaders know that we're not interested in maintaining the status quo. Now is the time to move health care to the front of the national agenda.

> Let's stop tinkering with a failure.
> We can change to a proven success.

The Pierpont Health Care System.

ROSS Z. PIERPONT, MD, F.A.C.S., D.A.B.S.

is a veteran of over 50 years in health care. A BS and MD graduate of the University of Maryland, he has spent the last five decades in medical practice, education and administration. Appointed to various state health services by five different governors, Dr. Pierpont was a member of the Maryland Board of Review of Health for twelve years. He is also a member of the Health Council of the Heritage Foundation.

A long-time opponent of our wasteful national heath care system, Dr. Pierpont is currently the CEO of both PSCI International, a health care consulting firm, and Gempro International, a manufacturer and distributor of alternative medical products. He currently resides in Timonium, Maryland with Grace, his wife of 57 years.

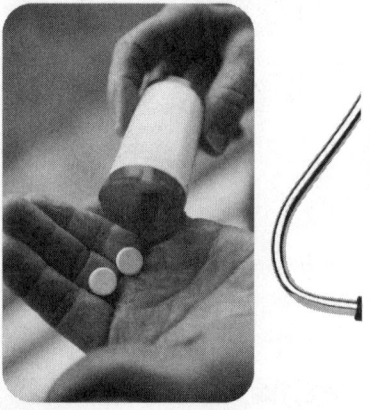

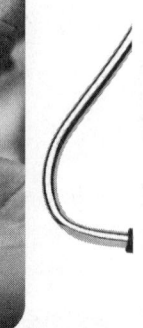

For more information about the Pierpont Health Care System, visit Dr. Pierpont's official website at www.pierpontusa.com, or write to:
215 Belmont Forest Ct. Ste. 408 Timonium MD 21093-7702